Collaboration for Inclusive Education

Collaboration for Inclusive Education

Developing Successful Programs

Chriss Walther-Thomas
Lori Korinek
Virginia L. McLaughlin
Brenda Toler Williams
The College of William and Mary

Allyn and Bacon

Boston ▪ London ▪ Toronto ▪ Sydney ▪ Tokyo ▪ Singapore

Senior Editor: *Virginia Lanigan*
Series Editorial Assistant: *Karin Huang*
Marketing Managers: *Ellen Dolberg and Brad Parkins*
Sr. Editorial Production Administrator: *Susan McIntyre*
Editorial Production Service: *Nesbitt Graphics, Inc.*
Composition Buyer: *Linda Cox*
Manufacturing Buyer: *Suzanne Lareau*
Cover Administrator: *Jenny Hart*
Electronic Composition: *Omegatype Typography, Inc.*

Library of Congress Cataloging-in-Publication Data
Collaboration for inclusive education : developing successful programs
   / Chriss Walther-Thomas ... [et al.].
      p.   cm.
   Includes bibliographical references and index.
   ISBN 0-205-27368-8 (pbk.)
      1. Inclusive education—United States.   2. Teaching teams—United
States.   I. Walther-Thomas, Chriss.
   LC1201.C63   1999
   371.9′046—dc21   99-11372
                                                                              CIP

Printed in the United States of America
10   9   8   7   6   5   4   3   04   03   02   01

*To all of the students and professionals
who will benefit from professional collaboration
and inclusive education done well.*

*And to our respective husbands,
Dennis, John, Scott, and Wayne,
and our children,
Adam, Andrew, Kyha, Laura, Lyndsey,
Melanie, Nathan, Shawn, and Stephanie
whose love and friendship mean so much.*

CONTENTS

PREFACE

This text has been designed to help school professionals serve as effective members of planning teams charged with the development of inclusive education programs for students with disabilities and others at risk for school failure. The learning needs of both novice and more experienced professionals have been considered in the book's development. As coauthors, we have assumed that readers represent a variety of professional roles and responsibilities, such as special educators, general educators, administrators, and staff development and related services specialists (e.g., school psychologists, counselors, occupational therapists). Although roles, responsibilities, and years of experience may vary, we also assume that most readers have had limited opportunities to plan, implement, and monitor inclusive programs for students with disabilities and their peers.

As coauthors, we represent more than 100 years of collective experience working in public schools and university settings. From various vantage points as teachers, specialists, supervisors, administrators, researchers, teacher and administrator educators, staff development consultants, and program evaluators, we have participated in dramatic changes that have taken place in special education. As education has become increasingly inclusive over the years, we have found that appropriate and lasting inclusion for students with disabilities is based on effective planning and ongoing support. Comprehensive planning and administrative support are central to facilitating the process and sustaining needed inclusive education over time.

Throughout the text essential planning and support considerations at the classroom, school, and district levels are presented to facilitate successful inclusion. Some of our recommendations are aimed primarily at district-level planners who can facilitate systematic change and broad-based support for new initiatives. Initially, some readers, particularly those who work in school systems in which little support exists for inclusive education, may view this information as irrelevant and possibly frustrating. Nevertheless, it is important for school- and classroom-level advocates to understand how the presence or absence of district-level actions affects practices at other levels.

Most of the content of this text is targeted directly at classroom-level practitioners. These are the individuals who have day-to-day implementation responsibilities. We present an array of collaborative adult and student support structures and proved instructional practices to facilitate and accommodate academic and social skills development. Structures such as assistance teaming, collaborative consultation, and co-teaching can enhance planning, problem solving, instruction, and progress monitoring. Student-based structures such as peer tutoring and cooperative learning can facilitate both individual and group learning goals. Some readers, particularly those with administrative or supervisory role designations, may be tempted to skip chapters focused on basic day-to-day implementation issues; we strongly encourage those readers to KEEP READING. Effective instructional leaders must understand appropriate practice in inclusive classrooms to facilitate staff growth and development, supervision, staff evaluation, and program advocacy.

Understanding the importance of district-level participation may help some readers anticipate and, hopefully, avoid common problems found in systems in which top-level administrative support for inclusive education is lacking. Committed school- and classroom-level advocates can begin to create conceptual frameworks for action. Strategies to facilitate information sharing and increase district-level involvement can be developed. These strategies may be as simple as distributing newsletters and article reprints, and encouraging classroom visits to model sites. In some settings, readers who understand the importance of top-level support may recognize their need to explore alternative support mechanisms when it is evident that district-level support will be difficult to obtain. In many resistant systems, pockets of successful inclusion continue to flourish at the school and classroom levels.

Understanding the barriers that exist, such as a lack of district-level support, helps individuals and teams set more realistic goals and more appropriate timelines for implementation and service expansion. This knowledge and planning can reduce the potential frustration of advocates by helping them take a long view of organizational change rather than get bogged down by these barriers.

Many of our recommendations are aimed at building-level teams that often consist of teachers, specialists, and administrators. It is important for these school leaders to understand how building-level planning can help or hinder inclusive education efforts. Working together enables school teams to pace themselves effectively to sustain commitment, action, and momentum over time. School-level efforts often stimulate the development of alternative sources of support when district-level support is missing. Schools accomplish this through other initiatives that facilitate collaboration with colleagues, PTA and community volunteers, family members, university faculty and students, community agency representatives, and others. These efforts lead to increased community visibility, gradual change in top-level support, and potential opportunities for small-scale funding to facilitate local development efforts. Many professional and business organizations, as well as local, state, and federal agencies, provide money for pilot projects, model development, or program demonstration grants.

This book addresses different levels of concerns and interests related to inclusive education. In the first part of the book, we set the stage and present the case for change in practice. We provide information that is often *not* included in many teacher and specialist preparation programs. Typically, this information is saved for administrative leadership programs. We believe, however, that *all* effective participants in inclusive education need to understand leadership, planning, and organizational change. Without a solid understanding of these concepts, many otherwise dedicated and enthusiastic advocates may give up on the process too quickly—believing that appropriate inclusion is impossible.

In Chapter 1, "inclusive education" and "collaborative service delivery" are defined and an explanation of why momentum for inclusive education is building is given. In Chapter 2, seven essential features of inclusive education which need to be cultivated to ensure appropriate and lasting inclusion are discussed. Chapter 3 offers an overview of effective organizational change and strategies for effective change agentry. Chapter 4 provides an overview of collaborative structures to support school-based professionals in their work with students and families.

Next, the structures for implementation are presented. Specifically, Chapters 5 and 6 explore the implementation basics for communication, problem solving, and support development. Chapters 7, 8, and 9 provide step-by-step procedures for developing assistance teams, collaborative consultation, and cooperative teaching or co-teaching models. Finally, we address many instructional issues that need to be considered when planning inclusion classrooms. In Chapter 10, a process for designing individualized education plans for students in inclusive schools is presented. In Chapters 11 and 12 research-based strategies and academic accommodations are presented to facilitate classroom instruction and social skills development. These chapters emphasize techniques aimed at effective instruction and community building for all students. Finally, some key points are revisited and future considerations for collaboration to support inclusive education are discussed in Chapter 13.

It is our hope that this text will be both informative and provocative. Reading one book on collaboration for inclusive education will not make any reader an expert on this subject; however, we hope that the content, practice, and references provided help readers to develop a conceptual framework that will facilitate their effective planning and collaborative practice in inclusive settings.

Acknowledgments

We want to acknowledge the many innovative classroom teachers, specialists, administrators, families, and students in school districts across the country who have taught us to design and manage learning environments that are truly inclusive. In particular we thank the many friends and colleagues whose work and insights influenced our thinking throughout the book, especially the suggestions shared in our concluding chapter. We appreciate the scholarship of our colleagues at the College of William and Mary and at many universities and public agencies in the United States and Canada. Over the years their work has broadened our understanding of inclusive education and professional collaboration. Their efforts helped us think about education in new ways, sharpened our professional skills, and improved our practice as educators, writers, and researchers.

Over the years, many talented students in the School of Education at the College of William and Mary helped us conceptualize and develop this manuscript. We are indebted to literally hundreds of dedicated and creative undergraduate, master's, and doctoral students. As these students pursued degrees and advanced certificates in elementary and secondary education, special education, counseling, school psychology, gifted education, and educational leadership programs, they provided reflective dialogue, feedback, suggestions, and constructive criticism of the concepts and ideas presented in this book. Their innovative and informative practice, research, and writing, as well as their candid and insightful reflections about the complexities of effective collaboration and inclusion taught us more than we could ever have imagined.

We are grateful for the ongoing work of friends and colleagues at the Eastern Virginia Training/Technical Assistance Center (College of William and Mary Center) whose tireless efforts help thousands of Virginia professionals find creative ways to solve challenging problems and provide more appropriate learning experiences for students with disabilities and their peers. In particular we want to thank Carolyn Ito, the Center's director; specialists Mary Holm, Tracy English, and Judy Hazelgrove; office manager Margaret Jones; and support staff members Lea Lawson and Catherine Triplett. All of them helped with this manuscript in myriad ways as readers, editors, critics, coaches, graphic designers, and friends; all provided us with good ideas and support.

We are also grateful for the conscientious and committed efforts of two tireless research assistants, Heather Fitz-Randolph and Susannah Wood, graduate students in the School of Education Counseling Program. They performed a broad array of exciting—and tedious—tasks with humor and good cheer as they handled the seemingly endless requests for rereading and editing chapters, distributing copies, securing permission, and tracking down elusive references. In addition, they were instrumental in the development of the test bank. Sue Melka and Teri Ancellotti, graduate students in the School Psychology Program, and Yannis Mavropoulos, a doctoral student in Special Education, also contributed greatly to manuscript preparation. We are especially grateful for the extensive support of Beth Stokes, assistant to the dean.

Allyn and Bacon made this a stimulating and rewarding project for us. We appreciate the confidence, assurance, guidance, and genuine kindness that Ray Short, retired senior editor, showed us. His faith in us and support for our work helped us try harder to do our best. The book was enriched by the perceptive comments and constructive feedback we received from all of the Allyn and Bacon field reviewers: Sandra R. Lloyd, University of Texas at El Paso; Scott Sparks, Ohio University; Earle Knowlton, University of Kansas; and Pamela Campbell, University of Connecticut. We appreciate the attention to detail, focused and prompt assistance, and supportive guidance offered by Karin Huang, editorial assistant at Allyn and Bacon and Bridgett Dougherty, project manager at Nesbitt Graphics.

We value the financial support we received over the years from the U.S. Department of Education and the Virginia Department of Education for several funded projects. Funding helped us prepare advanced master's and doctoral students for practice and research related to professional collaboration and inclusive education. It also enabled us to work directly with teachers, specialists, and administrators through the Eastern Virginia Training/Technical Assistance Center (College of William and Mary Center) who are engaged in the daily challenges of "doing inclusion right." In particular, we wish to express our gratitude to the doctoral students in the Leadership Preparation for Collaborative Service Delivery Project for their assistance with this project.

Finally, we want to acknowledge the unfailing support, encouragement, and commitment we received from our spouses, children, extended families, and many caring friends throughout this project.

Collaboration for Inclusive Education

1 Inclusive Education

Building the Case

LEARNING OBJECTIVES

1. Compare and contrast traditional schools and inclusive schools.
2. Identify and describe key elements of inclusive schools and collaboration.
3. Discuss the rationales for inclusive education and collaboration.
4. Summarize current criticisms of inclusive education.

Recently two middle school teachers from neighboring districts discussed their experiences related to the inclusion of students with disabilities in their classrooms. Kara, an enthusiastic seventh-grade teacher, reported the successes in her school district. "Inclusion has been one of the best things that has ever happened in our system! It has given us all a greater sense of community and belonging. Five years ago, we began designing our district's restructuring plan and inclusion was an important part of the plan from the very beginning. Since then, we have been amazed at the progress most kids have made in inclusive classrooms. In particular, students with disabilities have made better academic and social skills gains than we ever imagined possible. These kids are succeeding—they are happy and are making real friends. Inclusion has also helped a lot of other kids who struggled in school but never qualified for special education. These kids, who used to 'slip through the cracks,' now get a lot more classroom support and help. This happens because teachers, specialists, students, administrators, and families are all collaborating with each other. We are sharing ideas and working together in ways I've never seen before. There's very little of the old 'my kids' versus 'your kids' attitude among the teachers. Instead we are planning and teaching as a school team to help all kids. If you were to ask teachers in my building about inclusion, I think most of them would tell you it's been incredibly satisfying. I won't tell you it's been easy—because it hasn't been. We've worked hard, but I think we've grown a lot professionally because of inclusion and collaboration."

Elizabeth, also a seventh-grade teacher, shook her head and sighed, "After all you've said I hate to sound so negative but, I've got to tell you, inclusion has probably been the WORST thing that has ever happened in our district. It's been a nightmare for everybody—kids, teachers, administrators—and a lot of parents really hate it. Basically, the central office told us to 'just do it'. We didn't get much help figuring out a good plan for our school. We received very little training, no extra planning time, no other supports, and everybody—even those who hated it from the beginning—had to do it. I feel for the poor special education teachers who race in and out of classrooms going a million miles an hour. It's obvious that they don't have a clue about what's happening to those special education kids because there is never any time to talk about how they are doing. Consequently, it's really easy for identified kids to fail. Everybody involved with inclusion is frustrated. Even my principal, who *never* says anything against the central office, is furious. Some of the parents and teachers now refer to inclusion as 'the *i* word'. What's really sad is that nobody is willing to admit that we went about this all wrong. The central office still doesn't understand that implementing inclusion isn't just like turning on a light switch. We can't provide traditional services for kids with disabilities one day and then magically flip a switch and be truly inclusive the next day. It just doesn't work that way!"

The teachers' comments in the opening vignette represent the vastly different viewpoints on the topic of inclusion that exist in schools today. Some readers, especially those new to this debate, may find it difficult to believe that two teachers could hold such different opinions about the same topic. Seasoned veterans of public education, however, recognize the reality of these disparate ideas. As a result of efforts by advocates for inclusive education, record numbers of students with disabilities who were excluded from general education classrooms just a few years ago are now attending neighborhood schools and learning in classrooms with age-appropriate peers (U.S. Department of Education [USDOE], 1998).

Inclusion has become a topic of passionate discussion and heated debate among advocates of students with disabilities (Gallagher, 1995; Hallahan, 1998; Kauffman & Hallahan, 1995; Lipsky & Gartner, 1997a; 1997b; National Research Council [NRC], 1997). Inclusion advocates present a wide array of arguments based on social, legal, and educational practice to support their case; so do those on the other side, who speak in favor of the prevalent resource, or "pull-out," model of service delivery. In general, pull-out approaches provide special education and related services to identified students outside general education classrooms. Some students with disabilities may be assigned to pull-out programs on a full-time basis for a year or more. Others with disabilities may be assigned to general education classes but also spend a portion of their school day in resource programs in which specialized instruction is provided in small groups. Pull-out models are based on the belief that specialized instruction is provided most appropriately outside the general education classroom (Friend & Bursuck, 1996).

Typically, students in pull-out programs receive daily special education services. These small-group sessions range in length from 30 minutes to slightly less than half the school day. Given the inherent philosophical and structural differences that exist between inclusive and pull-out models, it is not surprising to find that many professionals and families have difficulty assessing the legitimacy of the arguments that each side presents.

Many outside observers may wonder why the concept of inclusive education creates such a furor. On the one hand, it seems logical and sensible to provide supportive learning environments for all students. Basically, it is the right thing to do. It is hard to imagine that anyone, especially recognized advocates of students with disabilities, could possibly oppose this effort. On the other hand, watching inclusion practiced poorly in many schools makes it easier to understand why caring and concerned advocates speak out against inclusion. Appropriate and effective inclusion is no easy task; in fact, it is difficult to achieve. It requires concerted effort by committed advocates to ensure that appropriate practices are implemented and supported over time.

In general, effective models of inclusion are characterized by comprehensive planning, support, and resources (Lipsky & Gartner, 1997b). Well-run programs offer families and professionals hope for the future of diverse learners. Unfortunately, many programs that claim to be inclusive are inclusive in name only. Many schools' "model" programs are actually poor examples that violate basic tenets of inclusive education; that is, educators are poorly prepared, classrooms are over-populated with identified and low-achieving students, and specialists have unwieldy caseloads that prevent meaningful classroom support (Kauffman & Hallahan, 1995). School systems that jump on the inclusion bandwagon without using a thorough and thoughtful planning process quickly encounter problems. When any worthwhile innovation is poorly implemented, the likely result is student and professional frustration and failure. Schools that have been through a poorly conceptualized attempt at inclusion usually espouse a "been there, done that" attitude when the topic is raised. Unfortunately, many administrators, teachers, specialists, and families who were involved in failed attempts assume that inclusion is a faulty concept rather than recognize that some difficulties were the result of inadequate implementation plans.

Despite failures in some districts, many school systems have adopted inclusive education with great success. Many of these systems have woven inclusion into other ongoing school reform efforts. During the past 10 to 15 years advances in instruction have provided more support and have enabled more diverse student learners to grasp concepts and participate in general education classes more effectively (Falvey, 1995; Gersten, 1998; Slavin, Karweit, & Madden, 1989). Some of these efforts include multiage grouping (Oakes & Quartz, 1994), cooperative learning (Slavin et al., 1989), classwide peer tutoring (Greenwood et al., 1992), and innovative academic programs such as Accelerated Learning (Levin, 1997). Although it is unnecessary for schools to implement some of these changes before taking on the challenge of inclusive education, schools that can build on their previous successes may have an easier time. In addition to the possibility of using one initiative to support the development of another, these schools also know more about making meaningful changes and sustaining these efforts over time (Fullan, 1991).

While the merits of inclusive education are being debated in faculty lunch-rooms, homes, school board meetings, universities, and legislative halls, the reality is that inclusion is happening every day in more and more schools. U.S. Department of Education (1998) data show that the number of students with disabilities who are being assigned to general education classrooms is increasing. Most school districts currently are attempting some form of inclusive education. These fledgling efforts range in size from small classroom-level activities that have been initiated by teachers volunteering to co-teach to broad, sweeping district- and statewide mandates for change.

This book is not intended to debate the philosophical questions about inclusion. As teacher educators and field researchers, we believe in inclusive education if it is implemented appropriately. Consequently, this book is about the process of creating effective inclusive programs through collaboration. It is designed to serve as a guide for teacher leaders, administrators, specialists (e.g., special education teachers, English-as-a-Second-Language [ESL] teachers, speech-language patholo-gists, counselors, Limited English Proficiency [LEP] teachers, school psychologists), and families who are interested in developing inclusive programs that are effec-tive learning environments for all participants. Critical district-level, school-level, and classroom-level considerations are addressed.

In this chapter, two basic terms used throughout the book—*inclusive educa-tion* and *collaboration*—are clarified. In addition, the basic case in support of inclu-sive education is presented. To do this, three fundamental areas of influence are discussed. First, some of the issues related to underlying social beliefs and values that have motivated schools to create more inclusive learning environments are examined. Second, legal and legislative precedents are reviewed. Finally, research related to traditional and inclusive instructional practices is examined. The preva-lent special education service delivery model used for the past 25 years is also evaluated.

What Is Inclusive Education?

Over the past fifteen years, many authors have presented definitions of "integra-tion," "inclusion," "heterogeneous schools," and "inclusive education" (e.g., Falvey, 1995; Giangreco, Cloninger, Dennis, & Edelman, 1994; Lipsky & Gartner, 1997a; Reynolds, Wang, & Walberg, 1987; Stainback & Stainback, 1990; Thousand, Villa, & Nevin, 1994). Although variations exist among these definitions, most ad-vocates agree that inclusive learning environments are those in which "everyone belongs, is accepted, supports, and is supported by his or her peers and other members of the school community in the course of having his or her educational needs met" (Stainback & Stainback, 1990, p. 3). Students are educated in general education classrooms with their peers to the greatest extent possible. Some skills, such as toileting, swallowing, and using public transportation, might need to be taught outside the classroom, but with few exceptions students spend the vast majority of time in class with typical peers. This is not to say that all students study the same curriculum, but they learn together with curricular adjustments made to meet individual needs.

In many ways, this concept is neither new nor revolutionary (Bunch, 1997). Special education advocates have long held an inherent commitment to inclusion. For many years, researchers, teachers, and program developers have written passionate and powerful arguments supporting inclusion in education, employment, and independent living opportunities for persons with disabilities (e.g., Dunn, 1968; Lilly, 1970; Reynolds, 1962; Wolfensberger, 1972). As Reynolds and Birch noted in 1977, "[T]he whole history of education for exceptional children can be told in terms of one steady trend that can be described as progressive inclusion" (p. 22). In essence, the second half of the 20th century has been marked by active advocacy to guarantee the rights and opportunities of persons with disabilities to live as independently and successfully as possible within the context of mainstream life (Lipsky & Gartner, 1997b). Over the years continuous progress has been made but not without an ongoing philosophical and logistical struggle among experts and advocates to find the most appropriate ways to include students with disabilities (Bunch & Valeo, 1997; Dunn, 1968).

What Is Collaboration?

Friend and Cook (1996) have defined collaboration as a *style* of direct interaction that characterizes many types of processes and projects. Effective collaboration is based on the ongoing participation of two or more individuals who are committed to working together to achieve common goals. Typically, these contributors bring different skills and unique contributions to create, strengthen, and maintain these relationships (Friend & Cook, 1996). Professionals agree that effective and ongoing collaboration among stakeholders is an essential feature of effective inclusion (Bauwens & Hourcade, 1995; Cramer, 1998; Creasey & Walther-Thomas, 1996; Fishbaugh, 1997; Friend & Cook, 1996; Giangreco et al., 1994; Korinek, McLaughlin, & Walther-Thomas, 1995; National Commission on Teaching and America's Future [NCTAF], 1996; Villa, Thousand, Nevin, & Malgeri, 1996). In essence, inclusion is impossible without effective collaboration (Cramer, 1998; Skrtic, 1991).

Ideally, participation in collaborative relationships should be voluntary (Friend & Cook, 1996; Thousand et al., 1994). This helps ensure everyone's commitment to the process. Collaborative relationships are based on mutual respect for each participant's unique skills, perspectives, and knowledge (Bauwens & Hourcade, 1995). Because participants value and respect one another's contributions, parity exists among members (Friend & Cook, 1996). No person is valued more than another. Mutual support and a willingness to share information, knowledge, skills, responsibilities, and resources are established hallmarks of effective collaboration (Fishbaugh, 1997; Walther-Thomas, 1997b).

Many collaborative relationships emerge out of shared concerns of like-minded individuals (Villa et al., 1996). Working together, collaborators create a sense of synergy that enables them to accomplish much more than they could on their own (Orelove & Sobsey, 1996; Walther-Thomas, 1998), ensures a broader base of initial support for change, and creates greater momentum to sustain efforts over time (Fishbaugh, 1997; Fullan, 1991; Fullan & Hargreaves, 1996).

Characteristics of effective collaborative teams are often manifested through the distribution of various team responsibilities, accepted decision-making procedures, shared use of available resources, and well-developed accountability measures (Giangreco et al., 1994). Common examples of collaborative groups found in inclusive schools include school–community planning teams, assistance teams, co-teaching partnerships, and consultative relationships. In Chapter 2 collaboration is discussed in greater detail, and throughout this book many proven and promising procedures for achieving effective collaboration and lasting change are presented.

Values and Beliefs in Inclusive Schools

In essence, those involved with inclusive schools share common values and beliefs that influence classroom practices. The goals and objectives of most public school systems are based on several common tenets. First and foremost, all children and adolescents have the right to educational experiences that enable them to become capable students, skilled contributors, and respected members of their learning communities (Bunch & Valeo, 1997; Oakes & Quartz, 1994). Most citizens believe that, in addition to well-honed academic skills, students should develop the knowledge, skills, and attitudes to become caring and compassionate citizens (Bracey, 1996; NCTAF, 1996; NRC, 1997). To achieve these aims, schools must foster the development of (1) caring relationships and genuine friendships; (2) a sense of belonging for all students; and (3) holistic, heterogeneous, and flexible learning opportunities (Giangreco et al., 1994; Levin, 1997; Lipsky & Gartner, 1997a; Oakes & Quartz, 1994; Sapon-Shevin, Dobbelaere, Corrigan, Goodman, & Mastin, 1998; Stainback & Stainback, 1996a; Thousand et al., 1994; Walther-Thomas, 1997a).

Caring Relationships and Genuine Friendships

Faculty and staff in inclusive schools cultivate caring and supportive relationships among students in a variety of ways. They set high expectations for student cooperation, peer support, and personal responsibility. They also create ongoing opportunities for all students, with and without disabilities, to become capable and skilled individuals (Stainback & Stainback, 1996b). Students learn fundamental communication skills and develop relationships with peers and adults. They acquire a broad array of skills, such as making and keeping friends, working together, problem solving, and resolving conflict. Interpersonal skills are taught, modeled, practiced, and reinforced in conscientious, systematic, and ongoing ways (Slavin et al., 1989). Further, classrooms are designed to encourage ongoing cooperation and collaboration among students. Students learn, teach, work, and play with peers daily through participation in small- and large-group activities, such as cooperative learning groups, buddy systems, and peer tutoring.

A Sense of Belonging for All Students

In the past, few students who had significant support needs (e.g., physical disabilities, low cognitive functioning, medical needs) attended their own neighborhood schools or had the opportunities to belong to classroom and neighborhood groups. Many of these students were bused to designated sites where special education was provided. While "clustering" students with disabilities may have helped the specialists' schedules, it wreaked havoc on students' social lives; they were segregated and isolated from families, peers, and classmates (Villa & Thousand, 1990).

Specialized classrooms or day programs away from students' neighborhoods offered limited occasions for them to learn how to "belong" because they didn't spend time with siblings, peers, and others (Kunc, 1992). In addition, students who attended these remote, specialized classes had few interactions with typical students; they spent every weekday with adults and others with disabilities. Commonly, these special programs were housed in segregated hallways away from general education classrooms or in separate buildings where students were physically and psychologically removed from other students. In many school systems, special education was treated like a second-class program. Space limitations resulted in "nomadic" special education programs that were moved from one building to another as shifts occurred in neighborhood enrollments. Special education students and their teachers had little time to interact formally or informally with others. Limited visibility in schools, coupled with busing and few opportunities for ongoing interaction, impeded students' development of meaningful relationships with others outside the special education circle (Kunc, 1992).

By contrast, inclusive communities are designed to surround *all* participants—students, families, educators, administrators, staff, and others—with support and encouragement to nurture a strong sense of belonging. Belonging is also facilitated by valuing the unique contributions that each person makes to the community's well-being. Although each person's contribution may be somewhat different from those of the other members, all contributions are recognized, appreciated, and celebrated. As Kunc (1992) noted:

> [W]hen inclusive education is fully embraced, we abandon the idea that children have to become "normal" to contribute to the world. Instead, we search for and nourish the gifts that are inherent in all people. We begin to look beyond typical ways of becoming valued members of the community and, in doing so, begin to realize the achievable goal of providing all children with an authentic sense of belonging. (p. 38)

Insights from the Field

When my daughter, Lyndsey, was in the second grade we moved to a new community. One November weekend I let her host a slumber party so she could get better acquainted with some of the girls from her class. I didn't know any of her guests, so as we addressed six or seven invitations and prepared for the party she told me a little about each girl. For example, I learned that Kizzie *always* wore purple and Cari had sold more Girl Scout cookies than anybody else in the *entire* school the previous year.

Several days before the party I received a call from the mother of one of the guests. She asked if I knew anything about her daughter, April. Proudly, I affirmed that I did. I told her that April was the "best artist" in the class, "a little shy," and "very sweet." Her mother added some additional details to my profile of April. She was a child with multiple disabilities who was in her first year of public school experience. She had never spent a night away from home. Candidly, her mother asked if I really wanted April to come to the party. Hiding my underlying concerns, I told her we really wanted April. I also pointed out, to reassure her—as well as myself—that I was a former special education teacher, so things would be fine. Toward the end of our conversation, and with considerable difficulty, she told me that this was April's first party invitation and that her daughter was thrilled. She was relieved to find that the invitation was "still good," and she indicated that I could call her at any time if April presented problems during the party. I must admit I was already feeling somewhat intimidated by the prospect of all those little "sleepover" guests, and to learn that one had identified disabilities heightened my anxieties.

Fortunately, the party was a smashing success. The girls loved the activities Lyndsey had planned and they all played well together. I found it interesting that the guests were just like Lyndsey had told me they would be. Kizzie did wear purple; Cari had lots of Girl Scout stories, and April *was* a magnificent artist. By bedtime two girls had gone home to their own beds—but not April.

Several hours after tucking them into their sleeping bags in the family room, I was awakened by crying. I knew immediately it was April. As I hurried down the stairs, the crying stopped abruptly and was replaced by hushed whispers. I stopped on the stairs and listened to the girls' quiet conversation. Working well as a team, the girls assured April that everything was okay and that "sleeping over" was hard. Kizzie told April she had probably had a nightmare. Another guest, Lauren, offered her stuffed animal for support. Melody said she was scared, too. Another girl suggested that April and Melody share a sleeping bag. Lyndsey pointed out that donuts would be served in the morning. Then someone suggested that they all sing a song April liked from school—but quietly so they didn't wake "the mother." I tiptoed back upstairs to the refrains of "Itsy-Bitsy Spider." The next morning donuts were served, no one mentioned April's nightmare, everybody hugged each other, and went home. Lyndsey told me she was so happy that we lived in this nice, new neighborhood where she had such good friends.

The slumber party was a great "aha!" experience for me personally and professionally. I think of this party as *the* day I began to truly understand the value of inclusive education. To some people April was a child with lots of potential learning and behavior problems. But Lyndsey and the other girls saw her differently. They saw and valued her as a "great artist" and a "good friend." If these girls had not been in the same classroom as April, they would never have known about her skills and abilities. If she had been a student in a special education classroom, would she ever have been invited to a typical peer's home for the night? (Chriss Walther-Thomas)

Holistic, Heterogeneous, and Flexible Learning Opportunities

To ensure appropriate classroom balance and protect the educational rights of *all* students, students with disabilities and other unique learning needs should be included in general education classrooms in approximately the same proportion as they exist in the larger population (Brown, Ford, Nisbet, Sweet, Donellan, & Gruenewald, 1983, p. 17). According to U.S. Department of Education data, approximately 10% of the students in schools have disabilities (USDOE, 1998). Within this group, most have mild to moderate disabilities; a very small proportion have significant disabilities. Given the small number of students with significant disabilities, only two or three of these students may attend a neighborhood school of 800 students.

In the process of creating balanced student rosters for classrooms, inclusive planning teams need to consider all students' abilities and needs as student placements are made and as specialists' caseloads are developed. Ideally, in a balanced class of 25 students, approximately 10% have mild to moderate disabilities, that is, two or three students. In addition, another 10% to 20% of students may be low achievers in comparison with their classmates or considered to be at risk for potential school failure based on school or home factors such as English proficiency, family income, or low academic performance. Finally, the remaining 70% to 80% of students should represent a mix of average, above-average, and high-achieving abilities.

In some school systems this "ideal" mix may be difficult to achieve, especially in urban and rural communities where disproportionate numbers of students are considered at risk for school failure. Nevertheless, the same process should be used to make student placements and caseload determinations as in schools in which more heterogeneous populations exist (Walther-Thomas, 1997a). Again, this means that all students' strengths and weaknesses must be considered. If the very best readers in the sixth grade all perform below the sixth-grade level, they are still the top students. They should be viewed as top performers and distributed evenly across all classrooms. This topic is explored further in Chapter 6.

Today, heterogeneous grouping is becoming more widely accepted in many early childhood, elementary, and middle school programs, but it is more challenging to determine the most inclusive, appropriate, and heterogeneous placements for high school students and young adult learners. Typical high school programs continue to divide students into multilevel offerings geared toward different visions of the future (e.g., college preparation, technical training, functional living, compensatory education). In making decisions and assembling resources to assist older students, it is essential to explore and acknowledge each student's long-term educational plans and personal and vocational aspirations. For some high school students, the most inclusive environment may not be full-time enrollment in traditional academic programs. Some may benefit more from community-based vocational training or apprenticeship programs, short-term resource classes, mentorships, and tutorials geared toward specific skill development (e.g., social skills, independent living, vocational preparation) to enhance their prospects for more active community participation, independent living, and vocational well-being in the post–high school years.

Students participate in multilevel learning through shared activities. Although all students participate in labs, field trips, discussions, and cooperative learning groups, they do not all learn the same concepts or skills from these experiences. Inclusive educators individualize students' learning objectives to ensure that unique learning needs are met within a shared content curriculum (e.g., science, language arts, social skills, physical education). Teachers and specialists work together to plan learning experiences that allow students to progress at their own rate (Collicott, 1991). For example, students studying the life cycle of frogs in an eighth-grade science class may have different learning objectives based on current skills and learning needs. During this unit, Susan, a typical student in the class, learns about the process of mitosis. Laurie, a student with mild mental retardation and poor social skills, learns to identify frogs at various life stages and improves her group participation skills. In inclusive settings, teachers use various "curriculum overlapping" strategies to teach important social skills, study skills, and learning strategies within the academic content (Giangreco & Putnam, 1991).

Most schools believe in fostering the development of caring relationships and genuine friendships; a sense of belonging for all students; and holistic, heterogeneous, and flexible learning opportunities, but clearly some schools achieve these aims better than others (Levin, 1997; Lipsky & Gartner, 1997b; Oakes & Quartz, 1994; Stainback & Stainback, 1996a). Figure 1.1 presents a comparison of traditional schools and inclusive schools to illustrate some of the common differences in practices that facilitate the development of these shared values and beliefs.

Think About It...

Some decision makers wonder if most inclusive schools can adequately prepare students with significant support needs to become independent and self-reliant adults. What are some of the potential risks and potential benefits teams should consider as placement decisions are made?

FIGURE 1.1 **Structure and Philosophy: Differences between Inclusive and Traditional Models.**

Traditional Models	Inclusive Educational Models
1. Some students do not "fit" in general education classes.	1. All students "fit" in general education classrooms.
2. The teacher is the instructional leader.	2. Collaborative teams share leadership responsibilities.
3. Students learn from teachers and teachers solve the problems.	3. Students and teachers learn from each other and solve problems together.
4. Students are purposely grouped by similar ability.	4. Students are purposely grouped by differing abilities.
5. Instruction is geared toward middle-achieving students.	5. Instruction is geared to match students at all levels of achievement.
6. Grade-level placement is considered synonymous with curricular content.	6. Grade-level placement and individual curricular content are independent of each other.
7. Instruction is often passive, competitive, didactic, and/or teacher-directed.	7. Instruction is active, creative, and collaborative among members of the classroom.
8. Most instructional supports are provided outside the classroom.	8. Most instructional supports are provided within the classroom.
9. Students who do not "fit in" are excluded from general classes and/or activities.	9. Activities are designed to include students though participation levels may vary.
10. The classroom teacher assumes ownership for the education of general education students, and special education staff assume ownership for the education of students with special needs.	10. The classroom teacher, special educators, related service staff, and families assume shared ownership for educating all students.
11. Students are evaluated by common standards.	11. Students are evaluated by individually appropriate standards.
12. Students' success is achieved by meeting common standards.	12. The system of education is considered successful when it strives to meet each student's needs. Students' success is achieved when both individual and group goals are met.

Source: Adapted from Giangreco, M. F., Cloninger, C. J., Dennis, R. E., & Edelman, S. W. (1994). Problem-solving methods to facilitate inclusive education. In Thousand, J. S., Villa, R. A., & Nevin, A. I. (Eds.) *Creativity and collaborative learning: A practical guide to empowering students and teachers.* Paul H. Brookes Publishing Company, P.O. Box 10624, Baltimore, MD 21285-0624.

Legal and Legislative Support for Inclusive Education

During the 1960s, families and professionals became vocal advocates for the educational rights of students with disabilities (Aiello, 1976). Many early advocacy efforts were stimulated in part by the 1954 landmark civil rights decision *Brown v. Board of Education, Topeka, Kansas*. In this decision, the United States Supreme Court ruled that separate education was not equal education for African American students. The Court recognized that separate educational programs interfered with educational opportunities and motivation of these students. As a result, their potential for long-term success was impeded. This ruling provided powerful impetus toward integrated education for African American students, and it set the stage for other advocacy groups to challenge commonly accepted practices that discriminated against other students because of disabilities or differences in language, gender, or ethnicity.

After many years of legislation and litigation, the Education of All Handicapped Children Act, P.L. 94-142, was passed in 1975. This law, now updated and reauthorized as the Individuals with Disabilities Education Act of 1997 (IDEA, P.L. 105-17), was a legislative landmark in many ways. Congress founded IDEA on six fundamental principles that include:

1. a commitment to *"zero reject,"* so that no student is excluded from public education because of the severity of his or her disability.
2. *procedural due process* to ensure student rights at every stage in the identification, eligibility, program development, and placement process.
3. *parent participation* and involvement at each stage.
4. *fair and unbiased assessment* to ensure that students are not penalized because of differences in their native language, culture, race, or ethnicity.
5. *free and appropriate public education* (FAPE) for every student who qualifies for special education in the *least restrictive environment* (LRE) possible.
6. *confidentiality of records* to protect student and family rights (Turnbull, Turnbull, Shank, & Leal, 1995).

In addition to these powerful safeguards for students with disabilities and their families, IDEA also represented a massive educational reform effort. It guaranteed an individualized educational program (IEP) for students with disabilities and ensured support for ongoing personnel preparation. Never before had Congress made such a widescale attempt to educate so many learners with diverse needs (Turnbull et al., 1995).

Implementation of the Least Restrictive Environment Principle

Since the initial passage of IDEA, more than two generations of students with disabilities have participated in mandated special education. During this time, policy makers, educators, families, and researchers have struggled to translate the law into effective practice. Unfortunately, LRE has proven to be a challenging concept to operationalize (Bunch, 1997; Korinek et al., 1995). Over the years many local, state, and federal courts have examined LRE issues and attempted to provide clearer interpretations of what constitutes appropriate learning environments for students with disabilities (Fishbaugh, 1997; Lipsky & Gartner, 1997b). Many LRE difficulties stem from IDEA's focus on the unique and individual academic and social learning needs of students (Stainback & Stainback, 1996b). Consequently, no one interpretation of LRE will work for all students with disabilities.

Development of a Parallel System. Many advocates believed that IDEA heralded a new day of home–school cooperation that would facilitate more appropriate general education opportunities for students with disabilities. Unfortunately, this didn't happen. Instead, mandated special education emerged as a massive, parallel system (Friend & Bursuck, 1996). IDEA regulations clearly indicated that general education classrooms were appropriate starting places for teams to consider as they planned IEPs for students with disabilities and determined appropriate placements for IEP implementation. Clearly, the law directed teams to remove students with disabilities only when general education classrooms were shown to be inappropriate learning environments. In practice, however, most educators and families continued to believe that effective special education had to be provided outside general education in classes often referred to as pull-out programs. As a result, billions of education dollars were invested in maintaining separate learning environments, such as resource rooms, self-contained classes, and special schools to provide services for students with disabilities (Lipsky & Gartner, 1997b; USDOE, 1998).

Two Interpretations of Least Restrictive Environment. Reviewing practices over the past 25 years, two distinctly different interpretations of LRE have been seen in school practice (Bunch & Valeo, 1997; Giangreco & Putnam, 1991; Lipsky & Gartner, 1997a; National Center on Educational Restructuring and Inclusion [NCERI], 1995; Salend, 1994; Skrtic, 1991). In the first, more prevalent model, practitioners have maintained their commitment to parallel systems of education for students with disabilities and their peers. Concerned advocates assumed that specialized settings provided more protected learning environments away from critical and unsupportive peers. Ideally, in smaller, more intensive classes, specially trained experts could use specialized teaching techniques, materials, equipment, and student management systems to help students learn at a better pace (Kauffman & Hallahan, 1995).

In the second LRE interpretation, students with disabilities have been placed in full-time general education programs or those that are as close as possible to general education classes. This interpretation has recognized the educational and social value of general education learning environments (Brown et al., 1983) and represents a significant move toward a more unified single system for educating all students.

Lingering Resistance to Inclusive Education

Over the past decade many advocates for students with disabilities have changed their views on inclusive education as a result of emerging research, increased acceptance and practice, changing state and local policies, and encouragement from the federal level to implement more inclusive programs (Heumann & Hehir, 1994; USDOE, 1998). Advocates have also acknowledged that inclusive education is harder to accomplish than some initially had hoped, but emerging research and practice are providing information and strategies to help schools make the transition.

Some opponents have lingering concerns about inclusion despite growing support. Clearly some of these concerns are rooted in philosophical differences and long-standing practices that are hard to resolve. Many legitimate and thought-provoking questions must be resolved, however, to ensure protection of the educational rights of students with disabilities as well as those of typical learners. The most frequently noted arguments against inclusion are presented in the subsequent discussion.

First, it is important to consider the interest and willingness of the general education community to educate students with disabilities in general education classrooms (Fuchs & Fuchs, 1995; Kauffman & Hallahan, 1995; Lloyd, Repp, & Singh, 1991). For years, special education has served an important function in schools by providing general educators with a convenient way to remove from their classrooms students who were perceived as difficult to teach. General education historically has endorsed special education and supported its need for significant resources because it has been an effective mechanism for removing the most difficult and challenging students from classrooms, allowing teachers to focus their attention on a smaller band of the student population.

Second, opponents question general education classrooms as appropriate learning environments for many students with disabilities, even those with relatively mild disabilities. Many students who end up in special education have experienced previous failure in these classrooms. Many of these students continue to experience difficulty even in smaller special education classes because of problems related to their disabilities such as distractibility, poor memory, visual and auditory processing problems, and poor self-control. Without adequate planning and support, many students with disabilities are likely to fail again in larger classrooms.

Third, opponents fear that, in inclusive classes, students with disabilities may not receive the more intensive and individualized instruction intended in pull-out programs. Some special education researchers contend that this type of instruction is especially critical in early elementary grades when fundamental reading skills are developed. If students fail to learn these skills, they may not catch up with their peers or develop the survival skills needed when the content becomes more demanding in the upper grades (Vaughn, 1997).

Fourth, some students need more significant support than many systems can provide (Klingner, Vaughn, Hughes, Schumm, & Elbaum, 1998). As a result, students with disabilities may be penalized by inappropriate instruction, insensitive peers, limited attention, and unrealistic expectations from general educators (Klingner et al., 1998). The complex needs of some students may also jeopardize typical students' learning if inadequate classroom assistance is available. Unless schools are willing to reallocate money to create better support networks, general education classrooms will not provide appropriate aid.

Fifth, given increasingly complex concerns about education today (e.g., violence, drugs, low achievement), greater diversity in language and culture, and new state and local policies demanding higher student performance, this may be a poor time to add more students with special needs to general education classrooms. Negative experiences with inclusion in some schools may actually create a backlash that results in more isolation for students with disabilities in the future (Council for Exceptional Children [CEC], 1996).

Sixth, because inclusive support services are relatively new in many schools and research is limited, their real effectiveness has yet to be proven. Inclusion may put undue stress and pressure on teachers that results in sagging morale and reduced professional confidence (Kauffman, 1989).

Finally, opponents worry that a more unified system of public education will undermine much of the progress that has been made in special education during the past 40 years. Today legislators, educators, and the general public recognize the unique needs of students with disabilities. Local, state, and federal funds are specifically designated to ensure that these students are educated appropriately. Opponents fear that other, high-visibility priorities (e.g., at-risk youth, technology, global competition, drugs) are likely to capture the attention of general education and that unguarded special education resources may quickly be diverted to other efforts (Hallahan, 1998; Kauffman, 1989; Kauffman & Hallahan, 1995).

These concerns must be addressed to satisfy critics and, more important, to ensure that students with disabilities receive an appropriate education. It is impossible, however, to ignore the mounting evidence against pull-out models. For a variety of reasons, some based in organizational issues and others related to students' disabilities, these programs have been, for the most part, ineffective. The data regarding the poor outcomes of students who participated in these programs have graphically illustrated the need for more effective alternatives.

Mounting Concerns about Student Outcomes

Despite years of intervention research, legislation, and mandated services, many students with disabilities continue to fall through the cracks of the public education system (USDOE, 1998). Some of the most disheartening postschool outcomes occur among students with mild to moderate disabilities. These are the students with whom it is generally assumed that teachers and specialists should be most effective (Carlson, 1997; Edgar, 1988; Malmgren, Edgar, & Neel, 1998; Wagner et al., 1991). These students also represent more than 90% of those served in special education programs (USDOE, 1998). As more student outcome data have become available, numerous areas of concern have been identified. Five of these areas will be examined briefly: (1) low rates of declassification, (2) high student dropout rates, (3) weak transition skills, (4) poor independent living skills, and (5) high rates of incarceration.

Low Rates of Declassification

Clearly, the impact of a disability cannot be discounted. Inherent problems that bring low-performing students to the attention of the special education system are not likely to be eliminated despite diligent efforts by students, their teachers, specialists, and families. Although effects of a disability may be minimized over time, most disabilities are likely to have lasting effects on student performance regardless of the support students receive (Bender, 1992). The prognosis for successful remediation of identified students' academic and social skills problems in traditional special education programs is not optimistic (Wagner et al., 1991; Wagner, Blackorby, Cameto, Hebbeler, & Newman, 1993). In traditional special education programs, once students qualify for special education services, less than 10% of all identified students, including those with mild disabilities, are ever declassified and returned to general education on a full-time basis (Carlson, 1997; Levin, Zigmond, & Birch, 1985; Madden & Slavin, 1983; Slavin et al., 1989; USDOE, 1998; Zigmond & Baker, 1990).

High Student Dropout Rates

A disproportionate number of students with disabilities fail classes and drop out of school before graduating (Wagner et al., 1991). Overall, almost 40% of students with disabilities leave school, whereas less than 25% of the general education student population drop out (Wagner et al., 1991, 1993; USDOE, 1998). Special education dropouts are also less likely than typical students to return to school to complete General Education Diploma (GED) requirements (Wagner et al., 1993). Students with disabilities reenter the education system at approximately half the rate of their peers (Stainback & Stainback, 1996a).

Unsatisfactory Transition Skills

Most special education students are poorly prepared for the future. Numerous studies have shown that students with disabilities fail to meet both teachers' and families' expectations despite years of extensive and expensive special education (Carlson, 1997; Edgar, Levine, & Maddox, 1986; USDOE, 1998; Wagner et al., 1993). Because these young adults have few relationships with peers, many must remain dependent on their families for social and emotional support. Young adults with mild disabilities remain at home long after their typical peers. This situation puts additional stress on many families because the parents and young adults had expected this to be a time of greater independence (Carlson, 1997; Edgar, 1988).

Poor Independent Living Skills

Many young adults with disabilities are vocationally ill-prepared. For example, Edgar and colleagues (1986) reported that only 18% of young adults with mild to moderate disabilities earn more than minimum wage. Few of these former students have the knowledge, skills, and confidence needed to seek out postsecondary education and use available community resources (Edgar & Polloway, 1994; Malmgren et al., 1998). Wagner and Blackorby (1996) reported similar postsecondary education enrollment findings in the U.S. Department of Education–sponsored National Longitudinal Transition Study (NLTS) data. In comparison with their typical peers, few young adults with disabilities participated in postsecondary education programs. Approximately one-third of the former special education students engaged in postsecondary learning experiences compared with approximately two-thirds of the typical population.

High Incarceration Rates

More than half of all students with identified behavior disorders drop out of school, and approximately 75% of these students are arrested within 5 years after leaving school (Wagner et al., 1991, 1993). Although students with mild to moderate disabilities represent less than 10% of the school population, they are grossly overrepresented within the juvenile justice system. Studies and meta-analyses of incarcerated youth (e.g., Hynes, 1995; Keilitz & Dunivant, 1986; Nelson, Rutherford, & Wolford, 1987; U.S. Office of Juvenile Justice and Delinquency Prevention [USOJJDP], 1994) show that 12% to 70% have mild to moderate disabilities. Many experts speculate that the academic failure, social isolation, and dropout experiences of students with disabilities all contribute to their delinquent behavior (USOJJDP, 1994).

In summary, student outcomes for participants in special education have been poor. Clearly, the program strategies that have been used in the past have not met many of the students' social and academic needs. These discouraging outcomes likely are due to a number of factors that work against students with disabilities and their teachers (Slavin et al., 1989).

Some critics claim that traditional special education programs have lacked the academic rigor needed to prepare students for life (Lyon & Moats, 1993). For example, many secondary special education programs continue to offer watered-down versions of required content classes (Ellis, 1997, 1998). Although this approach may enable students to earn passing grades, it does not provide adequate academic substance (Lyon & Moats, 1993; Zigmond & Miller, 1991). It is unlikely that many students with disabilities who have participated in segregated programs have the in-depth content knowledge they need to perform successfully on exit tests that many states require to earn a standard high school diploma (Lyon & Moats, 1993; NRC, 1997), a minimal requirement for success in today's world.

Concerns about Implementing Pull-Out Models

As noted earlier in this chapter, many students with disabilities traditionally received support in pull-out programs. A growing body of evidence suggests that most students do not benefit from out-of-class support. Reviews and meta-analyses suggest that instructional programs outside general education learning environments produce few, if any, positive and lasting effects on student performance (Baker, Wang, & Walberg, 1994/95; Carlberg & Kavale, 1980; Cole & Meyer, 1991; Halverson & Sailor, 1990; Slavin et al., 1989). Emerging research suggests that students with disabilities do better in inclusive settings (Elliott & McKenney, 1998; Klingner et al., 1998). A number of factors work against student success in pull-out programs. As Slavin and colleagues (1989) noted in an extensive review of pull-out instruction literature, these programs "too often result in a disjointed educational experience for the very children who are most in need of the best possible educational experience" (p. 155). Many experts find pull-out services difficult to manage and ineffective for students. As Bunch (1997) observed, although pull-out approaches represented progress over self-contained special education classrooms and segregated schools, they have become more of a "Solomon-like compromise by educators which cleaves in twain the educational life of children" (p. 16). Three of the most common complaints about this model are summarized below.

Minimal Professional Communication and Coordination of Services

Given the large caseloads of many specialists, they have little time to discuss progress and problems with general educators. Specialists often have responsibilities for students in a number of classrooms that span several grade levels. Few specialists are provided with scheduled noninstructional time to confer and coordinate their efforts with general educators. Most acknowledge that monitoring student progress across content areas is almost impossible. Typically, communication among professionals is fragmented and conducted on a "catch as catch can" basis. Not surprisingly, instruction in the two environments is often duplicative, contradictory, or neglected completely (Deshler, Ellis, & Lenz, 1996; Friend & Bursuck, 1996).

Lack of Student Self-Management Skills

If resource program planners had realized the sophisticated skills needed by students with disabilities to participate in, let alone benefit from, pull-out programs, these programs might have been conceptualized in a different manner. Within this model, students must perform a series of complex self-management and transition-related tasks. It has been well documented in the literature that many students with disabilities struggle with simple transitions from one task to another, let alone multistep transitions requiring movement from one learning environment to another. This process is, undoubtedly, more difficult for younger students who are less skilled and unaccustomed to the rotating schedules that older students learn in secondary programs.

Students must complete a number of tasks in transitioning from general education to pull-out classrooms. First, they must monitor their time and mentally disengage from instruction when it is time to leave class for the resource room. Next they must put their materials away and gather any required supplies before traveling through the building independently, avoiding distractions along the way. Not insignificantly, students lose valuable instructional time as they travel to and from their resource classrooms. If students are consistently unable to perform this sequence, then professional or paraeducator time must be carved out of daily schedules to escort students. When students enter the special education classroom, they must orient themselves to this new setting, assemble their materials, and engage in the new content. Often they must deal with new materials, new instructional strategies, new class rules, and new teacher expectations that may be very different from the previous setting.

Typically, students in resource programs are grouped together because of classroom scheduling considerations (e.g., grade-level times or content-specific periods) rather than similar instructional levels and learning needs. As a result, multiple students on multiple levels are often working on different subjects clustered into the same resource period. Consequently, while most students spend at least 45 to 60 minutes a day in a resource room, it is unlikely that all of the time is spent on specialized instruction. Given the diverse caseloads of most resource teachers, many spend much of their time "hopping" from one student's desk to another to address specific questions and check student work. As a result, students must wait their turn for the teacher to answer questions that arise. Despite what proponents might say about the small-group benefits of resource programs, few resource specialists teach small, well-defined groups with common instructional needs.

Following instruction, students must reverse their paths, return to their general education classrooms, and reengage in ongoing classroom activities. Independently, in many cases, they must determine what the class is currently doing and what they have missed. They must also collect whatever materials, assignments, and missed directions were given while they were out of the classroom (Deshler et al., 1996; Friend & Bursuck, 1996).

Not only do problem learners lack necessary transition and self-management skills, most of them find it difficult, if not impossible, to generalize the requirements for one task to another related activity, let alone from one learning environment to another (Stokes & Baer, 1977). Given previously mentioned concerns about poor communication and lack of service coordination, it is unlikely that many students with disabilities generalize the new skills learned in the resource room to the larger, more complex, and less closely monitored general education classroom (Deshler et al., 1996).

In summary, a wide array of outcome indicators for students who were, for the most part, educated in traditional special education programs present a discouraging picture. Clearly, traditional pull-out services have not worked for most students. Advocates of these approaches can always point to individual specialists or therapists whose efforts outside general education classrooms have made a difference in the lives of students. Certainly there are some notable exceptions. These anecdotal cases are important and should be studied carefully to determine how to provide individualized instruction outside the classroom if it is an inappropriate learning environment for particular targeted skills such as toileting, personal hygiene, or self-feeding. It is more important, however, to recognize the plethora of reports showing that this model is not sufficiently powerful to warrant continued use. MacMillan and Hendricks (1993) concluded, in a review of the evolution of special education over the past 25 years, that most pull-out services have "failed to demonstrate substantive advantages over regular classes" (p. 39).

School Reform Initiatives: Finding More Effective Practices

Gradually special education criticism began to build during the 1980s as professionals became increasingly concerned about implementation problems and dismal student outcome reports. Growing unrest within the special education community was compounded by the general mood for educational reform taking hold across the country (Sage & Burrello, 1994; Sarason, 1993).

In charting the history of the current reform movement, *A Nation at Risk* (National Commission on Excellence in Education, 1983) is often referenced as the document that stimulated the current era of change in public schools. This powerful report, developed by leaders in private and public sectors, criticized schools for doing a poor job in preparing students for the 21st century workforce. Since its publication, additional reform reports have been issued that have received considerable public attention (e.g., NCTAF's *What Matters Most: Teaching for America's Future*, 1996; the National Governors' Association's *A Time for Results*, 1991). Most continue to endorse the fundamental concepts that were introduced in *A Nation at Risk* but suggest additional changes related to teacher preparation, school policies, educational goals, and organizational structures (Bracey, 1996).

Specifically, today's schools are being asked to modify existing practices to reflect higher academic standards, greater collaboration, and more sensitivity to local concerns. This era of standards-based reform has produced a powerful effect on decision making in public schools and higher education. For example, many federal, state, and local boards have enacted policies aimed at improving academic excellence through greater emphasis on basic subjects and more extensive progress monitoring (Southern Regional Education Board [SREB], 1998; Tewel, 1995; Turnbull et al., 1995).

Federal Support for Inclusion

As a result of special education unrest, poor outcomes, and general calls for reform, Madeline Will, then Undersecretary of the U.S. Department of Education,

Office of Special Education and Rehabilitative Services, and the mother of a child with a disability, issued in 1986 a call for special education reform (Will, 1986). She joined with others (e.g., Gartner & Lipsky, 1987; Reynolds et al., 1987; Stainback & Stainback, 1984) as they encouraged educators, administrators, and policymakers to work together more collaboratively to create more effective programs for students with disabilities. By sharing greater responsibility for *all* students, the public education system could provide more appropriate and more flexible educational opportunities for all learners. Since that time, there has been a steady increase in the number of school systems that have developed inclusive approaches as part of their overall school reform and restructuring efforts (NCERI, 1995; NRC, 1997; USDOE, 1998).

The Continuum of Support Services

More and more systems are recognizing that the "continuum" of services guaranteed under IDEA (1997) is not only a range of placement options (i.e., general education classrooms to residential hospitals) but also a range of support services that can and should be used in any learning environment. Students with disabilities need support to be successful in general education classrooms. Placing students in these settings without adequate support is inappropriate. As students' programs are developed, inclusive planning teams must consider students' support needs across various instructional domains such as academic, social-emotional, functional living, and vocational areas. Appropriate service plans should be tailored to meet specific learning needs of students with disabilities, regardless of the learning environment (Snell & Drake, 1994). Some services that students require to succeed in general education settings may be as simple as preferential seating; some may be more extensive, such as assistive technology, specialized instruction, or co-teaching support. Support needs should also be considered on the basis of frequency required to meet student needs. Again, this can vary from low-level assistance, such as extended time during math tests or weekly monitoring to greater assistance, such as one-to-one therapy twice a week for 30-minute periods or ongoing ventilator monitoring. Two students with the same identified disability may have very different academic, social, and vocational educational support needs. Because students differ in their abilities and skills, they may require more or less support and resources. Thoughtful and thorough support planning ensures that students and teachers receive the assistance they need to make general education classrooms successful inclusive learning environments.

Emerging Evidence in Support of Inclusive Education

As inclusive education has gained momentum over the past decade, preliminary research reports are offering support for current efforts. Although critics charge that many of these reports merely provide "feel good" documentation for the efficacy of inclusive education (Fuchs & Fuchs, 1995; Kauffman & Hallahan, 1995;

Lloyd et al., 1991), a growing number of qualitative and quantitative studies corroborate potential benefits for students with disabilities, their peers, and professionals.

Benefits for Students with Disabilities.   Students with disabilities are more likely to succeed in effective inclusive schools because teachers, administrators, specialists, paraeducators, volunteers, and typical classmates are working together to ensure that every student is valued, respected, and accepted for who he or she is and is provided with meaningful and appropriate learning experiences. Emerging data suggest that students with disabilities do better academically and socially in inclusive settings (Klingner et al., 1998; Rea, 1997; Sapon-Shevin et al., 1998; Stevens & Slavin, 1995; Tapasak & Walther-Thomas, in press; Walther-Thomas, 1997a). This is true for students with high-incidence disabilities (Bunch & Valeo, 1997; Rea, 1997; Walther-Thomas, 1997a) and those with low-incidence disabilities (Cole & Meyer, 1991; McDonnell, Thorson, McQuivey, & Kiefer-O'Donnell, 1997; Tapasak & Walther-Thomas, in press).

Although many studies are appearing in the literature that support the academic and social benefits of inclusion, a recent study by Rea (1997) is noteworthy for several reasons. First, Rea collected extant data on schools over time. Most of the data she used could be easily collected in school systems interested in comparing the efficacy of pull-out and inclusive approaches. Second, the results from her study provide additional support for inclusive programs. Rea compared the academic performance of middle school students with learning disabilities in inclusive schools with similar students who were served for comparable periods in pull-out programs. Demographic data showed the groups were comparable in age, gender, ethnicity, socioeconomic status, IQ, years of special education services, years of education in one model or the other, and mothers' educational levels. Students in the inclusive classrooms outperformed those in pull-out programs across a number of important school performance indicators: they earned higher grades, achieved higher scores on standardized tests, attended more school days, failed fewer classes, and were involved in no more behavioral infractions than students in more restrictive placements.

Benefits for Peers.   Studies have shown that typical to high-achieving students are not harmed in the inclusion process (Klingner et al., 1998; McDonnell et al., 1997; Sharpe, York, & Knight, 1994; Tapasak & Walther-Thomas, in press). Emerging studies suggest that the presence of identified students in general education settings may enhance classroom learning experiences for peers who may be at risk academically or socially (Walther-Thomas, 1997b) as well as high-achieving students (Stevens & Slavin, 1995). This is understandable given the extra help to all class members when a learning specialist is present who can target specific problems as students work and develop appropriate intervention strategies immediately to address these concerns (Levin, 1997; Slavin et al., 1989; Walther-Thomas, 1997b).

Valuable life skills, often unexplored in more traditional settings, receive greater attention in inclusive environments (Bunch & Valeo, 1997; NRC, 1997;

> ## Think About It...
>
> If a school system is not employing inclusive education practices at the present time, can a legitimate case be made to allow individual schools to include some, *but not all,* students with disabilities in general education programs? How do you think this idea would be received in your own community?

Sharpe et al., 1994). As noted earlier, inclusive schools design academic work to use structures that facilitate social interactions among students (e.g., peer tutoring, cross-grade and classwide tutoring, cooperative learning). Through these interactions, all students have opportunities to develop or enhance their communication, problem-solving, and relationship-building skills (Giangreco et al., 1994; National Association of State Boards of Education [NASBE], 1992). Adults in inclusive schools provide students with ongoing support, models of caring and accepting behaviors, constructive feedback, and encouragement to be supportive of one another (Kunc, 1992; Tapasak & Walther-Thomas, in press). When inclusion is implemented effectively, ongoing, daily involvement in each others' lives helps students to become more empathetic and understanding as they develop a better appreciation for unique qualities that all people possess (Kunc, 1992; Levin, 1997). Emerging studies suggest that these aims to improve student attitudes in inclusive schools are realistic (Bunch & Valeo, 1997; Rea, 1997; Sapon-Shevin et al., 1998; Stevens & Slavin, 1995; Tapasak & Walther-Thomas, in press; Walther-Thomas, 1997a).

Benefits for Professionals.   Both teachers and specialists report professional growth and enhanced personal support as a result of opportunities to collaborate with others in the development of inclusive services (Bunch, Lupart, & Brown, 1997; Bunch & Valeo, 1997; Sapon-Shevin et al., 1998; Walther-Thomas, 1997a). Collaboration facilitates knowledge sharing and skill development in these ongoing relationships (Walther-Thomas, Bryant, & Land, 1996a). This process enables professionals to become more skilled and more confident in their abilities to address diverse academic and social needs of students with disabilities and others with unique learning needs (Giangreco, Dennis, Cloninger, Edelman, & Schattman, 1993).

General educators' attitudes toward students with disabilities improve as a result of inclusive education experiences when adequate resources, support, and preparation are provided (Giangreco et al., 1993). Most teachers and specialists become more supportive of the model over time. They see inclusive education as an effective approach for student learning and for professional development. It is important to note, however, that many studies also identify common concerns that teachers and specialists share when inclusion is poorly implemented and fails to provide adequate support and resources (Bunch et al., 1997; Karge, McClure, & Patton, 1995; Vaughn, Schumm, Klingner, & Saumell, 1996; Walther-Thomas, 1997a).

> ### Think About It...
>
> Arguments for inclusive education are based on facts as well as values and beliefs. Discuss what you think are the most compelling arguments for and against inclusion.

Chapter Summary

This chapter introduced the central concepts of this text: *inclusive education* and *collaboration*. In addition, the basic case for inclusive education was discussed and concerns of opponents were presented. Over the past decade, many new and long-standing values and beliefs, legal mandates, school reform efforts, and research findings have supported the need to create more caring and inclusive general education learning environments for *all* students.

Although the lingering concerns of those who advocate traditional pull-out models of support must be addressed, the need to find better ways to educate students with disabilities and prepare them for more satisfying and productive adult lives cannot be denied. In subsequent chapters, these concerns are addressed and recommendations are presented to help teams avoid the problems inherent in poorly planned and implemented initiatives. In the next chapter, seven essential features of appropriate and effective inclusive programs are explored. In particular, the importance of a collaborative culture to achieve inclusive education is emphasized. Understanding these features enables readers to develop a conceptual framework for inclusive program development.

CHAPTER ACTIVITIES

1. Spend a day as a volunteer in an inclusive classroom. As you observe, consider the social, legal, and research-based influences that you have read about in this chapter. Share the experience with your classmates.

2. Individually spend 10 to 15 minutes listing inclusive education barriers and resources in a school with which you are familiar. Use the following questions to guide your work: "What resources exist in this school that can facilitate more inclusion and collaboration?" and "What barriers exist that might limit more inclusion and collaboration?" Following individual work, compare answers in a small-group discussion with several classmates. Try to participate in a group with others whose knowledge and experiences are different from your own. What common themes does your group identify? What differences?

3. Interview a general or special education teacher who has been involved in inclusive education. Before the interview, brainstorm possible questions with classmates. Consider the influences that you have read about in this chapter as you formulate your questions. After the interview, compare notes with classmates.

4. Review the comments made by the teachers in the beginning vignette (i.e., Kara and Elizabeth). What are the significant differences between these two experiences? How do these teachers' experiences compare with those of local teachers?

5. Interview a family member of a student with disabilities who has been in both traditional and inclusive special education programs. Before the interview, brainstorm possible questions with classmates. Consider the influences that you have read about in this chapter as you formulate questions. After the interview, compare your notes with classmates.

6. Share resources on inclusion in class or via a class web page. For example, read one or more of the research articles cited in the chapter; post the citation, and provide a brief written summary of the key points. Continue this process throughout the semester to develop a greater understanding of the literature related to inclusive education and professional collaboration.

2 Essential Features of Inclusive Programs

LEARNING OBJECTIVES

1. Identify seven features fundamental to appropriate and effective inclusive programs.
2. Explain the importance of collaboration for achieving inclusive education.
3. Summarize suggested practices for district- and school-level inclusion planning teams related to each of the seven essential features.
4. Explain how teams might proceed when not all essential features are in place.

The Inclusion Planning Team at Martin Luther King High School was anxious to begin serving students in inclusive classrooms. As they looked carefully at their situation, they realized that there was a great deal of anxiety and resistance among the faculty and staff. In general, the climate at Martin Luther King was not particularly collaborative; teachers tended to work very independently and not get involved in much beyond their own departmental teams or extracurricular activities. Although the school had a representative team for overall site-based management, it was clear that their role was strictly advisory and not decision making. The principal and assistant principals were perceived as strong leaders and generally well respected. Although it was true that Anita Grant, the principal, had appointed the Inclusion Planning Team, she was not a visible promoter of the concept.

Before long, the team felt overwhelmed. So much needed to be done, yet the team had to admit that conditions at this time were not conducive to more inclusive and collaborative services. Some team members began to express doubts about their assignment. Maybe it would be better to stick with the current system of pull-out services.

Chapter 1 introduced the concepts of inclusive education and collaboration explaining how their evolution has been influenced by core beliefs and values, legal mandates, and the school reform movement. As an abstract ideal, many people are able to accept the notion of inclusive education. The issues become more controversial when the ideals of inclusion and collaboration must be translated into classroom practice. Understandably, people want to see real programs that are working well for students, families, and professionals. Unfortunately, what many individuals experience or hear about are the unsuccessful ventures. When things go wrong, they readily conclude that inclusion must be a bad idea. It may be more accurate to recognize that inclusion is a good idea that can be implemented badly. Its potential benefits are fully realized only when educators, families, and communities approach inclusion as a major innovation and apply sound practices to ensure development of appropriate programs.

This chapter describes seven features that are fundamental to appropriate and effective inclusion programs. These essential features include (1) a collaborative culture, (2) shared leadership, (3) coherent vision, (4) comprehensive planning, (5) adequate resources, (6) sustained implementation, and (7) continuous evaluation and improvement. Figure 2.1 shows how these seven essential features provide the foundation for effective inclusion through collaboration. As illustrated, the success of inclusive programs rests on these seven key conditions.

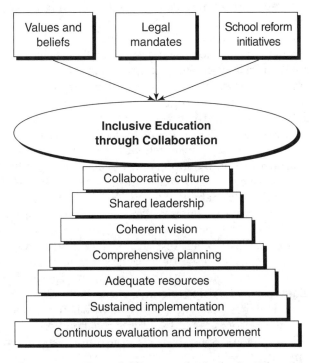

FIGURE 2.1   Essential Features for Inclusive Education.

A Collaborative Culture That Values Teamwork

Successful inclusive education requires members of school communities to share responsibility for all students and work together to support their learning and development. Although most schools aim to be collaborative communities, many encounter dissonance between professed values and actual experiences. Teachers and specialists may not feel empowered to take initiative and responsibility for new innovations if the overall organizational structure favors a more traditional authoritarian or hierarchical approach. Participants may be less inclined to take risks by attempting new service delivery alternatives if the system does not encourage—or actively discourages—such innovation. If school professionals have few opportunities to plan and problem solve with others in a collegial mode, it is unlikely that they will suddenly collaborate effectively to teach students with disabilities or those at risk.

Collaborative service delivery cannot simply be superimposed on a system that does not include professional collaboration in other forms. It is feasible only if the overall school culture supports the concept of professional collaboration. Teachers and specialists will find it easier to work collaboratively in support of inclusive education if they are accustomed to other forms of collaborative planning and problem solving. Many schools provide professionals with ongoing opportunities to collaborate for activities such as curricular planning, staff development, assistance teams, and school improvement initiatives. A number of practices currently associated with effective schools require collaborative interactions among educators. Pugach and Johnson (1995) cite examples of innovative approaches to school organizational structure (e.g., site-based management); changes in professional development and evaluation (e.g., peer coaching, peer evaluation); and curriculum and instruction innovations (e.g., interdisciplinary curriculum, cooperative learning). Middle schools are often good places to start pilot projects on inclusion because their organizational structure promotes teamwork (Dickinson & Erb, 1996; Walther-Thomas, Bryant, & Land, 1996). Typically teachers and specialists are members of grade-level teams that meet regularly to work together on issues of common concern. Collaboration by adults and by students has been the cornerstone of some comprehensive models of school improvement with demonstrated benefits for students of all levels of ability (Stevens & Slavin, 1995).

Group work becomes collaborative if the essential or defining elements are evident: voluntary participation; mutual goals; parity among participants; and shared decision making, responsibility, resources, and accountability (Friend & Bursuck, 1996). Successful experiences collaborating with others enable participants to develop enhanced trust, a stronger sense of community, and a greater willingness to take risks (Friend & Cook, 1996). Collaboration to support inclusive education is most likely to be successful when it is one facet of an overall school culture that encourages and supports collaboration among all members—students, families, teachers, specialists, administrators, and members of the surrounding community.

If the school culture truly values teamwork, then it follows that the development of inclusive services must be a collaborative effort. Successful initiatives

Think About It...

If collaboration should be voluntary, how can a school create a broad-based collaborative culture? Does everyone have to "buy into" collaboration?

involve key participants in all phases of planning and evaluation. Key participants include all those who have an interest or a stake in the inclusive education program, such as classroom teachers, special education teachers, related services specialists, support staff, central office and school-based administrators, board members, students with and without disabilities, and their family members. Some of these may be vocal advocates or leaders for inclusive education, others may be totally unaware of it, and still others may have serious concerns and even misconceptions about inclusion. Van Dyke, Pitonyak, and Gilley (1997) stress the importance of listening to the people most affected by the change. A pattern of open and honest communication helps educators, parents, students, and others to feel valued; in turn, they develop a sense of ownership of the process. Through large- and small-group meetings, focus groups, and individual conversations, it is possible to solicit a great deal of input from members of the school community.

Unfortunately, not everyone can be involved in in-depth deliberation and decision making. In most school settings, a representative group of stakeholders is appointed to a committee, team, or task force that is charged with responsibility for planning, coordinating, and evaluating the inclusion program. It is critical that the appropriate administrators and policymakers sanction the task force. For example, the superintendent should appoint members of a districtwide task force and ensure that the school board is kept informed and involved in the committee's work. Similarly, principals should appoint school-based task forces that may in turn work with members of their site-based management team to formulate plans for the individual school. Visible leadership at the top levels is vital to the success of the inclusion initiative.

The size of inclusion planning teams varies from groups as small as five in some settings to teams with more than 20 members in other settings. In general, a working group is most effective when it is as small as possible while assuring representation of all key constituents. The task force should intentionally seek members who bring diverse perspectives. Members are there to express and address different values or points of view—a far more constructive process in the context of planning than later on in the midst of implementation.

Effective and Shared Leadership at Every Level

The success of any innovation aimed at the improvement of educational programs and student learning depends not only on the active involvement but also on the leadership capabilities of key participants. The education of students with disabilities in more inclusive settings requires a "shared responsibility" among general and special educators throughout the system (Will, 1986). For inclusive education to be effective, leadership must be exercised by all who are involved with students and their families. Critical elements of effective leadership include the ability to establish direction, align key participants, motivate and inspire others, and produce useful changes in the organization (Billingsley, Farley, & Rude, 1993).

Advocates of inclusive education concur that effective leadership is needed at all levels of educational organizations. The National Association of State Boards of Education (NASBE, 1992) has emphasized the role of state boards in creating new visions for education reform that include *all* students. Policies at the state level have a tremendous influence on the tone and the content of the reform agenda. The NASBE report calls for a truly comprehensive approach that requires the leadership and collaboration of families, teachers, specialists, administrators, local school boards, and university faculty in preservice preparation programs. Figure 2.2 presents the NASBE Special Education Study Group (1992) recommendations regarding roles of these key constituents in the creation of inclusive systems. Only through such a comprehensive effort can fundamental shifts occur in educational delivery systems.

School principals and teachers are in especially critical positions to influence the change process. As instructional leaders, principals articulate school missions, promote an instructional climate, manage curriculum and instruction, supervise teaching, and monitor student progress (Krug, 1992). More specifically, effective principals can foster collaborative interactions among teachers for the purpose of improving teaching and learning for students with special needs. They accomplish this by communicating a vision for teacher collaboration, demonstrating that they value teacher collaboration, leading faculty planning for development of collaborative approaches, providing and participating in professional development opportunities, providing resources including time to collaborate, and recognizing student and teacher accomplishments (Tindall, 1996).

Teachers and specialists play a critical role in this process. Both general and special educators must be leaders for inclusive education. Because they work most closely with students and their families, teachers have the most direct influence on the educational program. For meaningful improvements to occur, teachers must become *change agents*. They must see themselves as leaders who are actively committed to making a difference and capable of doing so (Fullan, 1993; O'Hair & Odell, 1995; Pellicer & Anderson, 1995). Teachers and specialists who are advocates for inclusive education can be particularly effective when they coalesce with like-minded colleagues to provide services that are more responsive to student needs. Studies of effective collaborative efforts have reinforced this notion of shared leadership. Neither top-down nor bottom-up leadership is sufficient to initiate and sustain effective programs. Based on her research with co-teaching teams, Walther-Thomas (1997a) concluded that inclusive programs were most effective when shared leadership prevailed. Central office and building-level administrators must work closely with committed teachers, specialists, school staff members, paraeducators, families, and community members to design, deliver, and continuously monitor inclusive education programs.

FIGURE 2.2   **A Comprehensive Approach: A Checklist for Other Actors Creating an Inclusive System.**

Creating an inclusive system of education for all children will require the cooperative efforts of many key actors. These include parents, teachers, special educators, local school board members/local administrators, and state legislators. State boards must act early in the planning process to include these constituencies and gain their active support. Similarly, creating such a system is a strategic process. Planning for change must be ongoing and comprehensive. It must encompass all aspects of education, from finance and teacher training to facility construction, classroom instruction, and curriculum development. With this in mind, the Study Group provides the following recommendations for other constituents in this process.

For Parents and Families

- Offer the teacher in your child's inclusive classroom support and tips for working with your child. Good communication and information are the best ways for a general education classroom teacher to feel comfortable working with your child.
- Request neighborhood school placements for your child with special needs at every individualized educational program (IEP) meeting.
- Become active in your neighborhood school/parent association to reaffirm your child's inclusion in the school program.
- Become active in after-school, community-oriented activities to reaffirm your child's inclusion into community life.

For Teachers

- Seek out assistance in your classroom from other professionals, emphasizing a cooperative or team teaching approach for all students.
- Explore/observe a variety of teaching methods to learn different ways to tailor instruction to the multiple needs and learning styles of your students.
- Accept that not all students cover the same material at the same time, and that a variety of curricula (e.g., functional literacy, community mobility, and college preparation) are equally valid for different students.
- Above all, be flexible. This type of change takes time and every teacher makes mistakes along the way as he or she learns to work with increasingly diverse students.

For Local Boards and Local School Administrators

- Place a high priority on sustained teacher training for an inclusive system. All teachers will need ongoing training on how to work with a diverse student population. Such training must be tailored to the needs of the teachers in individual buildings, rather than using one generic program for the entire district.
- Creating an inclusive system should be integrated into everything a district does, including its hiring policies, evaluation instruments, architectural planning and construction of buildings, and overall budgeting. Local boards should review all policies to ensure that they promote an inclusive system.
- Regardless of state reporting requirements, local boards and local administrators should not use labels to identify student or to determine their placements. Students should be identified by the types of services they need, not by a medical-type diagnosis of their disability.

For Special Educators (Teachers and Administrators)

- Recognize the best service a special educator can provide his or her student is to enable the student to function independently in the real world. Each school should model that environment rather than create asylums for children. Special educators should define their role as enriching or supplementing the general education program, through consultation and in-class support, rather than providing an alternative program.

(continued)

FIGURE 2.2   Continued

- Creating an inclusive system will not mean there will be fewer special educators, but that special educators will do a substantially different job. Discretionary monies should be focused on joint special education–general education staff development efforts that build on the strengths of both fields.
- The school restructuring movement provides a window of opportunity for truly including students with special needs into the general student population. Special educators should be a part of every school governing council that has teacher representatives.

For State Legislators

- State legislators should create an inextricable link between special education funding and general education funding and remove any requirements that children be labeled according to disability category in order to receive services. Rather, when children are identified for services, it should be based on educational needs.
- State legislators should adopt new funding formulas that are neutral with respect to their influence on placement decisions and that do not encourage the overidentification of students for special services.

For the Federal Government

- The U.S. Department of Education (USDOE) should review current testing exclusion guidelines, and should seek to include all students in the National Assessment of Educational Progress and other assessments. The USDOE should increase efforts to ensure that states and districts do not abuse the exclusion guidelines in areas where they are established.
- The USDOE should conduct a comprehensive review of the regulations pertaining to special education with an eye toward creating flexibility to allow and encourage states and local districts to move toward truly inclusive schools.
- The USDOE should ensure that federal personnel conducting monitoring visits to states are fully oriented to the inclusive model of education, and that monitoring efforts should be refocused on the outcomes of inclusive programs.

For Higher Education

- The deans of colleges of education should endorse the theme of inclusion and move toward abolishing categorical teacher education programs.
- Teacher education faculty should undertake a strategic planning process to determine the content of a merged training system for preservice teachers.
- Once merged teacher education programs are developed, deans and college presidents should actively seek the necessary waivers from the state board to implement the new programs. At the same time, they should take the initiative to develop a new appropriation plan for the state legislature to fund the new professional preparation system.
- College presidents and deans should seek to make appointments in the schools, colleges, and departments of education with inclusion in mind. This means appointing special educators to positions of leadership in general education programs and committees, and vice versa.

Source: Adapted from National Association of State Boards of Education. (1996, October). *Winners all: A call for inclusive schools.* Alexandria, VA: Author.

A Shared Vision for the Future

Over time, as effective teams work together to design and implement innovations, most develop a shared and coherent vision of the future. Shared vision is a critical feature of effective collaboration; it enables teams to be focused and productive while maintaining their individual and shared commitment to change over time (Senge, 1990). This shared perspective facilitates teamwork, focuses energy, and aids decision making (Miles, 1995).

Shared visions emerge from personal visions possessed by individual members before joining the group, or they develop as everyone's knowledge, experience, and commitment expand as a result of working together. It is important to recognize, however, that most productive teams do not have a shared vision set in stone as soon as they begin. Many change process experts contend that trying to formulate a shared vision a priori is counterproductive and may actually stifle the group's creativity and productivity (Fullan, 1993; Senge, 1990). Authentic visions of the future emerge over time as a result of the teamwork, actions, and outcomes that occur (Larson & LaFasto, 1989).

One of the major responsibilities of the inclusion planning team is visioning. Through extensive dialogue with one another and with the broader community, the task force shapes and articulates a vision for inclusive education through collaboration that is unique and appropriate for the specific school setting. Although there is no formula for a good vision statement, such statements typically assert the overall program philosophy and goals by specifying the school's belief that all students can learn; its desire for all to succeed; and a shared commitment to education by staff, professionals, parents, and the community (Van Dyke et al., 1997). The NASBE Special Education Study Group (1992) emphasized the need for new visions to address the *whole* student, encompassing at least three spheres of development: (1) academic, (2) social and emotional, and (3) personal and collective responsibility and citizenship. Villa, Thousand, and Rosenberg (1995) note that successfully restructured schools explicitly include in their vision statements the concept that all students have the right to be educated with their peers in age-appropriate heterogeneous classrooms within their local schools. The exact content and wording of the statement must reflect the collective vision of the particular community. Conceptualizing the vision is just one essential step; continually articulating it promotes shared ownership of the vision and focuses subsequent planning and implementation activities.

Think About It...

Can a vision for public education be attentive to *both* excellence and equity? How can a vision assure students with disabilities access to inclusive education without compromising public expectations for high standards?

Comprehensive Planning

> "Here we go again," Drew remarked. "Last year it was whole language, but the system couldn't afford all of the materials we needed to teach with that approach. The year before that it was the Boys' Town behavior management. This year the hot topic is collaboration, and they've dumped most of the special education students into general education classes. But our staff development days have been cut, so we're supposed to implement this great new idea without enough training to know what we're doing. I can't wait to see what bandwagon our school jumps on next year!"

The frustration voiced by Drew and the clear lack of connections between new initiatives in his school reflect a lack of comprehensive planning. Without a long-range plan for improvement, schools are prone to "start over" each year with new ideas and strategies. Over time, haphazard approaches to school reform create frustrated and cynical professionals, many of whom learn to resent and resist innovations because they have lost faith in their system's ability to make meaningful changes (Fullan, 1993). It is easy to see why many veteran educators are tempted to take a "this too shall pass" attitude toward inclusive education initiatives.

Comprehensive plans serve as tools for articulating and communicating the vision of inclusive education. They demonstrate the organization's commitment to sustained support over time. Inclusive schools will happen only if school systems are willing to make long-term commitments to this effort. To accomplish this aim, comprehensive planning must be undertaken collaboratively to ensure shared commitment and support among all stakeholders. The teachers, specialists, and administrators charged with implementation responsibilities must believe that these plans are appropriate and manageable. Students, families, and professionals must all believe that key decision makers will provide support, monitor progress, and make appropriate changes as needed. Comprehensive plans help guide appropriate immediate and long-term decisions about resource allocation, staff development, personnel assignments, student scheduling, and evaluation.

Designing Inclusive and Collaborative Programs

In the process of visioning, inclusion teams and other key participants have created new focus and direction for their educational programs. To formulate meaningful vision statements, they have wrestled with important "why" questions: *Why* are we concerned about our programs? *Why* should we move toward more inclusive and collaborative services? *Why* change? Comprehensive planning takes the process one step further translating the vision into action. It enables inclusion teams to address the now-important questions: *How* will we accomplish this? *Who* needs to do *what*? *When* and *where* will we begin? The planning process is essentially a matter of the teams' working through these basic questions (Korinek, McLaughlin, & Gable, 1994).

Teams can call on many resources for help. To learn from the experiences of others, teams should visit successful programs, review their program guides and other written materials, and talk openly with teachers, specialists, and administrators in those settings. To what do they attribute their success? In hindsight, what should they have done differently? What advice would they give to teams just starting out? Most schools are very willing to share what they have learned along the way and to gather some new insights as well. Workshops and conferences offer additional opportunities for teams to acquire information about effective practices and network with teams in other schools. With the growing interest in inclusive education, most professional associations and publishers have a number of materials available to assist schools in planning: handbooks, guides, descriptions of model programs, and videotaped presentations. The professional literature includes hundreds of journal articles and other reference materials. Many provide rich descriptions of recommended practices, and some report the findings of research studies that have examined the efficacy of inclusive and collaborative approaches. Generally, teams find it useful to consult these sources as they develop their own programs.

It is important for planning teams to consider all essential program components. Typically, comprehensive program descriptions address the following: program goals, student needs, curriculum and instructional methods, program structures and management systems, professional roles and responsibilities, community involvement, procedures for students to enter and exit the program, and program evaluation (George & George, 1993). Teams must examine proposed initiatives in the context of other relevant programs and priorities. How do the proposed approaches fit with other expectations for students and teachers? How do existing practices facilitate or impede more inclusive education and collaboration? Also critical is attention to allocation of fiscal, human, and physical resources necessary for successful program implementation. Finally, teams must establish reasonable timelines to guide their implementation efforts.

The challenge for planning teams is to conceptualize complete and coherent program designs. The written program description represents the team's best thinking about how their particular program should work. In essence, each team creates its own model or theory for its program by saying that, if these resources are used in these ways, we expect to achieve these outcomes. Good program descriptions make sense. They appear logical and feasible, incorporate sound educational practices, and are attentive to legal and ethical issues (McLaughlin & McLaughlin, 1993).

The time required for comprehensive planning may seem overwhelming. In fact, many teams abbreviate the planning process in the mistaken belief that they are moving ahead expeditiously. Unfortunately, there are no shortcuts. The time invested in the development of a detailed blueprint is pivotal to a school's success in serving students in inclusive environments.

Beginning with a Pilot Initiative

Many schools find it helpful to implement a new vision in the form of a pilot initiative. Villa and colleagues (1995) note that change can often be introduced effectively by recruiting and supporting early experimenters to create successful examples of the desired program that those within or outside the organization can study and emulate. Many people feel less threatened by a pilot or field test because the very terminology conveys that the initiative is still in its formative stage. They may be more tolerant when difficulties are inevitably encountered, since the purpose of a pilot is to work out the "kinks" in the program.

Several points should be kept in mind, however, when inclusive education through collaboration is introduced as a pilot initiative. First, the plan for the pilot program must be developed with care to ensure that all necessary supports are provided so that the experimental effort is highly effective. The goal is to demonstrate success. Second, the pilot initiative must be highly visible. People must see the desired change in action in order to be convinced. Third, the pilot initiative must include a solid evaluation plan. It is important to have a complete description of the program (i.e., what is supposed to happen), as well as thorough documentation of the implementation process (i.e., what actually happens throughout the pilot phase). Although outcome measures are always critical, the nature and duration of a pilot program allow only preliminary, formative assessment of the program's potential influence. Once a pilot is under way, its success and the receptivity of the specific environment will determine how quickly the program can be expanded to other sites.

The following example illustrates the value of comprehensive planning to create more inclusive schools.

Three years ago Dr. Adele Brown, superintendent of Bayside School District, and the members of the school board decided it was time for their schools to become more inclusive. Growing dissatisfaction with traditional special education services, suggestions from educators and families, and the emerging literature on inclusion helped convince the administrative leadership of the district that there were better ways to serve students with special needs. Dr. Brown and members of the Board visited school sites in neighboring communities where inclusive approaches were being used. A school–community task force was asked to investigate inclusive schools and make recommendations to the Board during the spring. Task force members conducted site visits, read, interviewed teachers and administrators, held meetings with families, and surveyed students. The task force found strong support for inclusive education among families and educators; they recommended the development of appropriate programs to support this effort. The Board and the superintendent's staff developed a vision statement regarding inclusive education during the summer. They shared this vision with staff and families when schools opened in September. It said:

All Bayside School District students have the right to appropriate education in the least restrictive environment possible. For most students this environment is the general education classroom. It is the responsibility of Bayside teachers, specialists, administrators, families, and interested community members to help all students achieve academic and social success.

During the second year another committee investigated a number of research-based interventions that were used at various sites within the district. These included team teaching, cooperative learning, curriculum-based assessment, various classroom accommodations, and peer tutoring. This group was asked to determine validated practices that most Bayside educators could support to improve classroom teaching and student learning. As practices were investigated, staff members and families were given opportunities to review plans, voice concerns, and make suggestions for alternative approaches and strategies. In January the group presented three classroom interventions for districtwide support and adoption. The following interventions were recommended to facilitate effective inclusive education: co-teaching, cooperative learning, and peer tutoring. The Board supported the plan and agreed to provide funds for summer staff development to help interested professionals prepare for fall implementation.

During the remainder of the year school-level teams worked together to formulate local implementation plans. Multiyear plans were designed to support the district's existing master plan and build on the unique strengths and characteristics of each school. Local school planning teams were instructed to design realistic objectives and activities that could be accomplished given current resource support (e.g., staff development, time, materials). District-level administrators and specialists worked closely with building-level teams. Concerns, especially those related to fiscal resources, were discussed openly. Several planning teams researched the literature on inclusion and found studies that showed how other communities had changed their practices and saved money to provide more direct classroom support, such as more specialists, more paraeducators, smaller class sizes, and more technology. Strategies for district- and building-level cost-sharing and cost-saving were explored; plans for appropriate reallocation of funds were formulated. Specific components within each school's plans addressed common concerns that appear in the literature (i.e., staff development, classroom support, student and teacher scheduling, planning time, and teacher evaluation).

Every school planned for the following year during the spring semester. Local teams developed team teaching, consulting, and cooperative planning schedules for the following year. Balanced classroom rosters were also established. Multifaceted staff development was initiated. Teachers and administrators visited model schools, attended workshops, coached one another, read, studied, discussed, and planned. By September all of the self-contained classrooms in Bayside were eliminated. Most pull-out programs were significantly reduced. The year was characterized by many teaching and learning successes.

In summary, well-designed plans provide the frameworks for action. Key players know what is expected and how to proceed to implement desired services. Decision makers know what resources are required and the kinds of supports

---

Think About It...

Why might some schools adopt a "just-do-it" approach rather than engage in comprehensive planning for inclusive education? Are there ever conditions that justify implementation without planning?

---

necessary to sustain inclusive education over time. It is important to note, however, that good plans are also flexible. Through ongoing monitoring and evaluation, teams can refine their plans regularly as data about student and program performance are collected.

Adequate Resources

Appropriate and effective inclusion demands adequate resources. Assigning students with disabilities to general education programs without adequate support is not inclusion; it is inappropriate education. It is, as critics of poorly conceived and underfunded efforts contend, merely student "dumping" (Kauffman & Hallahan, 1995). Giving lip service to inclusion without providing the resources needed to implement effective collaborative service delivery raises serious ethical questions for decision makers. At all levels, psychological, human, and fiscal resources are needed to ensure responsible implementation of inclusive programs.

At the state level, policies and procedures must support and promote local initiatives designed to educate students with disabilities in inclusive settings. States can encourage more creative programming by easing categorical restrictions and allowing schools to leverage funds from different programs targeted for students with special needs. Standards for general education class size and specialist caseload limits must be examined and set low enough to enable educators to teach reasonable numbers of students in general education classrooms. State regulations should reflect current thinking about teacher preparation and licensure, staffing ratios, flexible funding, innovative service delivery, and appropriate outcomes assessment for all students. In the area of teacher licensure, it is critical that state requirements ensure that *all* teachers, novices as well as experienced veterans, are well prepared to work together in inclusive classrooms.

Implementation of inclusive education across the school district minimizes the unevenness and resistance associated with many change efforts. At the district level, leaders must support inclusive education to gain the endorsement of many critical stakeholders (e.g., school board members, principals, teachers, specialists, families, community representatives). Without district-level encouragement, it is easy for innovative ideas to get lost at the school level. Most principals face such a broad array of competing demands and expectations that they need encouragement, recognition, and resources from district leaders to change current patterns of special education service. Leaders must find creative ways to earmark new funds or reallocate existing funds to provide sufficient resources to develop school-level initiatives and support these efforts over time.

Today, many school districts are reorganizing and moving beyond rigid categorical programs, obtaining waivers if necessary, to integrate resources (e.g., special education, English as a second language [ESL], remedial reading and math programs) to extend their service capabilities. Cross-categorical programs allow specialists to concentrate their efforts on fewer schools, classrooms, and students. For example, in some large rural school districts, specialists such as special educators and Title I teachers no longer travel from school to school but combine their caseloads to share various instructional and management responsibilities. If these specialists meet regularly for consultation, collaborative planning, and problem solving, they can concentrate their efforts and provide more intensive support to students and teachers. Some districts have realized savings in their transportation budgets, for example, by reducing out-of-district placements for students with disabilities and serving more students in their home schools (Casey & Dozier, 1994). Another practice is the reduction or elimination of some or all pull-out classrooms; specialists are assigned to share classrooms with general educators. In many communities it takes more than $50,000 per year to maintain a typical classroom (i.e., utilities, furniture, supplies, janitorial services, maintenance). Recognizing that all school systems have limited funds, finances are an inevitable concern as services are reconceptualized. District-level leadership helps ensure that resources are used effectively and efficiently across schools. Many principals need district-level encouragement and permission to reallocate school funds, reconceptualize staff responsibilities, and create long-term professional development plans to support inclusive education.

At the school level, administrators must work closely with teachers and specialists to cultivate inclusive communities. School leadership must recognize and appreciate the value of teamwork. To understand the professional development needs and resource requirements that are essential to implement collaborative service delivery, principals must work closely with their teams. Because making changes is a disruptive process, administrators must provide all staff members with opportunities to hone their communication and problem-solving skills. During the spring, school teams must create classroom rosters for the following year that reflect an appropriate balance of student needs and abilities. Accompanying specialist caseloads and schedules must be designed in tandem to ensure that appropriate support will be provided to promote student success. These administrator-led teams must design weekly planning time and teaching schedules that enable professionals to meet with colleagues to create and implement collaborative plans (Creasey & Walther-Thomas, 1996). More specific information about resources for effective school-based implementation is provided in Chapter 6.

Sustained Implementation Support

> "After what we thought was a great year of co-teaching, we found out that we could no longer co-teach because our new principal said reading scores in our school were too low. She thinks it's because the special education kids were integrated into our co-taught classes."

When plans have been well conceived and the culture, leadership, and resources support collaboration, inclusive education is more likely to be successful. Yet many programs fail at this stage for lack of sustained effort. If participants and those to whom they are accountable expect a "quick fix," they may become discouraged when there is no evidence of immediate effectiveness. Maintaining the commitment over time requires an understanding of the change process and the importance of consistent support.

Support over Time

Meaningful change takes time. Inclusive education and collaboration are significant innovations in most schools, and change of this magnitude cannot be rushed. Those who study the change process now estimate that significant change takes years to accomplish (Fullan, 1993). Some estimates suggest that large-scale, system-wide changes may require as long as 10 to 20 years before these innovations are fully embraced as fundamental components of the system (Senge, 1990).

Successful implementation of innovations requires "steady work" over time (Sarason, 1993). Unfortunately, this is often hard to do in schools. Most veteran teachers can tell stories about abandoned programs, plans, and curricula that are reintroduced as "new" and "innovative" concepts 5 to 10 years later. This often happens because of several factors. School systems are constantly bombarded with an array of new and exciting innovations that promise improved student performance and demand time, money, and attention. Competing priorities are inevitable within school organizations and it is a difficult challenge for decision makers to find the approaches that truly offer the greatest potential. Leadership may change as frequently as every 3 or 4 years in many districts. Often new leaders arrive midway through the implementation of their predecessors' innovative plans. New leaders also bring their own agendas and initiatives that they want to implement. These new plans may look better to constituents than programs that are several years old. This happens because yet-to-be plans are unspoiled by the hard realities of day-to-day implementation. Setbacks or "implementation dips" inevitably occur as organizations move beyond the familiar ways to newer, more effective approaches (Fullan, 1993). Without an understanding of the change process, individuals and systems are prone to abandon innovations before they have had adequate time to prove—or disprove—their ultimate worth (Fullan, 1991).

Ongoing Professional Development

A comprehensive approach to professional development is perhaps the most critical dimension of sustained support for successful program implementation. Professional development for inclusion and collaboration ensures that all participants within the educational organization become students of school improvement and the change process. Everyone should become knowledgeable about (1) group decision making, (2) options for professional development, (3) collegial implementation of curriculum, (4) action research for school improvement, and (5) change as a personal and organizational process (Joyce, Wolf, & Calhoun, 1993).

The National Foundation for the Improvement of Education (Renyi, 1996) defines high-quality professional development as that which meets the following criteria:

1. Has the goal of improving student learning at the heart of every school endeavor.
2. Helps teachers and other school staff meet the future needs of students who learn in different ways and who come from diverse cultural, linguistic, and socioeconomic backgrounds.
3. Provides adequate time for inquiry, reflection, and mentoring and is an important part of the normal working day of all public educators.
4. Is rigorous, sustained, and adequate to long-term practice.
5. Is directed toward teachers' intellectual development of leadership.
6. Fosters a deepening of subject-matter knowledge, a greater understanding of learning, and a greater appreciation of students' needs.
7. Is designed and directed by teachers, incorporates the best principles of adult learning, and involves shared decisions designed to improve the school.
8. Balances individual priorities with school and district needs and advances the profession as a whole.
9. Makes best use of new technologies.
10. Is site based and supportive of a clearly articulated vision for students.

Generally, individual participants move through a series of predictable stages as they first become aware of an innovation until it is successfully implemented (Hord, Rutherford, Huling-Austin, & Hall, 1987). Early on, individuals tend to be most concerned about the personal ramifications of change (e.g., "What will inclusion mean for me and my students?" "How will co-teaching affect my job and my professional role?" "Will I be able to meet the new expectations of colleagues and supervisors?"). As people learn more about the innovation and how they will be involved, their concerns then center around tasks to be accomplished (e.g., "What does it take to teach special education students successfully in inclusive classrooms?" "What are our roles on the assistance team?" "How can we teach together effectively?"). In the most advanced stage of change, successful implementers focus more on the lasting impact of the innovation; they begin to think of ways to make it even more effective (e.g., "How can we improve our teamwork?" "Suppose we try to make our current co-planning process more effective?" "How can we prepare our students more effectively for adulthood?"). Individuals move through these stages of acceptance at different rates; they need different kinds of support along the way. Leaders at all levels can be helpful in providing information, encouragement, incentives, and rewards for continuous implementation and effort.

Just as schools are different, so are their reasons for changing to become more inclusive. One thing that is constant in all schools, however, is the need for ongoing, research-based professional development. Beninghof (1996) suggests three factors that are essential for effective professional development in support of collaboration for more inclusive educational services. First, the district must offer a spectrum of professional development activities to address the individual needs of staff and students. Second, planning for professional development should take into consideration that staff members will be at the various stages of readiness to accept major changes, as explained earlier. Specific development activities should be tailored to the needs of participants as they move through the different levels of the change process. Figure 2.3 presents Beninghof's suggestions for a spectrum of staff development activities for inclusion. Third, implementation is most successful when broad input is encouraged and staff is involved in the planning of professional development options from the beginning.

In summary, as state-, district-, and school-level visions are redefined and inclusive approaches are adopted, it is important for collaborative teams, at all levels, to be vigilant. Shared leadership is an essential part of this process. Rather than vest the future of inclusive education in one or two people, advocates must develop a broad base of support to ensure that the initiative can survive the loss of a significant player, inevitable implementation dips, and impressive campaigns waged by advocates of new innovations. Inclusive education supporters must understand the change process and work proactively to keep this topic a priority among school leaders, educators, and families.

Continuous Evaluation and Improvement

"Parents of students without disabilities are pushing us to prove that their kids are not 'losing out' in classes where students with special needs are included. Families of the kids in special education are concerned that their children will not get the individualized attention they received in their pull-out classes."

"With the push to have all students master the new standards of learning, we're afraid that the gains we've made toward successfully integrating students with special needs will be lost as general educators worry that these kids will lower class scores on the statewide assessment."

These scenarios are common in schools where systematic evaluation is not an integral part of inclusive program development and collaborative systems.

FIGURE 2.3   **Staff Development Spectrum for Inclusion.**

Stage	Activity
0—Awareness	A brief introductory workshop Awareness-level videotapes, such as *Regular Lives* (Goodwin & Wurzburg, 1988) Ongoing updates at faculty meetings Brief professional or newspaper articles on inclusion Discussions in the faculty room and other informational settings about experiences
1—Informational	Full-day workshops on general inclusion issues Presentations by parents of students with disabilities Brief presentations by practitioners of inclusion Brief professional or newspaper articles on inclusion
2—Personal	Group discussions around certain issues Presentation with questions and answers from practitioners of inclusion Conference attendance Reading and discussion groups Visitations to inclusive classrooms
3—Management	Practical books and articles Problem-solving sessions with a group or consultant Videos showing practical strategies, such as *Facing Inclusion Together through Collaboration and Co-Teaching* (Burrello et al., 1993) Visits to inclusive classrooms with opportunities for dialogue Internet resource sharing and dialogues Library and resource investigations
4—Consequence	Research articles on outcomes Discussion with colleagues about outcomes Research projects within own settings Highly focused skill-building workshops Meetings with representatives from the state department of education Study groups Videotaping with self-analysis
5—Collaboration	Problem-solving meetings with peers E-mail problem solving Peer coaching Team teaching with analysis Districtwide or regional networking Staff meeting updates Curriculum development committees
6—Refocusing	Reading club Peer coaching Conference attendance Presenting own experiences to others Authoring articles on inclusion Discussions with advocates for inclusion Independent study plans Leadership opportunities Demonstrations Inviting external evaluation programs

Source: Beninghof, A. M. (1996, Summer). Using a spectrum of staff development activities to support inclusion. *Journal of Staff Development, 17*(3), 12–15.

Without good information, educators are simply unable to support the claims that they are making about the benefits of their program or respond to the concerns expressed by others. In contrast, the hallmark of excellent organizations is that they can communicate to multiple audiences what results they are aiming for, how they will accomplish these results using certain resources according to specific timelines, and how they will know that they have achieved these results (McLaughlin, 1997). The set of features discussed thus far has set the stage for schools to function as excellent organizations while they create more inclusive systems. Diverse constituents have shared leadership responsibility for shaping a vision of inclusive education, developing a comprehensive plan, and following through with resources and support for sustained implementation. But how do educators know they are moving in the desired direction? How do they demonstrate that inclusive services are meeting student needs? How can they make their programs even better? The final component essential to effective inclusive education is systematic, ongoing evaluation and improvement.

Simply put, evaluation is a process that yields information to support decision making about the program being evaluated (McLaughlin & McLaughlin, 1993). The current economic and political climate has heightened demands for accountability in nearly all program areas, particularly those supported by public tax dollars. Policymakers and citizens at large expect both effectiveness and efficiency from their schools. Families need assurances that their children are being well served, are making good progress, and will be able to function successfully after graduation. Teachers and specialists have to be convinced that program expectations are feasible and that the necessary supports are in place for them to perform their roles effectively. They also seek data that enable them to refine their efforts and constantly improve their programs. Administrators need evidence that programs are working well so that they can be effective advocates for resources to continue or expand inclusive services. Clearly, different stakeholders are likely to have different information needs. To a great extent, evaluation is a matter of determining who needs to know what about the program.

Earlier emphases on collaborative culture and shared leadership underscored the importance of a team approach to the development of inclusive programs. A carefully configured inclusion team or task force will ensure that the diverse needs of important constituent groups are represented throughout the planning and evaluation of innovative programs. As noted earlier, the team should also seek input from the broader community. Additionally, it is often helpful for the team to include one or more persons with specific expertise in program evaluation. With more specialized knowledge and skills, evaluators can assist the team in planning and conducting evaluations that are useful, appropriate, and technically sound.

The process of framing specific questions provides a bridge between planning and evaluation. Teams that are conscious of this integral link find themselves posing important questions throughout their planning processes. They have no trouble defining what they would like to know about their inclusion effort. More often, the challenge for the team is to focus on several specific evaluation questions that are most meaningful at the particular stage of the process. Good evaluations require personnel time and other resources; they can be costly. It is simply impossible to evaluate everything at once. When teams realize that evaluation is a continuous process, they find it easier to focus on their evaluation priorities and postpone investigation of other evaluation targets to subsequent years. At the very least, framing the questions allows teams to anticipate future information needs and to put data collection systems into place.

Evaluation questions may address the design of the inclusion and collaboration model, its implementation, or its impact on students, adult participants, and the system as a whole. Given the current emphasis on accountability, most teams immediately associate evaluation with the measurement of results or outcomes. Certainly, evaluation of the program's impacts is critical; the effects on student performance and progress establish the "bottom line" for judging the merits of inclusive programs. Design and implementation evaluations are also critical, for they enable the team, administrators, and other users of the information to make sense of the outcomes observed. For example, the planning and evaluation team at Rosemont Elementary School focused on the effects of inclusion on students' academic achievement. Based on their analyses of standardized test scores, grades, and individualized educational program (IEP) objectives, they concluded that the inclusion program was effective for their students with disabilities. Despite feeling proud of these outcomes, the team soon realized that their evaluation was incomplete. The school board asked them to what they attributed their success at Rosemont. Principals and teams at neighboring schools wanted to adopt their inclusion model. The Rosemont team itself wanted to refine the program to make it even stronger. Without having evaluated the design of the model, Rosemont was unable to describe its strong points. Furthermore, they were not exactly certain how the inclusion program and the collaboration services had been provided. Many of the activities had evolved over time. The planning team needed more information about the program—how it was supposed to work (its design) and how it actually worked (its implementation)—before they could interpret the results achieved. It is not hard to see that the situation is even more difficult for school teams when the outcomes observed fall short of the standard. What do those disappointing results mean? Is the inclusion model poorly conceived and doomed to fail? Or maybe the resources never came through as promised and the model was implemented without some essential components. Most importantly, what should be changed to improve the program? Teams need design and implementation information as well as the outcome data to support their claims and to improve their programs. The process of continuous evaluation helps to ensure that divisions and schools are results-oriented and not merely innovative (Carnine, 1995).

Good evaluation questions also shape the processes for collection, analyses, and reporting of information. Generally, there are several different information or data sources relevant to any evaluation questions. Teams need to select the methods and measures most appropriate to their needs. The use of multiple sources of information and multiple measures strengthens the conclusions that can be drawn from analyses of the data. In the Rosemont Elementary School example, the team examined several measures of achievement—test scores, grades, and IEP objectives. Each measure has some real limitations, but collectively they create a more credible picture of the impact of inclusion on students' academic performance.

For help in identifying useful sources and measures for specific evaluation questions, teams should consult the professional literature and evaluation specialists, as needed. Figure 2.4 is an adaptation of the work of Bauwens and Hourcade (1995) and a statewide task force (Virginia Department of Education, 1993) to guide program evaluation efforts. The figure outlines some of the measures frequently used to address evaluation questions posed by inclusion teams and is intended to be suggestive rather than prescriptive. Teams may address several different evaluation questions and select several different information sources for each. They must decide what is most useful and feasible for their own settings. A word of caution is in order about the interpretation of evaluation findings. It is tempting for teams to make claims about the relative effectiveness of their programs (e.g., "Students do better in inclusive programs than in pull-out programs") or to attribute success to certain program features (e.g., "The achievement gains resulted from our co-teaching"). Such judgments can be made only through carefully designed studies that control for other factors that might account for program performance. If teams lack experience with research and evaluation, they are well advised to seek help from specialists within the school district or external consultants.

Toward More Inclusive Programs

What if some of these essential features are not yet present in a particular setting? What can a planning team do when the conditions are less than ideal? A planning team does not have to abandon its vision for more inclusive and collaborative services. Instead, it should build into its plan specific strategies for moving *toward* more inclusive and collaborative programs in a very intentional and careful manner. Strategies should approach needed change at two levels: one set of strategies at the systems level to help create the overall conditions essential for inclusion through collaboration and a second set of strategies at the classroom level to progress incrementally toward more effective inclusive practices. In fact, that is exactly the approach taken by the team at Martin Luther King High School. Let's return to the scenario introduced at the beginning of this chapter.

> Before giving up, the Inclusion Planning Team at Martin Luther King High School decided to gather more information about successful inclusion initiatives. After learning that certain features are critical to support effective inclusion programs, the team recognized that it had some work to do to create a more collaborative culture and more shared leadership at Martin Luther King before they could go much further with inclusion itself. The team agreed on several important strategies at the school level:

FIGURE 2.4   Useful Sources of Information to Address Evaluation Questions Frequently Asked about Inclusion and Collaboration Programs.

If your evaluation focuses on…, then consider these sources of information.

1. **The adequacy of your inclusion program design**

    Reviews and ratings of your written program descriptions by "experts" and by potential participants

2. **The provision of required resources**

    a. Reviews of relevant documents (e.g., budgets, staffing assignments and schedules, staff development schedules and attendance records, inventories of resource materials, lesson plan with instructional adaptations)
    b. Interviews with key participants

3. **The actual implementation of program activities**

    a. Reviews of relevant documents (e.g., records and agendas of staff development and parent programs, class roles and schedules of students and teachers, numbers of requests for assistance, minutes and action plans from team meetings, sample co-teaching plans)
    b. Direct observation of key activities (e.g., staff development sessions, team meetings, co-teaching in classrooms)
    c. Interviews with key participants
    d. Surveys of teachers, specialists, administrators, and families

4. **The impact on student participation**

    a. Reviews of student attendance records, retention data, and graduation rates
    b. Data on student participation in extracurricular activities
    c. Observations of student interactions in classrooms and other settings
    d. Interviews with students, families, teachers, and others

5. **The impact on student achievement**

    a. Data from curriculum-based assessments and standardized tests
    b. Grades
    c. Review of individualized educational program (IEP) and transition objectives attained by students with disabilities
    d. Credits and types of diplomas earned (e.g., special education, general, advanced)
    e. Admission and matriculation data for postsecondary education programs
    f. Data on school completers and graduate follow-up surveys of employers
    g. Interviews with students, families, and teachers

6. **The impact on students' social skills and adaptive behavior**

    a. Reviews of data on student referrals, detention, suspension, and expulsion rates
    b. Rating scales completed by students themselves, peers, parents, and teachers
    c. Observations of students in classroom and other settings
    d. Interviews with students, families, teachers, specialists, and administrators

7. **The attitudes and perceptions of key participants**

    a. Individual and group interviews with students, families, teachers, specialists, administrators, policymakers
    b. Surveys of these key participants

8. **The impact on the school system**

    a. Review of records (e.g., referral rates, fiscal reports, transportation reports, recruitment and retention of personnel, scheduling practices, out-of-district placements)
    b. Review of information on curricular and instructional approaches (e.g., curriculum guides, unit and lesson plans, materials purchase and use, IEP/transition goals and objectives)
    c. Interviews and surveys on professional collegial relationships

1. The team would meet with Ms. Grant and members of her advisory council to share their assessment of school readiness for inclusion. Together they would determine ways to encourage more collaborative involvement of faculty.
2. During the spring elections process, the team would nominate two new members for the advisory council, Tony Cirilli and Jill Bates. Both are popular with colleagues and have strong collaborative leadership abilities.
3. Every member of the planning team would function as an advocate and model for more collaborative interactions across settings. In departmental team meetings, Child Study Team meetings, and even one-to-one conversations with colleagues, team members would consciously shape more collaborative processes.

Beyond these general strategies to set the stage for inclusion, the team also defined some strategies at the classroom level:

4. At IEP meetings this year, there would be greater attention to explicit preparation of students for successful functioning in inclusive classrooms. More care would be taken to align the special education curriculum with state and local curriculum standards. Additionally, general education teachers would be encouraged to take a more active role at IEP meetings in planning specific accommodations for mainstream classes.
5. Since most students with disabilities were already mainstreamed for several periods each day, more emphasis would be placed on the provision of collaborative support for general education teachers. Two special education teachers would work together to combine several resource classes and free up more time for consultation on a regular basis. They would also try to apply and document collaborative consultation practices more systematically.

These five strategies represent an ambitious agenda for Martin Luther King High School. Although they cannot move immediately to serve all students in more inclusive programs or to provide a full array of collaborative supports for teachers, they are advancing their vision in a very deliberate manner that, in the long-term, will position the school for success.

Chapter Summary

This chapter has identified seven features that are essential for effective and appropriate inclusive education through collaborative service delivery: a collaborative culture, shared leadership, coherent vision, comprehensive planning, adequate resources, sustained implementation, and continuous evaluation for improvement. Ensuring that these key conditions are in place to enable teachers and students to have successful experiences with inclusion is clearly no easy task. Those responsible for program planning are best advised to move at a steady, deliberate pace to facilitate change of this magnitude.

CHAPTER ACTIVITIES

1. Review the case study about Bayside School District. In a small group with your peers, identify and discuss how the seven essential features are evident or not evident in this illustration. Which of the seven features are clearly present in the Bayside scenario? For those features that are less evident, consider strategies that Bayside might apply to strengthen their chances for success.

2. Think about the concept of shared leadership as it applies to your current professional role or the role to which you aspire. Write a brief description of some specific ways you envision yourself as a leader in this role. What special qualities and attributes can you contribute? How can you work collaboratively with others to provide leadership for inclusive education? After writing your response, share your ideas about leadership with a colleague. In what ways do your thoughts reflect your uniqueness as an individual? What insights did you gain about shared leadership?

3. If possible, arrange to visit a school where inclusive education and collaborative programs are in place. As you observe and interact with teachers, specialists, and administrators, focus on the seven essential features emphasized in this chapter. Which of these features are evident? How are they manifest in the school setting?

3 Understanding Organizational Change

Challenges and Opportunities

LEARNING OBJECTIVES

1. Describe factors influencing school reform and inclusive education program development.
2. Identify types of organizational change.
3. Discuss organizational structure, organizational culture, professional development, and ethics as important dimensions of change.
4. Describe guidelines to facilitate comprehensive planning for change.
5. Explain why teachers and specialists need to be knowledgeable about the change process.

A Conversation with Riverdale School District

BONITA DAVIES *(Riverdale Staff Development Director)*: I appreciate your returning my call.

DONNA SANTOS *(University Professor)*: It's always good to talk with you. Your voice mail message sounded serious. How can I help?

BONITA DAVIES: Well, as we have begun to implement more inclusive practices in our schools we are finding great variance in what inclusion means to educators. Our superintendent, Dr. Elva Johnson, believes in the concept and has communicated her desire to have all schools become "fully inclusive" environments. School administrators have interpreted this in a variety of ways. Some are assigning all special education students to general education classes with specialists reassigned to provide consulting support. In other schools, only students with mild disabilities, who can achieve successfully without any special supports or modifications, are considered for primary enrollment in general education classes. It is apparent that moving to implementation without providing adequate staff development and support for teachers and administrators has resulted in expressions of concern from all involved, including our students' families and the school board. I'm afraid that we may have violated much of what we've now become aware of as "best practice" in implementing inclusive programs. We need to step back and reassess the situation. Our leadership team would appreciate it if you and your colleagues at the university would be willing to assist us in planning a better approach for the district.

DONNA SANTOS: I'll need to check with them but I'm confident that we would be willing to meet, review your current status, and examine your present needs. Then we might be in a better position to work with you to generate some possible strategies or solutions.

BONITA DAVIES: Thanks. I'll get back to you with some possible dates and times. I know we've talked about the challenges of change before but some days it certainly feels harder than others!

DONNA SANTOS: Yes, I know what you mean! Hang in there. I look forward to hearing from you soon.

Perhaps this dialogue is a familiar one to those who have experienced the "birth" of an educational innovation implemented without careful consideration of the variables needed for effective and efficient change. Movement from traditional programs for students with disabilities to more inclusive education, as described in Chapters 1 and 2, constitutes a major shift that needs to be grounded in research on change. Educators can best plan effective implementation of new practices if they understand the themes emerging from research on the change process. This chapter reviews dimensions of the change process that support the sustained implementation and institutionalization of the essential components of inclusive programs described in Chapter 2. These dimensions support appropriate inclusion and quality educational experiences for all students. The information found in this chapter is usually provided in administrator preparation programs, but it is important here because teachers and specialists are increasingly becoming active participants in team approaches to educational planning and shared decision making. This chapter incorporates literature on innovation, school renewal, organizational behavior, leadership, change, staff development, school culture, and action research.

During the 1990s research on professional development and published information on field experience have led to a more complex view of the change process. There has been a shift from linear, step-by-step models, to circular or "rolling" models of change in which several aspects of an organization are addressed concurrently (Whitaker, 1993). For example, school districts develop detailed, comprehensive professional development plans for administrators and teachers designed to foster inclusive practices. Such plans must also consider the impact of proposed professional development and subsequent implementation on the school calendar, teacher workload, student placements, family involvement, and other factors. Fullan (1993) refers to change as a journey rather than a blueprint and suggests that plans for change should provide sufficient flexibility to create new "maps" in order to reach desired destinations or achieve desired changes. In an effort to manage change and achieve improvement, educators are faced with a range of opportunities and challenges. A primary challenge underlying change in educational organizations is to create structures that are open, nurturing, creative, collaborative, and responsive to the needs of all students (Hargreaves, 1994; Senge, Kleiner, Roberts, Ross, & Smith, 1994; Speck, 1996).

Understanding the change process enables professionals to fulfill their leadership roles in ways that further encourage collaborative educational environments and also facilitate sustained implementation of innovations. When teachers or specialists as advocates become skilled at integrating the desired change and the change process, they can become the most powerful sources of change (Fullan & Hargreaves, 1996; Maeroff, 1993).

Educational Context for Change: Inclusion and School Reform

A review of school reform movements in general and special education, as well as an understanding of the rights assured students under major federal and state legislation, are helpful in assisting professionals in understanding emerging roles and responsibilities (Lipsky & Gartner, 1997a; Sage & Burrello, 1994). As the movement toward a more unified system of public education continues, the recognized educational challenge of the 21st century is to achieve higher levels of learning for *all* students. In the scenario at the beginning of the chapter, it would probably help if all of the school-level personnel involved in implementation could explore the superintendent's vision and examine the benefits and challenges of inclusive educational opportunities. Yet, even when presented with supporting data, some educators might still continue to question the need for change. Perspectives held by internal and external stakeholders provide insight into why change is necessary in educational organizations.

When speaking about schools overall, many educators, as well as the general public, agree that something is seriously wrong with current educational programming. When discussing their own schools, however, many stakeholders often claim that everything is fine (Elam, Rose, & Gallup, 1996). They suggest that their schools are doing all they can under difficult circumstances. Often these professionals are unable or unwilling to acknowledge that anything is amiss and, therefore, are not in a position to alter the situation. Any effort to reform or create something new presupposes that educators can recognize institutional deficiencies and can propose more desirable alternatives to improve educational opportunities for students. Regrettably, some cannot or will not (Tewel, 1995). It is well recognized that social and economic systems have changed immensely during the past 50 years as information about teaching, learning, and human motivation has also expanded. Schools now serve increasingly more linguistically, racially, ethnically, economically, socially, and ability diverse student populations than ever before, and the data indicate that schools must change to better meet the needs of all students (U.S. Department of Education [USDOE], 1998). Yet, fundamental components of schools such as curriculum and approaches to organizing students for learning have remained basically unchanged (Lee, Bryk, & Smith, 1993; Murphy, 1993; Tewel, 1995).

The case for change is strengthened by an awareness that the larger society in which schools operate and the support structures for students are changing. Today there are more single-parent families and more children growing up in poverty than in the past. Increasing numbers of children and youth experience abuse and out-of-home placements. Statistics abound which indicate that the students entering schools today differ in some significant and educationally relevant ways from students of past years (Children's Defense Fund [CDF], 1998; USDOE, 1996). Therefore, conducting "business as usual" in educational enterprises is not appropriate.

External constituents continue to express concern and criticism of current educational performance (Barth, 1990). They offer countless recommendations to respond to these concerns. Some frequently mentioned suggestions include: (1) improving discipline in schools; (2) reducing the dropout rate; (3) increasing achievement levels in math and science; (4) extending the school day, the school year, or both; (5) developing enduring intellectual skills, such as critical thinking and problem solving; (6) providing opportunities for cooperative learning; (7) creating school environments that celebrate diversity and foster a sense of belonging for all students; and (8) improving transition services for students with disabilities (Barth, 1990; Cuban, 1990; Eisner, 1991; Stainback & Stainback, 1996a).

As public organizations, schools must respond to these public demands for change. In addition, to further understand the educational context for change with a view toward inclusion and school reform, professionals must focus on what special education services should be provided and how they should be implemented. One contemporary perspective calls on educational organizations and environments to be modified, enhanced, or prepared to address the needs of all students. From this point of view segregation, tracking, and resource-intensive practices such as identification and labeling are discriminatory, denying the provision of skills for participatory citizenship (Stainton, 1994).

Think About It...

What are some factors that indicate a need for educational change? What might schools do differently to address these factors?

Themes of Change

A review of school renewal literature of the past three decades (Bliss, Firestone, & Richards, 1991; Elmore, 1992) shows a consistent progression of ideas for improving education. Two areas of study illuminating this progression focus on school change and leadership for change. Research in both of these areas supports the understanding that change and innovation are constantly evolving, multidimensional processes rather than mechanical, linear sequences of events (Whitaker, 1993). Effective leadership for change requires people who are effective problem solvers and community builders. Hord, Rutherford, Huling-Austin, and Hall (1987) used the following underlying principles about the change process as the foundation for their research and the subsequent development of a model for change:

   1. *Change is a process, not an event.* There is sometimes a tendency by those who do not understand the complexities of change to equate change with the implementation of a new program rather than to view change as a process occurring over time, usually a period of several years. For example, implementing a whole language reading approach or block scheduling requires careful consideration of the need for ongoing professional development, family involvement, coordination, and communication across content areas. In addition, an implementation timeline that includes program evaluation should be developed.

   2. *Change is accomplished by individuals and is a highly personal experience.* Change affects people; therefore individuals should be a focus of attention in implementing new initiatives. As noted in Chapter 2, individuals will react differently to change and these individual differences should also be considered in planning the necessary and varied supports to facilitate effective change. For example, some view teaming as unsettling and threatening, whereas others will be energized and excited by the opportunity to participate in more collaborative experiences.

   3. *Change is best understood in operational terms.* Resistance to change can be reduced by anticipating answers to questions related to how a proposed change will directly impact current practice (Janas, 1998). For example, educators will want to know how much additional preparation time will be required. What will teachers or students have to do differently? How will change be measured?

   Given the complex nature of this change process, school change can have different meanings to educators in individual schools and districts. Because change is an increasingly constant feature in educators' lives, it is useful to help them place personal and professional experiences against a wider backdrop to broaden their understanding of the change process. Fullan (1993) suggests that an initial step in preparation for change is to engage each member of the educational organization in a study of the nature of change. Others who propose strategies for school improvement agree that this study of change is necessary across role groups—administrators, teachers, specialists, and support personnel (Fullan & Hargreaves,

1996; Knudson & Wood, 1998). In addition, there is a need to examine critically those ethical issues concerning justice and caring that emerge with heightened understanding of the change process. Discussions should address the tension that often exists between meeting legal mandates and selecting approaches that are more compassionate and in the best interest of families and students (Gable, Arllen & Cook, 1993). The ultimate goal is that all personnel develop an openness to change and learn to work together to improve the quality of educational experiences for all students.

Types of Change

Change can be accomplished in a variety of ways. It is helpful to explore the major types of organizational change in which schools may become involved. One such categorization offered by Herman and Herman (1994) gives insight into the emerging practice of shared decision making in schools. The roles and responsibilities of instructional and support staff members are changing to include more teaming and active participation with administrators in planning for improvements in educational programs. Sometimes representative groups of teachers and specialists actually initiate the change rather than having the change mandated by the school board or administration. This type of change is referred to as *optional change*. For example, two teachers volunteer to co-teach to facilitate academic and social development of their assigned students.

When school district employees and other stakeholders, such as family members, business leaders, or agency professionals, agree that minor changes will assist in improving current operations, *incremental change*, or change by degrees, occurs. Incremental change takes place when the school's or school district's operations are essentially working well. For example, in a school in which inclusion is being implemented effectively, the staff agrees to pilot a peer tutoring approach to enhance student learning and use of instructional time.

A third type of change, *transformational change*, involves comprehensive and systematic changes within the organization. Transformational change occurs when internal or external influences indicate a need for major changes in the way instruction, support services, or governance matters are being conducted. Transformational change would be required, for example, to determine the effectiveness of inclusive practice, a school district decides to use its assessment data, a graduate follow-up report, a special education compliance report, and a variety of consumer and teacher satisfaction surveys to support future planning.

Ideally, considering current educational, social, and political contexts, transformational change is the kind of change needed for meaningful implementation of inclusive educational programs. As implementation proceeds, optional and incremental types of changes also occur. This doesn't happen in all settings. Sometimes the move toward inclusion in a school district starts with individual teachers or within individual schools before it is embraced as a districtwide initiative. A transformational change effort, however, is advocated to avoid student regression and fragmented service delivery, for example, students who successfully complete elementary school in inclusive settings only to be placed in segregated programs at the middle school level.

Maintaining the organization while learning new ways of working together is another challenge in the change process (Drucker, 1985). The organization must keep going while changing and some of the tasks that are accomplished regularly must continue. For example, specific individualized education program (IEP) goals and objectives for students with disabilities need to be addressed even as teachers are collaborating and planning for increased access to general education programming. Given this challenge, the goal is to plan for change in such a way that some service delivery will be subtly or gradually altered in line with the desired directions for change.

Keys to Effective Change

Many researchers identify optimal conditions for ensuring that desired changes will be implemented successfully (Carlson & Awkerman, 1991; Fullan, 1993; Herman & Herman, 1994; Hord et al., 1987; Joyce, Wolf, & Calhoun, 1993; Knudson & Wood, 1998). Not surprisingly these keys for successful change correlate highly with the essential elements for building inclusive environments presented in Chapter 2. Consistently referenced throughout the literature on change is the need for a clear, shared *vision* of what the school or school district will look like when the change is completed. A detailed *plan* should be developed which includes clear-cut strategic goals that are to be reached as the organization undergoes the change process. Milestones or benchmarks should be established to guide the path of change. In addition, adequate *resources* (time, finances, materials, and personnel) must be provided. There must be a *commitment to change* by the leaders and by a critical mass of stakeholders. Frequent, high-quality, comprehensive, understandable, and two-way *communications* must occur throughout the change process. *Professional development* must be provided for those individuals who are to initiate or implement the change if they do not possess the necessary knowledge and skills. Adjustments must be made during the formative stages of the change process based on *progress assessment* during initiation and implementation, with an eye toward *sustained implementation*.

The supporting literature on change is extensive and represents a variety of types of research that yields a grounded set of themes to guide educators in planning for effective change. The following sections discuss these themes within the context of three important dimensions of change: organizational structure, organizational culture, and the ethics of change. Considerable emphasis is placed on organizational structure because change in this area overarches the others. Organizational structure sets the stage for cultural and ethical considerations related to change within the organization. Professional development, addressed in Chapter 2, is often thought of as a fourth dimension of change that requires considerable attention to achieve sustained implementation of inclusive programs.

Organizational Structure in the Change Process

From a historical perspective, Kuhn (1970) contributed the concept of a "paradigm shift." This is a profound change in the thoughts, perceptions, and values that form a particular view of reality (e.g., moving from a belief that students with disabilities should be educated in separate settings to understanding how inclusive service delivery enhances the total development of all students). Paradigmatic theorists conceptualize organizations as paradigms or shared systems of meaning. They are interested in understanding how existing systems of meaning affect and constrain thought and action in organizations. From this perspective, an organizational paradigm is a system of beliefs about cause-effect relationships and standards of practice and behavior (Skrtic, 1991). Sage and Burrello (1994) define paradigms as mental models that are used to place opportunities and challenges in perspective. These models are helpful in determining what information people perceive as relevant and useful in understanding and resolving the discrepancy between their actual situations and their goals.

There is general agreement in research on the change process and educational reform that what many professionals currently need is a fundamental shift of mindset about the concept of educational change and the provision of more inclusive programs and services. Such a shift facilitates the achievement of a learning, self-renewing organization characterized by shared understandings and the increased collective ability to study and change educational practice (Fullan, 1993; Hargreaves, 1994; Murphy, 1990; Senge, et al, 1994; Whitaker, 1993).

The concept of "the learning organization" has emerged as a powerful concept in the understanding of organizational change. Garratt (1987) suggests that the learning of the organization and its people improves the potential for survival in the longer term. He indicates that there are limitless opportunities involved in applying what is known about organizational learning processes with emerging thoughts on generating visions, refining thinking processes, developing policy and strategy, and changing views on management and leadership to achieve a more holistic process. Addressing these same variables, Senge (1990) proposes that learning organizations are those that have destroyed the illusion that the world is comprised of separate and unrelated forces. He offers a set of five learning disciplines that converge to create effective organizations of change. Four of these disciplines—personal mastery, mental models, building of a shared vision, and team learning—are structured around the fifth discipline—systems thinking. Systems thinking integrates the other disciplines into a coherent body of theory and practice. It keeps these factors from becoming gimmicks or organizational change fads. It allows the members of the organization to see how the disciplines interrelate (Senge, 1990).

Patterson (1993) suggests that viewing educational organizations as systems facilitates creative problem solving as educators seek to improve learning for all students. He defines a system as a "collection of parts that interact to function purposefully as a whole" (p. 67). Applying this definition of a system to organizations, it can be concluded that whenever people and materials are brought together to achieve an organization's purpose, a system is created. Most systems exist within larger systems. For example, a teacher, a classroom, instructional materials, and 20 students constitute a system. Sixteen of these systems within a building constitute a larger system called a school. Twenty of these schools make up a school district. The school district, in turn, is part of a larger, more complex system serving the needs of citizens living in a community. A comprehensive plan for change would include consideration of the impact of proposed changes on the specific system (e.g., the classroom) as well as the larger systems (i.e., the school, district, and community).

Patterson (1993) offers planning guidelines, shown in Figure 3.1, which provide a framework for initial problem solving and facilitate the move to more inclusive practices within districts. Systems thinking can allow an educational organization to develop proactive, long-term solutions to the educational challenges of serving all students in the least restrictive environment.

The next section illustrates application of each problem-solving guideline as Riverdale School District considers the improvement of educational services for students with disabilities.

Case of Riverdale School District

The Riverdale School District is experiencing changing conditions in its educational programs. Enrollment in alternative education, remedial and compensatory, and special education programs has doubled over the past 10 years. In response the district has increased staff and developed additional separate classroom units to serve these students. Yearly evaluation reports indicate a lack of educational progress for these students as well as an increase in student referrals for consideration of services outside of the general education classroom.

The superintendent, Dr. Johnson, is concerned about these trends and has encouraged building administrators to involve instructional and support personnel in shared responsibility for all students in a building. She further suggested team problem solving to develop more inclusionary settings and reduce or eliminate separate classrooms for exceptional students. The resulting implementation models that have emerged have created a general state of chaos within the district and the community.

FIGURE 3.1   **Guidelines for Initial Problem Solving.**

1. **Focus on the system, not the people.** Although change has a highly personal dimension, as comprehensive planning is initiated care should be taken to avoid assigning blame to individuals or groups within the organization.
2. **Learn how the current system evolved and how it connects to related systems.** The goal should be a common understanding of related history, which explains how the system was put together in the first place.
3. **Expect the system to resist interventions meant to disrupt the stability of the current system.** Conflict and disagreement are fundamental parts of successful change (Fullan, 1993). Because each participant has his or her own ideas about the innovations that are taking shape, developing institutional attitudes inevitably involves conflict. Successful teams use effective problem-solving strategies to deal with conflicts that arise (Garmston, 1998).
4. **Evaluate the system according to the organization's core values or collective beliefs.** This step involves the shaping of a shared vision and the identification of a common purpose toward which all the organizational systems should be working.
5. **Look beyond the symptomatic problems and symptomatic solutions to fundamental systems issues.** This requires avoiding "quick-fix" solutions. Forums should be created to engage constituent participation and ensure that organizational practices are consistent with identified core values.
6. **Think whole-system, long-term solutions and remain patient for the solutions to take effect.** Once values are clarified, examine all the systems affected. Remember that effective change takes time, a minimum of 3 to 5 years, with some initiatives requiring 10 years or longer.
7. **Anticipate new systems problems arising from current systems solutions.** Consider the downside of implementing new solutions and prepare to address the new problems.

Source: Adapted from Patterson, J. (1993). *Leadership for tomorrow's schools.* Alexandria, VA: Association for Supervision and Curriculum Development.

A representative group of staff members is convened to discuss current conditions. Bonita Davies, Director of Professional Development, is a member of this group and after considerable discussion suggests to the group that perhaps problem-solving and planning sessions might best be facilitated by someone from outside of the district. The group agrees and requests that Ms. Davies locate such a facilitator. This was the telephone conversation that opened this chapter. The following illustrates the application of Patterson's guidelines to the Riverdale planning process.

1. *Focus on the system, not the people.* As the initial administrative planning session begins with a status report, the conversation quickly turns to concern over the lack of student progress and the increase in referrals. "Which schools are doing poorly?" "Which principals have been unable to implement inclusion effectively?" "Which teachers are referring heavily?" "Who says we need to do anything differently?"

The facilitator, Dr. Donna Santos, quickly refocuses the discussion on the system and away from individuals. She suggests that the group begin by reviewing the related history.

2. *Learn how the current system evolved and how it connects to related systems.* The Director of Pupil Personnel Services, Warren Schmidt, provides a brief history lesson. Over the past two decades, state and local education agencies have received financial incentives for students qualifying for both special education services and compensatory education services. These incentives, however, fall far short of the actual costs of educating students with special needs. The budget for these students has increased much faster than the overall division budget.

In addition to special education legislation and corresponding litigation, another primary but subtle system is influencing special education: the general education system. As increasing numbers of students are at risk for failure in school, the general education system has frequently turned to special education for help. This dependency has created almost parallel systems within the division. The current delivery system involves specialists providing educational services to identified students in separate classrooms or pull-out programs for most of the school day.

3. *Expect the system to resist interventions meant to disrupt the stability of the current system.* In this school district the system of referrals for special education can be described linearly as follows. A classroom teacher or parent expresses concerns about a student's performance and ability to succeed in the general education classroom. The student is referred for evaluation and consideration for a special education placement. If the student qualifies, placement occurs in a special education class. The referring teacher is satisfied that the student will get some much-needed assistance. The special education teacher is pleased to be able to provide specialized services. In general, most families are pleased that the school district is so responsive to special needs students. The word spreads of this apparent satisfaction and referrals escalate. Why would anyone want to disrupt the stability of the current system?

4. *Evaluate the system according to the organization's core values or collective beliefs.* Dr. Johnson asks the group to consider seriously the question: Why would anyone want to disrupt the stability of the current system? One of the staff members refers to the school division's mission statement, displayed on a wall chart, which expresses "...care and concern for all students." Another staff member reflects that the school board recently endorsed another core value following a staff report that supports an integrated learning environment as beneficial for *all* students. Mr. Schmidt, citing the Students' Rights and Responsibilities Handbook, says that the division has pledged that all students will be treated with dignity and respect. Furthermore, reports indicate that enrollments in pull-out programs have increased significantly, yet student outcomes fall short of expectations.

This discussion continued through two more meetings focusing on these questions: What do we hold as core values regarding equal opportunity and access to success for all students? Are our practices consistent with our beliefs?

5. *Look beyond the symptomatic problems and symptomatic solutions to fundamental systems issues.* During the continued discussion of best options to serve special education students and others who are educationally challenged, someone raises the question: Is the increase in the number of students receiving special education the problem or a symptom of the problem? The group discusses that the intent of special education legislation was to ensure a free, appropriate public education in the least restrictive environment.

Not long after the special education legislation was passed, the group notes, student demographics began to change. Classroom teachers face more diversity and increasingly complex student needs. There is a greater mismatch between teacher expectations and student performance in classrooms in the Riverdale School District. The group concludes that this mismatch is really the fundamental problem. Special education and other specially funded projects offered a seemingly "quick fix" which, by its very nature, has prevented the district from pursuing more fundamental long-term solutions.

The group agrees to problem-solve toward a more lasting solution. Dr. Santos cautions that such solutions have a built-in delay factor; the positive effects of fundamental change take much longer to appear than the positive effects of symptomatic, short-term solutions.

6. *Think whole-system, long-term solutions and remain patient for the solution to take effect.* As an outgrowth of these initial meetings, several districtwide committees accept the challenge of examining current district practices and recommending a broad set of strategies to address the fundamental problem. A list of Riverdale's recommendations follows:

- More broadly educate the entire district's personnel on the implications of shared core values for practice.
- Discuss the implications of site-based management in making decisions about the distribution of resources to best serve students.
- Ensure that school-based planning teams represent the perspectives of students with disabilities.
- Outline the necessary professional development needs for all staff as solutions are proposed.
- Remove systems barriers and excuses that block the district's movement toward solutions.
- Remain patient and committed to the core values. Don't take the easy way out.
- The next level of committee work should add meaning to the above suggestions and then develop concrete action plans to enable the division to move forward.

7. *Anticipate new systems problems arising from current systems solutions.* The district's leadership recommends that all the progress Riverdale has made could be eroded or eliminated if the leaders of the change process fail to anticipate new systems problems. Similarly, some of Riverdale's anticipated challenges include:

- Rethinking the roles of administrators, teachers, and support staff.
- Creating additional time for joint problem solving around the needs of individual students.
- Addressing the barriers posed by state bureaucracies and legislation.
- Responding to the anxieties of families and teachers who found satisfaction with old solutions and fear that gains on behalf of students with disabilities will be lost.
- Proving that student performance will be better under the new system.

As the Riverdale School District case study illustrates, changing schools from clusters of isolated, compartmentalized, specialized units into communities of educators who share a commitment to a set of common goals requires diverse strategies (Knudson & Wood, 1998; Newmann, 1991). Learning communities require pursuing "a common agenda of activities through collaborative work that involves stable, personalized contact over a long term" (Newmann, 1991, p. 7). It is helpful to think of organizational restructuring as having multiple dimensions along a continuum. Reconceptualizing school organizational structure, therefore, requires an understanding that restructuring cannot be achieved by a single initiative but must include a series of actions designed to embrace a diversity of learners at the level of the individual school as well as the district level (Cawelti, 1994; Sage & Burrello, 1994).

Organizational Culture in the Change Process

Although considerable time has been spent addressing organizational structure, there are other important dimensions of change that should not be overlooked. Clearly one of the significant considerations is organizational culture. Several researchers have used the concept of "culture" in discussing the nature of the human environment in which school change occurs. The cultural change dimension refers to the social relationships and understandings that generate the self-renewing organization and allow the other dimensions to function in an appropriate social matrix (Joyce, et al., 1993). Culture can be defined as the guiding beliefs and expectations evident in the way a school operates, particularly in reference to how people relate to each other (Fullan & Hargreaves, 1992). Nias, Southworth, and Yeomans (1989) suggest four features of school culture: (1) beliefs, values, and understandings; (2) attitudes, meanings, and norms; (3) symbols, rituals, and ceremonies; and (4) preferred behaviors, styles, and stances. They suggest an interesting balance between two aspects of organizational culture—what people believe and think and how they behave and interact. Often attention is given to behavioral change—discrete, observable, describable, and tangible actions—and too little is given to the values or normative core of the school's culture. The culture of a school and efforts to bring about planned change are inextricably linked (Deal & Peterson, 1998). Changing structures without considering organizational culture often results in fragmented efforts. Careful attention to the multiple dimensions of school culture helps to identify potential sources of resistance to change. A cultural analysis requires careful observation, cross validation of perceptions, and pilot testing of assumptions.

Organizational culture is also affected by the cultural identities of individuals within the organization. Communication patterns and quality of interactions are influenced by culturally determined frames of reference as well as the unique experiences of individual members of a cultural group. The world views or cultural perspectives of administrators, teachers, specialists, family members, and students should be acknowledged and shared as educational change is being considered. This allows for identification of similarities and differences among those who need to collaborate to accomplish effective change.

As the opening scenario of this chapter illustrates, the leadership team in Riverdale School District, eager to provide inclusive educational experiences, has been confronted with differing views regarding the actual implementation of inclusionary practices (e.g., the belief that inclusion is considered only for students with mild disabilities who require minimal modifications, the belief that inclusive practice is for elective areas of the curriculum rather than core courses). Carlson and Awkerman (1991) provide a set of questions, found in Figure 3.2 on page 64, which might prove useful as school planning teams seek to gain insight and perspective by observing the important symbols within a school's culture.

Thinking about these questions and discussing them with colleagues provides additional insight into aspects of school culture. This process is a necessary part of capturing the school's and community's culture and subcultures. As a result of individual and group analyses, educational leaders can identify strategies to help preserve and enhance what is working and modify practices that are not consistent with overall goals. Strategies to consider include raising consciousness about both the healthy and debilitating aspects of the current culture; introducing new symbols, rituals, and slogans; and engaging in pilot efforts aimed at clarifying new purposes (Carlson & Awkerman, 1991).

Fullan (1996) offers two additional sets of strategies that appear likely to bring about systemic change on a large scale when implemented concurrently. One set of strategies, viewed by Fullan as essential, is *reculturing*. Reculturing is the process of developing new values, beliefs, and norms. For systemic reform it involves building new conceptions about instruction (e.g., cooperative learning and portfolio assessment) and new forms of professionalism for teachers (e.g., problem solving through collaboration). The process of reculturing is actually a process for changing one or more components of school culture, as discussed earlier. A second set of strategies can be described under the broad label of *networking*. Networking is described as a large-scale attempt to link significant numbers of schools through support networks organized around themes for improvement. This approach was designed to extend reform to those schools that were willing to change but were stymied without some organized assistance (Honig, 1994).

As described in Chapter 2, a fully collaborative culture allows for the expression of strong commitment of staff, collective responsibility, and a sense of pride in the organization. In such a climate, educators indicate a commitment to valuing

FIGURE 3.2   Observing a School's Cultural Symbols.

Space

- How are classrooms arranged in a school?
- How do teachers, administrators, and other staff people arrange and decorate their space?
- What is publicly displayed and where?

Rituals

- How do people dress?
- What is stressed in verbal and written communications?
- What ceremonies are followed during the school year (especially at the beginning and ending of the school year)?
- At the various events, how is space arranged? Who sits where, who speaks, and what is said?
- How do people react to critical incidents?

Stories

- What past experiences or shared experiences are elaborated on and frequently repeated?
- What stories are told to strangers, visitors, or new persons in the school?
- How is humor used? What is the content of the humor? Who is involved?

Time

- How do teachers and administrators use their time (particularly discretionary time)?
- Where and to what do people seem to devote considerable time?
- When people complain about a lack of time, what is it they feel cannot get done?

Extraorganizational Ties

- What is the nature of external relations? Who talks to whom and why do they talk?
- What attitude is expressed toward "outsiders"?
- What attitudes are expressed by outsiders toward the school?
- What close ties have been established and for what purpose?

Source: Adapted from Carlson R., & Awkerman, G. (Eds.). (1991). *Educational planning: Concepts, strategies and practices.* New York: Longman Publishing Group.

people as individuals and also valuing groups to which individuals belong. The examination of school culture is a continuous process. The Riverdale School District has begun such a process. The superintendent, Dr. Johnson, demonstrates an open style of educational leadership that encourages participation in the planning and decision-making processes. Her approach also fosters individual growth and ownership and creates greater responsibility and interdependence. Such a culture facilitates commitment to change, and improvement by creating communities of teachers who are responsive to change, which leads to improved learning opportunities and increased academic achievement of students (Whitaker, 1993).

Ethical Issues in the Change Process

There are several ethical issues inherent in an understanding of the change process as it relates to inclusive and collaborative programs. An awareness of these issues sets the stage for the evolving roles and responsibilities of school personnel. Included are ethical issues related to the professional and personal commitment to serve all students; provision of appropriate services in inclusive learning environments; professional attitudes and interpersonal skills; time and resource management; confidentiality; classroom diversity; and contradictory demands imposed by legislation and policies (Gable, et al., 1993; Howe & Miramontes, 1992). In order to address these issues appropriately, administrators must understand their roles in planning for inclusion, as described in Chapter 2. Kauffman (1994) suggests that one of the most important reforms we could make in special education would be to provide a much higher level of administrative and collegial support for teachers and specialists.

Views of ethical practice must take into consideration the rights of individuals as well as groups of students, while maintaining high professional standards in the face of rapid educational change. Several professional organizations have developed policy statements and guidelines to ensure sound practice in support of a unified educational system that is responsive to the needs of all students. These provide helpful frames of reference to both individuals and organizations. Since 1992, the Association for Supervision and Curriculum Development (ASCD) has endorsed inclusion of special programs through instructional environments that eliminate tracking and segregation (ASCD, 1992). ASCD further supports educational services that address the prevention of learning problems rather than labeling students after problems have been identified. The organization also encourages flexible use of funding to promote educational success for all students. The Council for Exceptional Children (CEC) suggests that inclusive schools must be located in inclusive communities and calls for interagency agreements and collaboration with local governments and business to help students assume constructive roles in such communities (CEC, 1994a). The Council of Administrators of Special Education (CASE) suggests that to bring about the change toward more inclusive educational services, there should be a responsibility of all stakeholders for all students. CASE further recommends a unified funding system emphasizing shared resources without labels and a unified curriculum framework as a means to conduct dialogue about outcomes for planning and organizing (CASE, 1993). The National Association of State Boards of Education's (NASBE) Study Group on Special Education, in its report *Winners All: A Call for Inclusive Schools* (1992), advocates for a unified educational system and recommends major changes in organizational and instructional practices, preservice and in-service personnel preparation, licensure, and educational funding. Several other professional organizations, including the National School Boards Association (NSBA), the National Education Association (NEA), the National Association of School Psychologists (NASP), and the National Association of Elementary School Principals (NAESP), have developed documents that suggest ethical obligations to ensure responsible inclusionary practices. Others, like the

American Federation of Teachers (AFT) and the Learning Disabilities Association of America (LDA) have voiced strong opposition to "full inclusion" practices that suggest the same treatment for all students. Many of these organizations have also published case studies and guidelines for implementing inclusive programs (e.g., *Creating Schools for All Our Students: What 12 Schools Have to Say*, published by the Council for Exceptional Children). Figure 3.3 provides contact information for

FIGURE 3.3   Selected Organizations with Policy Statements on Inclusive Education.

American Federation of Teachers (AFT)
555 New Jersey Ave., N.W.
Washington, DC 20001
(202) 879-4400
E-mail: AskAFT@aol.com
Web: http://www.aft.org

**Association for Supervision and
   Curriculum Development (ASCD)**
1250 N. Pitt Street
Alexandria, VA 22314-1453
1-800-933-ASCD (2723)
Fax: (703) 299-8631
E-mail: info@ascd.org
Web: http://www.ascd.org

**Council for Exceptional
   Children (CEC)**
1920 Association Drive
Reston, VA 22091
(703) 620-3660
E-mail: service@cec.sped.org
Web: http://www.cec.sped.org

**Council of Administrators of Special Edu-
   cation (CASE)** *A Division of the CEC*
615 16th Street, N.W.
Albuquerque, NM 87104
(505) 243-7622
Fax: (505) 247-4822
E-mail: info@icase.org
Web: http://www.icase.org

**National Association of State Boards of
   Education (NASBE)**
1012 Cameron Street
Alexandria, VA 22314
(703) 684-4000
E-mail of web page updater:
   carlac@nasbe.org
Web: http://www.nasbe.org

National Education Association (NEA)
1201 16th St., N.W.
Washington, DC 20036
(202) 833-4000
E-mail: neaworks@aol.com
Web: http://www.nea.org

**National Association of School
   Psychologists (NASP)**
4340 East West Highway, Suite 401
Bethesda, MD 20814-9457
(301) 657-0270
Fax: (301) 657-0275
E-mail: nasp8455@aol.com
Web: http://www.naspweb.org

Council for Learning Disabilities (CLD)
P.O. Box 40303
Overland Park, KS 66204
(913) 492-8755
Fax: (913) 492-2546
Web: http://coe.winthrop.edu/CLD

**National Association of Elementary
   School Principals (NAESP)**
1615 Duke Street
Alexandria, VA 22314
1-800-38-NAESP
Fax: 1-800-39-NAESP
E-mail: naesp@naesp.org
Web: http://www.naesp.org

International Reading Association (IRA)
800 Barksdale Rd.
P.O. Box 8139
Newark, DE 19714-8139
(302) 731-1600
Fax: (302) 731-1057
E-mail: pubinfo@reading.org
Web: http://www.reading.org

selected organizations to facilitate further review of their policies and guidelines for inclusive practice.

Vaughn and Schumm (1995) address other ethical considerations by defining "responsible inclusion" as the development of school-based educational models that put students first and make service delivery decisions based on individual needs of students. Consequently, if a student is unsuccessful in an inclusive setting, alternative interventions are provided rather than a quick change in placement to a more restrictive setting. Although a placement change may be easier for administrators and teachers, it may not be the best alternative for the student's education.

Another ethical dilemma growing out of inclusive programming is the need to provide adequate resources in classrooms (e.g., consultation, paraeducators, special materials, technology). Classroom teachers require and should receive appropriate support to plan and provide instruction for students with disabilities. Inclusion is not an opportunity to reduce the cost of providing services to students with disabilities. In fact, schools that have developed and implemented effective inclusion programs have done so with increases in financial expenditures (McLaughlin & Warren, 1993).

Additional ethical dilemmas are sometimes created by the very legislation designed to protect the rights of students and families. For example, assurances for confidentiality have to be respected at the same time that collaboration between teachers and specialists is encouraged. A teacher who wants to collaborate with others to problem-solve on behalf of a student is confronted with a school law which indicates that certain information can be shared only with personnel who directly serve the student. Another challenge is that appropriateness of educational services has to be ensured while considering the impact of inclusion on the time and personal stress levels of teachers and specialists.

Sound ethical decision making requires consideration of the perspectives of all involved. Failure to pay attention to the critical success factors for inclusive programming and the themes of change research can create ethical dilemmas that impede the achievement of educational goals. The extent to which these issues can be resolved through collaboration has a significant impact on the effective delivery of inclusive education for all students.

Figure 3.4 on page 67 illustrates what can happen when educational organizations do not address essential elements for successful change toward inclusion in a systematic way. School districts, school sites, or individual classrooms may be at various stages of implementation of each element but each must be addressed to avoid the possible negative consequences that will impede progress of inclusive efforts. Failure to do so poses serious threats to sound and ethical educational practices.

Think About It...

What is your current professional and personal commitment to serve *all* students?

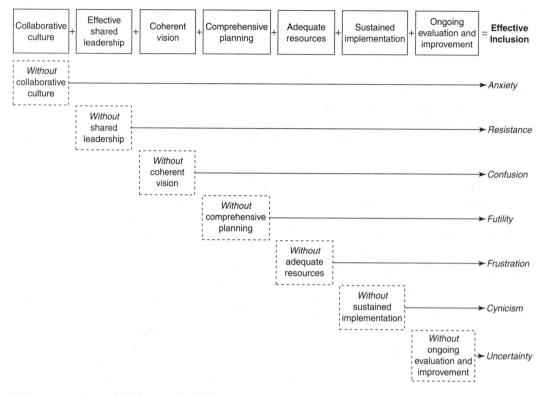

FIGURE 3.4   Essential Elements of Effective Inclusion.

Chapter Summary

Educators must be knowledgeable about the change process but not be paralyzed by it (Schaffner & Buswell, 1996). Although all of the considerations presented in this chapter may seem overwhelming, it is critical that change theory not be used as an excuse to resist making changes on behalf of students in a moral and coherent way. There is general agreement in the literature on change that members of an

Think About It....

As shown in Figure 3.4, when the collaborative culture element is missing, the outcome is anxiety. Why do you think anxiety occurs when the culture is not truly collaborative? Why do you think the absence of each other element produces the outcome listed at the end of each row?

educational unit in which change is being considered should study the change process to be better informed about the complexity and challenges that can be anticipated. Understanding the important dimensions of change, that is, organizational structure, organizational culture, and ethical implications, assists educators in developing coherent plans for change. Although administrative support is crucial, the evolving, shared leadership roles of teachers and specialists as change agents should not be overlooked. Continuous refinement of skills required for collaboration facilitates the kind of problem solving that overcomes barriers to change.

Schaffner and Buswell (1996) also suggest that the most detrimental result of putting inclusive education on hold until all individuals are prepared or of phasing it in gradually is that these methods ignore the urgent need for inclusion. Thoughtful dialogue and strategic planning that involve all stakeholders are essential. A long-term plan that includes careful focus on each of the essential elements for appropriate and effective inclusion against a backdrop of strategies for lasting and meaningful change yields the desired results.

CHAPTER ACTIVITIES

1. Use the chart on cultural symbols (Figure 3.2) to observe an educational setting. Summarize your findings. What cautions would you suggest in collecting and analyzing these kinds of data?

2. State your philosophy of education, which encompasses your values and beliefs. Describe your vision of a school district that would allow you to put your professional values and beliefs into practice. Identify characteristics of the organizational structure, culture, professional development, and ethical practice that you would seek.

4 Creating Collaborative Support Networks for Professionals and Students

LEARNING OBJECTIVES

1. Explain how collaboration supports individual reflective practice.
2. Identify and give examples of types of collaborative support for teachers, specialists, and other school personnel.
3. Discuss partnerships with families as a primary source of support.
4. Describe an array of supports for students that parallels the professional support network.
5. Summarize factors that influence the choice of specific collaborative structures.

Mike McCormick arrived early and sent an e-mail message to his boss, Steve Ingle, principal of Wasatch Elementary. It read:

Dear Steve,

Here is my first e-mail message of the year: HELP!!!!!!!!!!!! (I thought that would get your attention.) You know I love the challenge of an "interesting" mix of students more than just about anybody else in this school—BUT I've got to tell you the more I look at my class roster, the more anxious I get. With only 2 days left before kindergarten starts I've decided I really need some EXTRA help to get ready.

As you may recall, three of my 20 kids have identified disabilities. When we talked about student placements last April or May, I didn't know much about the students. Karen had served on the preschool transition planning team but has since moved to Montana. Mary Alice, Karen's replacement, seems great but has admitted that, as a new person, she doesn't know much about support services in this county. I would like to talk to teachers who really know the three kids; they were all in early intervention programs. Can you suggest the best way to approach this?

One child's parents came to see me today. Their expectations for classroom support seem very high. Their son has been in special education programs since he was 18 months old, and they obviously know their rights. Their son attended an inclusive preschool program and they are adamant that they do not want any pull-out services. They think he will have a full-time assistant in my classroom. This wasn't my understanding. Was it yours?

Thanks, Mike

Many educators like Mike sometimes encounter challenges that are not resolved despite their best efforts. They recognize the need for additional support to help them design and implement more effective strategies. By working together collaboratively, professionals can provide programs for students who present very unique needs.

The concept of collaborative service delivery to support inclusive education was introduced in Chapter 1 and further explained in Chapters 2 and 3 in terms of essential organizational features and the change process. This chapter examines collaboration as a means of deepening and extending individual professional practice. It presents an array of options for collaborative support and some considerations to guide educators in selecting among them. The notion of a parallel network to support students in inclusive communities is also introduced.

Reflective Practice

The process used by educators for systematic planning and problem solving is often described as *reflective practice*. Basically, reflective practice involves a deliberate ongoing application of the following sequence: plan, act, describe, and evaluate (Tripp, 1995). As Schön (1983, 1987) explained it, professionals learn to frame and reframe the complex and ambiguous problems they face, test out various interpretations, then modify their future actions as a result. Reflective practice conveys a dynamic conception of the educator's role. It involves thinking in action, thinking about action, and then acting on that thinking (Richardson, 1990). Reflection occurs on many different levels, from basic description (e.g., "I used these questioning strategies to stimulate the students' understanding of the concept") to higher level critical analysis (e.g., "How did these strategies facilitate learning for the different students in the class? How did this particular practice affect Craig, a student with a learning disability?"). Reflection may focus on the technical aspects of practice or on the more personal dimensions of professional development. It may also involve critical analysis of the values embedded in specific educational activities (Clift, Veal, Holland, Johnson, & McCarthy, 1995).

The importance of reflection occurring within the context of professional community has been emphasized consistently in the literature (Clift, Houston, & Pugach, 1990; Darling-Hammond, 1997; Fullan & Hargreaves, 1996; Little & McLaughlin, 1993; Pounder, 1998). In essence, reflection is "the conversation of practice" (Yinger, 1990). It is listening to one's own voice (alone or with others) exploring alternative ways to solve problems in professional situations (Hatton & Smith, 1995). Although reflective practice is viewed as an integral dimension of individual professional competence, the opportunity to engage in dialogue with one's peers introduces an additional collaborative dimension that enhances the value of reflective practice. This is, simply put, the intent of collaborative support. The basic processes for reflective planning and problem solving are the same whether they are applied by an individual, a dyad, or a small group. Because others contribute their own unique perspectives and expertise, a collaborative or team approach heightens the power of reflective planning and problem solving. The goal for program development, therefore, should be the creation of a full network of collaborative options that teachers and other professionals can access as needed to support their individual reflective practice. Individuals should be able to access the specific type and amount of collaborative support that they need at a particular point in time.

Resource Materials to Support Reflective Practice

Reflective practice involves examination of one's personal theories, conceptions, and values within the context of experiences. Reflective practice is most effective when individuals continue to expand and challenge their professional knowledge base and philosophy of education. For most people, reading the professional literature is one of the primary ways of keeping abreast of issues, trends, and research. Most teachers, specialists, and administrators cherish their personal libraries of texts, journals, guides, and other materials collected throughout their careers. They also access the resources of school, university, and community libraries as needed.

Published materials support reflective practice in a number of ways. At the most basic level, books and articles in professional journals can stimulate new insights that are immediately relevant to one's situation. At a second level, educators can turn to the literature and actively seek more information on a specific issue. The availability of on-line electronic reference systems, such as the Educational Resources Information Center (ERIC) and Education Abstracts, has greatly facilitated the search for useful sources. When looking for suggestions about testing accommodations in an inclusive classroom, for example, a high school history teacher was able to locate several articles including one in *Intervention in School and Clinic* that described specific types of test modifications to meet student needs (Salend, 1995).

Beyond textbooks and journals, a number of other publications exist to support teachers, specialists, and administrators in their reflective practice. Handbooks and desk references often provide quick sources of ideas to address specific needs (e.g., Algozzine & Ysseldyke, 1995; Beck & Gabriel, 1989; Choate, 1997; Jenson, Rhode, & Reavis, 1995). Although most of these resources are in text form, some now use multimedia formats. Additionally, the World Wide Web provides immediate electronic access to a wealth of educational resources.

When educators seek support for reflective practice, they often find it helpful to begin by consulting informational resources. They can access these materials on their own schedules to find help unobtrusively. When their reading efforts are not sufficient to assist them with a particular challenge, teachers, specialists, and administrators typically turn to other human resources for support.

A Network for Collaborative Support

The various ways that individuals work together to support one another are referred to as *collaborative structures* (Laycock, Gable, & Korinek, 1991). Figure 4.1 depicts an array of structures that can be used to create a full network of collaborative

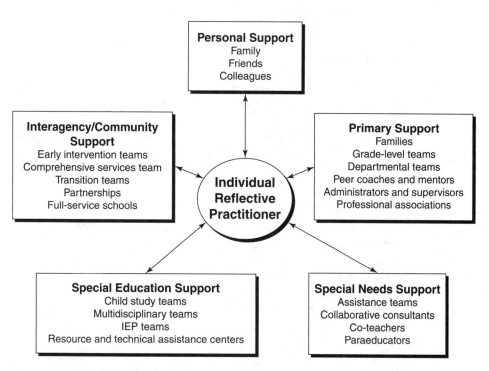

FIGURE 4.1   **A Network of Collaborative Support.**

> ## Think About It...
>
> Is it okay to bypass resource materials and immediately ask for help from colleagues? What would be some advantages and disadvantages of doing so?

support for individual reflective practitioners. The network acknowledges that there are different types of support, including personal, primary, special needs, special education, and interagency/community support. For each type of support, there are several different options or structures identified. These lists are not intended to be exhaustive but simply to illustrate the major structures of relevance. What follows is a brief description of the structures within each category. Those structures most critical for inclusive education are described in much greater detail later in this text in Chapter 7, on assistance teams; Chapter 8 on collaborative consultation; and Chapter 9 on co-teaching.

Personal Support

Professionals have personal lives that transcend the boundaries of the schools. Members of immediate and extended *families,* close *friends,* and trusted *colleagues* can be an intimate and powerful circle of support. Although family members and friends may not have professional expertise in education or human services, they can be highly effective in facilitating planning and problem solving. Many times, all that is needed is a good sounding board, someone who will listen attentively while an individual works through a pressing problem. Family, friends, and colleagues provide important moral support, affirmation, and encouragement to keep trying in the face of adversity. In their own unique voices, those closest are able to say: "This situation has really gotten you down, but you're a great person and you care deeply. Hang in there. I know that you'll be able to figure this out."

Primary Support

Typically, much of the support educators receive is provided through daily interactions and ongoing teamwork in their own schools. These primary relationships offer the most immediate support for professional concerns. Some are loosely structured arrangements that emerge as individuals work together, become better acquainted, and develop trusting relationships with one another (Dickinson & Erb, 1996). Among the most critical relationships are partnerships with students' *families.*

Families as Partners.   The importance of family–school collaboration has been well documented in the literature. Family–school collaboration has been positively linked with improved academic performance of students, as well as decreased absenteeism and discipline problems (Henderson & Berla, 1994; MetLife, 1998; National PTA, 1998; Pelco & Ries, in press; Rasmussen, 1998; Swap, 1991; U.S. Department of Education [USDOE], 1995). Active involvement with families also enhances the professional standing of teachers in the eyes of parents (Epstein, 1995). Family–professional collaboration has been so strongly and consistently supported by research that it is no longer considered an option but a professional obligation (Corrigan & Bishop, 1997).

The nature of family involvement has evolved in recent decades. Until the early 1990s, the focus was almost exclusively on "parental" involvement. More recently, professionals have recognized that partnerships should not be limited to parents alone but should also involve other family members (e.g., siblings, grand-parents) and even close family friends who are vital in providing support for students (Turnbull & Turnbull, 1997). Family involvement has also grown from narrowly defined relationships centering mainly on children's achievement to newer emphases on mutual partnerships involving all types of families in a broad range of activities that reflect their interests and values (Shartrand, Weiss, Kreider, & Lopez, 1997). Building on the work of Epstein (1995), National PTA has developed the following National Standards for Parent/Family Involvement (1998, p. 5) to increase awareness of effective practices and to promote meaningful family participation:

1. *Communicating.* Communication between home and school is regular, two-way, and meaningful.
2. *Parenting.* Parenting skills are promoted and supported.
3. *Student learning.* Families play an integral role in assisting student learning.
4. *Volunteering.* Families are welcome in schools and their support and assis-tance is sought.
5. *School decision making and advocacy.* Families are full partners in the decisions that affect children and families.
6. *Collaborating with the community.* Community resources are used to strengthen schools, families, and student learning.

When educators partner with families in these ways, they become important sources of support for one another. Collaboration between families and school per-sonnel enables the exchange of valuable resources and ideas for improving the qual-ity of education for all students (Pelco & Ries, in press). Effective family–professional collaboration hinges on the development of trusting relationships in which family

Think About It...

In your experience, have professionals behaved as if they honestly believed that fam-ilies were equal partners and, in fact, the experts on their own children? How does this conception of parity require many traditional school practices to change?

members and professionals work together to ensure the best services for each child and family (Bishop, Woll, & Arango, 1993). Schools that are truly family-centered recognize that families are the constant in students' lives, while educational systems and personnel are continually changing. Family-centered approaches emphasize family strengths and individuality, honoring the racial, ethnic, cultural, and socioeconomic diversity of families (National Center for Family-Centered Care, 1990).

Cultural Differences Affecting Family Partnerships.   The challenges of creating collaborative partnerships are often intensified when educators and families are from different cultural, racial, and ethnic groups. As the population of school-age children and youth becomes increasingly diverse, school professionals will be working to a greater extent than ever before with families whose language, experiences, values, and beliefs differ from their own. Although exact estimates vary, demographers concur that by the year 2000 more than one-third of the students in K–12 schools will come from culturally diverse backgrounds (Hodgkinson, 1993; USDOE, 1996). Already in the largest urban areas, more than 70% of those enrolled in public schools are students of color (Jerald & Curran, 1998), and it is predicted that minorities in the majority will be the pattern nationwide by 2020 (Vobejda, 1991). Hispanic Americans and Asian Americans will be the fastest growing segments of the U.S. student population (USDOE, 1996). Additionally, during this decade, more than 5 million children of immigrants are expected to enter U.S. public schools (Karp, 1993). Some schools, such as those in Fairfax, Virginia, report that over 100 different languages are spoken by the students that they serve.

Although the notion of the "traditional" American family has been shown to be mythical to a great extent (Coontz, 1995), the composition of families continues to change dramatically. The number of interracial couples in America has increased by 78% since 1980 (Steel, 1995), and the birth rate of interracial babies has multiplied 26 times faster than that of any other group (Smolowe, 1993). Additionally, the numbers of foreign and transracial adoptions have increased in recent years (Steel, 1995). Overall, fewer children are being raised in two-parent homes. For children born since 1980, it is projected that 50% of Caucasian children and 80% of African American children will live with one or no biological parent (Hernandez, 1994). Moreover, the age at which women are bearing children has changed at both ends of the age spectrum; more women are deferring childbearing to later years and more teens are becoming parents (Hanson & Carta, 1995). Children who live with a single parent who is poorly educated, relatively young, racially diverse, or has a disability are more likely to be poor and to experience poverty for longer periods of time (Center for the Future of Children, 1997). Overall, the poverty rate, as officially defined by the federal government, has risen dramatically among young children since the mid-1970s until one in four of America's children now live in poverty (National Center for Children in Poverty, 1996–1997). Children in cities are far more likely than other youngsters to live in extremely impoverished neighborhoods, those where more than 40% of the residents are poor

(Jerald & Curran, 1998). The Children's Defense Fund (CDF) notes that "poverty matters" (Sherman, 1997) in that extreme or prolonged poverty tends to stunt children's development and has damaging effects on school performance and completion.

In both urban and rural settings, increasing numbers of children are homeless (Vissing, 1996; Waxman & Hinderliter, 1996) as families with children constitute the fastest growing segment of the homeless population (Shinn & Weitzman, 1996; Walther-Thomas, Korinek, McLaughlin, & Williams, 1996). Many children do not live with their own families; approximately 502,000 children were in foster care at the end of 1996, nearly 25% more than in 1990 (CDF, 1998).

As students and families become more diverse on every dimension, all educators must develop new ways of thinking and behaving to enable them to interact effectively with members of different cultural, ethnic, and linguistic groups (Jordan, Reyes-Blanes, Peel, Peel, & Lane, 1998). The term *cross-cultural competence* is often used to describe this ability to conduct one's professional work in a way that is congruent with the behavior and expectations that members of a distinctive culture recognize as appropriate (Green, 1982; Lynch & Hanson, 1992). Cross-cultural competence does not mean knowing everything about every culture. The most important features include (1) an awareness of one's own cultural limitations; (2) openness, appreciation, and respect for cultural differences; (3) an acknowledgment of the value and integrity of all cultures; (4) a view of intercultural interactions as learning opportunities; and (5) the ability to use cultural resources in interventions (Green, 1982).

Cross-Cultural Communication.   Some of the most insidious roadblocks to cross-cultural communication and collaboration involve faulty assumptions that are made in the absence of genuine knowledge. Without adequate information, people are inclined to interpret the behaviors of others from their own cultural perspectives or based on common stereotypes or generalized attributes. At best, these assumptions blur the real meaning of individuals' words and actions; at worst, they can perpetuate dangerous biases against certain individuals and groups. Lack of parent participation, for example, is a well-documented concern (Lynch & Stein, 1987; Turnbull & Turnbull, 1997). How educators interpret this behavior reflects their underlying views and assumptions. What might be considered passivity may instead signify within Asian cultures a reverent regard for teachers as authority figures (Hyun & Fowler, 1995). Parents may decline active partnership and defer out of respect to professionals. Harry (1992) notes that lower rates of participation by African American families in the special education process has generally been attributed to mistrust, apathy, logistical constraints, stressful life circumstances, and disagreement with disability classifications. She emphasizes that this "deficit view" has deterred professionals from examining how their own attitudes and behaviors disempower parents and from restructuring the system to support more egalitarian participation.

It is difficult to make valid generalizations about any cultural group because a number of factors can mitigate the influence of cultural identity. Factors such as

Think About It...

What are some reasons why parents may not come to a scheduled meeting with teachers? What attitudes and beliefs are reflected in your response?

socioeconomic status, age, gender, educational background, duration of residence in the United States or in a particular region of the country, and, in the case of immigrants, the reason for the immigration may play a more dominant role than does the cultural framework within which the individual was socialized (Hanson, 1992).

Moving beyond one's own limited perspectives and developing cross-cultural competence is truly a lifelong process. Lynch and Hanson (1992) recommend a number of "steps in the right direction" to make educational interventions more appropriate for families from diverse cultures, and these are summarized in Figure 4.2. Their suggestions complement and extend the basic communication strategies discussed in Chapter 5.

FIGURE 4.2   Establishing Culturally Appropriate Family-Professional Partnerships.

- Learn about the families in the community that you serve. What cultural groups are represented? Where are they from? When did they arrive? How closely knit is the community? What languages are spoken? What are the cultural practices associated with childrearing? What are the cultural beliefs surrounding health and healing, disability, and causation?
- Work with cultural mediators or guides from the families' cultures to learn more about the extent of cultural identification within the community at large, the situational aspects of this identification, and regional variations.
- Learn and use words and forms of greeting in the families' languages if families are limited-English or non-English-proficient.
- Allow additional time to work with interpreters to determine families' concerns, priorities, and resources and to determine the next steps in the process. Remember that rapport building may take considerable time, but that it is critical to effective intervention.
- Recognize that some families may be surprised by the extent of parent-professional collaboration that is expected in intervention programs in the United States. Do not expect every family to be comfortable with such a high degree of involvement. However, never assume that they do not want involvement and are not involved from their own perspective. Likewise, do not assume that they will become involved or will feel comfortable doing so.
- For limited-English or non-English-proficient families, use as few written forms as possible. If forms are used, be sure that they are available in the family's language. Rely on the interpreter, your observations, and your own instincts and knowledge to know when to proceed and when to wait for the family to signal their readiness to move to the next step.

Source: From Lynch, E. W., & Hanson, M. J. (1992). *Developing cross-cultural competence: A guide for working with young children and their families* (p. 362). Baltimore, MD: Paul H. Brookes. Copyright 1992 by Paul H. Brookes Publishing Co., P.O. Box 10624, Baltimore, MD 21285-0624. Reprinted with permission.

Primary Support from other Professionals.   While collaboration with families offers one major source of support, educators also have many ongoing opportunities to collaborate with professional colleagues. For example, members of the same academic department (e.g., science, foreign language, special education) or grade level (e.g., the fourth grade) work together through both informal and formal mechanisms. These *departmental and grade level teams* enable professionals to share ideas, improve school programs, and problem-solve issues of common concern. Some departmental teams, such as the English department in a large urban high school, consist of more than 20 members. Other teams are very small. Two kindergarten teachers in a rural elementary school, for example, may comprise their own team. Today many team structures in schools are purposely designed to be more interdisciplinary and collaborative in nature, creating a rich context for support, problem solving, and professional growth (Dickinson & Erb, 1996; Pounder, 1998).

In recognition of the special support needs of novice professionals, many districts provide *mentors* for beginning teachers to help them adjust to their new professional lives and ensure that new teachers develop the essential professional skills, knowledge, and attitudes desired by the systems (Halford, 1998; Joyce & Showers, 1995; Stedman & Stroot, 1998). More experienced members help novice peers during the first year or two of their professional lives. In most cases, volunteers serve as mentors or "buddy teachers" with little or no reduction in teaching responsibilities (DiGeronimo, 1993). In other cases, however, professionals are freed from their regular assignment to serve as full-time mentors (Dollase, 1992; Ganser, Freiberg, & Zbikowski, 1994). Mentors provide colleagues with emotional support, information about overt matters (e.g., school policies and procedures), more covert considerations (i.e., school culture), and general assistance with professional responsibilities such as curriculum, classroom management, and testing (Ganser, 1996; Walling, 1994).

Peer coaching is another professional support structure. Colleagues may either volunteer or be assigned to work together. Typically, partners share similar professional roles, responsibilities, and professional status. Unlike mentoring programs where one partner has considerably more knowledge and professional experience, peer partners are co-equals who possess comparable professionals skills. Peer coaching facilitates the reflective collaboration necessary for positive change by breaking down the isolation of teachers and instilling a climate of trust and collegiality (Robbins, 1991). In peer coaching, one teacher observes a colleague's lesson; then, on the basis of the results of the observation, provides assistance in developing or improving instructional skills, strategies, and techniques (Joyce & Showers, 1995). Peer coaching is also effective when used in conjunction with school-level study groups pursuing selected instructional topics (Crowther, 1998).

A variation for colleague support is *peer collaboration* (Pugach & Johnson, 1988). It involves pairs of general education teachers who work together over time as voluntary problem-solving partners. Using a prescribed format to stimulate reflective dialogue, partners resolve their classroom concerns effectively and efficiently. Working together, peer collaborators clarify individual and shared problems that emerge in their classrooms, generate intervention plans, and evaluate student progress as plans are implemented (Pugach & Johnson, 1995). Partners alternate their roles as problem solver and peer facilitator as issues of concern emerge. Self-questioning and reflection by the teacher presenting a problem is encouraged; support is provided by the other partner who serves as the facilitator during the discussion.

Educational leadership is a critical aspect of professional support (Goor, Schwenn, & Boyer, 1997). Effective *principals, supervisors, and department heads* provide ongoing support and professional growth opportunities for new and experienced professionals. Building leadership is widely regarded as the most significant variable associated with effective schools (Algozzine, Ysseldyke, & Campbell, 1994; Fullan & Hargreaves, 1996; Goor et al., 1997). Supervisors provide a mixture of professional and personal support that contributes to teachers' job satisfaction and efficacy (Ashton & Webb, 1986). When teachers feel supported and empowered, positive changes occur in both teaching behavior and student learning (Felner et al., 1997; Ganser et al., 1994).

Affiliation with local, state, and national chapters of *professional associations* (e.g., American School Counselors' Association, American Speech and Hearing Association, Association for Supervision and Curriculum Development, Council for Exceptional Children, International Reading Association, National Association for School Psychologists, National Middle School Association, National Association for Secondary School Principals, National Education Association) provides excellent opportunities for professionals to stay abreast of significant changes in their fields and expand their knowledge and skills through conferences, workshops, journals, and leadership opportunities. Professional organizations enable individuals to see "the big picture" in ways that are difficult without these connections to a broader professional network (Walling, 1994).

Robyn Parks is a social studies teacher on a middle school team. Every day she and the four teachers on her team who teach math, language arts, social studies, special education, and science meet for an hour to discuss instructional issues related to the 108 students they share. Robyn is the only new member on the team. The others have worked together for at least 3 years.

Monday morning Robyn met with Mitch, the team leader, before school. She asked him if the team's agenda for the day's meeting would allow her time to share her concerns about the "disastrous" unit test she had just finished grading. Mitch, seeing how upset she was, assured her that they would make time to talk. During the team meeting Robyn explained the key features of the unit as well as testing problems her students had encountered. She also vented her frustrations. Team members shared their own vivid memories of failure when they were beginning teachers and tried to reassure her that making mistakes as a teacher is inevitable. Together the team brainstormed some possible unit development and test construction strategies. During the meeting and later in one-on-one interactions, each team member reassured Robyn that she was doing a fine job as a new teacher. What they particularly respected was her trying to improve.

Special Needs Support

Whereas structures of the previous types are routinely available to teachers and other school professionals, those for special needs support are triggered by a direct request for assistance. The individual practitioner actively seeks help in order to provide more effective education in an inclusive setting. To deal with specific academic or behavioral concerns, teachers or other professionals may request support from an assistance team. *Assistance teams* are school-based, problem-solving groups of peers who can help a teacher generate intervention strategies and develop an action plan to meet a specific need (Chalfant & Pysh, 1989; Chalfant, Pysh, & Moultrie, 1979; Whitten & Dieker, 1995). As an alternative, teachers may work with a single colleague or specialist to address their concerns about students' programs. When the planning and problem solving is highly interactive, enabling individuals with diverse expertise to clarify and solve classroom problems, the process is described as *collaborative consultation* (Friend & Cook, 1996; West & Idol, 1990). Through both assistance teams and collaborative consultation, teachers can access indirect support to assist them in meeting student needs. The support is considered indirect in that team members or consultants work with the teachers rather than directly with the students.

> Bob Ruiz thought about the sources of potential support he could get at Hyjotepe High School for help in working with Michelle, an honors student in science who had a knack for disrupting class from the moment she walked in the door. Her loud, disrespectful, and defiant behavior was really getting to him. Bob could ask the assistant principal who handled discipline issues to have a chat with Michelle. His colleagues in the science department might also have some ideas. Then there was Michelle's guidance counselor. He might meet with her at lunch and design a behavior change plan. After considering these options, Bob decided to start with Dell Scott, the gifted education specialist. He liked her ideas about science instruction and they had worked well together on the School Improvement Council last year. Given Michelle's interest in science, Dell seemed like a logical source of support through collaborative consultation.

Other structures for special needs extend beyond indirect support and engage collaborators in direct work with students. One such option is cooperative teaching, often called *co-teaching*. Co-teaching generally involves a specialist with a classroom teacher jointly planning, instructing, and evaluating heterogeneous groups of students in general education classrooms (Bauwens & Hourcade, 1995; Bauwens, Hourcade, & Friend, 1989; Cook & Friend, 1995; Walther-Thomas, 1997b). The teachers share responsibility for the class and alternate lead roles in delivering instruction.

In co-teaching, both teachers are fully credentialed professionals. Different types of collaborative relationships are also possible when one of the parties is a paraeducator. By definition, *paraeducators* do not have the professional preparation and licensure to practice independently; they work under the supervision of licensed teachers or specialists. Despite the role differential, paraeducators are important members of the team. With appropriate preparation, role expectations, and supervision, they can contribute significantly to planning and delivering educational programs and provide much needed collaborative support to teachers and other professionals (French, 1996; French & Gerlach, 1998; Pickett & Gerlach, 1997).

Support for special needs enables teachers and other school professionals to serve students with a broad range of abilities and difficulties. When professionals are able to bolster their own reflective practice by accessing the necessary support through assistance teams, collaborative consultation, co-teaching, and paraeducators, they can educate nearly all students in inclusive general education programs. Because these collaborative structures are so critical to the provision of inclusive education, assistance teaming, collaborative consultation, and co-teaching are described in detail in Chapters 7, 8, and 9, respectively. Additional information about working with paraeducators is provided in Chapter 6.

Special Education Support

The structures described thus far have been available to educators to assist them in serving any students who present special academic or behavioral challenges. When concerns are more severe and persistent, more intensive collaborative support may be necessary. The Individuals with Disabilities Education Act (IDEA) requires that all states and localities have a systematic plan to screen and identify children and youth with disabilities. Although IDEA does not explicitly mandate it, all states either require or recommend some prereferral assistance prior to comprehensive evaluation for a suspected disability (Turnbull, Turnbull, Shank, & Leal, 1995). Many schools have resource or *child study teams* who oversee this process. These teams are typically comprised of an administrator, a specialist, and one or more classroom teachers. It is unfortunate that many of these teams have served a very restricted role creating the impression that they are nothing more than gatekeepers for special education. Effective child study teams function much like assistance teams and provide support to teachers in attempting classroom interventions (Hayek, 1987). When performance does not improve after reasonable modifications, the child study team may decide that a full multidisciplinary evaluation is warranted in order to determine whether or not the student has a disability.

Multidisciplinary teams have responsibility for planning and conducting a comprehensive assessment of student strengths and needs in all areas of concern. The process is governed by specific procedural safeguards to ensure student and parent rights to an unbiased evaluation and to active family involvement in decision making. This multidisciplinary team, comprised of teachers, specialists, administrators, and parents, must determine a student's eligibility and need for special education services according to the criteria for recognized disabilities specified in federal and state regulations. The findings of the multidisciplinary evaluation team should also provide detailed information to support development of an appropriate instructional program for the student.

When a student is found eligible for special education, a written individualized education program (IEP) must be developed to specify the nature of the special education and related services the student will receive. This plan is developed by an *IEP team* that includes the parents, the student if appropriate, at least one general education teacher, one or more specialists from the multidisciplinary evaluation team, a representative of the educational agency who is qualified to provide or supervise the provision of services, and others at the discretion of the parent or school. An active IEP team provides invaluable support to the teachers and specialists who work directly with the student. Although the IEP must be reviewed at least annually, many teams meet more frequently to monitor progress and update shorter-term strategies.

Beyond what is available within a school or district, state or regional *resource and technical assistance centers* often provide additional support for teachers, specialists, and administrators. These centers may be federally, state, or locally funded (usually by several school districts) and provide specialized services to school personnel (Briggs, 1994; Buckley, 1994; Feichtner, 1993; Firestone, Rossman, & Wilson, 1983; Zorfass, 1994). Most federally- and state-sponsored technical assistance programs have a specific charge related to the goals of the sponsoring agency. For example, the National Center to Improve Practice (NCIP) exists to promote the use of technology in programs for students with disabilities (Zorfass, 1994), while a certain state-level technical assistance center focuses on supporting inclusive education for students with severe disabilities and serious behavior problems (Janney & Meyer, 1990). Services may include professional development, on-site and telephone consultations, information searches, lending libraries, newsletters, regional network information, and facilitation of communication among clients, schools, and sponsoring agencies (Ayers, 1991; Brinckerhoff, 1989; Haslam, 1992). Successful technical assistance providers help make school personnel aware of new information, regulations, and practices and help them choose among alternatives that meet specific local needs. They may work with administrators and decision-making teams to set priorities, plan initiatives, assess available resources, arrange staff development, and plan support for implementing and continuing innovations (Cox, 1983; Janney & Meyer, 1990). The type of assistance provided depends on the mission of the center and the perceived needs of school personnel. Classroom teachers, specialists, and administrators may access technical assistance providers for help with challenges unique to their roles or related to their work as a school-based team.

Think About It...

Why are resource and technical assistance centers typically available on a regional basis? How might services of regional centers complement services available within a local district?

Interagency Support

The types of collaborative structures described thus far have been primarily school-based options. At particular age levels and for more complex needs, school personnel may also interact closely with professionals from other agencies. These interagency teams can provide extensive support to the individual practitioners who work directly with students and their families.

In both early childhood and secondary programs, interagency teams contribute perspectives especially critical to transition planning. Although transitions in early childhood involve entry into school programs and those in secondary education involve exiting from school programs, the roles of interagency teams for these levels are parallel in many respects (Repetto & Correa, 1996). Professionals from health care, employment, social services, recreation, and other fields can become members of the *transition teams* responsible for development of individualized plans. For early intervention, a transition plan is a required component of the Individualized Family Service Plan (IFSP); the team must determine eligibility for preschool services and plan the staff development and student orientation activities necessary for a smooth transition into the receiving program. The transition team may also assist in arranging for necessary nonschool services (Rosenkoetter, Hains, & Fowler, 1994). For school-age students a transition component addressing instructional, employment, community, and postschool adult living services must be incorporated into student IEPs by age 14. The interagency transition teams provide opportunities for professionals across disciplines and settings to share observations and expectations and to devise more integrated, coherent intervention plans. More specific information about the IEP process and transition planning is provided in Chapter 10.

> Steve Ingle responded quickly to Mike McCormick's e-mail message. Steve knew that he and the teachers needed more information about the identified students to ensure they got off to a good start as kindergartners. He met with Mike and Mary Alice, the new special education teacher, that morning to discuss the situation. Together they reviewed the three student information folders that had been provided last spring by Victoria Kaplan, the district's early intervention specialist. They listed their questions and concerns. Steve called Victoria that afternoon for clarification on several points. She offered to set up meetings with the members of the three students' early intervention teams (e.g., preschool teachers, early intervention specialists, therapists, family members, social workers, nurses). Mike and Mary Alice called the three students' families to apprize them of their efforts, gather basic information that was missing from the folders, and let the families know that Victoria would be calling them about a team meeting at the school. After talking to Victoria, Steve sent an e-mail message back to Mike:
>
> > Mike, Victoria indicated that she is eager to work with us to ensure smooth transitions for these students. She's confident that enough support has been built into the students' IEPs to ensure appropriate stu-

dent *and* teacher support. I'm glad you brought this to my attention. Your proactive efforts will help us get off on a better foot with our new students and their families. See you tomorrow.

Interagency teams are also essential when student and family needs extend well beyond the capabilities of the schools. These interagency collaborative partnerships are gaining popularity as more education and human service agencies at local, state, and national levels seek solutions to complex problems with shrinking resources (Karasoff, 1998). The basic premise of these interagency relationships is the acknowledgment that working together is likely to produce better outcomes than acting alone (Melaville & Blank, 1991). Although each locality has its own array of agencies that provide services to youth and their families, most communities include public and private day care, public health, mental health, social services, parks and recreation, vocational rehabilitation, juvenile justice, and United Way Information and Referral Services (Haley, VanDerwerker, & Power-deFur, 1997). These agencies can support the efforts of school personnel to educate students in inclusive communities. In most communities, interagency collaboration involves professionals from relevant specializations working together to overcome traditional barriers of "turf," organizational structure, and scarce resources to create more integrated and efficient service delivery systems.

Structures for interagency collaboration have been most formally defined for serving students with severe behavior disorders, and many states have developed systems for comprehensive service delivery to this population (Hill, 1996). *Comprehensive services teams* engage professionals from relevant agencies, including education, mental health, social services, and juvenile justice, in the development and delivery of a wide array of community-based prevention and intervention services tailored to the unique needs of the student and family. As team members work together to reduce the fragmentation and increase the coordination and effectiveness of services, teachers and other school personnel discover new allies who can provide collaborative support.

An increasing number of communities are defining even closer relationships among professionals in education, health, and human service agencies by actively linking a full range of community services to the schools. This model of *school-linked services* streamlines the process of accessing support to create a more "user-friendly" network (Sullivan & Sugarman, 1996; Skrtic & Sailor, 1996). Many professional service providers have moved into school buildings to improve access through co-location of staff. Some communities create *full-service schools* with professionals such as social workers, psychologists, child care providers, nurses, pediatricians, job placement advisers, mentors from business and industry, and others on-site to provide "seamless," "one-stop" educational and community services (Dryfoos, 1994, 1998). With this extensive and intensive interprofessional support, professionals are able to address a broad range of educational and noneducational issues impacting students and their families.

In addition to the interagency teams of professionals, educators also access support from other sectors of the community. *Educational partnerships* that involve businesses, churches, civic organizations, federal agencies, and higher education institutions in support of schools have proliferated in recent years. Among the many different services provided through community partnerships are tutor/mentorship programs and school-to-work transition programs. Many partners choose to target particular groups of students, such as dropouts, noncollege-bound students, and students at risk (USDOE, 1996). Teachers who work with more challenging students, therefore, often are able to access extra support from the community at large.

Determining Appropriate Support

Although it is unlikely that all of the structures depicted in Figure 4.1 would be available in a single school, each setting should offer different types of collaborative support so that teachers and other professionals can access whatever help they need at particular points in time. The nature and extent of collaborative support should vary depending on the complexity and severity of student needs; the curriculum and setting demands; the skills, comfort level, and preferences of the teacher; and the class configuration.

Complexity and Severity of Student Needs.   As student needs become more challenging and persistent, more structured and intensive support may be required to ensure success in inclusive environments. Ms. Klemkowski, a sixth-grade teacher, might consult the specialist for learning disabilities once or twice for help with strategies to teach Scott, a student with attention difficulties. She needs much greater assistance from a team of specialists to work effectively with Louise, who is frequently truant from school, aggressive toward her peers, and performing far below grade level in most academic areas.

Curriculum and Setting Demands.   At the heart of most educational "problems" is a gap between expectations and performance. Teachers typically seek help when students are floundering in the ongoing program, despite modifications that have been attempted. The nature and level of the subject matter, classroom rules and routines, instructional activities, and testing formats are just some of the considerations affecting the kind of collaborative support that may be necessary. Mr. Federico, for example, may find that he needs support during the language arts block when he clusters students into small groups for intensive skills instruction. For the social studies block, he is able to manage the same class on his own because he uses a variety of cooperative learning activities.

Skills, Comfort Level, and Preferences of the Teacher.   The voluntary nature of collaboration means that teachers and other professionals are able to choose the nature and level of support that they need for a specific purpose. Mrs. Rogers, an experienced second-grade teacher, has had many students with disabilities in her class and feels comfortable with most aspects of Christopher's program. She just wants some ideas from other teachers who have worked with students who have cerebral palsy, so she enlists support from an assistance team. Next door, Mr. Spence has not had direct experience with students with mental retardation and is anxious about providing an appropriate program for Paula, a student with more intensive support needs. Mr. Spence welcomes the special educator as a co-teacher for his language arts class.

Class Composition.   The overall demands on a teacher are greatly affected by the range of needs presented by the entire group of students. If there are other students in the class who are functioning near the same level as the student with a disability, it sometimes makes it easier for the teacher to differentiate instruction. On the other hand, too many students with special needs may stretch the abilities of even a master teacher. In one of the examples above, Mrs. Rogers wanted only minimal support to help her meet Christopher's needs. Another year, she may have an especially diverse class that includes some students who are highly gifted and several with persistent behavior problems. She may then seek more extensive support to provide an effective program for them and for the two students with learning disabilities included in her classroom.

Student Support Network

The primary focus of this book is professional collaboration to support inclusive education. Just as adults need a full array of collaborative support structures to fulfill their responsibilities, so too students need a strong network of support to be successful in inclusive environments. The ideal is to provide an array of supports for students that parallels the adult support network depicted in Figure 4.1. Figure 4.3 on page 88 illustrates some of the possibilities. *Positive discipline policies, diversity programs,* and *skill and interest clubs* are sources of support that should be available to all students schoolwide on an ongoing basis. In addition, monthly school themes (e.g., courtesy, cooperation); shared songs, games, and rituals; suggestion boxes; school spirit committees; student service and volunteer groups; and student representation on school committees create a culture that is welcoming and supportive. The intent is to ensure that every student is involved in some extracurricular activities and has positive relationships with caring adults to develop a sense of belonging in the school community.

Other structures support more specific student academic or social needs. *Cooperative learning groups* and *peer and cross-age tutoring* are widely used to include and support students in heterogeneous classes. *After-school tutoring* and *homework hotlines* provide extra help for many students. Similarly, students may join *social clubs* or *friendship clubs* for structured support with interpersonal skills. Special groups are often configured to help students deal with common needs such as divorce in their families or eating disorders.

Student-to-student activities and service projects afford opportunities for student involvement in planning and provision of peer support. *New student orientation*

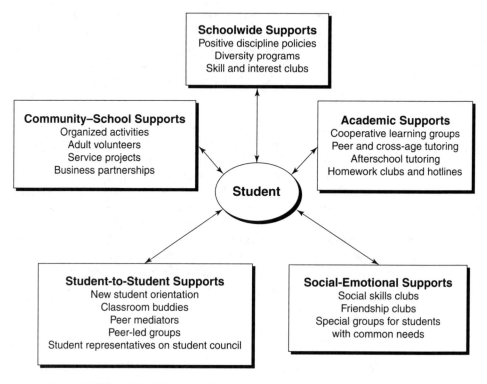

FIGURE 4.3   A Network of Student Support.

activities help students feel welcome, and *classroom buddies* are often recruited to provide ongoing assistance. Many schools prepare students to serve as *peer mediators* to facilitate problem solving and conflict resolution. Small *peer-led groups* also help students address specific needs. *Student representatives on student council* or other school committees broaden perspectives and ensure student voices in decision making. Every student, even those with significant support needs, should be involved in providing some type of assistance to others in order to develop a sense of efficacy and responsibility (Downing, 1996).

Support for students to function in inclusive communities must extend beyond the schools to involve entire communities. Students develop greater skills and a sense of belonging by participating in a range of *organized activities,* such as recreation, scouting, church, and neighborhood activities. Relationships with *adult volunteers* from churches, businesses, universities, and retirement centers are also important. Many students volunteer for *service projects* in which they work in hospitals, soup kitchens, or other service settings. Others benefit from *business partnerships* that provide mentors, tutors, or other relationships with adult role models.

> ## Think About It...
>
> Describe personal experiences with different student supports identified in Figure 4.3.

The more consistently that students receive messages that school is a place where everyone belongs, is cared for, receives needed support, and has much to contribute, the more likely that schools will be effective. Additional strategies for translating positive school norms into healthy classroom communities that promote positive behaviors are addressed in Chapters 6 and 12.

Chapter Summary

In inclusive schools, adults and students are freely able to access many different types of collaborative support. Although the specific support structures vary, the networks for both professionals and students are parallel in many respects. To support individual reflective practice, teachers, specialists, and administrators often find it helpful to consult resource materials for new insights and strategies. In addition, the benefits of dialogue with others make collaborative opportunities particularly appealing and effective. This chapter introduced the concept of a network of collaborative support for the reflective practitioner that includes personal, primary, special needs, special education, and interagency supports. Although a single school is unlikely to provide every structure described, it is important for educators to have access to an array of collaborative options when trying to serve students in inclusive programs. In this way, they can select the types of support best suited to student needs, the curriculum and setting, their personal skills and preferences, and the mix of students in particular classes.

A rich network of support for students includes general schoolwide structures, as well as specific supports for academic and social-emotional needs. Peer-based support systems are also critical to student development. Support from individuals and organizations beyond school enables students to participate to the maximum extent possible in inclusive communities.

CHAPTER ACTIVITIES

1. For your own setting or a selected school site, determine the specific collaborative support structures that are currently available to teachers and other professionals. Develop a graphic similar to Figure 4.1 that depicts the array of collaborative structures for your school. How adequate or complete is the network for collaborative support?

2. Similarly, identify and create a graphic of the specific types of support available to students in this same setting. How does the student support network compare with the professional support network?

3. In this chapter, issues of diversity were introduced with reference to collaborating with families. To what extent do the same considerations regarding diversity apply to collaborative relationships with other professionals? Give some specific examples of ways that cultural, ethnic, and linguistic differences might influence collaboration.

5 Building Fundamental Skills

Communication Basics for Collaborative Service Delivery

LEARNING OBJECTIVES

1. Explain the importance of effective communication to collaborative service delivery.
2. Discuss a model of the communication process.
3. Identify potential communication barriers that might interfere with effective collaboration.
4. Identify strategies for overcoming barriers to communication.
5. Describe the following skills and strategies for effective teaming in school settings: consensus building, conflict management, and negotiation and persuasion.

Superintendent Paula Rivera stepped away from the podium feeling confident that her presentation to all of the instructional personnel of the school district had gone well. She had explained the district's plan to provide more inclusive educational programs for students with identified disabilities and those at risk for academic difficulties. After reviewing the work of the Inclusion Task Force, Dr. Rivera had emphasized the broad-based involvement of all segments of the school community over the past year in defining a vision for more inclusive and collaborative services. She had pledged the necessary staff development and other resources from the central office for individual schools to support students and teachers throughout the implementation process. In closing, Dr. Rivera had stressed that this school district was approaching inclusive education the right way and would move toward this goal in a careful and responsible manner.

Those in the audience had different reactions to the superintendent's presentation. Many of the teachers and specialists left the auditorium stunned to learn that this was a new priority for their school district. This was the first time they had heard anything about an inclusion initiative.

For example, Floyd Knight, a special education teacher, believed the superintendent was not disclosing the full plan in her remarks. He wondered if the rationale for inclusion was only thinly disguised to reduce the number of special education teachers in the division. He worried that his job was in jeopardy.

Ben Edwards, a school psychologist, noted that Dr. Rivera did not mention the implications for school psychologists. He wondered if this meant they would no longer be critical members of child study teams.

Liz Klein, a ninth-grade English teacher, was mostly concerned about her son, Sean, a third grader with a learning disability. It sure sounded as though all students in special education were going to be dumped back into the general education classes.

Joe Lerner, one of the principals who served on the Inclusion Task Force, was pleased with the superintendent's overview of their effort. However, he wished she had gone into more detail about school-based planning and implementation. He knew this information would be helpful for teachers and specialists in his school.

This case demonstrates the importance of effective communication skills to successful implementation of educational initiatives. It illustrates that the message intended by the speaker is not necessarily the message received by the listeners. It also underscores the need to consider carefully the diversity of those who will be involved in the initiative and to incorporate two-way communication throughout the planning and implementation process. Additionally, this example provides insight into the need to ensure that planning group representatives are communicating throughout the process with those they are representing. For example, teacher task force representatives should report progress and receive concerns, questions, and suggestions from other teachers. School psychologists, school social workers, and other professional representatives should do the same for their peers. Family members networking with other families should also provide input. Advanced analysis of feedback from each constituent group as well as a question-and-answer period following her presentation would have enabled Dr. Rivera to communicate her support for more inclusive educational opportunities for all students more effectively.

An underlying theme present in Chapters 1 through 4 has been the important role of educational leadership in creating a *collaborative culture* that supports inclusive delivery of services to all students. A review of these chapters and reform reports referenced in them reflect continuing concern about how educators work together. In order for the collaborative process to be effective, educational leaders are expected to inspire and motivate staff, students, and families toward a district or school *vision*. Traditionally, leadership preparation programs for principals and other administrators have included coursework and field experiences that support development of the skills necessary for sharing this vision, *comprehensive planning,* management, and working with various school constituencies (Bagin, Gallagher, & Kindred, 1997; Carlson & Awkerman, 1991). In contrast, traditional teacher preparation programs have focused almost exclusively on delivery of instruction in isolated settings with little or no preparation for leadership, collegiality, or teamwork within the school setting (Fullan & Stiegelbauer, 1991; Sage & Burrello, 1994). If the essential feature of *shared leadership* described in Chapter 2 is to be realized, teachers and other school professionals will need to be equipped with the skills necessary to engage in a collaborative process of participation, cooperation, and interdependence (De Bevoise, 1986; Kraus, 1984; Maeroff, 1993).

There is general agreement on the skills that are essential to effective collaboration (Cramer, 1998; Fishbaugh, 1997; Friend & Cook, 1996; Idol & West, 1991; Thomas, Correa, & Morsink, 1995). This chapter outlines some basic skills and strategies that facilitate effective professional interaction in support of improved educational services for students. These skills include communication and consensus building, conflict resolution or conflict management, and negotiation and persuasion.

Communication Basics

Communication, the lifeblood of every school organization, is a process that links the individual, the group, and the organization. Educational leaders in today's schools have multifaceted jobs that require effective communication. For example, the results of two separate studies across a spectrum of organizational types and administrative levels indicate that administrators spend 80% of their time in interpersonal communication (Cohen, 1990; Walton, 1989). Similar findings ranging from 70 to 80% have been reported for elementary school principals, high school principals, and school superintendents (Kmetz & Willower, 1982; Martin & Willower, 1981; Pitner & Ogawa, 1981). These findings support the need for school leaders to have a clear understanding of the communication process. As collaborative school cultures develop, professionals interact in new and different ways. Teachers and specialists also need to understand communication basics in order to be better equipped for new roles that require increased interaction with other professionals (Goor, 1995; Maeroff, 1993). All members of the school team—professionals, paraeducators, and family members—need opportunities to develop communication and interaction skills previously reserved for administrators.

Fullan & Stiegelbauer (1991) indicate that all successful change processes are characterized by effective collaboration and good communication among those central to carrying out the changes. They suggest that such interactive professionalism serves simultaneously to increase access to and scrutiny of each other's ideas and practices. Effective communication skills allow professionals to recognize and address barriers that interfere with the sharing of individual needs, interests, and perspectives and the achievement of consensus.

The Communication Process

The communication process involves the exchange of information between a sender and a receiver. Figure 5.1 shows the key components of the communication process, which follows a sequence of steps: (1) *conceptualizing the message* is developing an idea, message, or information to transmit to an individual or group; (2) *encoding* is selection of symbols (e.g., words, nonverbal cues, pictures, or diagrams) to communicate the message that the sender wishes to transmit; (3) *transmitting* is the channel or method (e.g., memorandum, e-mail, fax, telephone, face-to-face communication) selected to send the message; (4) *receiving* is the receipt of the message by another person, requiring good listening skills, if oral, or attention to stated and implied meaning, if written; (5) *decoding* is translation of the received message into a perceived or interpreted meaning; and (6) *acting* is the final step of the communication process, which involves the receiver giving feedback to the sender that the message was received accurately (Bagin et al., 1997; DeFleur, Kearney, & Plax, 1993).

Although this model appears linear, the reality of interpersonal communication is that it is often more complex. Individuals engaged in conversation or other interactive message exchanges are actually simultaneously encoding and decoding messages, transmitting them to each other, and formulating replies even as the other person is transmitting. Moreover, there are a number of factors that affect the process as individuals communicate in various settings for many purposes.

Unfortunately, the potential for misunderstanding or miscommunication exists at every step in the process. Crucial to effective and accurate communication between senders and receivers is a set of symbols that have an agreed-on meaning. As reflected in the vignette about Riverdale School District in Chapter 3, when terms such as inclusion, collaboration, and co-teaching are discussed by educational professionals, it is important to establish common meanings to facilitate accurate communication. The communication process is also influenced by our previous experiences, cultural and ethnic backgrounds, social relationships, emotional involvement, mental and physical state of being, interest in the topic, and the physical setting within which the interaction takes place.

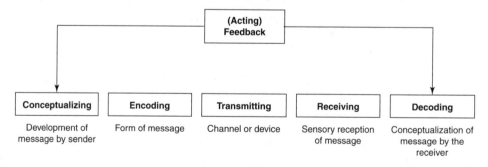

FIGURE 5.1   A Model of the Communication Process.

Barriers to Communication

Effective communication is essential in accomplishing collaborative service delivery; however, barriers may interfere with effective communication and adversely impact planning and implementation. A *barrier* is defined as any condition, either contextual or personal, that reduces accuracy in communication (DeFleur et al., 1993). In addition to the impact of personal, social, and cultural influences, there are other potential barriers to effective communication in collaborative situations. These include frame of reference, filtering, structure, information overload, semantics, and status differences (Bagin et al., 1997; DeFleur et al., 1993; Friend & Cook, 1996). These terms are described subsequently.

Frame of Reference

This type of communication barrier involves the encoding and decoding components of the communication process discussed earlier in this chapter. If the sender and the receiver have a common frame of reference, that is, the encoding and decoding of a message are similar, communication is likely to be effective. If the communicators have different frames of references, communication is likely to be distorted (Littlejohn, 1991). Interpretation of the same message can vary depending on the education, culture, and experience of the sender and receiver. Connotative meaning—the personal, subjective, and unshared interpretations of verbal and nonverbal symbols and signs—influences the accuracy of communications. People from different cultural backgrounds may react quite differently to the same message. For example, the response of some African Americans to the term *inclusion* may be influenced by past experiences with the term *integration*. It might be difficult for some Native Americans to accept parity as appropriate in collaborative school relationships with older, more experienced colleagues, given their cultural value of respect for eldership. Other examples of communications involving different frames of reference include those present in the interactions between superintendents and principals, principals and teachers, teachers and students, teachers and families, teachers and specialists, and school district personnel and agency personnel. The unique educational and professional experiences, roles, and responsibilities of each of these groups can result in unintentional distortions in the communication among them.

Filtering

Filtering involves the transmittal of partial or incomplete information between senders and receivers. This can be unintentional as a result of errors in encoding or decoding messages, or it may be intentional, when a sender assumes that parts of the message are not needed by the receiver. In the opening scenario, Dr. Rivera made a decision to announce central office support for inclusion without providing many of the important details desired by Mr. Lerner, the principal, and others in the audience. Either intentional or unintentional filtering results in distortions of the original meaning of the message.

Some educators may be reluctant to discuss negative information and may even withhold information that might create staff anxiety and delays in accomplishing team goals. Lack of understanding of colleagues' roles and responsibilities may affect horizontal communication between personnel at the same hierarchical level within the district's organizational structure (e.g., between a classroom teacher and school psychologist, learning disabilities specialist and occupational therapist, transition specialist and guidance counselor). Such difficulties may also arise in diagonal communication, which occurs directly from central office staff to personnel assigned to schools without going through the formal "chain of command" (e.g., special education administrator to school health professionals, homeless education coordinator to school office personnel). The resulting quality of communication often impedes change efforts.

Structure

The structure of educational organizations can affect the quality of communication within them. The complexity of the hierarchical levels of authority within a school district increases the chances that the message will be changed, modified, shortened, amended, misinterpreted, or totally fail to reach intended receivers. Generally, communication efficiency decreases with the increasing number of levels through which information must pass before reaching its intended receiver. In larger districts with more complex organizational structures, individuals tend to communicate more with colleagues, but communication from personnel above and below might be poor, distorted, or nonexistent. For example, information on the state assessment program that affects planning for inclusive service delivery is sent from the state education agency through the superintendent's office. This information might then be routed to other central office staff for distribution and may not reach principals and teachers in a timely manner. In smaller districts with less complex structures, this information might move faster from the superintendent's office to schools, but the superintendent might suffer from information overload caused by being the primary recipient of all such correspondence.

The structure of the organization and established communication patterns should also be considered as collaborative planning teams are formed. Teachers, specialists, and other school professionals who assume leadership roles need to work with team members to determine the best organizational scheme to enhance effective, accurate, and timely sharing of information.

Information Overload

Frequently, educators are bombarded with more information than they can handle effectively. Given increasing public concern about the quality of education, advances in communications technology (e.g., e-mail, fax, voice mail), decreased role specialization, responsibility consolidation, and task complexity within school environments, there is a need to consider carefully the amount of information to which educators are expected to respond. Callahan, Fleenor, and Knudson (1986) identified several common ways that people respond to information overload. These include failing to process some information, processing information incorrectly, leveling the amount of information by holding some of it until a period of less activity occurs, separating out less relevant information, categorizing information and using a general response for each category, and simply ignoring or avoiding the information. Some of these responses may impede communication, however, and both the positive and negative impact of these coping strategies must be considered as the amount of information disseminated between collaborating professionals increases. Although cited earlier for increasing the amount of information available, the use of multiple channels such as memoranda, e-mail, voice mail, telephone trees, and routing slips may also facilitate effective communication when time for face-to-face interactions is limited.

Semantics

Semantics can be a communication barrier because words may be misinterpreted. Classroom teachers and specialists may speak the same language but still not transmit understanding because the same words may have different meanings to different people. Meanings are not in the words but in the minds of the people who receive them (DeFleur et al., 1993). Meanings of concrete words do not differ much from senders to receivers. Little misunderstanding is likely when we speak of "book," "paper," or "pencil." The possibility for misunderstanding increases with the use of more abstract terms such as "ethic of care," or terms that evoke emotional responses such as "full inclusion." Other terms that constitute schools' professional jargon (e.g., co-teaching, looping, paraeducator) or acronyms (e.g., IEP, IDEA, LEP, SLD) are also easily misinterpreted.

Status Differences

Regardless of the symbols, status differences may interfere with effective communication between personnel at different levels of the formal and informal organizational hierarchy. Some obvious symbols of status differences are position on the formal organizational chart; degrees and titles; salary; stationery; access to paraeducators; computers; telephones; and size, furnishings, and location of offices or classrooms. Status symbols, such as educational attainment, dress, and income levels, may interfere with communication, especially when school professsionals are interacting with families and other members of the community. Individuals

---

Think About It...

How have you experienced each of the communication barriers identified in this section: frame of reference, filtering, structure, semantics, and status differences?

---

with higher status have more communication demands on them and often, out of necessity, must limit their communications.

Overcoming Barriers through Effective Communication Skills

As one reviews a description of the potential barriers to communication, some of the solutions appear obvious. However, because effective communication requires sustained effort on the part of senders and receivers, it is helpful to examine those communication skills that facilitate the development of a two-way communicative climate—listening, repetition, empathy, understanding, and feedback.

Listening Skills

Effective listening is one of the most important of all communication skills. Fortunately, it is one that can be learned. This means that it can be analyzed, understood, and improved. Listening skills affect the quality of personal and professional relationships (Freshour, 1989). Education reform reports, discussed in Chapter 1, recommend formal instruction in listening skills. Failure to work actively at listening well has been identified as the weak link in the chain of two-way communication (Bagin et al., 1997; Hersey, Blanchard, & Johnson, 1996). Some organizations include techniques for improving listening skills in their team building activities.

Recommendations for improving listening skills are found in numerous resources on communication skills (Barker, 1990; Brammer, 1993; DeVito, 1994; Eitington, 1989). DeFleur and colleagues (1993) suggest that an effective way to personalize and incorporate suggestions is to develop a comprehensive personal plan for effective listening. Assessing current listening skills is a primary step in such a plan. There are several tools available to assist in this self-assessment of listening behavior; Figure 5.2 is an example of one. The information received from such an assessment can be used to establish personal goals for improving listening behavior. Critical to the attending, hearing, encouraging, and processing behaviors outlined in Figure 5.2 are other essential skills for effective, active listening including paraphrasing content, reflecting feelings, and summarizing. Examples of each skill follow.

FIGURE 5.2 Listening: A Self-Check.

1. Am I **ATTENDING** to the speaker(s) and the message(s) through
   ____ open posture?
   ____ comfortable eye contact?
   ____ avoidance of distracting thoughts and behaviors?
   ____ constant monitoring through interaction?

2. Am I **HEARING** the message(s) communicated in terms of
   ____ the speaker's point of view?
   ____ voice quality, pace, and rhythm?
   ____ body language?
   ____ the feelings as well as the content?

3. Am I **ENCOURAGING** open communication through
   ____ subtle verbal and nonverbal cues?
   ____ paraphrasing when it seems appropriate?
   ____ reflecting the speaker's feelings when it seems appropriate?
   ____ asking clarifying questions when it is necessary and appropriate?
   ____ monitoring my facial expressions and body language?

4. Am I **PROCESSING** the message(s) to respond when appropriate through
   ____ identifying key themes and supporting points?
   ____ relating information from other relevant sources?
   ____ making notes when it seems appropriate?
   ____ summarizing when it seems appropriate?

Source: McLaughlin, V. (1998). Listening: A self-check. Unpublished class material, The College of William and Mary, Williamsburg, VA.

Paraphrasing Content.   Paraphrasing content is not simply repeating the content but editing the speaker's words to get to the core of the message. It involves making a concise response to the speaker, as illustrated by the principal's response in the following example. This conversation takes place between Mr. Garcia, a special education paraeducator, and the principal, Mrs. Olivera, about his reassignment:

> MR. GARCIA: I need to meet with you about this situation. Maybe I need to meet with the superintendent. I don't know what needs to be done! But something has to happen. Maybe you need to help this teacher understand why I should have been a participant in the planning for this change. Maybe someone should apologize to me. Maybe I need to take my case to the union or go to the school board.

MRS. OLIVERA: I understand your desire to have been more involved with the decision making in this matter and that you want something to happen as a result of our meeting.

MR. GARCIA: Yeah, I really am frustrated by this!

Another illustration of paraphrasing is taken from an interaction during a teacher assistance team meeting between Mrs. Brown, a team member, and Mrs. Gray, a teacher who is seeking assistance from the team.

MRS. BROWN: Mrs. Gray, please tell us what you're concerned about.

MRS. GRAY: I thought this would work but I can't tolerate having another teacher in the classroom with me. It really makes me nervous. The specialist, Mr. Franklin, has to leave my classroom.

MRS. BROWN: You're saying that you thought it would work out but at this point you would like to end the co-teaching relationship?

MRS. GRAY: Yes, that's right, I guess.

Reflecting Feelings.   This skill is similar to paraphrasing content except that the feelings associated with the verbal content are reflected. Reflecting feelings is more challenging because it requires listening for the feeling words used in the conversation, as demonstrated by Ms. Ramos in the following example. Ms. Ramos is the fourth grade teacher in the classroom to which Mr. Garcia has been reassigned.

MR. GARCIA: I am so angry! I can't believe that I was reassigned to work with my students who are in your classroom without anyone consulting with me or explaining what was to take place. I thought I was more respected than that.

MS. RAMOS: You are angry about how the reassignment was handled and feel that you are not respected.

MR. GARCIA: Damn right I am!

Summarizing.   This skill involves integrating the content and feelings that have been expressed. Summarizing is useful if the conversation has lasted a long time or if you are meeting for a second or third time with the other person and want to remind him or her of previous discussions. It is also used to conclude meetings and conferences. For example:

MRS. OLIVERA: If I can summarize what we have been saying here, Mr. Garcia, it seems that you are angry about the way you were informed of the change in your position responsibilities, feel disrespected because of the way it was handled, want something to be done about it, but at this time you are not quite sure what should be done. Is this an accurate summary?

MR. GARCIA: Yeah. That about does it.

Additional strategies in a systematic plan to improve listening skills involve remaining open and sensitive to communication from different people; actively concentrating on what is being said; showing alertness and interest; searching for the full meaning of a message; and avoiding premature judgments about a person's intentions, qualifications, or actual positions. In other words, wait until the entire message has been heard. Learning to listen well is an important part of getting along with and influencing others. Frequent self-checks and continued development of this skill improve collaborative interactions.

Repetition

Another skill that is important in creating a positive communication environment is repetition. Repetition is one of the most frequently used techniques for overcoming communication barriers (Bagin et al., 1997). This technique involves sending the same message over and over again, using multiple channels (e.g., face-to-face discussions, written meeting summaries or minutes, audiovisual presentations, electronic media, e-mail). This strategy provides several opportunities for the intended audience to receive and assign meaning to the information that is being communicated. For example, initial activities designed to increase families' awareness of inclusive practices might include an oral presentation using overhead transparencies at Back to School Night, followed by a booklet that addresses the most frequently asked questions or myths and facts about inclusion. These strategies could then be followed by a PTA meeting with roundtable discussions on specific strategies that support student learning in inclusive settings (e.g., cooperative learning, peer teaching) and a presentation on the school district's television station.

Empathy

Empathy is a technique for understanding the other person's frame of reference. Effective communication means that the sender can make predictions about how the receiver will respond to a message. For example, specialists should place themselves figuratively in the shoes of classroom teachers and attempt to anticipate personal and situational factors, such as time constraints, multiple reporting responsibilities, and formal educational preparation, that might influence teachers' interpretation of messages. The greater the gap between the learning, culture, and experiences of the sender and the receiver, the greater the effort that must be made to find common ground for understanding.

Understanding

In order to achieve understanding it is important that messages contain clear and concise language. Educators must encode messages in words and symbols that are understandable to receivers. Some research has found that written communication that is transmitted to employees in business settings has been rated, using readability formulas, as beyond the level of satisfactory reading for typical adults (Enos, 1990). Given the earlier discussion of professional terminology and jargon as potential barriers, it is important to ensure common understanding of terms by providing concrete and relevant examples whenever possible. This becomes increasingly important as professionals foster collaborative relationships with families who may not have previously interacted in problem-solving situations on behalf of students. For instance, giving specific examples of what each teacher might do during a co-taught lesson helps to explain the concept of co-teaching to family members.

Feedback

As participatory management and site-based decision-making practices increase in educational settings, the skill of providing and securing feedback is important to ensure effective communication. Feedback also clarifies the degree to which a message has been received and understood. Questions such as the following can be helpful in eliciting verbal feedback about the reception of a message: How do you feel about my statement? What do you think? What did you hear me say? Do you see any problems with what we have talked about? (Enos, 1990).

In summary, effective communication requires a sustained effort on the part of all school professionals involved in collaborative service delivery. The goal is to recognize and overcome communication barriers and arrive at mutual understandings. Refining active listening and feedback skills and approaching interpersonal interactions with empathy and understanding will improve all communications.

Consensus Building

One of the essential features for effective inclusive education described in Chapter 2 is *comprehensive planning*. A collaborative planning process also serves as a communication and consensus building strategy, especially in determining goals and priorities. Consensus building provides the greatest opportunity for each participant to contribute his or her ideas. Consensus is a cooperative effort to find a solution acceptable to everyone (Kayser, 1994). Agreement comes by "talking things through," rather than by voting. Opportunites for stakeholders to bring relevant issues into the open and to analyze and discuss these issues with respect for each other's views are crucial to reaching commitment toward common goals (Carlson & Awkerman, 1991).

Think About It...

Generate communication strategies that could be used to develop an understanding of inclusive practices. What other channels could be used to facilitate awareness?

Numerous consensus building techniques have been developed to help planning groups reach agreement on topics of discussion. Some of the most frequently used techniques include Polling, Nominal Group Technique, Delphi Technique, Fishbowl Technique, and Telstar (Herman & Herman, 1994; Hoyle, English, & Steffy, 1990; Kaufman & Herman, 1991). These are described briefly in the next paragraphs. Professionals are encouraged to consult the references provided for more detail on how to facilitate these consensus building techniques.

Polling

Polling involves representative individuals indicating their preferences or predictions. This can be done through telephone interviews, face-to-face interviews, or mail opinionnaires. The results of polling can provide information that assists planning teams to develop action plans. For example, in a school in which co-teaching is to be piloted, a survey would be developed and distributed to teachers in order to determine the degree of teacher interest, willingness to participate, and staff development needs. The information is then compiled and used by the planning team to establish specific implementation objectives.

The Nominal Group Technique

The Nominal Group Technique (NGT) is devised to stimulate new ideas and arrive at a consensus. It is useful for identifying problems and determining causes as well as generating ideas for solutions to the identified problems. Although NGT brings people together for problem solving, it limits their interaction so that ideas will not suffer due to premature evaluation, social pressures, and the like (Murnigham, 1981). In NGT all are encouraged to participate, discussions are focused on specific questions, and consensus is reached through a series of voting exercises.

Advantages cited for NGT are that it separates the fact-finding and idea-generation activities from the evaluation phase of the problem-solving process. It also balances participation, avoiding discussion takeovers by more assertive members of the team or group. Good results can be produced in a short time (60 to 90 minutes) and it is easily learned by participants. Limitations of NGT are that it requires a skilled facilitator; the question to the group must be very precisely stated or the results will be less than expected; and it may not produce a true consensus since group interaction is limited. See Figure 5.3 on page 104 for the steps in using this technique.

The Delphi Technique

The Delphi Technique is a structured process for achieving consensus without the requirement of face-to-face contact by the participants. It was originally developed for achieving consensus in forecasting but has been modified for group use in problem solving. The Delphi Technique works best when participants cannot

FIGURE 5.3   Nominal Group Technique.

1. Small groups of five to nine team members are given a written question and asked to generate ideas for 5 to 10 minutes, individually and silently. A more complex problem may take additional time.
2. Going around the table, each team member presents one idea at a time from his or her list.
3. The facilitator records these ideas on a chart.
4. After all ideas have been posted, the team discusses them, providing clarification, support, or challenges for the posted ideas.
5. Team members individually rank-order the ideas. The team is then asked to come up with one powerful solution or the best idea. This is accomplished by having team members present their top idea from the list, which is not evaluated but may be discussed to ensure understanding. Each idea is then rated by the other participants on a five-point scale. Participants rate only their colleagues' ideas, not their own. The best idea from each small group may be subjected to another round of ratings by the entire team. The best idea is the one that receives the highest point score.

be brought together for group discussion because of geographical or scheduling problems; participants are strong individual thinkers, working better without group interaction; the process of writing solutions facilitates a careful thinking through of the complexity of the problem; and the Delphi participants are treated on an equal basis because all ideas are pooled (Eitington, 1989). Figure 5.4 outlines the general procedures for this technique using an example specific to collaborative service delivery.

FIGURE 5.4   Delphi Technique.

1. Teachers, administrators, and specialists from districts in which inclusive education is being successfully implemented are requested to serve on a panel of experts to address a given problem, policy, or issue challenging a district planning team in which such practice is just being considered (e.g., ways to find time for co-planning).
2. Questionnaires are developed and mailed to the participants in the study.
3. The respondents complete questionnaires individually and mail them back to the team.
4. Designated team members summarize all responses, develop a second questionnaire, and mail it back to the respondents with a request to reconsider their ideas in light of the new or composite opinions.
5. Respondents vote on or rank-order ideas as to feasibility and return their responses to the team.
6. The team prepares a final summary and feedback report. Three to five rounds of questionnaires and rankings may be necessary to secure a consensus that will enable the decision-making team to move forward.

The Fishbowl Technique

The Fishbowl Technique is one in which a group of representatives is selected from broader groups to discuss and negotiate points that will lead to consensus while the larger membership observes the dialogue. A variation includes providing a rapid input opportunity to anyone who is not a part of the representative discussion group. For example, a group of eight educators who represent grade levels and specialist areas within a building is arranged in a close circle of chairs to discuss scheduling options for collaborative teaching, but an empty chair is also included in the circle for use by an audience member who might wish to give input to the discussion. Once the information is shared by this temporary participant, she or he must return to the audience while the eight representatives continue their dialogue for the purpose of achieving consensus.

Telstar

Telstar is another consensus building technique that is similar to the Fishbowl Technique, but it allows for even broader participation. Telstar can best be used when very large, diverse stakeholder groups have an interest in the planning results (Herman & Herman, 1994). The initial goal of Telstar is to divide large groups into subgroups. Figure 5.5 outlines an example of the Telstar technique used in a districtwide initiative.

Knowledge of and skill in using these techniques allow educators to work together more effectively and efficiently on behalf of all students. Consensus building skills and processes are important to problem solving and to minimizing

---

FIGURE 5.5 Telstar Technique.

---

1. Begin the process with participants from each school.
2. Those in attendance are asked to nominate six persons to serve as spokespersons for the local school's interests when meeting with the total school district's group.
3. In this example, if there are 10 schools in the district, 60 persons (six from each of the 10 schools) would be asked to come together to achieve consensus on the issues to be discussed.
4. Each of these six-member teams would next be asked to select its primary spokesperson, and the group of 10 spokespersons would be seated in chairs in a closely aligned circle. The five other team members would be seated in close formation behind their selected spokesperson.
5. Discussion would begin among each of the 10 spokespersons with their team members and the audience observing. The audience could contact spokespersons between meetings but could not interact during official meetings.
6. Any of the five members from any group could call for a caucus of his or her group by calling "time out." During this caucus the group gives the spokesperson ideas or directions. All 10 groups could caucus until the individual who originated the caucus called "time in." After the caucus is over, only the 10 spokespersons can discuss consensus possibilities.

conflict within collaborative settings. Consensus is recommended when owner-ship and commitment to a decision are fundamental to successful implementation (Richardson, 1997).

Conflict Management

Maurer (1991) defines conflict as a disagreement resulting from incompatible demands between or among two or more parties. Because conflict is an active pro-cess rather than a state of being, it is possible to analyze, influence, and ultimately manage or resolve conflict. Conflict management is the process whereby the par-ties work out their disagreements in order to end the conflict successfully. Although it is usually impossible for an individual to respond to all of the elements involved in a conflict, it is possible to become skilled in procedures that facilitate conflict management.

Causes of Conflict

The word *conflict* is usually interpreted negatively. While conflict can pose a threat to the achievement of organizational goals, it can also be helpful to an organiza-tion and viewed as constructive if the following occurs after the conflict has been resolved: the relationship is stronger and the parties are better able to interact or work with each other; the parties like or trust each other more; the parties are sat-isfied with the results; or the parties have improved their ability to resolve future conflicts that might arise (Johnson, 1986). Conflict has the potential to produce growth, opportunity, and success. A moderate level of conflict is usually construc-tive. If there is no conflict, the organization may become stagnant and may lose much of the energizing force that conflict often creates.

In completing the Think About It exercise, you may have identified one or more of the following: communication barriers; role ambiguity; unclear expecta-tions, regulations, or rules; unresolved prior conflicts; conflicting interests; dis-agreement on tasks or content issues; competition for scarce resources; differences in values or ideologies; incongruent thought processes or perceptions; or inconsis-tent outcome preferences. In addition, lack of trust, integrity, benefits, informa-tion, or in clarity can create conditions that can cause conflict (Maurer, 1991).

Types of Conflict

Normally, in the best circumstances, change and innovation mean conflict (Fullan, 1993). Coombs (1987) identified three types of conflict that might be encountered

---

Think About It...

Conflict exists in organizations for a variety of reasons. Think for a moment about your present setting (e.g., school, work, home). What are some conditions that cause conflict?

in educational settings. The first type of conflict involves parties who must choose an outcome but whose goals are incompatible. An example of this is the scheduling of students within a school setting. The administrator may choose to place all students with disabilities on the same homeroom team to facilitate communication between the teachers and specialists and to justify lower student–teacher ratios or assignments of co-teachers. The teachers and specialists, however, may see the importance of distributing the students across teams to allow for increased interaction with typical peers. This difference of opinion about what is most important in planning for students could become a conflict. Researching and sharing information on promising strategies for student placement might facilitate a solution.

A second type of conflict is one in which parties want different things but must settle on one solution. This type of conflict involves finding a mutually acceptable solution that satisfies the needs of all concerned. For example, a mathematics teacher who wants to give a grade of "C" to a student with learning disabilities because of the instructional accommodations that this student has received may be in conflict with the student's parents who believe that the student has earned an "A." There is a need to preserve the relationship between the two parties and to resolve this conflict in a manner that results in a "win" or gain for both. One approach would be for the teacher and parents to revisit together the level or quality of performance assigned to each letter grade and to review the evidence of student achievement to support the proposed letter grade.

The third type of conflict involves parties who want the same thing but only one can have it. This type of conflict is described as the most difficult type (Maurer, 1991). An example would be co-teachers who develop a plan to use the paraeducator for instructional support within the classroom in conflict with an industrial arts teacher who wants the paraeducator to accompany any students with IEPs to his class during the same time period. The parties involved here must find mutual interest in resolving this conflict. A third party or negotiator might be necessary to reach points of agreement. Reviewing student needs and the prerequisite skills for the industrial arts class might facilitate resolution of this conflict.

Conflict Management Strategies

As noted earlier, the nature of conflict is complex. There is general agreement among those who conduct research in this area that there are some conflict situations that cannot be resolved but must be carefully managed. What constitutes a conflict situation for one person may not constitute a conflict situation for another. Accordingly, the way one person effectively manages conflict may differ greatly from the way another person manages conflict. Because personal strategies are learned, individuals can change them by learning new and more effective ways of responding to conflicts. Knowing personal preferences for conflict management as well as the styles of others helps one in interacting and collaborating on behalf of students.

Johnson (1986) suggests that there are two major issues which affect how we act in conflict situations: the importance assigned to the achievement of personal or professional goals, and the importance of maintaining a good relationship between the persons involved in the conflict. Depending on the relative importance assigned to goals and relationships, there are five styles or strategies for managing conflict that might be used. These include avoiding, dominating, obliging, compromising, and integrating. Although most people have a preferred approach to managing conflict, certain responses are more effective for certain situations. However, interpretations vary and responses are often influenced by the beliefs, values, age, and experience of those involved.

Avoiding or Withdrawing.   People who use this strategy withdraw (physically or psychologically) from a conflict situation rather than face it. They have low regard for the relationships and the goals involved in the conflict. It is appropriate to use avoidance when the issue is trivial or the potential negative effect of confronting the other party outweighs benefits of resolving or managing the conflict (e.g., one name plate is omitted from the door when two teachers begin to co-teach; a team member has a communication style of interrupting near the end of comments as he begins his own). Avoidance is not appropriate when prompt attention is needed, the issue is of personal importance, or an individual has the responsibility to make a decision.

Dominating or Forcing.   This strategy involves forcing others (by directing, mandating, attacking, overwhelming, or intimidating) to accept a solution to the conflict. People who use this approach seek to achieve personal goals at all costs. Relationships are of minor importance. A dominating response might be viewed as appropriate when an ethical or legal requirement has to be met, a speedy decision is needed, or in situations in which others may lack the skills to make technical decisions and an unfavorable response by the other party may prove costly to you or the organization. For example, a teacher assistance team recommends proceeding, as quickly as possible, with evaluations to answer questions related to a student's learning problems. A specialist on the team disagrees with the accelerated timeline being proposed because parental notice and consent must be given prior to such an assessment. A dominating style or response is inappropriate if the issue is complex, (e.g., a causal hearing), or a decision does not have to be made quickly.

Obliging or Smoothing.   This approach is used when the relationships involved are perceived as more important than personal goals. There may be an emphasis placed on what one person has in common with the other rather than on differences. This accommodating response might be viewed as appropriate when the issue is more important to the other party or you are willing to give up something in exchange for something from the other party in the future. For example, disagreement arises over the format for a worksheet developed for co-planning. The sequence of the items on the form is not as important to you. You concede to the format desired by your partner.

Compromising.   Compromising people are moderately concerned for their own goals and their relationships with others. A compromise is an adjustment or settlement by which each party makes concessions. This method resolves conflict as long as each party perceives that sacrifices are equal. If someone senses the final solution is weighted in one person's favor, the conflict could emerge again. Compromise can be a quick solution, but often it is not permanent. It is appropriate when consensus cannot be reached or a temporary solution to a complex problem is needed. For example, controversy emerges over the scheduling of tests and major assignments on Friday and the impact that this has on students. No teacher wishes to adjust the examination schedule or assignment due dates. A compromise would be to make the adjustment that would best meet student needs and have teachers alternate each marking period between Fridays and other days of the week. A compromising style would not be viewed as appropriate when the problem is complex enough to require more extensive problem solving.

Integrating.   Individuals who choose this strategy simultaneously have a high regard for their own goals and for relationships with others. They view conflicts as problems to be solved and seek a solution that achieves both their own goals and the goals of the other person in the conflict. This method involves collaboration between people, openness, exchange of information, reduction of tension between parties, and examination of differences to reach a solution acceptable to both parties. This response is appropriate when issues are complex, consideration of others' ideas is needed to reach better solutions, time is available for problem solving, and commitment is needed from other parties for successful implementation. Making judgments about students' programs and developing co-teaching schedules are two examples of when an integrating style of conflict management is appropriate. It might be viewed as inappropriate when issues are simple (e.g., deciding between an 11:30 A.M. or 12:00 noon lunch period), an immediate decision is needed, or other parties are unconcerned about the outcome.

Unfortunately, many conflicts are ones in which one party achieves his or her goal at the expense of the other. People often use the win-lose approach because they view the conflict as either-or: Either I get what I want or you get want you want. There are some cases in which the win-lose approach may be necessary, such as when there is only enough money for one computer to be purchased; when only one position is available for promotion; or when an individual is committing an illegal act. Often, however, there are ways to reach a more acceptable solution.

Think About It...

Identify specific situations in which each of the styles for managing conflict might be appropriate and situations in which each style might be inappropriate.

Therefore, the aim is to find a solution that satisfies the needs of everyone involved and allows all parties to reach their goals. This win-win outcome is often a challenge to achieve. It requires a noncompetitive attitude and a high level of cooperation from all those involved. A win-win approach requires effective communication among team members that is regular, direct, constructive, and nonthreatening. Along with communicating effectively, team members must display behaviors that encourage communication and thereby assist in resolving conflicts. Encouraging behavior occurs when a team member (Walker & Harris, 1995):

1. Avoids remarks that imply the other person is wrong or needs to change.
2. Communicates a desire to work together to explore a problem or seek a solution.
3. Demonstrates respect for the concerns and ideas of others as reflected in a genuine willingness to listen.
4. Identifies with another team member's problems, shares feelings, and accepts the team member's reaction.
5. Focuses on factual issues and behaviors and not on personalities in working to resolve conflict.
6. Demonstrates a willingness to self-assess critically his or her own behaviors and ideas based on the facts presented.

In addition to encouragement, successful conflict management requires effective communication skills and creative thinking to develop voluntary solutions acceptable to those involved in a dispute. These skills are useful not only for teams working within a school or district but also for working with families and representatives from community agencies.

Collaborative Negotiation and Persuasion

The Case of Bay City School District
An inclusion planning team from Bay City School District comprised of general education teachers and specialists (special education, reading, mathematics, and computer literacy) returned to their district following attendance at the annual symposium sponsored by a local state university. As the team planned the follow-up session to share information from the symposium with colleagues in their respective departments, several team members expressed an interest in establishing co-teaching relationships within their buildings in order to improve learning opportunities for students. Other team members responded with comments that their principals would never allow it. The group began to discuss possible approaches to gain administrative support.

As reflected in the Bay City School District case, when teachers and specialists assume the roles of internal advocates for more inclusive practices on behalf of their students, they often find themselves in negotiation situations with educational leaders, family members, paraeducators, and other professionals. Johnson (1993) suggested that the word *negotiation* suffers from overuse, as it is commonly applied to almost any kind of interaction between individuals or groups. Negotiation is a process in which individuals or groups seek to reach goals by making agreements with others. This process often includes offering concessions and demanding them from other parties, but it functions best when it serves as a method for discovering mutual interests and joint payoffs (Johnson, 1993). Negotiation requires participants to identify points of difference, teach each other about their respective needs and interests, create various possible solutions, and reach agreement about what will be done. Negotiating is the principal way that old relationships are redefined and new relationships are created (Girard & Koch, 1996; Johnson, 1993; Walker & Harris, 1995; Ury, 1991).

Negotiation can also be viewed as a technique for problem solving. The chances for successful conclusions to negotiation efforts are greatly enhanced if the participants have a clear understanding of the problem to be solved, that is, the issue(s) that separate them from reaching agreement (Walker & Harris, 1995). Three questions are helpful in the initial planning for negotiation:

- What are we trying to achieve?
- What is the environment in which we must operate?
- What problems are we likely to encounter?

These questions can be applied to the situation involving collaborative service delivery described in the Bay City vignette—securing administrative support for co-teaching. First, what is the team trying to achieve? Possible responses to this question could be improved educational opportunities for students with disabilities, increased opportunities for all students to receive improved instruction, and an educational environment that allows for continued professional growth and development as professionals work together to address factors that impede student success.

Second, what is the state of the current environment in which the co-teaching approach is being proposed? This question leads to a series of other questions that the team must consider. What practices are already in place that signal administrative willingness for shared decision making? What opportunities for professional collaboration already exist? How receptive is the principal to staff input or suggestions for improvement? Which current academic challenges will co-teaching help to address? How much information do principals have about the benefits and challenges of inclusive service delivery for students with disabilities? How have family members reacted to past changes in educational services? What school and community resources exist to support the proposed change? What has been the fate of recently initiated innovations? What factors contributed to the success or failure of these innovations? These questions provide a framework for an environmental scan that gives the team insight into those current factors that will impact future negotiations.

Third, what problems are we likely to encounter? Based on the environmental scan and anticipating points of disagreement, a list of "what ifs" should be developed. What if the principal asks for some evidence that co-teaching is effective? What if the principal is opposed to any changes in the current delivery system due to concern about low test scores? What if the principal is fearful of adverse responses from parents? What if there is concern regarding adequate time for teacher–specialist planning? Anticipating potential concerns in this way better prepares the team to face possible issues during negotiations rather than being surprised when these issues arise.

Walker and Harris (1995) suggested that every negotiation situation, no matter how simple, should have similar scrutiny before discussion. This allows the opportunity to "think before speaking" and to bring the elements of sound planning to even the simplest negotiation. The negotiation planning process facilitates the development of specific, measurable statements of what is to be accomplished. In addition, an action plan is developed that includes how meetings will be scheduled, what information will be shared, and who will constitute the team. Additionally, these preliminary discussions assist in constructing stronger position statements or arguments that are intended to persuade and gain support.

After assessing the negotiation environment, it is important to consider the communication model and to conceptualize the message that will be communicated. One goal of communication is to influence others' thinking, feelings, or actions. Daily, situations are experienced in which an individual or group is trying to get someone else to make a change that seems desirable by developing and transmitting messages aimed at modifying thinking or conduct. Such attempts to effect change by using strategies of communication are collectively referred to as *persuasion* (DeFleur et al., 1993; Perloff, 1993; Ross, 1994).

Persuasion can also be viewed as a transaction that occurs between two parties in communication (Hogan, 1996; Reardon, 1991). The sender and the receiver of a message play equally important roles in achieving whatever change takes place. One of the decisions that needs to be made is whether to develop a message that will present just one side of a persuasive argument, to include both sides, or to use both sides and refute the opposing arguments. Returning to the case of Bay City School District, the team must frame their persuasive presentation to principals. They must decide whether their communication should include only the anticipated benefits of co-teaching, discussion of benefits *and* challenges, or discussion of benefits *and* challenges along with suggestions for minimizing challenges in the proposed implementation. Results from a number of studies supported this last strategy of using the two-sided message which responds to disadvantages and serves to refute the criticism of an approach (Allen et al., 1990). Other decisions include the selection of a channel or device to transmit the information (e.g., verbal presentation with an executive summary of goals, objectives, and clearly stated action plan).

Finally, an important aspect of the negotiation and persuasion process is to listen carefully to the response of the other party in order to identify and define points of agreement and points of disagreement that might be conceded or reframed and addressed in another manner. Although concessions do alter the content of the proposed option, they establish a perception that an agreement can be reached. For example, following persuasive presentations by teachers and specialists, the principals in the Bay City School District case indicate support for co-teaching pilot sites but state that they are unable to rearrange schedules that have already been planned for the fall semester to provide common planning time. A point of concession might be that teachers will use before- and after-school times during the fall semester for planning, and principals will adjust spring semester schedules to provide the requested time during the school day.

It is important to plan negotiation and persuasion strategies carefully. Teachers and specialists who are attempting to influence change toward more inclusive educational services should continue to read and share information on emerging practices, nationally and locally, that have demonstrated promise for improving achievement and enhancing growth and development of all students. Critical analysis of successful initiatives increases credibility and positions of negotiation. The data gathered from this analysis also strengthen the persuasive message that collaboration among all stakeholders in the educational process yields benefits for students, professionals, and families.

Chapter Summary

This chapter established the importance of effective interpersonal communication skills as teacher and specialist roles are changing in response to the complexity of student needs. The field of education is experiencing a paradigm shift from providing isolated services for students with special needs to collaborating within schools to include all students in the school and community to the greatest extent possible. Simultaneously, teaching is evolving from an isolated act to one requiring increased interaction with other professionals, paraeducators, families, and community agencies in order to meet new educational goals. Teachers and specialists have increased opportunities to share in the decision-making process with administrators. To enable all educators to share in this process as confident and knowledgeable team members, professional development should be provided to ensure competence in the communication basics outlined in this chapter.

Although professional development experiences in support of communication skill development can take many forms (e.g., classes, workshops, school-based support and practice groups), it should be noted that decisions to improve in this area are very personal. One goal of professional development support is to assist educators to identify and develop personal communication competencies that would improve the quality of their interactions with others. Additional self-improvement activities might include audiotaping or videotaping interactions and evaluating them for active listening skills (e.g., summarizing or paraphrasing), establishing a system to receive feedback from colleagues on a targeted skill, or maintaining a journal of collaborative experiences. Another professional development goal is to enable educators to make informed decisions about interpersonal communication with sensitivity for and in anticipation of responses from others. Understanding potential communication barriers and mastering strategies for overcoming these barriers in support of this goal is a never-ending learning process.

CHAPTER ACTIVITIES

1. Review the potential communication barriers discussed in this chapter. Consider which skills serve as tools for overcoming each barrier.

2. Each of the three conflict types discussed in this chapter are listed below. For each type, identify one specific conflict that you have had to manage in the past. List the sequence of events and explain why you think the conflict belonged to that specific type. Which was the easiest and which was the most difficult to resolve?

   • Type I: Parties have incompatible goals.
   • Type II: Parties want different things but must settle on one solution.
   • Type III: Parties want the same thing but only one can have it.

6 Implementation Basics

Getting Started

LEARNING OBJECTIVES

1. Discuss the importance of school-level efforts in laying the groundwork for effective and inclusive classroom practice.
2. Describe practices that facilitate effective school and classroom planning.
3. Describe effective support strategies for professionals and students in inclusive schools.
4. Compare and contrast implementation issues at the school and classroom level.

Jeff Krutch was an assistant principal when he was selected to oversee construction of Longview Middle School and become its principal the following year. During the construction year, he also worked with a community/faculty committee appointed by the superintendent to design an appropriate middle school master plan for Longview. Jeff and the committee studied various models, visited recognized schools in the region, and met regularly to develop a plan that would address diverse academic and social needs of Longview's student body.

Early in the planning process, the committee decided that the master plan should emphasize academic and social inclusion of all students. As teachers, specialists, paraeducators, office staff members, and others were hired, individuals who were supportive of inclusive education and other key components of the emerging plan (e.g., peer mediation, interdisciplinary teaching, cooperative learning) were selected. In particular, the hiring committee looked for individuals with good communication skills who enjoyed working with others. In addition to positive attitudes, they looked for people who had previous coursework or experience working collaboratively.

Recognizing that many staff members might benefit from additional preparation in various emphasis areas, the committee offered an array of summer learning experiences for interested personnel that included options such as independent readings, university courses, school-sponsored mini-workshops, and informal weekly "coffee and chat" groups that helped the staff "get up to speed" on key topics in the master plan before school started.

Five years later, key tenets of the initial master plan are still guiding Longview's efforts. There are two or three teams at each grade level. Students assigned to grade-level teams represent a heterogeneous mix of abilities. Typically, most teaching teams consist of four general educators and one specialist such as a special education, reading, alternative education, or Title I teacher. Each teaching team is responsible for the core subjects (e.g., math, language arts, science, social studies). Teaching teams have two daily planning periods: one for team planning and one for individual and/or collaborative planning. Most general education team members co-teach with each other as interdisciplinary units develop. Specialists provide both co-teaching and consultative support for students and teachers. Grade-level teams work together to determine where and when co-teaching takes place. Most decisions are based on learning needs of students and complexity of unit content. Some co-teaching also emerges as a result of shared professional interests, previous co-teaching successes, and teacher requests. Typically, most teams provide low-achieving students with co-teacher support in their language arts and math classes because of difficulties many experience in these subjects. Some teams rotate specialist co-teaching assignments systematically every 2 or 3 years. This allows all team members to collaborate and expand their classroom accommodation skills as well as access more direct support from specialists.

Recently, after analyzing student achievement and grade report data, the Longview Leadership Council, which represents teachers, specialists, administrators, and community members, found that some students have more academic and behavior problems in elective classes (e.g., health, technology, foreign languages) than in their core subjects. As a result, the council has recommended some changes for next year to ensure that specialists provide more indirect and direct support in these classes.

When asked about Longview's accomplishments related to inclusive education, Jeff observed:

> "We have reached a point where we're beyond the basics. Now we're trying to tackle some of the more difficult issues such as the student evaluation process. We want to know to what extent an inclusive approach helps students perform more successfully. We need to collect more complete data to substantiate our good feelings. We also want to improve co-teaching. Clearly, some co-teachers are better than others; as a school, we want to know what we can do to help less skilled performers. Finally, our state curriculum standards are rising and we need to keep pace. We must do everything we can to instruct all students effectively, especially those with special needs. As a school we're good—but we want to be better. I think members of the Longview team are truly committed to something that Dr. Vernon, our superintendent, likes to call "the next level of excellence.""

Longview is a good example of an inclusive learning community resulting from long-term planning. Inclusion at Longview isn't viewed as an add-on program; instead, it is an integral part of the master plan. When a master plan is in place, revisited regularly, and modified as needed, school leadership teams can design and develop improvement activities in a more focused and systematic manner. For example, as professional development opportunities are considered at Longview, the planning team discusses how various proposals will dovetail with ongoing activities. Will new efforts also improve classroom support services and learning opportunities? How will ongoing collaboration among teachers and specialists be affected? How will instruction be enhanced?

Undoubtedly, Longview's teachers, specialists, and administrators, like most public school employees, would like more resources to better implement and evaluate their master plan goals. Resource limitations aside, Longview's master plan for program development and improvement facilitates more focused and effective use of available resources to achieve identified goals.

In this chapter, basic "nuts and bolts" questions related to effective school and classroom implementation of inclusive programs are addressed. In Chapter 2 seven essential features of effective inclusion were presented. They include (1) collaborative culture, (2) shared leadership, (3) coherent vision, (4) comprehensive planning, (5) adequate resources, (6) sustained implementation, and (7) continuous evaluation and improvement. These features provide the foundation for successful and lasting inclusive education programs; they also help guide decision making in effective schools. This chapter describes specific actions, based on these features, that must be taken in schools and in classrooms to ensure that inclusion is implemented effectively and appropriately.

Creating Inclusive Schools

As emphasized in Chapter 2, effective school-level leadership is an essential component in the development of inclusive programs (Creasey & Walther-Thomas, 1996; Lipsky & Gartner, 1997a; Korinek, McLaughlin, & Walther-Thomas, 1995; Tindall, 1996; Van Dyke, Stallings, & Colley, 1995). Principals and assistant principals who are charged with responsibility for special education and other special programs such as English as a second language (ESL), limited english proficiency (LEP), gifted, and remedial reading play pivotal roles in changing instructional practices in their schools. It is well recognized that administrative leadership sets

Think About It...

Identify specific activities at Longview Middle School described in the vignette that support each of the seven essential features of effective inclusion.

the direction, tone, and pace for innovation and lasting change (Barth, 1990; Fullan, 1993; Hord & Hall, 1987).

In many schools, other school leaders also play important roles. These individuals may not be involved in day-to-day school management but they are viewed by the school community as knowledgeable and trustworthy. They may include master teachers, PTA officers, teachers' union representatives, department heads, and local community leaders. Overall, as inclusive efforts emerge in schools, the broader the base of leadership, the better. Shared leadership encourages greater participation, stronger commitment, ongoing support, more creative problem solving, and better program monitoring and improvement (Adams & Cessna, 1991; Cramer, 1998; Pugach & Johnson, 1995). In addition, broad-based leadership also ensures that inclusion remains a schoolwide priority and that a cohesive plan of action is developed, implemented, and monitored over time (Creasey & Walther-Thomas, 1996).

In the following sections, important roles and responsibilities of school-level leaders are addressed. In essence, administrators and other influential school leaders provide specialists, classroom teachers, and paraeducators with the resources they need to create meaningful inclusive environments for all students.

Build School-Level Teams

As mentioned in the opening vignette, Longview Middle School has a leadership council comprised of highly respected members of the school faculty, staff, and community. Typically, these teams include school administrators, competent and enthusiastic faculty members (e.g., classroom teachers, special educators, related services personnel), supportive community representatives (e.g., parents, grandparents, community leaders, agency personnel), and, in many cases, student representatives. School-level planning and leadership teams formulate comprehensive plans that address a broad array of topics including inclusive education. These plans are based on local needs, resources, and values. Depending on the size, needs, and resources of schools, one or more planning teams may be needed to deal specifically with inclusion issues and ensure that the policies and procedures they propose will fit with the school's master plan. Inclusion planning teams also help define and demystify inclusion, correct misconceptions, and problem-solve issues that naturally arise. Together they plan and monitor initial implementation efforts and provide information, encouragement, and appropriate models. Visible support by respected leaders helps reduce the likelihood that skeptical members of the school community will see inclusion as a passing fad that can be ignored (Janney, Korinek, McLaughlin, & Walther-Thomas, 1994; Korinek et al., 1995; Lipsky & Gartner, 1997a).

Principals play critical roles in setting the tone for inclusion and developing a collaborative culture in their schools (Tindall, 1996). If the principal is positive, supportive of staff, and committed to inclusion at all levels, it is reflected in beliefs, attitudes, and practices of the teaching faculty (Van Dyke et al., 1995; Walther-Thomas, 1997a). Tindall (1996) noted in her study of principals in inclu-

FIGURE 6.1   Principal Actions That Foster Collaboration.

- Express a philosophical commitment to teacher collaboration and put words into action.
- Encourage shared decision making among faculty, staff, students, and families.
- Provide clear, written expectations and constructive feedback for all staff members.
- Recognize and acknowledge individual and group efforts and accomplishments.
- Trust professionals to be responsible decision makers.
- Be willing and ready to provide needed assistance.
- Attend and participate actively in professional development sessions.
- Listen, brainstorm, and problem-solve regularly with staff members.
- Ensure that staff members have essential materials, skills, and other resources.
- Demonstrate flexibility, positive mental attitude, and creative problem solving.
- Provide scheduled time for co-planning and preparation.
- Develop an array of collaborative support structures (e.g., teacher assistance teams, consultative relationships, co-teaching partnerships).
- Seek volunteers for new initiatives that include students, families, community members, and businesses.
- Provide opportunities for continuous professional growth.
- Spend time in classrooms observing, co-teaching, and teaching while others plan.
- Encourage staff attendance at meetings on collaborative projects.
- Monitor students' academic and social growth on a variety of formal and informal measures.
- Keep stakeholders informed through activities such as information-sharing forums, monthly newsletters, roundtable discussions, and open houses.

Source: Adapted from Tindall, E. (1996). *Principal's role in fostering teacher collaboration for students with special needs.* Unpublished doctoral dissertation. College of William and Mary, Williamsburg, VA.

sive schools that their actions served as catalysts for others. As one principal observed:

> The number one thing we are all here for is the kids and for them to learn and grow. As long as its good for the kids, then I will be for it. If it isn't good for them, then I would question what they are doing.... I tell prospective teachers who come here that we're big on relationships; we're big on getting along together, working together, and that if they're not willing to do that I'd rather they not come.

Figure 6.1 describes actions that effective principals perform to facilitate communication, support, monitoring, and evaluation in collaborative schools.

Start Planning Early for Next Year

Many new teams feel overwhelmed and unsure about where to begin planning for successful inclusion. Unfortunately, there are no exact formulas to follow. Planning appropriate inclusion is hard work, even for experienced teams. In many ways, every school is different—even within the same district. Student needs, professional skills, and potential resources all must be considered. To ensure thorough consideration of all important issues, teams should begin early in the school year for the following year (Creasey & Walther-Thomas, 1996; Tilton, 1996; Villa & Thousand, 1995; Walther-Thomas, 1998). This means that it is *not* too early to start planning in December or January. This is especially important in schools new to inclusion. Taking a semester or more to consider student placements and needed support services helps ensure better long-term program success. In addition, the extended timeline for decision making provides better opportunities for communication, creative brainstorming, and more effective problem solving. It also helps set the stage for more productive individualized education program (IEP) meetings with families in March and April. Early planning enables the central office to be more responsive when school teams need additional resources. If school planning teams gather information early and present their needs for additional support to central office decision makers in February or March, before district budgets are finalized for the following year, chances are better that the issues can be addressed.

Recruit and Support Capable Participants

Planning teams should recruit capable and willing professionals to serve as role models for others during the initial phase of implementation. Well-respected members of the faculty who possess effective communication skills are excellent candidates for pioneering efforts. As noted in Chapter 2, effective implementation of new programs is highly dependent on a number of factors. Clearly, meaningful professional development that enables participants to master new skills and practice them with support is a key consideration. In addition, a collaborative culture can provide individuals with participation and skill development opportunities, ongoing classroom support, and a safe environment for personal and professional risk taking.

Professionals who have worked together successfully in the past often make good candidates for initial implementation teams. When pilot-test participants engage in some form of ongoing collaboration, such as daily co-teaching or weekly consultation, with previously established relationships in place and mutual respect for each other's professional skills, the process moves more quickly (Friend & Cook, 1996). This does not mean, however, that educators must be friends in order to be effective classroom collaborators. Nevertheless, the need to respect and value each other's potential contributions is critical to their effectiveness as a team.

Under the best of circumstances, effective collaboration is hard work. If capable participants face the extra burden of mentoring an incompetent colleague, it may be unrealistic to implement meaningful changes. Professionals should not be disqualified solely on the basis of limited experience, however. Today, many preservice programs are providing instruction and supervised practice working in inclusive environments, and many recent graduates may be well suited to collaborative roles.

Unfortunately, some collaborative relationships fail despite earnest efforts and well-honed professional skills. Some partners become frustrated and give up prematurely before they have had sufficient time to work out the "bugs" that collaborative teams often encounter and before they have witnessed potential benefits. Common bugs often include the need for extra time to meet and plan with partners; discomfort with their partner's working style, philosophy, or classroom management; or a loss of faith in the process to meet many complex student needs.

Before discouraged partners give up, it may help to revisit with their leadership team the seven essential features introduced in Chapter 2. In particular, resource considerations need to be addressed. For example: Have participants had opportunities to develop basic skills in effective collaboration? Do collaborators have regularly scheduled time for weekly planning and problem solving? Is the number of students with special needs in each classroom appropriate? Do specialists' caseloads enable them to spend sufficient time each week in general education classrooms? As noted earlier, many worthwhile initiatives are poorly funded—and fail quickly. If resources are not infused into the system to support new efforts, leadership teams must decide how to reallocate existing resources. The old adage, "To do more, we must do less" applies in these situations. For example, if specialists want to spend more time in general education classrooms helping students with special needs, they must spend less time teaching these students in pull-out settings. Making this change is much easier said than done! Clearly, specialists' attitudes must change but so must those of students, families, classroom teachers, administrators, and others. All of these stakeholders must adjust their expectations regarding traditional pull-out services for testing and tutoring students.

Even when teachers and specialists are well prepared, competent, and enthusiastic about the process, effective collaboration takes time (Cramer, 1998). Ideally, educators should commit to working with their designated partners for at least 2 years. This allows them adequate time to establish positive working relationships; develop effective roles and responsibilities; and design, implement, and evaluate appropriate classroom curricula. Most experienced collaborators report that working with others gets easier over time as they develop and refine their own effective "routines" for working together (Pugach & Wesson, 1995; Karge, McClure, & Patton, 1995; Walther-Thomas, 1997a).

Provide Ongoing Professional Development

Unfortunately, many competent and motivated educators cannot "just do it" when it comes to collaborating effectively with others. Traditionally, preservice programs taught aspiring educators how to work with children and adolescents—not other adults. In most schools, veteran educators have spent years working alone with few opportunities for ongoing dialogue and collaboration with colleagues (Bauwens & Hourcade, 1995; Friend & Cook, 1996).

Following preliminary preparation to ensure that a cohesive vision is developed, ongoing professional development and implementation support should be provided. Diverse and specialized professional development options must be provided that allow faculty and staff to choose experiences that can meet their needs appropriately. Well-planned opportunities that span an extended period of time should provide strong models, supervised practice, classroom coaching, time to reflect, and problem-solving support (Joyce & Showers, 1996).

As trust and communication skills develop, some classroom collaborators are capable of monitoring and critiquing their progress effectively. Some fledgling teams, however, especially those with limited preparation or experience working together, may find this process very challenging. To facilitate team development, veteran collaborators may help new teams as mentors and coaches. The support of knowledgeable and trusted colleagues, administrators, and supervisors can be reassuring as new teams explore areas of concern and clarify each member's roles and responsibilities.

Create Balanced Classroom Rosters

Student placement is one of the most challenging aspects of effective inclusive education. Successful inclusive classrooms are not overloaded with students with special needs. As class rosters are developed, it is important to keep the concept of natural proportions in mind (Brown et al., 1989). Ideally, inclusive classrooms should be designed to reflect a typical and heterogeneous mix of students who perform at different levels, have unique needs and talents, and can learn together under the direction of creative and supportive teachers.

Some schools serving high percentages of special education students and at-risk students may find it more difficult to create truly balanced and heterogeneous rosters (Stainback & Stainback, 1996a). Organizational procedures such as neighborhood school placements for all students, pooling resource funds, and creating noncategorical or cross-categorical caseloads can help reduce the problems that planners face in these schools. In some areas, these schools may qualify for additional funding to support special projects. Although high-risk schools have more challenges, overall, many of these schools actually have more resources such as specialists, paraeducators, computers, and funds to support smaller class sizes to develop a network of inclusive classroom support. Figure 6.2 illustrates examples of possible student grouping patterns and specialist support assignments to ensure that appropriate classroom support is available to meet student needs.

Creating balanced, mixed-ability classrooms and establishing manageable specialist caseloads are especially difficult when students with a wide variety of specific disabilities (e.g., hearing impairments, emotional and behavioral disabilities, mild mental retardation) are transported to one school. In the past, many school districts created "cluster" programs to serve students with specific disabilities more efficiently by combining special education resources at a single site rather than providing services at multiple schools. Although clustering may be more cost-efficient and facilitate the work of itinerant specialists, clustering is not conducive to effective inclusive education. Clustering makes it difficult, if not impossible, to create balanced classroom rosters if identified students are to be included in general education classrooms. For example, in Longview Middle School, there are three students with visual impairments. This is an average number

FIGURE 6.2   Examples of Possible Student Grouping Patterns and Specialist Support Assignments.

Class 1	Class 2	Class 3
High Performing (5)	High Performing (5)	High Performing (4)
Typical (10)	Typical (14)	Typical (15)
Low Performing (6)	Low Performing (5)	Low Performing (4)

Identified Needs: This class has three students with reading problems, two students "at risk" because of family-related concerns, and three students who are identified as gifted.

Support Resources: The reading specialist co-teaches 90 minutes a day during language arts. The guidance counselor and/or the social worker consult with the teacher during his planning period on Thursdays. The gifted education teacher co-teaches a 45-minute lesson on critical thinking skills on Fridays.

Identified Needs: This class has three students with learning disabilities (LD), one student with limited English proficiency (LEP), and three students who are identified as gifted.

Support Resources: The LD specialist co-teaches 90 minutes a day during social studies and math. A retired teacher volunteers two mornings a week. The LEP teacher consults during Monday planning, and the gifted education teacher co-teaches a 45-minute science lesson on Wednesdays.

Identified Needs: This class has one student with an emotional disability (ED), one student with physical disabilities (PD), and three students identified as gifted.

Support Resources: A full-time paraeducator is assigned to the class; he consults with a physical therapist who sees the student with PD weekly. An ED teacher co-teaches 60 minutes a day during science. The gifted education teacher consults weekly. The entire teaching team plans together on a monthly basis.

Note: All three classrooms are designed with a balanced mix of high-performing, typical, and low-performing students. Some of these students have been identified for special services; others have not. Classroom support is provided for all students by school specialists.

of students with this type of disability given the school's size and the low incidence of visual impairments. There are two seventh graders and one eighth grader who have special vision needs that the planning team and the specialists will consider as student placements and support plans are developed. If Longview were a cluster site for all of the district's middle school students with visual impairments, the planning team might need to address the needs of 15 to 20 students in addition to the number of neighborhood students with a wide range of mild to moderate disabilities.

As noted in Chapter 1, ideally, classroom proportions should mirror the larger society in which we live (Kochhar & West, 1996). This means approximately 10 to 20% of the students in any classroom may be targeted for special help because of significantly lower performance in academics or in other areas such as social skills, English language, cognitive abilities, self-management, or motor skills. Typically, many of these students qualify for special education, remedial reading, ESL, or LEP services. Others with performance problems do not qualify for extra services but require extra teacher time and support. Thoughtful consideration of all students' needs as placement decisions are made helps ensure better classroom balance, appropriate support service commitments, and classroom well-being. When classes include identified students who require extensive support, the total number of students with performance problems should be reduced.

High-performing students (e.g., gifted, high achievers) should represent approximately 10 to 20% of the students in mixed-ability inclusive classrooms. The majority of students in the classroom, that is, 60 to 70%, should be students who are considered "typical." With regard to classroom placements, it is important to think about the performance of students in a holistic manner. Some students may perform poorly in many academic and social skill areas; other identified students may have very specific, well-defined, and relatively narrow bands in which performance is a problem. A label may not tell decision makers much about a student's actual performance abilities. For example, Paul is a good student who is described as highly motivated, creative, very verbal, and performs well in most academic subjects. He also has cerebral palsy, significant motor problems, and uses a wheelchair. Belinda is described as hyperactive, has a visual impairment, and is socially immature. She is also a straight A student with an IQ of 150. These students present very different support needs in the classroom.

In general, balancing classroom rosters is easier in elementary and middle schools in which mixed-ability grouping is considered the norm. In high schools, however, students are grouped more homogeneously on the basis of their skills, interests, and future educational plans. Typically, classes are designated as basic, average, or advanced. Unfortunately, lower level courses are often overenrolled with struggling students who need considerable help for reasons such as undetected learning and behavior problems, language barriers, limited ability, motivational problems, or other risk factors. In these situations, available resources such as weekly consultation, paraeducator support, scheduled planning periods, reduced class size, and specialist caseloads must be evaluated carefully and distributed equitably (Tilton, 1996). For some students with disabilities, average or advanced classes may be preferable to lower level classes if adequate support can be provided (Kochhar & West, 1996; Stainback & Stainback, 1996b; Walther-Thomas, 1998). This is especially true for students who plan to pursue postsecondary education. Inclusive learning opportunities provide these students with the essential skills, strategies, and personal confidence needed to perform satisfactorily in college or vocational preparation programs.

Provide Scheduled Collaborative Planning Time

One of the most critical components in successful collaboration is regularly scheduled time for partners to share information, monitor student progress, solve individual and group problems, plan lessons, and develop interventions (Cramer, 1998; Murphy, 1997; Walther-Thomas, 1997a; Walther-Thomas, Bryant, & Land, 1996). Ongoing dialogue is an integral part of lasting collaborative relationships, regardless of the interaction structure (e.g., co-teaching). Ideally, collaborators should have at least an hour of uninterrupted time each week for these discussions. This time also allows participants to broaden their knowledge and skills. In addition to maximizing student and teacher support, these sessions serve as relationship "insurance policies." Time together discussing issues of common concern prevents minor issues from developing into major problems because busy stakeholders didn't talk through their concerns (Cramer, 1998).

Collaborative planning in elementary schools is often concentrated in times when students have art, library, computer technology, or other specialty classes during the course of the typical week (Murphy, 1997). Some schools arrange these times into larger blocks such as 45 minutes of music followed by 45 minutes of physical education to provide teachers and specialists longer periods for planning and preparation. In other schools, specialists' schedules are arranged so that 1 day each week is designated exclusively for testing, planning, colleague consultation, and other communication-related tasks (e.g., telephone calls, home visits, family conferences, written reports).

Typically, middle school schedules facilitate co-planning more easily than either elementary or high school schedules (Walther-Thomas, 1997b). Many middle school schedules are designed with two daily planning periods to accommodate both individual and team planning. Assigning specialists as members of grade-level teams also promotes co-planning and ongoing communication (Walther-Thomas, Bryant, & Land, 1996). High school collaboration is often the most challenging to organize given the size and complexity of most schools. Collaboration is facilitated when specialists are assigned to various academic departments (e.g., math, English, science). As core members of these departments, specialists can address the needs of identified students and others at risk more effectively in relationship to a particular content that spans several grade levels.

Unfortunately, finding common planning times for collaborators is one of the most challenging tasks that administrators and school teams face (Karge et al., 1995; Kochhar & West, 1996; Walther-Thomas, 1997a). Consequently, teams should begin developing a master schedule that includes common planning time for collaborators about 1 year in advance. One change in the tentative schedule can set off a series of chain reactions that may disrupt a number of staff members' teaching and planning schedules. Creating adequate planning time necessitates careful consideration of many dimensions of the schedule.

Given potential problems associated with finding common planning time, Figure 6.3 on page 126 provides some innovative ideas that schools have used when common planning periods are impossible to schedule for all collaborating teams. Although not all of the ideas presented here work in any given setting, these suggestions may stimulate creative thinking about some new or unexplored possibilities.

In summary, school-level actions provide classroom implementers, (i.e., teachers and specialists) with the organizational structure, resources, and moral support

FIGURE 6.3   **Planning Time Possibilities for Collaborators.**

- Create early-release days once a week or twice a month by restructuring the school day. Work with community recreation programs, local businesses, nonprofit organizations such as Boy Scouts, Big Brothers/Big Sisters, fire and/or police departments, and PTA groups to create early-release activity programs (e.g., films, lessons, sports teams, miniclasses, activity clubs, community service projects) for students.
- Combine two or more classes for activities that accommodate larger groups (e.g., films, demonstrations, guest speakers, peer tutoring). Encourage teachers to trade time blocks.
- Restructure the day to create a "zero hour" planning period before students arrive.
- Use e-mail communication to reduce scheduled faculty meetings and designate unused faculty meeting time for co-planning.
- Schedule specialists (e.g., gifted, art, music, physical education, library, guidance, technology) in back-to-back activity blocks.
- Create a monthly calendar of times when administrators, guidance counselors, school psychologists, and other school personnel are willing to teach classes.
- Ask staff members to stay an extra hour on Wednesdays and leave with students on Friday afternoons.
- Recruit and train retired teachers, PTA members, business partners, university students, service groups (e.g., Key Club, Kiwanis) to volunteer during planning time.
- Encourage PTA leaders to recruit, train, schedule, and supervise volunteers. (*Note:* Qualify skilled volunteers as substitute teachers to provide schools with greater protection against liability when teachers conduct planning sessions outside their classrooms.)
- Generate school funds and/or fund-raiser money (e.g., PTA-sponsored events; faculty-sponsored movie nights) to hire floating substitutes to cover planning meetings.
- Provide compensation (e.g., time off for personal use and/or professional development, additional pay, minigrants, conference registration fees, supplies, software) for staff members who agree to co-plan before or after school.
- Reduce teachers' nonacademic duty assignments (e.g., bus duty, cafeteria monitoring, recess supervision) by using community volunteers and/or paid employees to facilitate planning during these times.
- Identify community business partners who are willing to provide planning resources and incentives (e.g., snacks, resource materials, sponsorship of substitute teacher hours).

needed to create meaningful education programs for students. Without active involvement and leadership from school administrators and other school leaders, successful inclusion is much more difficult to achieve.

Think About It...

What are some potential forces outside schools that can either facilitate or block local efforts to become more inclusive?

Creating Inclusive Classroom Communities

Typically, specialists and teachers who are new to inclusion have many questions about classroom roles and responsibilities. "Who does what in the room to support effective teaching and effective learning?", "How can we help all students feel good about themselves as learners?", and "What can we do to promote cooperation and support among all students?" It is important to remember that no one has all the answers. Committed collaborators find that every setting has its own unique challenges and that effective solutions can be found when program advocates pool their collective skills and expertise. By acknowledging that ongoing collaboration and meaningful inclusion are relatively new concepts, participants can then be more honest with themselves and others, think more creatively, try new approaches, and persevere over time. Although there are no shortcuts to creating inclusive communities, there are a few fundamental principles that can facilitate the process.

Set the Stage for Classroom Community

Professionals' roles in building classroom communities are pivotal. In every interaction with students, they set the tone, model acceptance and celebration of diversity, and help students feel welcome and safe. They set expectations, select targets and methods for instruction, and provide feedback to students about their behavior. Educators have the power to focus on positive behavior and make students feel successful or to spend their time correcting, directing, and punishing challenging behaviors.

The first few weeks of school are critical for getting to know students, helping them to learn about one another, and providing clear messages about classroom expectations (Charney, 1991; York, Doyle, & Kronberg, 1992). Interest inventories, cooperative groups, and friendship activities focused on helping students (and the adults) in the classroom to learn each other's names, cultures, and personalities provide opportunities for students to see each other in a positive light. Examples of activities that are appropriate during the first weeks of school highlight common interests, special strengths or talents, and likes and dislikes. They include autograph hunts, identity boxes with personal artifacts, class bulletin boards, and paired interviews and introductions. Discussions about what it feels like to have friends, how to be a friend, how friends treat each other and how to make more friends, can promote positive relationships among classmates. Peer relationships develop that may not materialize without these focused and instructional activities.

Searcy (1996) recommended additional "friendship interventions" including structuring social interactions at recess, lunch, and free periods; providing assignments that require students to interact repeatedly outside class; setting up learning centers that promote interaction; and using activities with peers as reinforcers. Helping older students learn about extracurricular activities, clubs, teams, and other school groups also facilitates social connections. New students often miss out on these opportunities because they were not present at the beginning of the year when activities were announced, they do not know who to contact, and are not invited to participate by peers or adults. Teachers play a critical role in facilitating belonging. Without these efforts, students tend to associate only with other students whom they already know and who are most like themselves. Judgments about other students are then made on the basis of physical appearance, academic performance, or atypical behavior (Charney, 1991; Downing, 1996), and many opportunities to give and receive support are lost as students settle into familiar groupings and egocentric behaviors.

A classroom atmosphere of acceptance and belonging for all students can also be promoted through class discussions focused on the meaning and importance of community, how students benefit from being part of a community, specific behaviors that show caring and concern for others, ways to make the classroom a safe and inviting place for everyone, student rights and responsibilities, classroom chores, and so on (Langone, 1998; York et al., 1992). York and colleagues (1992) suggested that, as a follow-up to these discussions, teachers work with students to identify priorities and develop an action plan for community expectations that could be used instead of the traditional teacher-generated classroom rules. Well-known ongoing support structures that focus on positive social relationships and address student-to-student interactions include classroom meetings, buddy systems, lunch meetings to talk about friendship issues, lessons on problem solving and conflict resolution, and friendship or social skills clubs (Charney, 1991; Johnson & Johnson, 1995; Sapon-Shevin, Dobbelaere, Corrigan, Goodman, & Mastin, 1998; York et al., 1992). Some of these student supports were mentioned in Chapter 4 and are addressed in greater detail in Chapter 12.

Another important activity for the initial weeks of school and subsequent follow-up is clarifying classroom expectations for individual, small-group, and whole-class activities, as well as establishing and practicing classroom routines. Initial time spent helping students learn how to find and use materials, transition between activities, practice rules, and behave effectively when working alone and with others will save time for instruction in the long run. Behaviors such as greeting and using each other's names, sharing materials, asking for and offering help, joining activities and inviting others to join, taking turns, respecting each other's space and property, and expressing needs are typical social targets for demonstration and practice.

For older students with more experience working cooperatively, behaviors such as giving and receiving positive and negative feedback, active listening,

Think About It...

Identify several ice-breaker or community-building exercises that you have participated in at school, summer camp, professional meetings, or in other settings. What were the purposes of these activities? How could they be adapted for various age levels?

encouraging participation, reaching consensus, and resolving conflicts are important skills. Unless students see a need to use the target behaviors and discriminate when they should be used, they are likely not to demonstrate the desired behaviors. Discussing rationales for positive social actions and cues in situations that signal the need to engage in these behaviors is critical to developing prosocial skills (Deshler, Ellis, & Lenz, 1996). Taking the time to work through disagreements as they arise provides practice for students using an effective problem-solving process. Recognizing students who have successfully settled their own disputes helps them become more confident in their interactions (Dowd, 1997; Sapon-Shevin et al., 1998). Noticing what students do right and redirecting them to more appropriate behaviors when they lapse (e.g., "critique the ideas and not each other" when students in groups criticize each other) models supportive behavior and leads to more productive and cohesive classrooms. Being positive, encouraging, and specific (e.g., saying "That took courage to stand up for Mac when the other kids were teasing" rather than using generic phrases like "Good job") helps build classroom community.

Although many educators think that they already engage in the positive behaviors described previously, research has shown that they may actually interact differently with different students (Montague, Bergeron, & Lago-Delello, 1997; Tal & Babad, 1990; Wentzel, 1993). For example, one study found that students at risk received significantly more negative or neutral nonacademic feedback than their peers and much less positive and academic feedback. These students were also perceived more negatively and experienced more teacher rejection and negative discrimination (Montague et al., 1997). Teachers may not even realize their biases but they may profoundly affect students' views of themselves and their school.

Cultural Influences on Classroom Interactions.   Culture and language may also affect both educators' and students' perceptions and interpretations of classroom interactions (Garcia & Malkin, 1993). Culture often plays a significant role in educators' differential treatment of students and in students' interactions with peers and adults (Artiles & Trent, 1994; Patton, 1998). Professional expectations for various groups or types of students, definitions of what constitutes "appropriate" and tolerable behavior, and reactions to student behaviors are often based on cultural beliefs, values, and norms. When students' expressed values, attitudes, and behaviors are different from those of the professional in charge, these differences are often judged to be deficits, problems, or deviance rather than differences (Anderson & Webb-Johnson, 1995). For example, Native American and Hispanic cultures typically value cooperation and sharing with family and friends. A teacher may interpret a student's genuine attempts to share answers or help a classmate on a test as cheating.

Educators may also respond differently to behaviors exhibited by culturally diverse students than they do to similar behaviors demonstrated by students of the same cultural background. A student of the same culture may be judged to be "assertive" when he or she questions the relevance of an assignment, and the assignment may even be adjusted. When a student of a different culture objects to the assignment, she or he may be deemed "insolent" or "defiant." Higher rates of school suspensions and expulsions of African Americans and their overrepresentation in classes for students with emotional and behavioral disorders are attributed in part to cultural and interactional differences between students and teachers (Anderson, 1992; Kauffman & Hallahan, 1981; Patton, 1998).

Communication variations among cultures also contribute to differential interactions (Byrd, 1995). For example, use of dialects, slang, colorful language, simultaneous talk instead of turn-taking during conversation, nonverbal messages expressed through eye contact or avoidance of eye contact, and certain body language (e.g., hands on hips, folded arms) may be interpreted as disrespect, noncompliance, defiance, or lack of intelligence. These actions may actually reflect differences in cultural style rather than behavioral deficits or deviance. Although differential treatment to the disadvantage of students may not be intentional on the part of professionals, increased self-awareness of interactional patterns is a first step toward being more sensitive and responsive to cultural issues in classroom communities. The suggestions previously offered in Chapter 4 for developing cross-cultural competence and the discussion of effective communication in Chapter 5 are highly relevant to addressing cultural issues related to classroom behavior.

Methods that may be used for self-assessment to increase awareness include asking for feedback on teacher-student interactions from colleagues, co-teachers, students, and family members; videotaping or audiotaping; and counting specific behaviors (e.g., the number of positive versus negative or corrective statements made to students, the number of interactions with various students). Periodic assessment of the social climate of the classroom with instruments such as the *Learning Environment Inventory* and *My Class Inventory* (Fraser, Anderson, & Walberg, 1991) is helpful in obtaining student feedback for improvement. These instruments ask students to rate classroom features including satisfaction and difficulty with work assigned, cohesiveness of the class, adequacy of the physical environment, clarity of expectations, organization of the class, support for diversity, favoritism by the teacher, cliquishness among students, and emphasis on cooperation or competition. Research has shown that students learn more when they perceive their classes as satisfying, challenging, and friendly but with enough structure, direction, and organization to make sense (Walberg & Greenberg, 1997).

Disability Awareness Education.   An important part of building social relationships and support systems among students with disabilities and their typical peers is to help all students become more aware of disabilities (Haring, 1991; Sapon-Shevin, 1992). Helping typical students, students with disabilities, teachers, and families to understand the nature and possible needs of classmates with disabilities facilitates friendship development. Information about disabilities can be built into the curriculum through the use of guest speakers such as older students with disabilities, parents of students with disabilities, doctors, therapists, university instructors, or community members with disabilities; discussion of videos, television programs, books, magazines, and newspaper articles about individuals with special needs; research on celebrities with disabilities; exposure to assistive technology; and simulation activities that allow students to glimpse what it feels like to have physical, sensory, or cognitive disabilities. Special programs like *Kids on the Block* puppet presentations designed for elementary students or performing groups that deal with disabilities are also effective strategies.

At the secondary level, it may be most appropriate to infuse disability issues into classes such as civics, government, English, or psychology. The goal of awareness activities is to share information and realistically portray disabilities while building respect for and appreciation of differences. Students should be helped to see that peers with disabilities are not better or worse, just different in some ways, and very much like their classmates in most other ways (Downing, 1996; Friend & Bursuck, 1996; Haring, 1991; Sapon-Shevin et al., 1998).

Self-Advocacy Skills Development.   As noted in the previous section, typical students are not the only ones who need to be informed about disabilities. Many students with disabilities themselves have not been educated sufficiently about their conditions or been helped to analyze their strengths, interests, and abilities. Students need this information to be effective self-advocates. Special education professionals, advocacy groups, technical assistance centers, regional resource centers, public and university libraries, and the Internet are rich sources of information and resources for disability awareness efforts. As with other aspects of social skills development and support networks, sustained efforts with follow-up discussions to increase awareness throughout the school year have greater impact than one or two special events or presentations.

Student Choice and Self-Control.   If educators want students to exhibit more socially responsible behavior, they need to provide meaningful opportunities for students to practice self-management and decision making. Self-management involves self-regulation of identified behaviors and the conditions and consequences surrounding these behaviors. Comprehensive reviews of research have shown that self-management procedures have improved the academic and social behaviors of students in general education classes at all levels (Korinek, 1991; Utley, Mortweet, & Greenwood, 1997). For example, individuals might use pictures, reminders, checklists, or self-talk to remind themselves to engage in desired behaviors (e.g., offering support, turning in assignments, arriving on time, or contributing to class discussions). Students could monitor their behaviors with a simple assessment of whether or not they are engaging in the behavior at the designated time, or use a recording sheet or counter to keep track of the number of times they perform a particular behavior. Self-rewards such as self-congratulations, an activity with a friend, or a special treat to reward accomplishing goal-related behaviors or denial of these reinforcers for falling short of preset goals provide consequences for behavior. Greater self-management on the part of students increases their independence and personal responsibility and frees educators to focus more time on academic instruction with less time spent refereeing student

> **Think About It...**
>
> Consider the reminders and rewards you use to help yourself develop new behaviors. How could some of these techniques be used by students with whom you work to improve their performance? What adaptations might be needed?

disputes. As with any academic skill, self-management must be taught, practiced, and encouraged if students are expected to demonstrate this behavior.

Educators can also incorporate numerous opportunities for self-management and decision making into classroom procedures and routines. Allowing students to make choices about the order in which they complete assignments; the way in which they demonstrate learning (e.g., a book report, dramatization, radio review, commercial, or pictorial of a book just read); and selection of reading materials, research topics, classroom privileges, chores, and free-time activities give students practice in decision making. Even very young children should be given choices of materials and activities. Showing students how and where to obtain assistance (e.g., designated peers, reference materials, self-correcting materials, lists of procedures) from sources other than their teacher fosters independence and reinforces the concept of the classroom as a learning community.

Encouraging students to set goals for learning and social interactions helps develop self-regulation and provides students with a sense of control and self-efficacy. Peer-mediated self-management, wherein students assist their classmates with self-control through reminders, helping them count their behaviors, giving them feedback on the quality of their work, and reinforcing their positive behaviors, has also been found to be an effective bridge between adult control and self-management (Kerr & Nelson, 1998; Utley et al., 1997).

Preparation for the Arrival of Students with Disabilities. Teachers and specialists should learn about a new student with a disability before he or she joins the class in order to facilitate acceptance and support. It may help to talk with previous teachers and specialists who have worked with the student and to meet with the student and his or her family before school starts. Although teachers need to learn about students' specialized support needs, they should also learn about students' more typical qualities. They should become familiar with students' interests, likes and dislikes, hobbies, and talents, that is, the positive qualities that make them special. Learning about strengths and abilities of students with disabilities helps classroom professionals see these learners as multifaceted people. This also relieves potential concerns about the amount of aid that may be required. Understanding students' support needs, teachers are better prepared to provide more appropriate assistance and support. Teacher understanding and acceptance provides a good model for typical students, paraeducators, and other adults who work or volunteer in classrooms. If teachers show that they like a student with a disability and that he or she is an important and valued member of the class, it helps others develop positive feelings as well (Giangreco, 1996b). Downing (1996) suggested that in some instances, especially if the student is new or has extensive support needs, it might be helpful to have classmates watch a videotape of the student with disabilities before he or she joins the class. Following the videotape students can be encouraged to ask questions aloud or via a question box for class discussion.

Teachers and class members should take time to genuinely welcome new students who join the class after school starts and celebrate their arrival. This is especially important for students who join after the school year has started and for students with disabilities whose adjustment to new environments may be more difficult. As Giangreco (1996b) notes:

> Welcoming the student with a disability may seem like a simple thing to do…but you'd be surprised how often it doesn't happen. It can be devastating for such a student (or for any student) to feel as if he or she must earn the right to belong.… when children with disabilities come to your classroom, talk to them, walk with them, joke with them, and teach them. By your actions, show all of your students that the child with disabilities is an important member of your class and, by extension, of society. (p. 56)

Opportunities for All Students to Become Peer Assistants.   All students need opportunities to be recognized as capable people. "Helping" roles in the classroom, school, and community offer opportunities for students to develop valuable skills and demonstrate their capability, competence, and independence. In inclusive schools every student should have ongoing opportunities to be both a provider of assistance as well as a recipient of assistance or support. These opportunities build self-confidence, self-reliance, and peer understanding. When special education students are viewed as capable contributors, it helps demystify their disabilities and allows others to see them as "typical" in many ways.

Planned opportunities for students to spend time assisting one another also helps peers become better acquainted. Genuine friendships can develop more naturally when students have opportunities to interact without interference from well-intentioned adults. Caring teachers, specialists, and paraeducators often become barriers that make it more difficult for students with disabilities to establish relationships with their peers. Whenever possible, teachers and specialists should design classrooms so that peers provide each other with assistance and support rather than rely solely on adults to do so.

Peer assistance roles should be clearly delineated and, whenever possible, mutually beneficial. An array of support opportunities helps ensure that all students can participate. Many helping tasks can be designed to occur at convenient times during the school day. For example, Gwen eats lunch with Betsy on Mondays. Betsy walks Michael to the bus after school on Thursdays and Michael accompanies Kevin to keyboarding class at 2:00 P.M. every Thursday. Kevin meets

FIGURE 6.4   **Criteria for Peer Assistant Selection.**

1. *Every* class member should have opportunities to provide and receive peer assistance.
2. Select willing and interested volunteers; let these students lead the way.
3. Provide appropriate preparation for all roles and responsibilities.
4. Assign brief, "low-risk" tasks to those who may be interested in helping but hesitant to participate.
5. Work with administrators and teachers to facilitate cross-class and cross-grade helping experiences.
6. Rotate roles and responsibilities regularly to involve as many peers as possible.
7. Limit daily time helping so that helpers' learning is not compromised.
8. Provide appropriate supervision to ensure student safety and appropriateness in help provided.
9. Keep participating students' families informed and help them understand the educational value of these experiences.

Erin, a student in another class, at her locker after school on Wednesdays, and they walk together to the community art center for a class. Regularly rotating designated jobs helps all class members become better acquainted and keeps time commitments at manageable levels. Well-designed roles can ensure that neither student's learning (i.e., the recipient or the provider) is affected adversely.

As teachers and specialists select class members for various classroom roles, a few basic guidelines should be considered to ensure student safety and avoid potential issues regarding professional liability. Figure 6.4 provides some basic criteria for peer helper selection.

Paraeducators' Involvement

Many inclusive classrooms are supported, in part, by skilled paraeducators. Typically, these classroom assistants work closely with teachers and specialists to provide help for all class members. Paraeducators are often assigned to work in inclusive classrooms because of a specific student's more extensive support needs or because of large numbers of special-needs students in a class. As noted in the previous section, however, it is important for all adults in the classroom to encourage all students to be as independent and self-reliant as possible. As one wise paraeducator noted, "Good support doesn't mean that the adult and the student need to be attached with Velcro!"

Paraeducators, like teachers and specialists, should remember that when students with or without disabilities need assistance, peers should be seen as the "first line" of support. Whenever possible, paraeducators should avoid unnecessary academic assistance or intervention in social disputes among students. Data collection, materials preparation, supervision of review activities, modeling, providing constructive feedback, and offering general classroom support are examples of appropriate paraeducator involvement. In addition, paraeducators can also provide invaluable classroom assistance by handling tasks clearly inappropriate for peers (e.g., toileting assistance, feeding, self-help instruction, significant academic support) and other responsibilities that are too time-consuming for professionals to handle alone. During planning meetings, professionals and paraeducators often work together reviewing classroom data; updating student records; sharing strategies for data collection, instruction, and behavior management; and discussing other classroom concerns. Most effective paraeducators need preparation, supervision, feedback, and support to provide appropriate assistance to students with and without disabilities and their teachers. Clarifying paraeducators' classroom roles and related responsibilities is an important starting point for teams (Langone, 1998).

Unfortunately, few classroom teachers are well prepared to instruct and supervise paraeducators (Pickett, 1996). Many are unfamiliar with what paraeducators can and cannot do legally in classrooms to support students with disabilities and assist professionals. Many classroom teachers need guidance and support to ensure they make the most of these valuable resources. As appropriate, specialists should work with teachers and paraeducators to clarify both individual and classroom needs, develop realistic paraeducator performance expectations, and delineate clear strategies to facilitate ongoing communication (Pickett, 1996; *Special Education Report*, 1997).

In summary, well-planned inclusive classrooms provide all students with a broad array of academic and social skills learning opportunities. In addition, these learning communities are built on a flexible infrastructure based on both peer and adult support. These settings offer all students daily experiences that promote collaboration, cooperation, self-advocacy, and caring. Many beneficial, albeit indirect, learning opportunities are offered in these settings that are frequently missed in more traditional classrooms.

Collaborative Planning: The Key to Successful Classroom Inclusion

In many inclusive schools in which a solid foundation of support has been laid, effective collaborators report that the "secret" to success is ongoing teamwork focused on instructional planning (Pugach & Wesson, 1995; Walther-Thomas et al., 1996; Walther-Thomas, 1997a). Not surprisingly, effective planning, like all other aspects of collaboration, doesn't just happen. It cannot be done "on the run." Quality planning demands dedicated time reserved exclusively for this task, competent participants, and a genuine commitment to common classroom goals.

Effective and efficient planning enables collaborators to develop, implement, and evaluate appropriate student support programs (Langone, 1998). In addition, these relationships enhance participants' professional growth opportunities as they learn from one other (Walther-Thomas, 1997a). For example, teachers can help specialists develop a better understanding of the classroom demands that result when a broad array of student abilities, interests, and needs interact with a given curriculum. Specialists can help teachers develop a better understanding of disability characteristics, potential problems these conditions create, and potential classroom interventions for academic and behavioral concerns.

In this section, basic principles that can be used to develop effective collaborative interaction routines are presented. These principles apply regardless of the collaborative structure that may be used (e.g., co-teaching, teaming, consultation). In Chapter 9, more detailed information is presented about specific planning considerations for co-teaching.

Planning Practices

As noted earlier, it is not uncommon for planners to report that focused and productive collaboration often requires an hour or more each week. This time requirement seems to be true in most collaborative relationships—not just for daily co-teaching. Some planners report that their planning time needs decrease as they become more familiar with each other's contributions and with the basic content-related issues. Others hold the opposite view that more time is needed as team planning skills develop. In essence, they seem to set higher standards for themselves and for their collaborative efforts. Some co-teachers report that their relationships require more planning time than consultative relationships. However, others who are engaged in consultation report that planning is more time-intensive because teachers must explain ongoing classroom interactions to the consultant to identify primary problems adequately and develop appropriate interventions (Walther-Thomas, 1998).

Many effective consultants spend regularly scheduled time in partners' classrooms every week or two to stay apprised of student performance and provide support for their partners (Tilton, 1996; Villa, Thousand, & Nevin, 1994). For example, Fay, a classroom teacher, and Marge, a school psychologist, co-teach a 45-minute social skills lesson every Friday morning. Fay reinforces the skills introduced in the lesson during the following week. Marge feels that this time in the classroom is productive because she can observe specific students, monitor intervention plans, model new group and individual techniques, and role-play new strategies and skills for the students with Fay.

Efficient Meeting Routines.   Effective teams develop efficient routines that facilitate their meetings. Many teams incorporate familiar organizational structures such as written agendas for discussion of various items, defined roles for participants (e.g., timekeeper), rotating responsibilities, and written action plans to ensure that all required tasks are completed as planned (Walther-Thomas, 1998). Some teams establish routines that are highly structured; however, most develop patterns that are flexible enough to meet their preferences and interaction styles while helping to achieve the meeting objectives. For example, some teams have a set meeting time and place each week, whereas others make these decisions from one week to the next. Some teams snack while they meet after school, whereas others may prefer a "no eating" policy. Some teams use laptop computers during meetings to expedite the development of their action plans, whereas others meet at a coffee bar after school and rotate responsibility for taking notes and distributing action plans the following day.

Many planning teams start their sessions with a period of individual and group reflection and evaluation of their work together (i.e., "How are things going with Samuel this week?"). This systematic revisiting of previously discussed issues ensures that concerns are monitored over time. Discussion of specific roles and responsibilities promotes personal accountability and provides opportunities to give compliments, share constructive feedback, and offer encouragement. On-going evaluation of student and professional performance improves teaching efforts and strengthens collaborative relationships. Effective and efficient planners stay focused on the planning task at hand. Without a shared commitment to this effort, it is easy to lose valuable time discussing interesting, but extraneous, personal and school-related topics. Ideally, planners find other time to share this information.

Incorporating Both Generalist and Specialist Perspectives

Typically, general educators approach classroom instruction and management from a "big picture" perspective. Consciously or subconsciously, they analyze materials they will be teaching and ask themselves questions such as, "What do I need to do to teach this concept to 25 students? What are some strategies and practice activities I can use? How long will it take to cover this material thoroughly? What else is going on in class that needs to be considered? How will I measure my students' mastery of this material?" and "What did I do last time I taught this?"

Most specialists approach instruction and management from a different perspective that reflects their professional development and experience in more traditional programs. They are more likely to focus on students' individual needs and miscellaneous details related to content instruction and behavior management concerns (e.g., accommodations, modifications, alternative assignments). They may ask themselves questions such as, "Given her reading and comprehension difficulties, what problems is Susan likely to have with *Catcher in the Rye*? What kinds of modifications and accommodations might help?" and "I wonder if the school library has this book on tape? Knowing how easily she gives up on difficult reading material, how can I motivate her to hang in there until the story line captures her attention?"

Both viewpoints are legitimate—just different. Each perspective needs to be considered to ensure that individual and group needs are addressed appropriately. Over time partners learn to appreciate each other's perspectives. This process leads to better instructional programs, more productive teamwork, and a broadening of each person's professional skills. After studying effective planning among co-teachers over time, Walther-Thomas (1998) encourages planners in inclusive settings to address the "big picture" issues first. This makes sense for

> **Think About It...**
>
> What should university and college preparation programs do to better prepare professionals for future roles and responsibilities as collaborators and team planners? What should be done in staff development activities in schools?

general educators and allows participants to examine the standard requirements related to the content and established learning goals for all students. Once these fundamental issues are clarified, partners can then begin to address the specific concerns related to individual students.

Chapter Summary

This chapter has presented a number of considerations regarding the development and successful implementation of inclusive communities. Given appropriate resources and support, school teams can create academic and social learning environments that enable all class members to achieve. Effective school-level planning and action ensure that teachers and specialists have an organizational framework that facilitates classroom-level planning, instruction, and student support.

At the classroom level, teachers and specialists maximize their effectiveness when they employ proved instructional strategies and grouping structures that facilitate peer support, social skills development, and active student engagement. By involving all class members in student-to-student support, professionals' skills and other classroom resources can be used more effectively for the benefit of all students.

CHAPTER ACTIVITIES

1. Review Figure 6.3. Brainstorm additional ways that teachers and specialists can find regularly scheduled planning time.

2. Interview administrators, teachers, and/or specialists involved in implementing inclusive education programs. What have been their greatest accomplishments and greatest concerns?

7 Meeting Student Needs through Assistance Teams

LEARNING OBJECTIVES

1. Identify the nature, purposes, and benefits of assistance teams.
2. Describe the composition of assistance teams and considerations for team member selection.
3. Identify and apply the steps of the assistance team process to problem-solve student cases.
4. Describe the process for establishing and maintaining assistance teams in educational settings.

Sally Sparks is deeply concerned about Robert, an 8-year-old boy in her second-grade class. He demands so much of her time, does little on his own, and seems able to complete assignments only with a great deal of teacher attention. When he doesn't receive it, he disrupts the other students and refuses to try working independently, claiming "I can't do it!" He has difficulty paying attention and following verbal directions, yet he can read on a third-grade level and draws exceptionally well. He does not seem to have any friends, probably because of his sometimes aggressive and immature behavior (teasing, name-calling, blaming others for his behavior). Sally wants to refer him to special education because she feels he has learning and attention problems beyond those she knows how to address herself. Her preparation didn't include working with these kinds of students. She's frustrated, Robert's frustrated, and so are his parents, but they are reluctant to have him tested for special services.

What should Sally do? Even if she makes a referral, he'll still be in her class demonstrating the same behavior on Monday morning. She knows the process takes time, but she could sure use some help right now!

Every day teachers and specialists face many student challenges. Most are ones they can handle on their own or with informal assistance from friends or colleagues, but some problems require more help. This chapter presents information on assistance teams that work with educators to provide supportive ideas and information that address their educational concerns about students' academic and behavioral problems. Assistance teams help brainstorm strategies and develop specific plans to deal with the more challenging problems that educators encounter.

Definition and Function of Assistance Teams

Intervention assistance teams are school-based, problem-solving teams designed to enable all teachers to meet the needs of their students demonstrating difficulties. Known by a variety of names (e.g., schoolwide assistance teams, teacher assistance teams, student intervention teams, teacher support teams, instructional support teams), this collaborative structure or approach helps classroom teachers identify and plan interventions for academic or behavioral problems interfering with student success. Although not required for special education referrals, assistance teams help teachers document the need for more extensive services, such as special education or related services, when the students' needs warrant these additional supports.

Most assistance or intervention teams are based on the teacher assistance team (TAT) model developed by Chalfant, Pysh, and Moultrie (1979) to address problems encountered by teachers attempting to meet the needs of students at risk for failure and students with disabilities in general education classrooms. Often teachers lack the professional preparation, confidence, or experience needed to deal with difficult-to-teach students while meeting the instructional needs of 20 to 30 others in general education classes. When teachers refer students for special education evaluation, a lengthy process at best, there is no immediate assistance with the classroom problems that precipitated the action. Often referrals do not result in special education services. Even if they qualify for services, most students with difficulties continue to spend the majority of their school days in general education classes. The ultimate responsibility for most service delivery rests with classroom teachers like Sally.

The goal of assistance teams is more efficient, effective instruction for students and increased support for teachers (Chalfant et al., 1979). Chalfant and colleagues conceptualized TATs as a means of providing immediate support for individualizing instruction, dealing with challenging behaviors, reducing inappropriate referrals to special education, and using the expertise of both general and special educators more effectively. If the TAT process does not resolve the difficulties, these teams often help teachers document the need for more extensive services.

Over the years, many variations of TAT have evolved. These problem-solving teams serve the same student and staff support purposes as did the original TATs. For the remainder of this chapter, these teams are referred to as assistance teams (ATs), and the commonalities among the various adaptations are highlighted.

Assumptions and Attitudes Underlying Team Problem Solving

Assistance teams, like other peer problem-solving models, are based on the assumption that general education teachers possess the expertise to help students with learning and behavior problems if support and encouragement are provided (Chalfant et al., 1979). Professionals can share their challenges with colleagues, and as a result of peer-provided support, can then work successfully with the students presenting these challenges. This process empowers many teachers to work effectively with more diverse students (Sindelar, Griffin, Smith, & Watanabe, 1992). It is further assumed that professionals working together as a team can resolve many more problems than individuals working alone.

Another assumption underlying team problem solving is that decisions made by teams are typically superior to decisions made in isolation, especially when team members represent diverse backgrounds, experience, and expertise (Fuchs & Fuchs, 1989; Thomas, Correa, & Morsink, 1995). Group decision making also helps safeguard against errors in individual judgment while enhancing adherence to due process requirements (Pfeiffer, 1980). Interdisciplinary collaboration helps AT participants develop a common language, knowledge base, and understanding of diverse roles, responsibilities, and techniques among related professionals (Welch et al., 1992).

A criticism sometimes leveled at the AT process is that it is a "Band-Aid approach," that is, it deals only with superficial problems and does not deal with pervasive underlying causes of the classroom difficulties, such as dysfunctional family life, poverty, or lack of resources. The purpose of AT is to identify and develop a plan for dealing with specific student behaviors in order to interrupt the cycle of failure and frustration the student and the teacher are feeling. Once the student and teacher are experiencing even small academic or behavioral gains, other concerns can be addressed with greater likelihood of success. Assistance teaming assumes an incremental change process with the teacher and the student.

Benefits of Assistance Teams

Educators have reported numerous benefits of ATs, both for students and for themselves. As with any innovation, benefits accrue faster when assistance teaming is implemented conscientiously and supported by needed resources such as meeting time, staff development for participants, and administrative support.

Although efficacy research is limited, emerging data suggest that AT models have the potential to promote positive changes in student behavior, provide support for both students and professionals, and reduce and improve the quality of referrals to special education (Aksamit & Rankin, 1993; Bay, Bryan, & O'Connor, 1994; Chalfant & Pysh, 1989; Evans, 1991; Kovaleski, Tucker, & Stevens, 1996; Safran & Safran, 1996; Whitten, Bahr, Hodges, & Dieker, 1996). In a study of 96 teams (Chalfant & Pysh, 1989), team members reported that group problem solving was effective in generating useful intervention strategies, providing moral support and reinforcement, and improving student performance as a result of intervention plans developed. Sindelar and colleagues (1992) characterized AT or collaborative problem-solving models as enjoying "high consumer satisfaction, widespread adoption, and consensual validity" (p. 256). High satisfaction among AT members is important because lack of satisfaction decreases the likelihood of successful collaboration (Ostroff, 1992).

Administrative support is critical to realizing the benefits of ATs including team members' and consumers' satisfaction (Graden, Casey, & Bonstrom, 1985; Kruger, Struzziero, Watts, & Vacca, 1995; Rosenfield, 1992; Safran & Safran, 1996). Kruger and colleagues (1995) found that positive feedback more strongly related to AT satisfaction than other administrative support aspects, but release time was also significant. Lack of release time for ATs was a "prominent concern among AT members" (p. 208). Clarity of purpose of the AT was also cited by educators as a significant factor in their satisfaction with the teams. Helping teachers and helping students were ranked most highly among educators (Kruger et al., 1995). Although hours of staff development were unrelated to team members' satisfaction, their satisfaction with preparation for teaming was highly related to their satisfaction with the AT. Kruger and colleagues suggested that this showed that quality of preparation was more important than the quantity of the skills development process. Korinek and McLaughlin (1996) found that even a limited amount of quality staff development and practice with the AT process resulted in the development of viable intervention plans and an increased comfort level with the problem-solving process. Participants on teams also reported high satisfaction with the efficiency and effectiveness of the process used in assistance teaming, as well as with the diversity of ideas and perspectives offered.

Benefits for Students.   Assistance teams provide direct and immediate attention to students' educational needs. Whereas special education referral and evaluation may take months to complete with no guarantee that the process will result in special education services, typical ATs are much quicker in responding to educators' requests. Shortly after receiving the request, a contact member of the AT may meet with the teacher or other educator requesting assistance. The team usually meets as a problem-solving group within a few weeks (depending on the number of requests in a given situation). ATs provide more informal support structures in educational settings and are used as a prereferral step in many states to alleviate the need for a more comprehensive special education evaluation.

Prior to referrals, ATs help teachers try different interventions and document results. In many cases, these techniques are successful and formal referrals for special education are no longer necessary. As previously noted, if referrals are necessary, the team's documentation of student progress or lack thereof helps support the case for more intensive special education services. For example, if Sally Sparks can show that she has systematically implemented different intervention plans designed with her assistance team and Robert has shown little progress, the case for special education will be strengthened. Should Robert be determined eligible for special education, Sally could still access the AT for ideas about general classroom interventions to support him in her classroom. Naturally Robert's special educator and any other specialists serving him would be part of this team problem-solving process. Finally, ATs assist teachers in developing support plans to provide a smooth transition for students who may be returning to general education classes from pull-out programs or to ensure an appropriate level of support for those exiting special education if services are no longer needed. Again, the benefits of ATs for students are dependent on effective team functioning and conscientious implementation of intervention plans by educators (Safran & Safran, 1996). Careful monitoring of student performance before and during intervention helps to ensure positive outcomes of the AT process.

Benefits for Educators.   ATs help teachers and other educators become aware of and skilled with additional or more specialized assessment and intervention strategies (Chalfant & Pysh, 1989; Sindelar et al., 1992). It is widely recognized that there will never be enough specialists to provide all the direct services and classroom support needed by students with disabilities or those who are at risk for school failure. ATs help bridge this gap by using available school resources and expertise more efficiently. Including more diverse students in general education classes necessitates equipping general educators with more strategies to be successful with these students.

The AT process also provides a forum for discovering mismatches between curricula and the students' needs. For example, Letisha is a ninth grader who has been assessed but did not qualify for special education and who is struggling in prealgebra. The AT could problem-solve with the math teacher, Ms. Walker, to devise some modifications to help Letisha be more successful. The team may also discuss the appropriateness of Algebra II (scheduled for next year) to Letisha's education and postsecondary goals, and, considering graduation standards, brainstorm alternatives that may be a better curricular match for this student than Algebra II at this time.

Assistance teaming also provides teachers and specialists an approach for proactive planning as well as responsive problem solving. In Letisha's case, the team could involve the student and her family to assess the appropriateness of the current curriculum, available alternatives, and other resources related to Letisha's longer term vocational and educational goals. This would allow the team to engage in more appropriate planning for the future as well as attend to the immediate problems in Letisha's math class.

Staff development for and participation in the AT process also provides educators with more explicit and effective problem-solving skills and processes for teachers as well as team members. In many cases, collaborative problem solving has not been a part of general educators' or specialists' formal professional development, so they may not be particularly knowledgeable or skilled with this process. The structured format used in AT provides an efficient agenda for the problem-solving process and enables even beginning collaborators to be effective in their efforts using basic interactional skills.

Finally, many educators report the support from colleagues to be one of the best features of assistance teaming (Chalfant & Pysh, 1989; Safran & Safran, 1996).

> **Think About It...**
>
> Consider the school situation in which you presently work or have completed field experiences. Is an assistance team in place to assist staff and students? How does it operate?

Teaching can be a lonely profession given the challenges faced in today's classrooms. Teachers report feeling overwhelmed in their attempts to meet the diverse and often complex needs of growing numbers of students along with ancillary duties they are expected to assume in their schools. Many perceive a lack of support from administrators or colleagues. Consequently, teachers and specialists are leaving the field in record numbers (Billingsley & Cross, 1992). Assistance teams provide a cost-effective source of support to help educators persist in their efforts and to feel connected to colleagues and more effective in their work. Team members report that serving on the team expands their repertoire of skills, ideas for interventions, multidisciplinary perspectives, and appreciation for their colleagues (Korinek & McLaughlin, 1996; Ward, Korinek, & McLaughlin, 1998).

Assistance Team Composition and Qualifications

The original ATs were comprised of three elected general educators who served for a period of time and met with teachers requesting assistance (Chalfant et al., 1979). Election to a team by one's peers was considered a vote of confidence in a teacher's ability and willingness to support colleagues in their problem-solving efforts. Chalfant and colleagues (1979) suggested keeping a core of experienced members on the AT to provide team continuity, but systematically rotating one team member every quarter or semester once the team is established to give others an opportunity to serve and learn. Family members were also frequently invited to participate. Sometimes members of other multidisciplinary teams or other specialists (e.g., a guidance counselor, school psychologist, special educator, gifted/talented specialist, social worker, speech therapist, occupational therapist, reading specialist) participated on ATs on an ad hoc basis as needed.

Considerations for Team Composition. Today, AT composition varies from school to school. Members may be elected, appointed, nominated by their peers, or selected from volunteers (Phillips & McCullough, 1992). Some sites include administrators and specialists in addition to or in place of some of the classroom teachers. Teachers requesting assistance must feel comfortable with the team and all participants should experience a sense of ownership, parity, and responsibility. Family members and students are invited to participate in team problem-solving meetings to the extent possible and appropriate.

The AT process recognizes that each member of the team brings different but equal expertise to the problem solving. For example, the special educator may know about accommodations, behavioral interventions, and learning strategies to help a student such as Robert focus his attention and monitor his own work completion. A counselor or social worker may be added to the team to share insights about family dynamics that may be affecting Robert's performance in the classroom. An administrator may be involved to answer questions regarding resources needed for special interventions, rearrange schedules, expedite evaluations for special education, or assist in securing volunteers to help with implementation of action plans. Sally, even though she is requesting assistance, still knows more about her own classroom structure, expectations, and curriculum than any other member of the team. Her insights and ideas contribute the focus for the group's collaborative problem solving. Together, combining their collective knowledge and expertise, this team is better prepared to plan an intervention most likely to succeed with Robert.

It is important to note that administrative participation on ATs should be considered carefully. On the one hand, principals can offer valuable instructional leadership and resources. These resources may include release time, scheduling preferences, professional development, recognition, and support. Successful principal-led ATs have been implemented in many schools. On the other hand, principals are also responsible for evaluating professional staff. Consequently, teachers may not feel as open requesting assistance, sharing their problems, or admitting difficulties in front of their immediate supervisors. Whereas administrative support for AT is critical to success, Sindelar and colleagues (1992) found that teachers were more satisfied with collaborative problem solving when the principal was not the team leader. If this is the case, an assistant principal, department head, instructional supervisor, or team leader may serve as the administrative designee or representative on the AT. Administrators must understand and accept the AT concept, effectively communicate the process to the teaching staff and related services specialists, and work with staff to ensure effective AT implementation. Administrators must try to minimize teachers' feelings of discomfort in early stages of team development and provide members a feeling of ownership in the process.

Different combinations of team participants have been successful in accomplishing the goals of assistance teaming at different sites. Decisions about team composition should be made at the school level after broad-based discussion and

Think About It...

Consider your colleagues' or classmates' interpersonal qualities and professional expertise. Who would you recommend to serve on an assistance team? Why did you suggest each of these members?

careful consideration of existing staff responsibilities and resources available to support implementation at that site.

Qualifications of Team Members.   General qualifications of team members include classroom experience, knowledge of curriculum and materials, ability to assess learning and behavior problems and individualize instruction, effective communication, and interest in helping colleagues. Phillips and McCullough (1992) highlighted the need for team members who possess skills and attributes necessary for collaborative problem solving, including maintenance of confidentiality, credibility with colleagues, creativity, intrinsic motivation, and a collaborative orientation. They cautioned against potential members who are already overcommitted with other school responsibilities, reluctant to serve, skeptical about the process, or whose schedules preclude regular attendance at AT meetings. Other skills relevant to problem identification, goal setting, and brainstorming are also important to effective assistance teaming. The need for more complex skills such as negotiating and building consensus is minimized in assistance teaming, since the team is explicitly taught to accept and support the requesting teacher's choice of goals and interventions from among those brainstormed (Korinek & McLaughlin, 1996).

Relationship of Assistance Teams to Other School-Based Teams

In many schools, ATs are separate from mandated special education teams (sometimes called child study, screening, or resource teams) required to deal with referrals, evaluations, eligibility, and placement decisions. Generally, separate special education teams and ATs can accommodate more requests and involve more professionals in the benefits of collaborative problem solving than can a single team functioning in dual roles. Separate ATs may also be perceived as more approachable by general education teachers who may consider the child study team as a "gatekeeper" for special education.

In some schools, however, special education teams also function successfully as ATs. One team serving as both a child study and assistance team can help ensure that referrals for special education are appropriate and can offer support to teachers whose referrals do not result in a comprehensive evaluation. One team also offers the advantages of continuity and efficiency for students who proceed through both prereferral and evaluation for special education stages. For example, if a dual-function team considered Robert's case, members could review Sally's request for assistance to determine if special education evaluation is warranted. The team could also provide immediate support to Sally by offering suggestions, observing Robert, and brainstorming classroom interventions. A compromise between single and separate teams may be a common member who serves on both the AT and the special education team. When a referral for comprehensive evaluation is made, this member can provide some continuity between the teams which may expedite decision making.

As noted previously, the AT and child study/special education processes may occur simultaneously. For example, Sally might refer Robert for a special education evaluation because of her concerns about his long-term emotional and behavioral problems. While this team considers whether or not a comprehensive evaluation is needed, the AT may be meeting with Sally to offer her support and help her identify some immediate management strategies for Robert. This will help him be more successful in her classroom during the special education process. The strategies shared by way of the AT process are valuable to the general educator regardless of the outcome of special education eligibility.

In considering the special education and AT processes, it is important to ensure procedural safeguards in the identification of students with disabilities and protection of confidentiality. Although state or local policies may strongly encourage prereferral interventions, the AT process should not be a prerequisite for an evaluation for special education or consideration for eligibility for other services such as Title I or district-level math or reading assistance. A student may be referred by anyone at any time, whether or not a teacher participates in the AT process.

Many schools have grade-level or departmental teams organized to plan and deliver instruction to particular groups of students for whom teams have primary responsibility. Although typically these teams have regularly scheduled meetings, these sessions are often less formal and less structured than AT meetings. The AT process, however, can be used successfully by these teams when specific problems arise for a more focused approach to problem solving. In some schools, teams designate one of their regularly scheduled meetings (e.g., on a weekly or biweekly basis) as an AT meeting to address challenging student concerns. This approach does not require the formation of a separate AT to support the teachers involved, but capitalizes on the efficiency and effectiveness of the AT process to plan for more systematic academic or behavioral interventions for designated students served by the team. For example, the Gold Team at Farnsworth Middle School meets during a common planning time four times per week. The team has agreed to use the AT meeting format and procedures to address more significant concerns of teachers related to individual students on the team every other Friday. The first student for whom they used the more formal AT procedures was Sam, a sixth-grade student with Down syndrome who was causing major disturbances in Mr. Lieu's science class. The Gold Team (which included a special educator) asked the speech and language specialist to join them for this meeting because they suspected that some of Sam's behavior was related to his limited communication abilities in addition to his lower academic skills. They would devote the Friday

Think About It...

Do you think ATs should be separate from child study, special education, or other teams in schools with which you are familiar? Why or why not?

meeting to problem solving regarding strategies to make Sam more successful in his science class or others in which he was included.

Team Roles

Typically roles delineated on ATs include a facilitator/team leader, team contact person, recorder, the teacher requesting assistance, and ad hoc members such as other teachers, specialists, family members, or students. The roles of these participants are described next.

Team Leader. Prior to the AT meeting, the leader or facilitator encourages requests for assistance, screens requests, assigns teacher contact responsibilities, schedules meetings, invites participants, provides participants with copies of the request for assistance, and ensures that all members are aware of and understand their roles and responsibilities on the team. The team leader calls the meeting to order, appoints a team recorder, and sets the tone for the meeting. She or he tries to create a collaborative problem-solving atmosphere and to convey a "we can do it" attitude, that is, working together we can accomplish more than any one of us working alone. The team leader facilitates the problem-solving process and the completion of a structured implementation plan. She or he also ensures participation while keeping the meeting on task and on time. The leader poses nonthreatening questions, listens actively, restates and clarifies responses of team members, resolves conflicts among members, and schedules a follow-up meeting.

The team leader or appointed designee meets with the teacher requesting assistance as soon as possible after receiving the request. The "contact" person offers moral support and an empathetic ear, and assists the teacher in completing a request for assistance form. Often the contact observes the student in the requesting teacher's classroom to gain additional insight into the situation. At the beginning of the meeting, the contact reviews the reasons the teacher requested the meeting, which includes restating the problem and clarifying the goal or objective with input from the teacher. This helps the group work toward specific target behavior(s) in their problem solving.

Recorder. The recorder takes notes at the AT meeting, including decisions related to the intervention plan and suggestions offered during brainstorming. The recorder also checks the accuracy of notes with team members prior to the close of the meeting to ensure complete records and common understandings. This role should be rotated among members from meeting to meeting.

Team Members. Other members of the team review the completed request for assistance form submitted by the teacher prior to their meeting in order to identify problems, study interrelationships, and consider recommendations. During the meeting, these members actively listen, ask clarifying questions, and provide suggestions. Effective team members limit their comments to the points being discussed, contribute succinctly, and allow other members to contribute. Student participation in the team process is highly desirable. Student peers often offer unique perspectives and powerful insights into accommodations and interventions for a particular student. When appropriate, the student under discussion should also be invited to participate in the AT process in order to foster self-advocacy and promote the student's taking an active role in his or her education.

Once AT members have been identified, they must make the team operational in their particular setting. Key tasks in mobilizing an assistance team include determining (1) the length of service on the team; (2) how future team members will be selected or elected; (3) a procedure for handling requests; (4) a scheduled place and time for weekly organizational meetings and release time for members (e.g., substitutes for key personnel; meetings before or after school; meetings during planning time, lunch, centers); (5) a record-keeping system; (6) a location for collecting and storing requests, action plans, and completed forms; and (7) communication procedures with faculty, administrators, and team members. The process for carrying out these tasks may vary from site to site and should be tailored to specific circumstances existing at individual schools.

Team members, administrators, and other school personnel can encourage teachers to use the AT process in a variety of ways. Word of mouth, flyers, and faculty meeting presentations may be used to describe the AT process. Newsletters and e-mail messages can also be used. Many teams post or distribute lists of suggestions generated by the team for dealing with common student problems. Teams may invite interested teachers to observe the process (with the requesting teacher's permission) to help others understand the AT process. Requests can be encouraged especially after family conferences, school exams, or report cards. Probably the best advertisements for ATs are the teachers who have availed themselves of the process and received valuable assistance. These individuals can help "spread the word" to other faculty members.

Effective ATs require time, effort, expertise, and commitment from all team members. Incentives for team participation can enhance the likelihood that qualified professionals will serve as AT members. Incentives may include release time to meet during school hours, compensation time for AT time spent before or after school, preferential class scheduling, reduced duties (e.g., bus duty, hall monitoring, extracurricular expectations), preferred parking spaces, and free breakfast or lunch. Professional development opportunities such as conferences, meetings, or educational materials are also valued by many AT members. Public recognition from administrators and positive feedback on team efforts can also go a long way toward encouraging and sustaining AT member participation.

The Assistance Team Process

Premeeting Activities

As described earlier, the leader or a designated contact person meets with the teacher as soon as possible after a request for assistance is submitted. This meeting is designed to complete or clarify the request (see Figure 7.1 on page 150), discuss

FIGURE 7.1 Request for Assistance.

Demographic data (student, age, grade, school, teacher, date of request).

1. What specific student behaviors are interfering with classroom success?
2. Describe the student's individual strengths and interests.
3. What *exactly* does the student need to *do* to be more successful in your classroom?
4. What strategies or interventions have you tried thus far?
5. Provide any background information and/or available assessment data directly relevant to this request.

the teacher's concerns, and review the AT process. This ensures that established procedures are followed. Team members are provided with copies of the request and other useful information prior to actual team meetings. An observation may be scheduled to gather additional information and confirm the teacher's findings. For example, the designated team contact would schedule a meeting with Sally, Robert's teacher, at a mutually agreeable time to listen to her concerns about his performance. The contact person would assist Sally in completing her written request, schedule an observation of Robert, and explain briefly the next steps in the AT process.

The Request for Assistance

The request for assistance questions shown in Figure 7.1 have been adapted from Chalfant and Pysh (1979) and Project RIDE (Beck & Gabriel, 1989). They represent basic questions addressed by most ATs. The student-oriented questions have been expanded here to assist teachers in refining requests. These questions may also assist team members in better understanding the student in the context of a particular situation and in developing plausible intervention alternatives.

The first question regarding specific behaviors that the teacher wants the student to demonstrate and to stop demonstrating helps the teacher and the team to focus on specific, classroom-based behaviors as the targets for intervention. Teachers often use general terms to describe behaviors such as "disrespectful," "immature," "unmotivated," "hyperactive," "aggressive," "disruptive," or others that are open to different interpretations. More specific, observable, and measurable descriptions of behavior, such as "refuses to comply with teachers requests to complete work or remain in area," "has difficulty sharing toys, materials, space with other children," "seldom returns homework or completes seatwork," and "hits, kicks, pushes others when he gets angry" give a clearer picture of problem behaviors.

The second question regarding student strengths and interests serves to help the teacher and team identify and recognize positive attributes, interests, and skills that the student possesses. These serve as a foundation on which to build and provide important clues to interventions that are more likely to succeed.

Given the importance of student motivation and engagement in the learning process, the identified strengths and interests also provide opportunities to invest the student in his or her educational program.

Asking *exactly* what the student needs to *do* to be successful helps focus the teacher's and team's attention on replacing undesirable behaviors with more appropriate alternatives. Unless this is stressed and the focus of intervention is expanded to building positive behaviors (not just reducing negative ones), the student is likely to replace the behavior being decreased with other inappropriate actions. This question also forces teachers to articulate expectations for their classrooms and criteria for student success. Examples of appropriate behaviors may be to "complete work in spelling with 80% accuracy," "share toys and art materials without arguing," "solve problems without physical contact (hitting, kicking, pushing)," or "participate in group discussions and small-group projects."

The fourth question asks the teacher requesting assistance to identify strategies or interventions that have already been tried in an attempt to address the identified problem. This gives the team important information on previous attempts, if any, to deal with the student's behaviors and helps members during their brainstorming and intervention planning to go beyond strategies that have already been tried. Even if team members suspect that previous interventions had not been implemented systematically, the requesting teacher is likely to be more open to trying new interventions rather than repeating ones perceived as ineffective in the past.

Finally, the teacher is asked to provide relevant background information or assessment data, or both. The purpose of this query is *not* to review every bit of data available on the student or to request additional testing beyond that which is normally done in the classroom with all students. The latter would be a violation of the student's rights if testing is done without parental permission. This question is included, however, to prompt the team to look at existing data on the student directly relevant to the presenting problems and student strengths. Possible data sources may include records of observations, work samples, grade books, report cards, anecdotal records, attendance records, classroom testing data, skill or behavior checklists, parent or medical information, or learning styles indicators (Baron & Chalfant, 1987). These data may prove helpful in clarifying the problem and in generating effective solutions. A sample request for assistance form completed for Robert in Sally's class is shown in Figure 7.2 on page 152.

Meeting Format

The format for AT meetings that serves as both an agenda and an action plan for intervention implementation is shown in Figure 7.3 on page 153. The team leader opens the meeting by welcoming and introducing participants by name and position. Name tags or cards with this information (e.g., "Greg Hines—4th Grade Teacher," "Donna Schwartz—School Psychologist") may be useful if requesting teachers, family members, or other participants do not know all team members. The team leader establishes the role of recorder, reminds other members of their duties

FIGURE 7.2   **Request for Assistance Completed for Robert.**

Request for Assistance

Date: *1/7*

Student's Name: *Robert E.*   **Age:** *8 yrs., 2 mos.*

Teacher's Name: *Sally Sparks*   **Grade:** *2*

Team Contact:
(Assigned by Team Leader)

1. What specific student behaviors are interfering with classroom success?

   Doesn't complete assignments or work independently; off-task and inattentive; disrupts other students; difficulty following directions

2. Describe the student's individual strengths and interests.

   Reads on 3rd-grade level
   Draws well
   Likes adult attention

3. What *exactly* does the student need to *do* to be more successful in your classroom?

   Attempt and complete assignments on his level
   Follow classroom directions
   Stop disrupting others during seatwork

4. What strategies or interventions have you tried thus far?

   Frequent reminders and warnings
   Stay in from recess when he doesn't finish work
   Drawing when he gets his work done (but he seldom earns this)

5. Provide any background information and/or available assessment data directly relevant to this request.

   IRI scores = 3.2 level
   on grade level in math (2nd grade)

(see roles described previously), and reminds everyone present of the purpose of the meeting (i.e., to assist the requesting teacher in developing an intervention plan for his or her classroom to meet the needs of the student under discussion). The assigned recorder notes all persons in attendance in section 1 of the form.

The rest of the 20- to 30-minute problem-solving meeting proceeds as indicated on the form. The team leader or contact person begins the discussion by reviewing the reasons the teacher requested a meeting, then summarizing the stu-

FIGURE 7.3   **Format for Assistance Team Meetings.**

Agenda	Action Plan
1. Introduce participants	Persons in attendance:
2. Review Request for Assistance	Intervention goal:
3. Brainstorm interventions	List of ideas generated on reverse side or attachment:
4. Select intervention(s)	Teacher's chosen intervention(s):
5. Identify support needs	Materials and/or collaborative assistance needed:
6. Plan evaluation	Criterion for success and how it will be measured:
7. Schedule follow-up	Date set to review progress:

dent's problems and any additional information on the request for assistance such as student's present behaviors, strengths, interests, desired behaviors, techniques already tried, and other relevant background information. The teacher is given an opportunity to react, verify, correct, or add information, and with the team members, reaches consensus on the major problem and specific behaviors or goals to be targeted for intervention. A specific statement of the intervention goal ("What do I want?" "What is the desired behavior?") is critical to focusing the team on the central target and generating positive solutions toward desirable behaviors, rather than simply decelerating inappropriate behaviors. In Robert's case, Sally determined, with the help of the team, that she wanted him to complete more work independently and that she would start with his reading assignments, an area of strength for Robert. Suggestions for problem identification and goal selection with examples for another student, Ramona, are offered in Figure 7.4.

FIGURE 7.4   Tips for Problem Identification and Goal Setting.

1. **Assess what is happening—look at the "big picture."**
   - *Look for patterns and relationships.* Are problem behaviors linked to a particular type of task, setting, demand, or each other? Example: Ramona's frequent disruptive behaviors of touching others, taking their materials, and talking occur when she is out of her desk during seatwork.
   - *Consider strengths (successes) as well as weaknesses (deficits).* What is the student interested in? What does he or she do well? What specific behaviors are interfering with learning? Refer to strengths and weaknesses listed on the Request for Assistance form for insights into the problem.

2. **Set priorities.**
   - *Focus on central concerns.* Which behaviors are of greatest concern, most disruptive, the greatest obstacles to classroom success, or if changed, would make a real difference?
   - *Address manageable targets.* What can realistically be changed in a relatively short period of time so that the student and teacher experience success on which they can build?
   - *Strengthen desired behaviors whenever possible.* What appropriate alternative behavior do you want to replace the problem behavior? Example: Although the teacher wants Ramona to stop all of her disruptive behaviors, if the teacher focused on rewarding Ramona for staying in her seat and finishing her work, she would be strengthening positive alternative behavior that would automatically decrease the disruptive behaviors of concern.

3. **Define clear goals.**
   - *Pinpoint measurable outcomes.* What *exactly* do you want? Have you described the target behaviors in a way that you can count and measure them? Example: "on-task," "disruptive," and "respectful" are difficult to measure. "Finishes assignments in reading at ≥ 80 %," and "Gets through recess without hitting, kicking, or shoving others" are easier to keep track of to measure progress.
   - *Set reasonable criteria.* Can the student realistically meet the level of performance you have set in a relatively short period of time? Example: If Ramona is finishing only 10 % of her work at present, it would be unreasonable to expect her to finish 90 % of her assignments in the next 2 weeks. Assuming that she can do the work, starting at 40 % and then gradually increasing the criterion toward 90 % over a period of time may be a more reasonable approach. Focusing on one subject and gradually expanding to other periods once Ramona is meeting with consistent success is also recommended. Success breeds success!

Brainstorming Interventions

Brainstorming is a process of generating many possible solutions or strategies to address a specified problem or goal. In the AT process, all brainstormed ideas should be recorded to provide a permanent record of the suggestions generated. These ideas may be listed on the reverse side of the form itself, on the chalkboard, index cards, a flipchart, or overhead transparency. In order to improve the efficiency and effectiveness of the brainstorming portion of the meeting, members should:

- Generate as many ideas as possible.
- Encourage responses from every team member (including the teacher requesting assistance and the recorder).
- Expand on each others' ideas.
- Avoid judging, evaluating, commenting, or criticizing suggestions at this point in the process.
- Avoid attaching names to ideas.
- Save clarification of suggestions for after the brainstorming.

Three to 10 minutes has been suggested as the length of time for brainstorming (Beck & Gabriel, 1989; Chalfant & Pysh, 1979). As an alternative, Bauwens and Hourcade (1995) suggest that team members listen for naturally occurring pauses in the brainstorming process. Typically, there is an initial burst of ideas followed by a lull while team members think about additional alternatives, then another smaller burst with a lull. They recommend brainstorming be terminated after the second pause in the suggestions. Chalfant and Pysh (1989) reported that, across the 96 ATs they studied, teams typically generated a range of 12 to 22 suggestions per brainstorming session. Korinek and McLaughlin (1996) found similar numbers of suggestions generated by preservice interdisciplinary teams comprised of graduate education students completing fieldwork toward their respective majors. Figure 7.5 on page 156 shows a list of suggestions brainstormed by the AT for Robert to help him complete more reading assignments on his own.

Intervention Selection and Planning

After brainstorming, the requesting teacher may seek clarification on some ideas that were not understood or may seem promising. The teacher then chooses the intervention(s) that seems most feasible and is assisted by the team in developing an implementation plan detailing the steps (if any), materials, and collaborative support needed to implement it. Collaborative support may include assistance to help the teacher implement a selected strategy, help in data collection, or provide special activities or rewards for the student.

The AT process represents a departure from other problem-solving models because postbrainstorming discussion is limited to addressing only those items noted by the teacher. The interventions selected by the teacher are accepted as the "right" strategies by the team (Chalfant et al., 1979), rather than taking the time to

FIGURE 7.5   **List of Suggestions Brainstormed for Robert.**

Have an outline-daily plan

Paraprofessional assistance

Self-reward

Tape recorder

Small group or buddy system-peer helper

Consultation from the learning disabilities
    resource teacher

Set a timer

Behavior chart with self-checks

Behavioral contract

Token economy

Secret signal for off on-task

Subtle reminders, hidden notes

Alternative response modes to writing—
    more project-oriented

Notes home for good behavior

Home-school rewards

In-class leadership roles

Videotape and show him behaviors

Subject badge

Self-monitoring

Colorful work folders

Special pens to complete work

Permanent visual aids in classroom

Puppet friend

Out-of-class rewards (library, etc.)

Use of computer or typewriter

weigh advantages and disadvantages of every suggestion. This approach saves meeting time and acknowledges that the teacher is ultimately responsible for implementing whatever interventions are chosen. It is critical that the teacher feels ownership and confidence in the plan. Although other team members may prefer alternate interventions, it is the teacher requesting assistance who delivers the program, and therefore has the right to choose the suggestions he or she considers most feasible.

The team should discourage the teacher from trying too many interventions at once. Limiting the number of strategies implemented gives a clearer picture of the connections between the interventions and the observed student behaviors; a smaller number of strategies is also more manageable, and thus more likely to be implemented consistently. The number of interventions selected is also influenced by the nature of the interventions. If the selected strategies are simple, discrete, and compatible, it may be possible to implement several strategies at once. For example, it may be relatively easy for Sally to provide a colorful work folder, a special pen for completing reading assignments, and an increase in her social reinforcement, in addition to consulting with the resource teacher in learning disabilities about Robert. On the other hand, if strategies are more complex (e.g., if Sally had chosen a major curricular modification, a multifaceted self-monitoring system, a behavioral contract or token economy), best practice suggests limiting the number of interventions attempted at any one time.

Establishing the criteria for success and the method for measuring progress is critical to the intervention process. Educators are advised to keep their criteria reasonable in relation to the student's current performance and their progress recording simple yet sensitive enough to show progress or lack thereof (the KISS principle—*keep it simple, yet sensitive*). If data collection is perceived as cumbersome or too complex, busy general education teachers are less likely to track the behavior objectively. Initially, it may be sufficient to record the target behavior during one or two daily periods, rather than try to monitor all situations for the entire school day. Ideally, teachers should use existing measures whenever possible (e.g., records of completed work, grades, work samples, attendance/tardy records). Naturally occurring breaks in instruction, such as the end of the lesson, recess, and lunch period, may provide opportune times to make notes or tallies on behavior. Although the teacher may be working toward increasing appropriate behavior (e.g., reinforcing greater participation, more appropriate social interactions, more on-task behavior), it may be easier to keep track of the student's infractions, such as lack of participation during a lesson, major altercations with peers, or classroom disruptions for recording purposes and to monitor changes in behavior. To the extent possible, teachers should involve students in monitoring their own behaviors through the use of checklists, tally sheets, tokens, or the like. For example, Robert may keep track of his completed reading assignments by marking an "X" next to the date on a chart included in his reading folder for each assignment that is returned and has met the 80% criterion. Adjustments in the recording system (e.g., more frequent or a different type of recording) can be made if the data collected do not seem to reflect accurately the progress made by a student in the course of implementing the selected intervention. For example, if Robert is turning in his reading assignments but is still requiring excessive attention from Sally, a more sensitive recording system may be counting the number of times he requests help, or noting the number of assignments he completes with two or fewer requests for teacher help.

Follow-Up

As the last step in an AT meeting, a date is set for a follow-up meeting to check on the progress of the intervention. Typically, 2 to 3 weeks after the initial meeting is a reasonable time frame for follow-up. This provides enough time to allow the selected strategies to be implemented and have an effect, but not so long that if the strategies are ineffective the teacher and student meet with continued failure and frustration for an extended period. The contact person from the team may do informal follow-up prior to the official team follow-up meeting. A sample follow-up form is shown in Figure 7.6 on page 158.

The follow-up form identifies teacher, student, and dates of both the initial AT meeting and the follow-up meeting. Progress toward meeting the goal identified on the action plan is reviewed, and a decision to continue, modify, or terminate the intervention is made by the team. If the student has shown some progress toward the determined goal, the teacher may wish to continue the selected strategy or modify it in some way to improve progress. In the case of a modification, specific adjustments are discussed and described. For either an extension or modification, a

FIGURE 7.6 **Follow-Up Meeting to Monitor Progress on an Earlier Assistance Team Meeting.**

Teacher: _____ Student: _____

Date of Last Action Plan: _____

Date of Follow-Up Meeting: _____

1. *Evaluation of Progress:* Review of specific documentation of performance. To what extent have defined criteria for success been achieved?

2. *Decision:* What is the specific plan at this point?

___ Continue the intervention as originally planned until the goal is achieved.

    Date for the next follow-up meeting: _____

___ Modify the original plan as follows:

    Date for next follow-up meeting: _____

___ Terminate the intervention because the original goal has been achieved.

date is set for another follow-up meeting. If the problem is resolved (i.e., criterion is met), the case is closed or the teacher may request that the team assist with another presenting problem. Whether an initial or follow-up AT meeting, the content, recommendations, and action plan or follow-up form are officially recorded and the teacher leaves with a copy of the plan in hand or receives a copy soon after the meeting.

Monitoring Team Functioning

It is important for ATs to evaluate their functioning on a regular basis. The form shown in Figure 7.7 provides an example of questions that teams can use to assess their performance. This may be done weekly or every other meeting in the case of teams that are just getting started; at least quarterly evaluations are recommended for established teams. The AT process can also be used to problem-solve and improve the functioning of the team itself. For example, a meeting may be devoted to brainstorming ideas and developing a plan for promoting use of the team in a school in which this resource is being underused by teachers. If a team is having

FIGURE 7.7 Team Evaluation Form.

Name _____   Team Role _____

Student _____   Date of Meeting _____

1. How effectively did the team problem-solve to assist the teacher requesting assistance?

   Not very effectively   1   2   3   4   5   Highly effectively

2. How satisfied were you with your own participation in the teaming process?

   Highly dissatisfied   1   2   3   4   5   Highly satisfied

3. In order to make team problem solving more effective, list behaviors that you would like team members:

   To do more of: _____

   _____

   _____

   To continue: _____

   _____

   _____

   To do less of: _____

   _____

   _____

difficulty generating numerous alternatives during brainstorming or sticking to the topic during the meeting, the AT process can be used to plan more efficient and effective team functioning.

Chapter Summary

Assistance teams are school-based problem-solving teams designed to help teachers meet the needs of students demonstrating learning and behavioral difficulties in general education classes. The goal of ATs is more effective instruction for students and increased support for teachers. Teams assist teachers in defining problems, brainstorming possible interventions, planning implementation of teacher-selected interventions, and monitoring student performance through a structured format. Team composition may vary from school to school, but is comprised mainly of respected general education teachers. Specialists as well as administrators may serve on the team as ad hoc or regular members of the team. Professional development in the AT process, administrative support, resources (e.g., release time), and ongoing evaluation of team efforts are essential for effective ATs. The true measure of team effectiveness is increased success for students with academic or behavioral difficulties in inclusive classrooms and enhanced support for their teachers.

CHAPTER ACTIVITIES

1. Locate and interview one or two team members on an assistance team or other school team that operates in a similar fashion. Questions should focus on the positive aspects and challenges of assistance teaming in that setting and advice for establishing teams.

2. Consider a school with which you are familiar. Identify the advantages and disadvantages of having the administrator on an AT for that school. Discuss the merits of teams comprised of general education teachers versus ATs that are more interdisciplinary in composition.

3. Identify reasons for considering the purpose or function of challenging behaviors for the student when brainstorming interventions. Give examples of interventions that might be used if the function is: (a) attention, (b) avoidance, (c) control, and (d) stimulation.

8 Meeting Student Needs through Collaborative Consultation

LEARNING OBJECTIVES

1. Identify the nature, purposes, and benefits of collaborative consultation.
2. Describe and apply the steps in collaborative consultation to problem-solve student cases.
3. Explain behavioral and peer collaboration as variations of collaborative consultation.
4. Describe content and communication skills essential to collaborative consultation.

With over 20 years of teaching experience, Carla Taylor thought that she could handle almost anything in the classroom. She enjoyed working with the most challenging students, and other teachers recognized her ability to reach those with special needs. This year was no exception. Carla had three students with learning disabilities, one with attention-deficit/hyperactivity disorder (ADHD), and one with a hearing impairment. She had declined the offer of a co-teacher because she believed that others needed classroom support more than she did.

Despite her experience and comfort level in working with challenging students, Carla was suddenly at a loss to help Rachel Burns, one of the girls in her class. Rachel had been a good student at the beginning of the school year, but her performance had deteriorated dramatically over the past 2 months. She had many unexcused absences, was not turning in any homework, and was frequently unprepared for class. Rachel's grades were suffering to the point that she might fail for the semester. Whenever Carla tried to talk with Rachel, she got little response.

During a conference with Rachel's mother, Carla learned that there had been a lot happening at home. Mrs. Burns confided that she and her boyfriend had recently broken up and he had moved out of her house, where he had lived for the past 2 years. Although Rachel's father had left the state after their divorce several years ago, he had returned and was now pressuring her for a reconciliation. Mrs. Burns said that he had been spending more time at the house, and she knew that all of this was very hard on Rachel. Mrs. Burns was not surprised to hear that Rachel was doing poorly in school. Her behavior had changed at home as well. Mrs. Burns indicated that she would do what she could to help Rachel but admitted that she was having a difficult time herself.

Even the most skilled and experienced teachers like Carla become frustrated when tried-and-true interventions do not work with certain students. Despite their best efforts to find solutions, they may exhaust their own resources and need more help.

Collaborative consultation is one approach to meet support needs of classroom teachers. Although consultation may be appropriate for many different purposes, this chapter focuses on consultation as a collaborative structure for the specific purpose of supporting more inclusive education for students. Although there are many variations, generally collaborative consultation is defined as "an interactive process which enables people with diverse expertise to generate creative solutions to mutually defined problems" (Idol, Paolucci-Whitcomb, & Nevin, 1986, p. 1). The typical consulting configuration is a dyad involving a general education teacher and a specialist. The teacher requests assistance from a specialist who has expertise perceived as relevant to the particular concern (e.g., a special educator, reading specialist, guidance counselor, transition specialist, school psychologist). At times, teachers also seek out other classroom teachers for peer consultation.

Collaborative consultation is considered an indirect support service because, in most cases, consultants do not interact directly with students. Instead, consultants interact with the professionals who work directly with students. Given the structure of most classrooms and schools, teachers tend to be the direct service professionals who most often confer with consultants. Truly collaborative cultures, however, promote a heightened sense of shared responsibility for students. Collaborative consultation in these settings becomes a reciprocal process; all school professionals are comfortable both giving and receiving consultative support. A classroom teacher, for example, may be an effective consultant for the speech therapist who is having difficulty working with one of the students in the teacher's class. The teacher serves as a facilitator and shares alternative strategies for getting the student to respond more actively.

Although consultation typically begins as a one-to-one interaction or dyadic process, it sometimes expands to include others on the team. For example, a sixth-grade teacher and the learning disabilities (LD) specialist may invite the reading specialist to their meetings because they are seeking more effective ways to modify the curriculum for a student who has severe reading disabilities. Similarly, professionals may include family members in the consultation process. Parents or guardians contribute unique insights that enable teams to target important goals and to identify strategies that work in school as well as in the home and neighborhood.

Collaborative consultation can provide different types of support for teachers. Some need a colleague who understands and accepts their concerns as important. When consultants listen attentively, teachers gain a sense of validation. They feel safe to express their frustrations and self-doubts. For example, ninth-grade English teacher Theresa Fowler, similar to many teachers who initiate a consulting interaction, needed to vent some negative feelings about her students. She was angry with a particular student and accused him of being a "chronic trouble-maker" who was purposely disrupting her class. Because the consultant was not put off by her strong feelings, Theresa was able to admit that what bothered her most was "feeling so helpless because I just don't know what I can do to make a difference for this student who really needs me." Encouragement and support from professional colleagues often help teachers persist with students who present difficult challenges.

Collaborative consultation offers more than just moral support. Teachers also benefit from problem solving with an objective partner. Even the most competent reflective practitioners get bogged down when their repeated efforts are unsuccessful. Collaborative consultation provides teachers with opportunities to talk through issues with colleagues who share a commitment to the reflective teaching process and can contribute new perspectives. When the metacognitive monologue of an individual teacher becomes a collaborative dialogue between two colleagues, the possibilities for creative and effective problem solving are greatly enhanced.

Finally, collaborative consultation enables professionals to acquire new information and skills. Because both parties actively participate in the identification of the problem and the generation of solutions, they learn from one another. Partners expand their perspectives as well as their repertoires of assessment and intervention strategies. They are better equipped to deal with problems at hand and also similar situations in the future.

Think About It...

Why might a teacher seek support from a consultant rather than an assistance team? What factors might make consultation the collaborative structure of choice?

The Bases for Collaborative Consultation

To understand consultation in practice, educators need some historical perspective, familiarity with major theoretical orientations that have shaped contemporary models, and knowledge of the research on school-based consultation.

Origins of Consultation as a Service Delivery Option

Not long after special education classes were introduced into American public schools, professionals recognized consultation as an alternative model for service delivery. In the 1960s, the concept of a full continuum of services formalized the notion that students with disabilities could be served in general education classrooms with consultative assistance offered by school psychologists, consulting teachers, resource teachers, and others (Deno, 1973; Lilly, 1971; Reynolds & Birch, 1977). As consultation gained support as a viable service option, it was incorporated into the new roles of special education resource teachers, who provided both direct instructional services to students and indirect consultative support to teachers (Wiederholt, Hammill, & Brown, 1978). Several variations of the consulting teacher model, such as the diagnostic-prescriptive teacher (Prouty & Prillaman, 1970) and the crisis or helping teacher (Morse, 1971) models, were prominent in the 1970s. By the 1980s, consulting teacher models were well established in public school settings and in university programs for professional preparation (e.g., Friend, 1984; Idol-Maestas & Ritter, 1985; Paolucci-Whitcomb & Nevin, 1985).

The emphasis on consultation is not unique to the field of special education. Similar consulting approaches emerged in other professional disciplines that serve students with special needs. As Gutkin (1996) noted:

> Whether one examines the scholarly and professional literature in special education, school psychology, speech-language pathology, school counseling, or any other specialty area, it appears that each field has independently reached the same conclusion: School-based consultation services are a crucial and growing element of professional services for children with special needs. (p. 333)

Thomas, Correa, and Morsink (1995) attribute the rapid expansion of consultation approaches to its potential for reducing referrals for special education services, diminishing the necessity for labeling, helping teachers respond to changing school practices, contributing to the success of students in general education settings, dealing with the unique needs of secondary students, and supporting early childhood programs.

Major Orientations for Consultation

Since consultation has been used as a support service in many professional fields, variations have evolved to reflect different theoretical perspectives or orientations.

Idol and West (1987) delineated as many as 10 different types of consultation that have influenced educational practice, six of which have clearly identifiable theory bases. When the focus is specifically on consultation to support inclusive education, three orientations are particularly relevant: mental health consultation, process consultation, and behavioral consultation. Conoley and Conoley (1992) and West and Idol (1987) provide more complete descriptions of these perspectives.

Mental Health Consultation. With the longest history and the most traditional psychological roots, mental health consultation may be considered the prototypic consultation approach (Conoley & Conoley, 1992). Caplan (1970) introduced mental health consultation as a way for psychiatrists to support direct care providers and enhance their effectiveness with clients through discussion and problem solving. According to Caplan, mental health consultation could help teachers, nurses, and others who worked with difficult clients by enhancing their knowledge, skills, and professional objectivity. Contemporary versions of mental health consultation have broadened to include more of a systems perspective. These approaches focus on the reciprocal influences of settings, persons, and interactions and seek interventions to improve dysfunctional systems (Fine, 1985). For school-based professionals, Caplan, Caplan, and Erchul (1995) recommend mental health *collaboration* as a variation of the original mental health consultation. The more collaborative approach recognizes that, as a member of school-based interdisciplinary teams, specialists share equal responsibility for outcomes and often have some direct service responsibilities with students.

Process Consultation. Process consultation aims to improve interpersonal and group procedures used by administrators, teachers, students, and families to reach their educational objectives (Schmuck, 1995). Process consultation focuses more on *how* individuals or groups interact than on the content of their interactions. Consultees increase clients' personal awareness and understanding of problem situations. Together they examine environmental dynamics and explore ways in which these factors affect their work (Schein, 1969). Frequently, educators use a process consultation approach to improve team processes and productivity (Conoley & Conoley, 1992). Process consultation is also used for many strategic planning and systems change efforts. Fundamentals of process consultation are evident in peer coaching, in which experienced coaches (i.e., consultants) provide corrective feedback, communicate new ideas in a positive and nonthreatening manner, stimulate reflective thinking, and facilitate the consultee's own problem-solving and decision-making efforts (Joyce & Showers, 1983).

Behavioral Consultation. Behavioral consultants rely on a highly structured problem-solving process using the principles of applied behavior analysis (Babcock & Pryzwansky, 1983; Gable, Korinek, & McLaughlin, 1997). A primary role of consultants is to facilitate the functional analysis of the situations of concern. Functional analysis is often referred to as *ABC analysis,* because it focuses on the temporal sequence of antecedent events (A), target behaviors (B), and consequences (C) and on determining the function of student behavior in particular settings (e.g., control, attention, avoidance) (Kerr & Nelson, 1998). By recognizing the relationship between student behavior and specific environmental events, consultees are then able to apply appropriate interventions to increase desired behaviors and decrease undesirable behaviors.

The initial stage of the consultation process, sometimes characterized as the behavioral interview (Gable, Friend, Laycock, & Henderson, 1990), is devoted to a definition of the problem in clear behavioral terms. Consultants employ questions or statements to elicit descriptions of the behavior, setting, and evaluation or measurement of the behavior, for example, "When and where does the behavior occur?" "How frequently?" "What events happen just before the behavior?" "How do you and others respond to the behavior?" "What purposes does the behavior appear to serve; that is, what does the student get out of behaving this way?" Through this functional analysis, consultants and consultees clarify understanding of the environmental variables that may contribute to the problem (e.g., assignment difficulty, grouping arrangements, peer interactions, or teacher reactions). Consultants use summary statements to synthesize and review information, and they record it on a worksheet or form. Throughout the interview, consultants communicate empathy with their consultees, and they deflect or redirect credit and responsibility to the consultees.

Following detailed analysis of the problem, consultants and consultees develop intervention plans to change the target behavior by modifying antecedent events and/or consequences. Whenever possible, the aim is to strengthen desirable responses so that students learn more appropriate ways of behaving. Consultants encourage interventions that have been validated through research (Fuchs, Fuchs, & Fernstrom, 1993). Involving students themselves in goal setting, self-monitoring, or peer-mediated behavior change programs as often as possible gives students greater ownership and motivation. In the final stages of consultation sessions, consultants and consultees agree on clearly defined roles and responsibilities to ensure successful implementation, evaluation, and follow-up of the proposed intervention plan.

Collaborative Consultation.   Contemporary approaches to school consultation tend to be more eclectic, drawing primarily from mental health, process, and behavioral origins while accentuating the highly collaborative nature of consultation. Although the problem-solving tasks may be nearly identical to those in other consulting models, the *style* of interaction differs from earlier "expert" models of consultation (Friend & Cook, 1996). Underlying this shift in style of interaction was the recognized need for greater parity among specialists and classroom teachers if consultation were to be effective (Pugach & Johnson, 1995). Collaborative consultation requires the *sharing* of expertise (Dettmer, Dyck, & Thurston, 1996). Although specialists have unique expertise to contribute, they are not in a position to prescribe interventions to be implemented by a colleague. For teachers to feel a sense of ownership of the process, they must be respected as competent and committed professionals. They work most directly with students and bring knowl-

---

Think About It...

Compare and contrast models for colleague consultation. Identify and defend your preference.

---

edge and skills essential to the development of effective intervention plans. The most "user-friendly" forms of consultation encourage consultees to initiate consultations and to maintain control over the nature and extent of services provided, including meeting times, objectives, and timelines for achieving objectives (Ehly & Macmann, 1994). Consultation becomes a collaborative process when participants assume mutual responsibility for defining the problem, designing a plan, and monitoring the effectiveness of the interventions. At certain times as appropriate, consultants may have brief direct involvement with students as classroom observers or co-teachers to gather more information, try out interventions, model techniques, or monitor progress.

The Research Base for Consultation

Consultation has a rich history and is widely recognized as effective for school-based practice. The empirical research base for consultation is slowly accumulating (Fuchs, Fuchs, Dulan, & Roberts, 1992; Sheridan, Welch, & Orme, 1996; West & Idol, 1987). A consistent finding overall is that consultation has produced positive outcomes approximately three-fourths of the time (Mannino & Shore, 1975; Medway, 1979; Sheridan et al., 1996). Improvements have been evident through positive changes in consultee skills and attitudes, student behavior and academic performance, and referral patterns or other system-level indicators.

Theoretical differences and the lack of detail in defining and implementing consultation models have made it more difficult to interpret research findings. The majority of empirical studies have investigated behavioral consultation, and the most beneficial outcomes generally are attributed to the behavioral models (Fuchs et al., 1992). Another model using a highly structured questioning approach to problem solving, peer collaboration, has also demonstrated consistently positive outcomes. Although less widely researched, peer collaboration has been shown to reduce referral rates, increase teacher confidence in handling classroom problems, and expand teacher tolerance for cognitive and social differences (Johnson & Pugach, 1991; Pugach & Johnson, 1995).

Sheridan and colleagues (1996) concluded that well-constructed models with sound theoretical bases may be superior to those without clear conceptual frameworks. Others urge caution noting that research on behavioral consultation may be dominant as a reflection of its empirical roots, but available research may not do justice to the complex realities of school-based consultation (Safran, 1991). More detailed analyses of participants' verbal and nonverbal communication behaviors

(Benes, Gutkin, & Kramer, 1991) and increased use of qualitative case study methodology (Pryzwansky & Noblit, 1990) have been suggested as strategies for extending the research on school-based consultation.

The Collaborative Consultation Process

Most colleague consultation models incorporate a series of basic steps to facilitate the critical thinking and dialogue conducive to effective problem solving. In essence, these problem-solving models are variations of the reflective teaching process introduced in Chapter 4, in that they involve a cycle of planning, acting, describing, and evaluating. Generally, collaborative consultation models entail more than these four basic steps so that the reflective process can be made more explicit for active participation by two or more individuals. In many ways, the problem-solving process for collaborative consultation parallels the process used for assistance teaming described in Chapter 7. The differences are due to the distinctive grouping configurations. The more structured process for assistance teaming helps small groups to function effectively and efficiently; the process for collaborative consultation is slightly more elaborate to allow two participants to engage in more in-depth problem solving.

Different experts offer their own problem-solving sequences for collaborative consultation. Rigid adherence to any one sequence is not likely to prove helpful, because meaningful consultation does not follow a script. In natural settings, it unfolds as a focused conversation between individuals with their own unique needs, communication styles, and personal preferences. Consultation is a dynamic and fluid process, driven by the unique ideas and interactions of the participants involved. What school professionals need is a framework for collaborative consultation that can serve as a general guide for effective and efficient problem solving.

A 10-step process for consultation adapted from the work of Dettmer and colleagues (1996) is presented as a useful framework for collaborative consultation (Figure 8.1). The substeps illustrate what might be accomplished at each phase of the interaction. Not every step occurs in a given meeting; nor do steps always unfold in the suggested order. Again, the steps provide only a general guide to stimulate productive problem-solving interactions.

Preparing for the Consultation

Typically, school professionals initiate the consultation process by requesting assistance from colleagues who have expertise perceived as relevant to their concerns. A fifth-grade teacher, for example, might approach the school psychologist for help with a student who has suddenly become confrontational with adults and peers. Alternatively, she might seek assistance from the teacher for students with visual disabilities when she needs strategies for adapting instruction for a child with limited vision. Friend and Bursuck (1996) encourage teachers to do their homework prior to seeking consultation and to collect samples of student work

FIGURE 8.1   A 10-Step Process for Collaborative Consultation.

1. **Prepare for the consultation**
   - Focus on area of concern.
   - Organize materials.
   - Prepare several possible strategies.
   - Arrange for a comfortable meeting place.

2. **Initiate the consultation**
   - Establish rapport.
   - Focus on the tentatively defined concern.
   - Create collaborative climate.

3. **Collect information**
   - Solicit data and make notes.
   - Identify additional data needs.
   - Summarize information.

4. **Identify the problem**
   - Focus on needs.
   - State what the problem is/is not.
   - Propose desirable circumstances.

5. **Articulate the goal statement**
   - Identify issues, avoiding jargon.
   - Encourage expressions of concerns.
   - Develop a concise goal statement.
   - Check for agreement.

6. **Generate solutions**
   - Problem-solve collaboratively.
   - Generate alternative interventions.
   - Suggest examples.
   - Review options and likely consequences.
   - Select the most reasonable alternative.

7. **Formulate a plan**
   - Specify tasks for chosen intervention.
   - Establish responsibilities.
   - Generate evaluation criteria and methods.
   - Agree on a date for reviewing progress.

8. **Evaluate progress and process**
   - Conduct a review session at specified time.
   - Review data and analyze results.
   - Keep products to document progress.
   - Assess the collaboration process.
   - Make positive, supportive comments.

9. **Follow up on the situation**
   - Reassess progress periodically.
   - Support effort and reinforce results.
   - Continue the plan for further improvement.
   - Make adjustments as necessary.
   - Bring closure if goals have been met.

10. **Repeat consultation as appropriate**
    - Include others as necessary.

Source: From Dettmer, P., Dyck, N., and Thurston, L. (1996). Consultation, collaboration, and teamwork for students with special needs (p. 132). Needham Heights, MA: Simon & Schuster. Adapted with permission.

and other documentation demonstrating their concerns. Consultants should also begin to focus on the general concerns expressed in preparation for the initial meetings. Together, colleagues set times and places to meet free from interruptions and conducive to meaningful discussion.

Initiating the Consultation Session

Consultants usually take the lead in creating comfortable yet focused interactions. If consultees appear relaxed and ready to proceed, only a few introductory comments may be necessary before discussing the agenda for the session. However, consultees who are new to the process, more upset, or resistant to consultation may need more time at this stage. Consultants communicate acceptance and respect most powerfully by listening with care to consultees. It is often helpful for consultants to stress the collaborative nature of the process; that is, the intent of consultation is to work together to support the teacher in meeting the learning and behavioral needs of students. Agreeing on the agenda, that is, what each party hopes to accomplish in the session, is a good way to clarify expectations.

Collecting Information

Often teachers requesting assistance begin with a very general concern. It is not uncommon to hear initial statements such as "George is not doing any of his work in my class" or "Serbrina just can't function in a regular classroom." The role of consultants is to guide consideration of information from a variety of sources that is relevant to the expressed concern without getting bogged down in extraneous data. Meetings can become sidetracked when participants feel compelled to discuss everything that is known about a particular student. Skillful questioning helps to maintain the focus. For example, "Do we have any information that might explain George's poor performance in math?" or "What exactly is happening in class when Serbrina runs out of the room?" Pugach and Johnson (1995b) note that effective facilitators prompt and record questions and answers to ensure that *who, what, when, and where* aspects of the situation are adequately explored. This model of peer collaboration also encourages teachers to stay focused on issues over which they have control (Pugach & Johnson, 1995a).

Defining the Problem

Identifying the real problem is often the most difficult facet of the consultation process, yet it is absolutely critical to effective intervention planning (Bergan, 1995; Bergan & Tombari, 1975). Dettmer and co-workers (1996) emphasize the importance of clarifying what the problem is and what it is not, and they caution against jumping ahead to solutions. The guidelines for problem identification described with reference to assistance teams in Chapter 7 are equally helpful in collaborative consultation. The aim is to target needs that are central to success and possible to change. When teachers feel especially overwhelmed by many perceived needs, consultants can help to focus by posing questions, for example, "As a starting point, can we focus on one particular concern that, realistically, we can address to make a difference for this student?" Consultants can also remind consultees that additional concerns can be addressed in future sessions.

Articulating the Goal Statement

Once the problem is clearly identified, collaborators formulate an intervention goal. A simple prompt from consultants, such as "What would you like to see happen?" often elicits workable goal statements from consultees (Ozer, 1980). Phrasing the goal in clear, behavioral terms is often the greatest challenge. For example, the consultant can help by asking, "What do you want Serbrina to do?" "Under what conditions would you like to see her do this and how will we know when she meets this goal?" As noted earlier, consultation sessions do not follow a linear script. Attempts at this stage to target a manageable goal may evoke feelings of frustration about the student, the problems encountered, and the consultation process itself. Successful consultants recognize and accept consultees' needs to vent strong emotions. By employing effective listening skills (see Chapter 5), consultants can reflect both the feelings and the content communicated by consultees with comments such as, "It's really discouraging to be trying so hard yet seeing so little progress." Consultants with strong communication skills help consultees move through those feelings to more constructive action. It is important for consultants to summarize the goal statements, check for accuracy, and write them down before proceeding to intervention planning.

Earlier in this chapter, a veteran teacher, Carla Taylor, was struggling to help her student, Rachel. She decided to approach the school counselor, Deb Powell, for assistance. What follows is the portion of their consultation session focused on initiating the session, collecting information, defining the problem, and formulating a goal statement.

DEB: When you asked to get together, you sounded so concerned about Rachel. Tell me what's been going on.

CARLA: Well, I've never seen another student just shut down so completely. Over the past few months, I've seen such a dramatic change in Rachel's behavior that she's gone from being a good student who participated well in my class to someone who's hardly there.

DEB: Are you saying that she misses school a lot?

CARLA: Not really. I mean that Rachel seems so distant, like she's physically in class but not much more. But now that you mention it, she has had more unexcused absences over the past 9 weeks as well.

DEB: What seems to account for the changes in Rachel's performance?

CARLA: I honestly don't think it has much to do with school or the class itself. From my conversations with Rachel's mother, I think the family has been going through so many changes...Rachel is such a sensitive kid. I think she's very affected by what's been happening to her and her mother.

DEB: So you think Rachel's reacting to things that are happening at home?

CARLA: Yes. Mrs. Burns told me that her divorce 3 years ago was very hard on Rachel. She has not had much contact with her dad because he had moved to Ohio. When Mrs. Burns's boyfriend moved out, Rachel's dad came back into the picture. Rachel must feel pulled in so many directions. She and her mother are very close. Mrs. Burns admitted to me that she was not doing well herself, and I suspect that Rachel is being protective of her mother.

DEB: What a tough situation for a kid!

CARLA: It's so frustrating to watch. When everything else seems to be falling apart for Rachel, I just hate to see her losing out in school as well.

DEB: It's not hard to see how much you care about her. Rachel's lucky you're her teacher.

CARLA: Thanks. I can use some encouragement about now.

DEB: As you described the changes in Rachel over the past few months, I couldn't help wondering about possible abuse at home. Do you think that might be an issue?

CARLA: It's crossed my mind, but only because of the sudden behavior change. I've tried to pay close attention but haven't seen any physical evidence, and neither Rachel nor her mother have ever said anything to make me suspect abuse. I was very glad to learn from Mrs. Burns the other day that they have started family counseling. Hopefully, the counselor will explore the whole situation and help them begin to work things out.

DEB: That is good news. If they can get some professional support on the home front, it will allow us to focus more on Rachel's performance in school. Carla, are there any other factors that might explain why Rachel is having difficulty?

CARLA: Not that I can think of. Rachel has the ability—she has always been an average to high average student and, earlier in the school year, she had decent study skills.

DEB: As I reviewed her records, there was no evidence of problems prior to this year. She seems to have been making fine progress.

CARLA: Actually, I've talked with John, Rachel's teacher last year, to see if he could offer any insights, but he was surprised to learn that Rachel is having difficulty.

DEB: What about Rachel's relationships with her peers? How does she get along with the other students?

CARLA: She's never been especially outgoing, but she had several close friends. In my class, she and Donna and Ganine were pretty close. To their credit, the girls have been trying to support Rachel, but she's not having much to do with anybody these days.

DEB: Carla, you've talked in general terms about Rachel's "shutting down." Help me understand exactly what that means. What does Rachel do?

CARLA: It's definitely not a case of Rachel disturbing anybody else. When I say she shuts down…she just seems totally uninvolved in what's going on in class. Sometimes she puts her head down, but usually she just sits there—not participating.

DEB: Like she's not connecting with the people and activities around her.

CARLA: You got it. She doesn't join in group work; she doesn't raise her hand; and if I call on her, she just looks blank or shrugs it off.

DEB: What happens when you try to talk with her? Has she shared her side of things?

CARLA: Believe me, I've tried. I thought we had a good relationship. But recently, as I've approached her in class to encourage her participation or after class to talk privately, she just says she doesn't want to.

DEB: So Rachel's not ready to talk about it at this point.

CARLA: Another thing related to her shutting down. She has stopped doing homework and other assignments. I haven't gotten anything from her in weeks, and it is really affecting her grades. I want to be supportive but she has to give me something to work with.

DEB: It's discouraging to watch her failing when you know she has the capability to do so much better.

CARLA: So what can I *do* about all this?

DEB: As you've described it, Rachel has stopped participating in class and is not completing her classwork or homework. She seems to be reacting to some really stressful changes at home. The family has just started counseling, and you want to do whatever you can to improve Rachel's school performance.

CARLA: Exactly.

DEB: You have several different concerns, but can we focus on one specific goal as a starting point? What might interrupt Rachel's nose dive and begin to get her back on track as a student?

CARLA: Hmm…She's got to start doing some work. We could begin with the homework issue, because she would be able to do much better in class if she were keeping up with her homework assignments.

DEB: That's true. Any other goals that come to mind?

CARLA: Well, another major issue is participating in class. If she would join in and do some work, then she might see some progress and start getting decent grades again.

DEB: Any other possibilities?

CARLA: No, I don't think so.

DEB: You have two good goal possibilities: homework or class participation. Does one make more sense than the other as our initial priority?

CARLA: As I think about it, with so much instability at home, it might be hard to target homework as our priority right now. It is important though… can I come back to that later?

DEB: Certainly. I agree that class participation seems like the appropriate goal for now. Let's talk specifically about your expectations. What *exactly* do you want Rachel to do?

CARLA: Everything!

DEB: Of course, but considering her performance in recent weeks, what's realistic to expect?

CARLA: If she would only participate in the *major* projects, it would make such a difference.

DEB: So what are those?

CARLA: For the remainder of the semester, for example, a good percentage of her grade in social studies will hinge on the cooperative learning group project. If she doesn't get involved in that, she is likely to end up with a failing grade. If she did a good job, she could end up with a "C."

DEB: Participation in the group project sounds like a very workable goal.

CARLA: What I like about this goal is that it may accomplish two purposes. It will help Rachel to get back on track academically, and it will help her reconnect with some of her peers.

DEB: Good, let's go with it, but we'll have to be a little more specific about what "participation" means. Again, what *exactly* must Rachel do?

CARLA: I'd like her to take an active role, to contribute to group discussion, come through with the tasks she takes on…That's a lot, huh?

DEB: They're all reasonable expectations, but we need to focus on the most important ways for her to participate—and it would be helpful to define behaviors that we can observe and measure.

CARLA: Well, for the cooperative projects, each student agrees to take on at least one specific role. I guess the most concrete evidence of Rachel's participation would be completion of the task for which she's responsible.

DEB: Defining that as the outcome would work well. My only concern is that we are left with only one measure and it may come at the very end of the group experience. Are there any other indicators of participation?

CARLA: Well, I could try to observe how much she talks and contributes to the group. But in all honesty, I don't think I can do that while I'm monitoring the different groups in my class.

DEB: That does require some systematic observation. Is there any other way of monitoring Rachel's participation.

CARLA: Here's an idea. Sometimes when we use cooperative learning groups, I ask students periodically to complete self and team evaluations. It's a way of monitoring that involves the kids. Maybe we could have everyone do that regularly, and it would provide the information we need about Rachel. It's a simple checklist about how they participated. If Rachel made some contribution even half of the time, I'd be pleased for now.

DEB: Yes, and I like the way this requires her to reflect and keep track of her own behavior.

CARLA: Let me give you a copy of the form that I have used with groups in the past, and you might be able to suggest some ways to make it work even better for our purposes.

DEB: Sure, I'd be glad to do that. Now let's take a minute and make sure we can capture our goal in one clear statement: Rachel will participate in the social studies cooperative learning group by taking an active role in the majority of sessions and by completing her task for the group project.

CARLA: That's good.

Generating Solutions

Thorough discussion of the problem in steps 3, 4, and 5 generally stimulates the process of generating creative interventions. If the problem has been identified correctly and an appropriate goal has been selected, most teachers are ready to move on to solutions. It is critical at this point not to revert to an expert version of consultation, which can happen if consultants jump into—or are drawn into—prescribing solutions for the consultees. To ensure ownership by consultees, it often helps to have those who requested assistance be the first to offer some ideas. This can be done through brainstorming as described in Chapter 7. As long as consultees are actively contributing, consultants are free to offer additional ideas. Generating possible solutions is a shared responsibility, and all suggestions should be recorded verbatim.

In some instances, consultees have difficulty coming up with intervention ideas. It may help for the consultants to structure the process a little differently. Ozer (1980) recommended that teachers build on past successes when attempting to identify new interventions. Thinking about what has worked with the student in other situations often stimulates adaptations appropriate for the immediate goal. For example, the consultant might ask George's teacher, "What have you found helpful in working with George in other areas? In those instances when he experienced some success, what exactly were you doing that may have enabled that to happen? Are there some approaches that seem effective in those situations that we might apply here?" Both consultants and consultees may begin by writing down at least three intervention ideas that might be effective for this goal. If each idea is written on an index card, participants can share them and have a ready-made list of interventions to rearrange later in priority order.

Formulating a Plan

With the problem and intervention goal clearly identified and a list of alternative strategies generated, consultees and consultants are equipped to develop the

Think About It...

Review the vignette about Rachel and identify the specific steps of the collaborative consultation process within the dialogue between Carla, the teacher, and Deb, the school counselor.

intervention plan. Like any other plan, this should specify *who will do what, when, and where.* In collaborative consultation as in assistance teaming, the persons seeking help select solutions that seem most appropriate for their particular situations. As one way of actively engaging teachers in selecting interventions, Pugach and Johnson (1995b) suggest having them select three of the most promising ideas and predict what is likely to happen when these are implemented in the classroom. Typically, one strategy emerges as having the greatest potential for success. Consultants should encourage teachers to play out the intervention in very specific terms, so that it becomes evident exactly what the teacher will do and whether any special assistance or materials are required.

Part of the planning process requires specification of the criteria and methods for evaluating progress and outcomes. If the team has defined a truly measurable goal during step 5, then this task is not difficult. The suggestions in Chapter 7 for establishing reasonable criteria for success and manageable ways of collecting student performance data are as applicable to collaborative consultation as they are to assistance teaming. It is important that teachers plan to collect on a regular basis the information about student performance to determine to what extent the target goals are actually being achieved. On occasion, consultants may support teachers by also collecting observational data. Caution is advised once again, for the aim is to design intervention and evaluation strategies that teachers can reasonably implement in their classrooms.

As in assistance teaming, it is important to record the decisions made during consultation in a useful format that will guide implementation and monitoring. No one form meets everyone's needs; generally consultants and consultees write up their plans in formats that they find most straightforward and helpful for their own purposes. An example of the intervention plan completed by Carla Taylor and Deb Powell to address the concerns about Rachel Burns is provided in Figure 8.2. Note how the initial concerns, the identified problem, and the goal statement defined in their earlier dialogue are captured on the consultation worksheet. Carla and Deb continued their problem-solving meeting and generated alternative ideas for interventions, which they also recorded on the form. Carla chose to combine two suggestions in her plan, and she and Deb clarified their responsibilities for implementation and evaluation. Most consultation meetings, including the example with Carla and Deb, conclude with consultants briefly reviewing major points of the plan and facilitating agreement on when to meet again for follow-up. Copies of the complete intervention plan, such as the worksheet in Figure 8.2, should be provided for all participants.

Evaluating Progress and Process

Collaborative consultation does not end at the conclusion of the problem-solving meeting. The ultimate success of the consultation effort hinges on the effective implementation of the plan in the classroom or other school settings. Consultees and consultants touch base frequently to update one another on implementation

FIGURE 8.2   A Collaborative Consultation Worksheet.

Initiator:	Carla Taylor	**Facilitator:**	Deb Powell
Date(s):	November 12	**Time(s):**	3:15

Initial concern(s): A dramatic change in Rachel Burns's behavior—she has shut down and is not participating in class, not interacting with her teacher and classmates, and not doing any homework. Rachel has ability but is in danger of failing.

Identified problem: Rachel has stopped participating in class and is not completing classwork or homework. She seems to be reacting to stressful changes at home.

Goal statement: Rachel will participate in the social studies cooperative learning group by taking an active role in the majority of sessions and by completing her tasks for the group project.

Potential solutions: (Use the reverse side if necessary)

Include Rachel's friends in her cooperative learning group.
Allow Rachel to select the group she wants to work with.
Assign a peer partner.
Allow Rachel to opt out of a few group sessions if she chooses.
Have Rachel earn time with the teacher if she actively participates in the group.
Maintain contact with Mrs. Burns to encourage continued family counseling.

Selected intervention(s): Assign Rachel to the group that includes Donna and Ganine, two of her friends who can be supportive in a gentle way. Make an agreement with Rachel that if she participates actively in three cooperative learning sessions, she can earn a "pass" that allows her a session when she doesn't have to take an active role. She can use her passes whenever she feels like it.

Responsibilities: Carla will assign the social studies projects, form the cooperative learning groups, and monitor the participation self-checks and the completed group work. Deb will review the self-check form and suggest modifications if needed. Deb will also be the primary contact with Mrs. Burns regarding family counseling.

Evaluation method(s): Rachel will complete a participation self-check following each cooperative learning session. She and Carla will tally her progress and passes. Together, they will review her contribution to the final group project.

Follow-up strategies: Carla and Deb will meet briefly in 2 weeks to review preliminary progress. They will evaluate the plan at the end of the semester.

issues. Together, they review student performance data and determine the progress made. When evidence indicates improvement, there is the opportunity to reinforce the teachers' investment in the process and to celebrate shared success.

Participants should also spend time reflecting on the consultation process—what has been helpful and what might be improved on for future interactions. As trust develops over time, the partners become more comfortable sharing their perceptions and giving constructive feedback. Initially, consultants can prompt the evaluation process through questions, such as "What did you find most helpful as we worked together?" "What were the rough spots?" and "How could I be of greater help in future consults?"

Following Up on the Consultation

Although often neglected, this phase of the process is critical for sustaining teacher commitment and student progress. Partners may decide to meet periodically to reassess the situation, analyze trends in student performance, and make whatever adjustments are necessary in the program. It is important to continue to document changes in the plan and student performance data. When problems are persistent or complex, it is helpful to schedule additional meetings as follow-up sessions. In other instances in which problems have been alleviated, the consultant may simply check with the consultee at regular intervals. Experienced consultants may be actively engaged in follow-up interactions throughout the school day—in the hall before the students arrive, between classes, over lunch, and before the faculty meeting. This type of consultation "on the run" can be an efficient mode of follow-up only when sufficient time has been spent initially identifying the problem and developing a sound intervention plan. These miniconsults do not substitute for the more intensive, focused problem solving that is fundamental to the collaborative consultation process.

When intervention goals have been attained and student performance has stabilized at the desired level, partners can reach closure through mutual agreement. Typically, consultants express their openness to future interactions with comments, such as "I look forward to following George's progress" or "Let me know if I can be of any further assistance."

During the second scheduled follow-up meeting, Carla reported that, after getting off to a great start, Rachel's performance had leveled off with her actively participating in approximately 40% of the cooperative group sessions. As Carla monitored the teams in class, she had noticed that Rachel seemed to be off-task several times, talking quietly with Ganine while the rest of the group was working on their project. Although she was pleased to see Rachel interacting with peers, her conversations during group work were not helping her academically.

Carla and Deb discussed this new development. One of the intervention strategies proposed at their initial planning meeting had been assignment of a peer partner for Rachel. At their school, peer partners were student volunteers who had received special preparation to listen and provide support to other students in need. Although Carla and Deb had not selected this intervention at first, they agreed that it might be helpful now. Deb took responsibility for finding Rachel a peer partner as soon as possible.

Repeating Consultation If Necessary

Through regular follow-up interactions, both consultants and consultees are fully informed about the student progress being achieved. Recycling through all or part of the consultation process may be appropriate when there is little or no improvement in target behaviors after reasonable intervention periods. Partners need to encourage each other to try again. Sometimes it takes several attempts before effective intervention plans can be devised. After several intervention cycles, it may become clear that certain specialists or family members are needed on the team, and partners may agree to include other individuals who can contribute new perspectives to effective problem solving.

Many teachers choose to repeat the consultation process even when they have experienced success. If they began the process with many different concerns about a particular student, they may want to tackle another issue after the first has been resolved. Serbrina's teacher, for example, decided to work on a second intervention goal related to peer interaction. Carla Taylor asked to work on Rachel's homework completion once her family situation stabilized and her class participation improved.

Essential Consultative Skills

Advocates for consultation recognize that the process demands a high level of professional competence. Idol and West (1987) have compared effective consultation to effective teaching as applications of "artful science." Yet both the scientific and artful bases of consultation differ from those of teaching, and the two roles remain distinctive. Not every professional effective in the provision of direct service to students is equally effective as a consultant. Specifically, Idol (1990) characterized the bases of consultation as both scientific and artful. The scientific base is the content or knowledge base that the consultant brings to the consulting process. This knowledge base is usually the primary reason that a particular individual is consulted. The artful base of consultation is the way in which the consultant works with consultees to solve problems. This base is often referred to as the process skills of consultation.

Content Expertise

The content or knowledge base—what Idol described as the "scientific base" for consultation—is derived from research and professional practice. Chapters 11 and 12 address key instructional and prosocial strategies within the knowledge base that should be shared by general and special educators. Additionally, the knowledge base for each field of specialization (e.g., elementary teaching, counseling, physical therapy, school psychology, special education) includes the content unique to that discipline. The collective expertise of the different professionals in school settings, therefore, enables educators to address nearly all of their concerns effectively.

A first step in mobilizing this expertise is recognizing its existence. Figure 8.3 provides a list of professionals available within most school districts who have the specific expertise to serve as consultants when particular concerns arise. The list of common concerns and potential consultants is not intended to be exhaustive or prescriptive; it simply illustrates the many different sources of consultant support available. Although specialized expertise is generally associated with each discipline, other factors such as background, experience, and interest also determine a person's helpfulness for specific needs. When problems are more serious and complex, school-based professionals may also access consultative support from

FIGURE 8.3   Examples of Professional Expertise Relevant to Student Concerns.

Concerns	School Colleagues with Special Expertise
General education curriculum	Classroom teachers, lead teachers, mentor teachers, curriculum supervisors/specialists, principals
Learning difficulties	School psychologists, special educators, classroom teachers
Reading difficulties	Reading specialists, special educators
Behavior management	School psychologists, special educators, guidance counselors, classroom teachers
Language skills	Speech and language specialists, bilingual educators
Alternative communication skills	Special educators for hearing or visual disabilities, assistive technology specialists
Independent living	Special educators, transition specialists, occupational therapists, assistive technology specialists
Motor skills	Physical educators, physical therapists, occupational therapists, assistive technology specialists
Social adjustment	Guidance counselors, classroom teachers, special educators, school psychologists
Career/vocational skills	Vocational educators, vocational assessment specialists, transition specialists, guidance counselors
Orientation/mobility skills	Orientation and mobility specialists
Health issues	School nurses, physical education teachers

professionals in other agencies, such as social services, corrections, mental health, and others to comprise a comprehensive services team.

Process Expertise

The ability to use content knowledge within collaborative interactions with colleagues is the process or "artful" dimension of consultation. Despite the variety of consultation approaches, certain skills are considered central to collaborative problem solving. West and Cannon (1988) identified and validated essential collaborative consultation competencies needed by both general and special educators interacting to meet the educational needs of students in classrooms. Using the Delphi technique (explained in Chapter 5), a 100-member interdisciplinary, expert panel identified 47 specific competencies as essential to the consultation process. The competencies clustered into eight categories: (1) consultation theory/models; (2) research on consultation theory, training, and practice; (3) personal characteristics; (4) interactive communication; (5) collaborative problem solving; (6) systems change; (7) equity issues, values, and belief systems; and (8) evaluation of consultation effectiveness.

Thomas and colleagues (1995) noted that specific preparation to develop consultation competencies typically is included in programs for health and medical practitioners, school psychologists, and counselors, but such preparation is less often provided for special educators and is even more limited for general educators. Until more preservice preparation programs adequately prepare professionals for consultative roles, most teachers and specialists will need additional staff development to help them acquire important consultative skills. Many of the practices associated with effective staff development described in Chapters 2 and 3 apply to the acquisition of consultative skills. As noted earlier, educators need continual opportunities for guided practice, reflection, and feedback in order to develop the essential competencies for collaborative problem solving. The strategies suggested in Chapter 5 to refine basic communication skills are also helpful, since those skills are critical to collaborative consultation.

Educators who have experienced consultation as a collaborative process are sometimes reluctant to seek support from specialists who may approach consultation from an "expert" perspective. Yet, at times, the need for particular content expertise may outweigh the concerns about a truly collaborative orientation. For example, a teacher may need to consult with the physical therapist, even though she finds the individual more prescriptive than collaborative. Knowledge of the collaborative problem-solving process can equip teachers and other school professionals to be more educated consumers of consultation and to take more responsibility for the consultative interaction. Teachers should feel free, for instance, to structure the consultative process in ways that are helpful to them. It is perfectly appropriate for a teacher to begin the process by saying, "I would really like to work with you to plan some more effective ways of positioning Carol for group activities. Let's think this through together to devise some strategies that I can use in my classroom." Comments like these help clarify the teacher's expectations, establish parity in the relationship, and set the stage for shared responsibility. If later in the process, the specialist begins to prescribe solutions, the teacher can reinforce her right to choose the interventions that she will use in her class with statements such as, "Those are great ideas. Thank you. What I think would work best for me and my students is…" or "This has been really helpful, but I need some time to think about which strategy to implement in my classroom." In this manner, consultees can shape a more collaborative interaction to meet their needs.

Chapter Summary

Consultation has evolved over many decades as an effective means of providing indirect support for teachers and other professionals who request assistance as they work directly with students exhibiting special needs. Contemporary approaches to collaborative consultation are rooted in the traditions of mental health, process, and behavioral consultation. Although the specific steps may vary, collaborative consultation is essentially a problem-solving interaction in which partners share responsibility for problem identification, goal setting, intervention planning, evaluation of student progress, and follow-up. Effective consultation is both a science and an art that requires application of specialized professional knowledge through highly interactive dialogue between colleagues. Within a school district and the broader system of human service agencies, educators have access to a range of consultants who can contribute important expertise to the improvement of programs for students with disabilities and other special needs.

CHAPTER ACTIVITIES

1. Interview several teachers and other school professionals to learn their impressions of the consultation process. How often have they accessed consultative support? What have they found particularly helpful? What recommendations would they offer you to make the best use of consultative support?

2. Focus on a specific school setting, perhaps your current place of employment or a setting where you would like to be employed. Construct a resource list with names, titles, contact information, and areas of expertise for individuals who might serve as consultants.

3. Think about your own area(s) of expertise. As a result of your education, personal and professional experiences, interests, talents, and skills, what special perspectives would you be able to contribute as a consultant for one of your colleagues?

9 Meeting Student Needs through Co-Teaching

LEARNING OBJECTIVES

1. Describe the co-teaching process.
2. Summarize the characteristics of effective co-teachers.
3. Describe some of the roles and responsibilities of co-teachers.
4. Explain four effective co-teaching format variations and appropriate applications of each.
5. Discuss key components of effective co-planning.

Many visitors to Quincy Komalen and LeTeisha Brown's science class have difficulty determining who is the "real" teacher. They enjoy this comment and report that, as co-teachers, they work hard to achieve this level of role equity in the eyes of their students, families, and visitors—and to a certain degree, themselves. These efforts are evident on entering their classroom. Both names appear on the door, on the chalkboard, and on all materials sent home with students. Both teachers have desks in the room, as well as demonstration tables. Hanging on the wall near their desks both have family photos, framed diplomas, and pennants from their favorite sports teams to help their students get to know each of them better.

Quincy and LeTeisha agree their success as co-teachers is based in large measure on their shared commitment to high-quality teaching, each person's unique contribution to the team's effectiveness, and the willingness they had to "hang in there" during their first year of co-teaching. "It was truly the pits!" LeTeisha laughed. "We both felt like beginning teachers all over again. Co-teaching with Quincy was awkward and embarrassing. It was just weird having another adult in the classroom, hanging around—watching and listening to every goofy thing I said or did." Quincy agreed that it was difficult but noted that, "Every month got a little easier for us but the awkwardness and extra time it took to plan together lasted a long time. At first neither of us knew what we were supposed to do. In the beginning we were way too nice to each other. Then, about December, the honeymoon was over and we had to learn how to resolve natural differences that existed between us in philosophy, professional training, discipline, and so forth. But we kept trying to make the arrangement work because we could tell so quickly that working together was good for our kids."

As noted in earlier chapters, co-teaching involves two or more professionals teaching together on an ongoing basis for at least part of most school days (Cook & Friend, 1995). This model is used frequently by general and special education teachers to support students with disabilities and other at-risk students within general education classrooms. Most partners co-teach daily during instructional periods when identified students have the most difficulty. For example, in most elementary and many middle school programs, co-teachers work together during language arts and/or math periods. In high schools, co-teaching often expands to include courses required for graduation (e.g., algebra, English, health, world history), specialized vocational training programs (e.g., computer-assisted drawing, automotive mechanics, electronics), or other less academic but important skill development areas (e.g., career education, home economics, SAT preparation, and driver's education). Some co-teachers work together on a more limited basis. School counselors, school psychologists, and health educators often co-teach more focused, time-limited units with general educators to address various social and health-related issues. For example, middle school educators might co-teach a unit on self-advocacy or substance abuse prevention twice a week for a 45-minute period during the course of a semester.

Veteran co-teachers report that the first year of teaching and planning together is the most difficult; co-planning and co-teaching get easier and more refined as partners become more familiar with their shared classroom, curriculum content, students' needs, and partner's style (Walther-Thomas, 1997a). During the first year together, most co-teachers report that they work hard laying the groundwork for their partnership. In the second year, they enjoy the benefits of their labor. By the third year, co-teachers talk more about their co-planning and co-teaching efforts as "enhancing" the content (Walther-Thomas, 1997a).

Co-teaching enriches learning opportunities for all students by targeting students with unique learning needs and many peers who struggle in school but fail to qualify for extra help. Co-teachers share their unique perspectives with partners based on previous education, teaching experience, and expertise. Differences between partners' skills allow them to view the same classroom situation from different vantage points.

Ideally, school-level planning teams arrange professional schedules so that co-teaching partners work together for 2 or 3 years before new partner assignments are made. This means that many co-teachers work together at least one period a day for several years. Over time teams develop their co-teaching "rhythm" as they learn from each other and establish effective classroom roles and routines. Specialists also learn more about the general education content, and they develop better large-group strategies for instruction and classroom management. General educators often learn more about learning problems that students with disabilities and other low-achieving students experience. They also develop more effective strategies for individualizing instruction and improving group learning and performance.

It is unlikely that most school systems will ever have the resources to provide specialists for co-teaching in every general education classroom. Consequently, many school planning teams may find it necessary to rotate co-teaching partners every 2 or 3 years. Although co-teachers who find their work satisfying may be reluctant to change partners, periodic reassignments allow more students, teachers, and specialists to benefit from co-teaching. New assignments also provide opportunities for experienced co-teachers to share their knowledge and skills with others who are interested but inexperienced with the process or who may be new to the system.

This chapter describes the basics of co-teaching. Following a brief historical review of co-teaching, major characteristics of effective co-teachers are described. Next, key roles and responsibilities of co-teachers are presented. Finally, effective strategies for initiating co-teaching, designing appropriate support services, and planning instruction together are provided.

Historical Background

Co-teaching is not a new concept in education. For example, this teaching approach was popular in the 1960s and early 1970s when "open plan" schools were in vogue. During that time, geodesic dome architecture was used in many communities to create open-space schools that consisted of a series of learning "pods." In many schools, walls between classrooms were minimal or nonexistent as planners hoped that the open physical environment would facilitate increased professional teamwork and collaboration (Cohen, 1973; Trump, 1966). Unfortunately, most team teachers were not ready for their new assignments; they lacked the professional preparation, planning time, and coaching needed to create lasting relationships (Dickinson & Erb, 1997).

Just when team teaching was fading from the general education scene, it appeared briefly in special education literature as a strategy for facilitating early "mainstreaming" efforts following the passage of Public Law 94–142 (Garvar & Papanla, 1982). These early recommendations had little impact on actual classroom practice and special education service delivery. As pull-out programs lost favor, co-teaching resurfaced as a structure for facilitating professional collaboration and providing students and their teachers with direct classroom support (Bauwens & Hourcade, 1995; Friend & Cook, 1996; Walther-Thomas, Bryant, & Land, 1996). Although research regarding the efficacy of co-teaching is limited, the emerging data suggest benefits for identified students, their peers, and the professionals who serve them (Bauwens, Hourcade, & Friend, 1989; Boudah, 1994; Friend, Reisling, & Cook, 1993; Walther-Thomas, 1997a).

> ## Think About It...
>
> How can co-teaching help students with mild disabilities? How about students with more significant support needs? How can it help other students (e.g., gifted, typical, at risk) perform more successfully?

Walther-Thomas (1997a) studied 25 schools over a 3-year period as they implemented co-teaching models. Teachers and principals reported many benefits for students and professionals. Specifically, students with disabilities developed better attitudes about themselves and others; that is, they became less critical, more motivated, and more skilled in recognizing their own academic and social strengths. Their social skills improved, positive peer relationships developed, and many showed positive academic gains as well. As a result, fewer identified students were removed from their general education classrooms because of their inability to cope with academic or social demands. Many other low-achieving students also showed academic and social skills improvement in co-taught classes.

Participants in this study attributed improvement among these students to more teacher time and attention. Reduced pupil–teacher ratios facilitated better progress monitoring, more individual assistance, reteaching, and enrichment opportunities. Many general educators in this study reported a greater "sense of community" as their classrooms became more inclusive. Benefits for professionals included opportunities for professional growth, personal support, and enhanced motivation for teaching as a result of their co-teaching experiences (Walther-Thomas, 1997a).

Effective Co-Teaching Teams

In this section six common characteristics of effective co-teaching teams are described. These fundamental characteristics are recognized as important factors in the lasting success of co-teaching teams (Bauwens & Hourcade, 1995; Friend & Cook, 1996; Walther-Thomas, 1997a). The unique characteristics of co-teachers discussed here build on the generic characteristics of effective collaborators presented in Chapter 6.

Highly Skilled Professionals

Effective co-teachers take pride in themselves and are strongly committed to their professional growth. This attitude is reflected in their planning, preparation, and overall teaching skills. Effective co-teaching relationships provide excellent opportunities for partners to share their expertise, cultivate new skills, and refine existing ones (Walther-Thomas, 1997b). Co-teachers value their own efforts and provide strong support for the efforts of their colleagues. Consequently, it is important for administrators and planning teams to remember that co-teaching should not be used for teacher remediation. To be successful, both partners must possess well-honed professional skills and positive attitudes about co-teaching.

Shared Beliefs, Responsibilities, and Recognition

Co-teachers believe that students with disabilities and other students with unique learning needs have the right to learn with their typical peers. They also believe that *all* students in the classroom are their students. Initial questions about classroom responsibilities related to "my students" versus "your students" quickly disappear in effective classrooms where the available professional resources are used to help every class member succeed.

Effective co-teachers share all major responsibilities for planning, delivering, and evaluating classroom instruction during the instructional periods they teach together (Walther-Thomas et al., 1996). Individually and as a team, they manage and maintain the classroom, teach new concepts, monitor individual and group practice, provide individual assistance, and communicate progress to students and others.

Effective co-teachers must share classroom status, power, and authority. Both must feel comfortable and supported in making judgment calls as needed. Specialists must not be perceived as assistants. During their verbal interactions in class, in daily roles and responsibilities, and in behind-the-scene dialogues, co-teachers must convey to themselves and others that they are a team that respects and values each other's contributions.

Complementary Professional Skills

Working as equal partners may not mean that co-teachers perform exactly the same roles and responsibilities. In many elementary and middle school programs, for example, it is easy to "blur" role distinctions between general educators and special educators during basic reading, writing, and math instruction. Classroom observers may be unable to determine who is the general educator in these settings. Both teachers are actively engaged in instruction and supervision, and the instructional lead changes frequently.

However, in many middle school and almost all high school programs, it is a very different story, as each person's contribution to the content is easier to discern. For example, general educators possess specific content knowledge related to upper-level classes they teach (e.g., geometry, earth science, drama, art). Therefore, they are usually responsible for the team's subject matter. Typical secondary special educators have well-developed skills related to learning strategies, study skills, social skills, and self-monitoring techniques; consequently, they take the lead in developing the team's focus and direction related to these topics. Working together, effective secondary teams provide their students with rich academic content and advanced learning strategy instruction. Once decisions are made about the instructional leadership in secondary programs, co-teachers share the remaining roles and responsibilities in a manner very similar to co-teaching teams at lower grade levels.

Shared Resources and Other Symbols of Professional Status

Very few schools have enough resources. In many locations, classroom resources (e.g., extra student books, teachers' manuals, computers, paper, duplication privileges, paraeducator support) are highly valued commodities and often available in limited supply. Effective co-teachers quickly learn to share their resources with one another and combine resources for the good of all their students. Effective partners also share fundamental symbols of recognition that convey professional status and authority in the classroom. It is important for both partners to feel at home in their classroom. Consequently, both need dedicated space in the classroom (e.g., desk, blackboard access, bulletin boards, roll book access and use, storage) to signify their respect for each other, their involvement in the classroom, and their contributions. Also, both co-teachers' names should appear on the classroom door as well as on all documents that class members, administrators, and families receive (e.g., homework assignments, progress reports, grade sheets). Correspondence from the principal and staff should clearly communicate the school's commitment to ongoing professional collaboration and inform families that all specialists are actively involved in classroom teaching and learning.

Co-Teaching Roles and Responsibilities

Effective co-teachers work together in many ways to make the most of their teaching partnership. Initially, partners are likely to feel more comfortable performing certain classroom preparation and teaching duties than others. Despite the temptation to divide up responsibilities and keep these assignments over time, it is important, especially for new co-teaching teams, to share all responsibilities and create dynamic roles that will motivate participating teachers as well as foster continued professional development.

In this section, four basic dimensions of co-teaching roles and responsibilities are described. In essence, co-teachers (1) plan and teach together; (2) develop instructional accommodations; (3) monitor and evaluate student performance; and (4) communicate student progress to others.

Think About It...

What can school leaders do to help teachers and specialists develop the essential characteristics of effective co-teachers?

Planning and Teaching Together

Ideally, co-teachers participate actively in planning, teaching, and evaluating student performance. In most co-taught classrooms, both teachers introduce and teach new content, conduct review sessions, assign and supervise in-class and homework practice activities, and administer and evaluate tests. For example, on Mondays, Wednesdays, and Fridays, Anita Gomez, an eighth-grade language arts teacher, introduces new material, while her co-teaching partner, Kip Nelson, a reading specialist, provides related warm-up and wrap-up activities. On Tuesdays and Thursdays, they reverse their roles. Every day they both participate in skill modeling, role playing, monitoring, and supervision. They also divide their preparation responsibilities (e.g., materials development, modifications, duplication, homework correction) equally on the basis of such considerations as student needs, professional expertise, time available, and other competing responsibilities.

In many secondary programs, content specialists, such as calculus teachers or American history teachers, teach the new concepts, while learning specialists, such as learning disabilities teachers, Title I reading teachers, or gifted educators, teach related study skills and learning strategies to help all of the students, especially those with learning difficulties, learn new skills and content more successfully. Specialists may also lead daily review and reteach sessions on previously taught concepts. For example, Ned Craigmiles, a ninth-grade field biology teacher, always teaches the new science concepts, such as mitosis and photosynthesis, whereas Bonnie Bauserman, his co-teaching partner, always teaches the learning strategy or study skill as her part of their lessons. Skills and strategies to help students perform more successfully (e.g., three-column note taking, textbook usage, test preparation) have been paired with specific science units, such as recycling, habitat preservation, and bioethics. Both teachers supervise lab work, conduct review sessions, prepare tests, and develop projects.

Co-teaching offers opportunities for teachers to use a variety of large- and small-group teaching strategies. Four basic co-teaching format variations exist, each with its unique characteristics as well as potential advantages and pitfalls: interactive teaching, station teaching, parallel teaching, and alternative teaching (Figure 9.1 on page 190). Each of these variations are discussed briefly in the next sections. One lesson may involve more than one variation. This is especially true in secondary classes, in which 90-minute blocks of time are common. The object is to vary the format to meet student needs and to keep teachers and specialists from defining their teaching roles in a narrow and restrictive manner.

Interactive Teaching.   Through interactive teaching, both partners have opportunities to share the teaching "stage" in the classroom. Alternating the instructional lead for short periods of time (5 to 10 minutes), both partners have multiple opportunities during a lesson to serve as the lead teacher and the support teacher, respectively. The lead changes regularly and dialogue between teaching partners flows throughout the period.

FIGURE 9.1   Variations of Co-Teaching: Advantages and Disadvantages.

Variation	Advantages	Disadvantages
Interactive Teaching (Whole group) Partners alternate roles presenting new concepts, reviewing, demonstrating, role playing, and monitoring.	• Provides systematic observation/data collection • Promotes role/content sharing • Facilitates individual assistance • Models appropriate academic, social, and help-seeking behaviors • Teaches question asking • Provides clarification (e.g., concepts, rules, vocabulary)	• May be job sharing, not learning enriching • Requires considerable planning • Requires modeling and role-playing skills • Becomes easy to "typecast" specialist with this role
Station Teaching (Small group) Students in groups of three or more rotate to various teacher-led and independent workstations where new instruction, review, and/or practice is provided. Students may work at all stations during the rotation.	• Provides active learning format • Increases small-group attention • Encourages cooperation and independence • Allows strategic grouping • Increases response rate	• Requires considerable planning and preparation • Increases noise level • Requires group and independent work skills • Is difficult to monitor
Parallel Teaching (Small group) Students are divided into mixed-ability groups, then each partner teaches a group. The same material is presented in each group.	• Provides effective review format • Encourages student responses • Reduces pupil–teacher ratio for group instruction/review	• Not easy to achieve equal depth of content coverage • May be difficult to coordinate • Requires monitoring of partner pacing • Increases noise level • Encourages some teacher–student competition
Alternative Teaching (Big group; small group) One partner teaches an enrichment lesson or reteaches a concept for the benefit of a small group, while the other partner teaches and/or monitors the remaining members of the class.	• Facilitates enrichment opportunities • Offers absent students "catch up" time • Keeps individuals and class on pace • Offers time to develop missing skills	• May be easy to select the same low-achieving students for help • Creates segregated learning environments • Is difficult to coordinate • May single out students

Interactive teaching is not simply turn-taking by partners. Instead, it is a dynamic process whereby both partners are actively engaged in the teaching and learning process. Both partners work together to support, clarify, and extend each other's efforts to ensure that effective student learning is taking place. Experienced partners work together, constantly reading each other's cues regarding students' understanding and the effectiveness of their instruction. Both teachers should be moving around the room, talking to each other and to their students. Initially, the added movement and ongoing teacher dialogue may feel awkward and uncomfortable for some partners. For example, lead teachers may find their partners' movements and comments distracting. Sensing their new partner's discomfort, some co-teachers may be tempted to sit down and be quiet until it is time for them to be the leader. To make the most of their time together, members of co-teaching teams should talk about their feelings and work through their initial awkwardness.

In interactive teaching, while the lead teacher is presenting, the support teacher plays a variety of roles. For example, he or she may ask clarifying questions ("Ms. Zahn, I'm not sure we all understand what you are saying. Would you tell us again what you mean by 'cessation'?"). Partners also clarify student understanding by rephrasing concepts or assigned tasks ("Excuse me, Mr. Krustch, do you want us to read the three paragraphs on page 322 silently *before* we discuss them with our partner?"). Support partners monitor many student behaviors; they redirect student attention as needed, supervise practice, and facilitate task completion activities. Ongoing group and individual monitoring provides better opportunities for skill development, more individualized help, effective trouble shooting, and systematic data collection.

In addition to asking clarifying questions and monitoring classroom activities, support co-teachers facilitate student learning through modeling, role plays, and demonstrations. Modeling appropriate classroom behaviors through "good student" performances helps all students become more effective problem solvers and self helpers. For example, Helen Huber and Kevin Contos want their eighth-grade science students to become better note takers. Together they taught their students an effective three-column note-taking system. However, most of the class members needed more models and additional supervised practice. During planning, Kevin and Helen discussed this situation and agreed to alternate note taking several times each week for the next month. When a transition in the teaching lead occurs, the co-teachers stop instruction briefly to review the support teacher's notes.

Sometimes Kevin and Helen use two overhead projectors and two screens to illustrate good note taking in action. For example, while Helen teaches a 10-minute segment on three Virginia songbirds, she uses one projector to show students various shape, color, and size differences among the birds. She also provides students with correctly spelled models of key vocabulary words. Meanwhile, using the other projector, Kevin models listening carefully and taking notes just as their students should be doing. After Helen finishes her instruction, Kevin discusses his notes with the students before the teachers introduce the next activity. In addition, as students become more proficient note takers, transition periods are used to compare the support teacher's notes with those of class members, spot check individual students' notes, and provide note-taking feedback.

Co-teachers can also use role plays to elaborate on either academic or social skills content. For example, Helen and Kevin recently created a lively class discussion by role playing a conversation between an environmentalist and a developer who is interested in building a riverfront amusement park. Working together, Helen and Kevin also like to demonstrate the steps in completing new tasks, conducting various procedures, and improving students' communication skills (e.g., conducting a lab experiment, using a new computer program, asking a teacher for help).

Station Teaching.   Co-teachers use this approach simultaneously to present or review new content, supervise practice, and test student skills at directed or independent workstations for small groups, partners, or individuals. During the class period, students rotate through stations where they can engage in a variety of learning, practice, and testing activities such as playing a practice game, reading a story, or taking a quiz. Students can also rotate through a variety of independent stations and helper-directed stations where volunteers such as student teachers, paraeducators, older students, or class members manage individual and group practice activities.

Station teaching allows co-teachers scheduled time during class to review critical concepts with students needing more help and to assess student skill levels. Co-teachers can strategically group students for rotation in and out of specific stations. This approach facilitates high levels of student responding. In general, students enjoy the process of rotating from one station to another. Although station teaching is an effective mechanism for providing intensive classroom support for target students, it is important for teachers to mix the rotating groups regularly to avoid the social stigmatization of homogeneous grouping. Helen and Kevin like to use station teaching to explore unit topics in greater depth. Recently, while studying water pollution, the class spent 75 minutes rotating to various stations. The class of 25 was divided into five mixed-ability groups that spent approximately 15 minutes at each station. Groups examined pond water bacteria under microscopes at Kevin's station, tested pH levels at Helen's station, and discussed a recent three-page *Science* article on the declining shellfish population with Marisa, the special education paraeducator, who works in the classroom several times each week. Student groups also worked independently at two stations where they completed a Nature Conservancy survey that Helen had found on the Internet and played a computer game on industrial water use developed for middle schools by the Environmental Protection Agency.

Parallel Teaching.   Using this model, co-teachers divide their students into two mixed-ability groups. Co-teachers each work with one group and basically cover the same content or skills. Parallel teaching provides a good format for practice and review lessons since it allows for higher levels of student responding than are possible during whole-class activities, and helps teachers monitor student performance more closely. The smaller group also may be less intimidating for students who are reluctant to answer questions in front of the entire class. For example, a month or so before their students take a standardized eighth-grade science test, Helen and Kevin plan weekly 30-minute parallel teaching sessions to help students review and practice effective test-taking strategies. They also like to use this format to review major unit concepts and key vocabulary words before quizzes and unit tests.

The primary disadvantages of this approach are related to extra planning needed to ensure equal coverage of the material and coordinating the pace of instruction to allow both groups to finish at the same time. Like station teaching, this variation requires a higher tolerance for classroom noise as both groups are responding simultaneously.

Alternative Teaching.   This structure enables co-teachers to create small, strategically constituted groups to work on specific skills, concepts, and projects. Consisting of fewer than six or seven students, these groups typically meet no more than five or six times as a group. One co-teacher works with the small group, while the other teacher instructs the rest of the class. This structure is especially useful when several students have missed instruction on critical content or when their classroom performance suggests that they would benefit from additional instruction, guided practice, or both. The structure also lends itself to various extension activities or enrichment projects. On Fridays, Helen and Kevin typically offer a 20- to 30-minute alternative teaching session. They rotate weekly teaching responsibilities so each partner teaches the large and small groups. These co-teachers intentionally try to "mix it up" so students are never stigmatized by their participation. On the whole, the teachers and the students like these sessions. Some weeks, participation is based on test scores or student absences. These sessions are reteaching lessons designed to address specific content or quiz performance concerns. Some weeks these sessions are designed to enhance and extend learning opportunities for interested students, and as a reward for social or academic performance (e.g., highest score, greatest personal improvement). During some units, Kevin and Helen post proposed alternative teaching topics and interested students sign up in advance for selected groups.

It is important to prevent alternative groups from being seen as punishing experiences for students who need extra help or as exclusive opportunities for only the highest achievers. Every student should have multiple chances to participate in both types of alternative teaching sessions. Students with achievement problems benefit from active, creative, hands-on experiences that many enrichment lessons provide. Likewise, even high-achieving students may need additional instruction, review, and guided practice of some concepts following an absence when initial instruction may have been missed. Both co-teachers should lead reteaching and enrichment alternative teaching lessons. During a recent third-grade chemistry unit, Helen and Kevin taught an alternative teaching class called "The Science of Baking." On alternate Fridays, one taught a 45-minute

---

Think About It...

How would you design one or more lessons in your professional specialty area that would use all four variations of co-teaching?

---

cooking class in the cafeteria, while the other supervised more traditional science practice activities. Each week six or seven students were randomly selected for the baking session until all class members had the opportunity to participate. Baking class students created nutritious snacks that were shared with class members at the end of each session.

These four co-teaching variations (interactive teaching, station teaching, parallel teaching, alternative teaching) facilitate both innovative co-teaching and effective classroom learning. They provide creative opportunities for new concept instruction, supervised skill practice, review, individualized assistance, and progress assessment. It is likely that most co-teaching teams will prefer some variations more than others; however, they should use all four regularly to ensure parity in instructional assignments, provide appropriate student support, and minimize stereotyping professionals or students in these classrooms. Given limited classroom space, some co-teachers wonder how to arrange desks and tables most effectively. Figure 9.2 illustrates possible classroom arrangements to facilitate the four co-teaching variations.

Developing Instructional Accommodations

Another important co-teaching responsibility is to develop effective classroom accommodations and modifications for students as needed. Many simple support strategies can facilitate concept understanding and skill mastery. For example, guest speakers, hands-on labs, computer software, and audiotaped textbooks enrich concept learning for most students. New concept learning is also enhanced by instructional posters, interactive bulletin boards, and small-group learning centers. Many materials can be developed by students themselves, paraeducators, or other classroom volunteers. Older students who read above a third-grade level often benefit from learning to use effective cognitive strategies (e.g., mnemonics, self-monitoring) and study skills (e.g., highlighter use, keyboarding skills, textbook usage). Practice materials can often be adapted easily by adjusting the visual format, such as font size and shape, number of items per page, or amount of white space between lines. Relatively simple worksheet modifications often help students who may be easily distracted, overstimulated, or defeated by tasks that may visually appear to be more complex than they actually are.

Many accommodations are ones that effective teachers use instinctively every day. Although students with mild to moderate disabilities often survive in general education classrooms with few, if any, accommodations, effective support

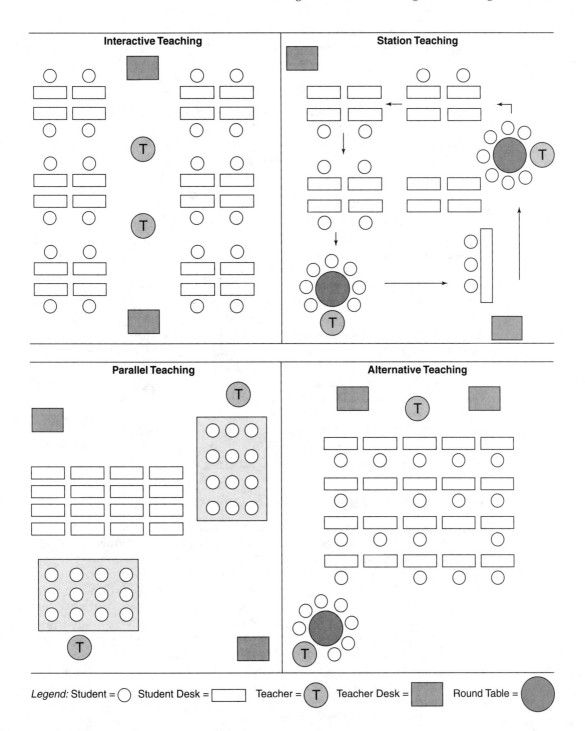

FIGURE 9.2 **Examples of Co-Taught Classroom Floor Plans.**

can greatly improve the performance of these students. Chapter 11 provides more information for developing appropriate classroom accommodations.

Monitoring and Evaluating Student Progress

Ongoing monitoring and evaluating of student progress is another important dimension of co-teaching. Combining their unique professional expertise and experience, effective co-teachers design classroom policies and evaluation procedures that facilitate effective monitoring, fair and comprehensive performance evaluation, and student self-evaluation. Like many effective classroom accommodations, comprehensive monitoring and evaluation are not necessarily complex and time-consuming endeavors. For example, classroom management plans should be developed with involvement from both teachers and class members. Plans should include consideration of basic classroom rules, classroom goals, performance expectations, individual and group consequences, and potential rewards. Students benefit from written criteria for daily homework, individual and group projects, written papers, presentations, and other creative projects. Teaching students to monitor, correct, and critique their own work according to class-developed criteria (e.g., personal journals, daily rating sheets) facilitates their growth and skill development; it also provides co-teachers with monitoring assistance. Co-teaching provides teams with more time to conduct regularly scheduled progress meetings with individual students. Sessions should be designed to encourage student reflection, the development of self-evaluation skills, and student-directed goal setting for the future. As with all co-teaching strategies, it is important for co-teachers to rotate their responsibilities for the individual sessions to ensure that all students spend time with each teacher assessing their performance and progress. Again, Chapter 11 provides additional information on performance-monitoring and evaluation procedures.

Communicating Student Progress to Others

Finally, effective co-teachers share ongoing responsibilities for communication with audiences outside the classroom. Oral and written communication from co-teachers addresses student progress, concerns, and other emerging social, vocational, and academic needs. Typical audiences include families, other school personnel (e.g., school psychologist, guidance counselor, administrators, English as a second language (ESL) teachers, transition specialists), and various community agency representatives (e.g., mental health counselors, physicians, social workers). Insights from both teachers provide a richer, more complete picture of student performance. Shared involvement in individual and classroom communication allows outside observers to understand more about co-teaching and how both teachers participate in student learning and development. Oral comments, written documents, and other communication strategies (e.g., classroom open houses, observation days) should reflect involvement by both teachers.

During the spring, it is helpful for co-teachers to discuss individual learning profiles with teachers, counselors, and vocational supervisors who will work with students the following school year. Classroom work portfolios that emphasize students' unique learning strengths, interests, needs, and characteristics help others who are unfamiliar with students more quickly develop effective working relationships. Sharing classroom and individual student insights with one another and developing communication documents helps co-teachers establish a stronger base of team support over time.

In this section, potential co-teacher roles and responsibilities related to classroom preparation and modification, content presentation, performance monitoring and evaluation, and communication were presented. The roles and responsibilities have been defined very broadly to offer an overview of fundamental ways effective partners interact to create enriched learning environments for their students.

Getting Started: Designing Effective Classrooms for Co-Teaching

Teams should begin in February or March to develop the following year's schedules. This allows time for careful matching of potential co-teachers and preparation for their roles. It also facilitates development of a master schedule that will include common planning time for partners.

Who Should Co-Teach

Co-teaching assignments should be based on thorough evaluation of identified student needs, such as disabilities, and academic and social skill levels; course content; and available school resources (e.g., special support funds, class size, specialist caseloads, professional skills). Based on needs and resources, general educators may be paired with one or more professional colleagues for in-class support through consultation or co-teaching. Effective inclusion is based on active in-class participation and support from all school specialists such as speech/language therapists, reading specialists, Title I teachers, ESL teachers, gifted education teachers, art therapists, media specialists, counselors, nurses, psychologists, technology specialists, and occupational and physical therapists (Bauwens & Hourcade, 1995). It is important to involve as many specialists as possible in the process for a few reasons. First, public schools will never have enough special educators to meet the diverse learning needs of all students—many of whom are not identified specifically for special education services. Involving all specialists in co-teaching increases the availability and appropriateness of classroom support schools can provide. Second, co-teaching models work well across content and unique student needs; they should not be limited to special education. Finally, co-teaching is more likely to become a lasting practice if it is seen as a schoolwide priority that is supported

FIGURE 9.3   Who are Good Candidates for Co-Teaching?

Listed below are some common characteristics of general educators and specialists who make good co-teachers. This list is not exhaustive; however, it provides a sample of qualities often found in effective teacher leaders.
Effective co-teachers have:

_____ Professional competence

_____ Personal confidence

_____ Respect of colleagues

_____ Professional enthusiasm

_____ Respect for colleagues' skills and contributions

_____ Good communication and problem-solving skills

_____ Personal interest in professional growth

_____ Flexibility and openness to new ideas

_____ Effective organizational skills

_____ Previous experience teaming with others

_____ Willingness to invest extra time in the process as needed

_____ Commitment to planning weekly with partner

_____ Voluntary participation in co-teaching

by all staff members, administrators, and families. Figure 9.3 lists some of the common characteristics of effective co-teachers.

Finding Appropriate Partners

Learning to value and respect a partner's professional viewpoint is essential to effective co-teaching. It is tempting for new co-teachers to select a close friend as a co-teaching partner because of shared philosophical beliefs about how classrooms should operate. Sometimes selecting a friend can be a successful approach; other times it is not. Effective collaborators intentionally contribute *different*—not similar—sets of knowledge, skills, and attitudes. Together, they share ideas and learn from each other. Partners who are "perfectly matched" may have little to offer one another from the perspective of professional growth.

Having said that it is okay—even preferable—to be somewhat different from one another, it is important to discuss fundamental aspects of teaching, such as philosophy, style, student grouping, and classroom leadership related to management, discipline, and grading *before* making any long-term commitments to co-teach. A candid and open discussion of critical issues can help professionals understand each other's views. Strong and differing opinions on various aspects of teaching need to be acknowledged. If it is apparent that there is little room for negotiation and flexibility it is important to admit this. Many identified points lend themselves to comfortable compromises easily; other points do not. For example, Lauren Huang, a 10th-grade English teacher, does not tolerate classroom profanity. Bruce Kirkpatrick, a high school alternative education teacher, does not have a strong opinion on this issue. Consequently, it may not be a point of concern between them—if Bruce can live with Lauren's rule. If, however, Lauren believes that all students who swear in class should be suspended, Bruce may find he has a stronger opinion than he originally thought.

Perfect agreement on *all* classroom rules is not essential; however, some factors, such as respecting others' opinions, valuing each other's professional skills, and demonstrating flexibility, are critical. If little room is available for negotiation on participants' key concerns, it needs to be admitted before making long-term commitments to work together. As difficult as it may be to acknowledge a mismatch, it is much easier than to live through a difficult year proving the partnership was a bad idea. Figure 9.4 on page 200 provides a list of preliminary questions potential co-teachers should discuss regarding their teaching philosophies, beliefs, and daily practices.

Based on previous experience working together, some questions may not be relevant. New questions may also emerge during this discussion. To facilitate an honest and open discussion, potential partners should consider the questions in advance and set aside at least an hour to explore them together. Some educators may find it easier to meet several times in shorter sessions.

Co-Planning: The Key to Effective Co-Teaching

Cooperative planning or "co-planning" is an essential part of effective co-teaching (Walther-Thomas, 1997a). This process helps collaborators clearly define and delineate their classroom roles and responsibilities. It also facilitates careful consideration of individual and group needs as classroom plans are designed, implemented, and evaluated. Despite the importance of co-planning, obstacles often stand in the way. It is important for educators to recognize these obstacles, find ways to deal with them effectively, and monitor their progress along the way.

Instructional planning has long been recognized as a critical component of effective teaching (McMurry, 1904). Most teachers in the United States, however, have little scheduled time built into their professional workdays for planning, materials preparation, grading student work, and family contacts (National Commission on Teaching and America's Future [NCTAF], 1996). In comparison to teachers in many other industrialized counties, U.S. teachers have significantly less time for planning and preparation. Unlike their Asian and European counterparts who spend more than half of their professional workdays planning instruction, preparing materials, and meeting with colleagues, students, and families, American teachers are given little dedicated time for these important tasks (Nelson & O'Brien, 1993). Typically, most American elementary teachers have about 8 minutes of scheduled planning time for every hour they teach; secondary teachers

FIGURE 9.4 Preliminary Questions for Potential Co-Teaching Partners.

1. What do you see as your greatest strengths as a teacher? What are your weaknesses?
2. How do you help new students feel comfortable in your classroom?
3. What are some of the daily instructional and organizational routines you like to use (e.g., homework box near the door where students leave assignments, 10 minutes of silent reading after recess)?
4. How do you teach new concepts?
5. How do you differentiate instruction within lessons?
6. Typically, do you differentiate instruction for students with special needs? If so, what are some examples?
7. What kinds of practice activities do you use (e.g., cooperative learning groups, labs, peer tutoring, learning stations)?
8. What are your basic classroom rules? What are the consequences?
9. (If not previously mentioned in question 8) What are your rules regarding restroom privileges? Gum chewing? Group work during class? Free time?
10. How much noise do you permit during practice activities?
11. What are your expectations for students regarding notebook organization? Daily note taking? Participation during class discussions? Written assignments? Homework assignments? Due dates?
12. How do you monitor and evaluate student progress?
13. Describe typical tests, quizzes, projects, and assignments.
14. How are grades determined for homework? For written assignments and projects? For the semester or the year?
15. Do you make evaluation modifications for students with disabilities? If so, what are some common types?
16. How is special assistance given to students with special needs during class? On assignments and projects? On quizzes and tests?
17. How do you communicate with families?
18. Describe your instructional planning process. How far ahead do you plan? Typically, how closely do you follow your plans?
19. What do you see as our potential roles and responsibilities as co-teachers?
20. What is your biggest hope for our work together? What is your biggest concern?
21. How will we find an hour a week to plan and problem-solve together outside of class?
22. What are some ways we can ensure equal status for both of us in the classroom (e.g., desk space, both names on the door, daily teaching responsibilities, shared grading)?
23. What are some ways we can share responsibilities for preparation, teaching, monitoring, and evaluating student performance?
24. What are some of your "pet peeves" in the classroom?
25. How can we give each other constructive feedback as our relationship develops?
26. What are some things we can do to ensure trust and confidentiality in our relationship as co-teachers?

Source: Adapted from Walther-Thomas, C. S., Bryant, M., & Land, S. (1996). Planning for effective co-teaching: The key to successful inclusion. *Remedial and Special Education, 17*(4), 255–265.

Think About It...

What are some other questions that potential co-teachers should discuss? What would you want to know about a potential teaching partner?

---

fare slightly better with about 13 minutes of planning time per instructional hour (National Education Association [NEA], 1992).

Despite the lack of scheduled planning time, most American teachers clearly recognize the importance of planning and preparation. They report spending 10 to 15 hours per week engaged in planning activities outside their classrooms (Stigler & Stevenson, 1992). Most teachers are socialized to plan alone—at home, after school, during summers, on holidays, and on weekends. Unlike educators in other countries who plan during the school day with colleagues, planning for many U.S. teachers is a solitary, isolated activity (NCTAF, 1996). Most have never experienced ongoing instructional planning with colleagues. Unfortunately, some teachers have developed inappropriate planning habits, that is, planning "on the fly," teaching only the bare minimums with limited consideration given to the content, let alone thoughtful assessment of students' group and individual needs.

Co-teachers, as co-planners, must learn how to plan together effectively. Initially, many partners report that the process is somewhat unfamiliar, awkward, and time-consuming. Although co-planning research is limited, effective co-teachers report that planning is an essential component in their success as teaching partners (Walther-Thomas, 1998; Walther-Thomas et al., 1996). One study suggested that good planning is basically a recursive process (Engeström, 1994). In essence, experienced partners develop lesson plans in an open-ended and spiral-like fashion. As noted in Chapter 4, when partners work together over time, typically they become more reflective revisiting common instructional issues on multiple occasions as they plan, teach, analyze, modify, and evaluate their instructional efforts. Experienced co-planners may not use conventional oral turn-taking, pausing, or decision-making procedures during these sessions. Instead, familiar with each other's styles and skills, they often plan in a lively manner, building on each other's ideas and suggestions. They revisit points made in earlier discussions as they create their instructional plans (Engeström, 1994; Walther-Thomas, 1998; Walther-Thomas et al., 1996).

Because of the complex nature of the co-planning process, it is easy to understand why successful planning takes time, good communication, trust in each other's professional competence, and commitment to this effort. Walther-Thomas (1998) studied co-teachers over time and found five general planning themes among practitioners who considered themselves to be effective co-planners. First, skilled co-planners trust the professional competency of their partners. Frequently they cite their partners' skills, contributions, and commitments as central to their success. Underlying confidence in their partners' skills helps create a structural framework that allows them to work through classroom and communication problems that are bound to occur over time. Second, accomplished co-planners meet regularly and develop effective planning routines to make the most of these sessions. Efficient routines emerge as co-teachers became familiar with each other's skills, interests, and working styles. As routines develop, more in-depth planning takes place during these work sessions. Third, effective co-planners create learning and teaching environments in which each person's contributions are valued. As a result, their ongoing classroom roles and responsibilities are distributed fairly. Classroom visitors have difficulty identifying who is the classroom teacher and who is the specialist because both teachers seem equally engaged and equally respected by students. Fourth, effective co-planners design learning environments for their students and for themselves that demand active involvement. Co-teachers report that the intensity of co-planned instruction, supervised practice, and more individual student attention enables them to accomplish more learning goals with students than if either teacher taught alone. Fifth, co-planners become more skilled over time. Effective co-planners report that they feel more productive, comfortable, and creative working together over time. Many co-teachers report that the amount of time they spend co-planning does *not* decrease significantly as their teaching team becomes more experienced; however, the quality of their plans, as well as the quality of group and individual instruction they provide, improves as a result.

Most co-teachers rely on their state and district curriculum guides as the basic framework for their instructional units, weekly plans, and daily lessons. Working together, co-teachers design essential linkages between classroom content goals and designated individualized education program (IEP) goals for identified students. They determine the extent to which content goals must be modified, if at all, to meet the needs of students with disabilities and other unique learning needs. Many experienced co-planners use a broad array of instructional strategies, practice activities, and monitoring procedures to create active and productive learning environments (Bauwens & Hourcade, 1995).

Implement Co-Teaching Slowly

As experienced educators will attest, many schools are notorious for throwing out the old and instituting the new with little planning and preparation. Currently, co-teaching is the new teaching innovation in many school systems. As a result, many inexperienced co-teachers are being assigned to work with multiple teaching partners. Innovation research, as well as common sense, suggests that large-scale implementation of new initiatives is destined to encounter serious problems (Fullan, 1993).

New co-teachers should start this process slowly with adequate preparation, planning time, and coaching support. New co-teachers should work with no more than one or two teaching partners during the first year. Although it is tempting for innovative administrators and teachers to think that competent co-teachers can do more from the very beginning, for the long-term success of co-teaching it is critical for teams to resist this temptation (Friend & Cook, 1997).

Developing effective co-teaching relationships takes time, skills, and commitment from partners. Co-teachers must work together to redefine their roles and responsibilities and to establish new ones. They must also create routines for effective co-planning and co-teaching (Walther-Thomas et al., 1996). As relationships develop, partners rely on each other's professional expertise and experience. Specialists need the support of their general education partners as they learn about general education classrooms (e.g., new content, large-group instruction, classroom management). General educators, in turn, look to the specialists for information about unique learner characteristics, classroom accommodations and modifications, and other strategies for individualizing instruction. Gradually, additional co-teaching partnerships can be added. For example, over time, experienced specialists often develop up to three ongoing co-teaching relationships with colleagues.

Summer planning can help new co-teachers prepare for their work together. In many classrooms the important decisions are often made before school starts (e.g., daily routines and rules, curriculum, student evaluation, and classroom management). Because co-teaching relationships benefit when both teachers participate in critical classroom decision making, working together during the summer helps them be ready for the first day of school as a team. Experienced co-teachers may also want to use summertime to evaluate the success of the previous year's efforts. Considering classroom data over time (e.g., office referrals, report card grades, child study referrals, student work) can help co-teachers make appropriate modifications (Cook & Friend, 1997).

Prepare in Advance for Effective Planning

For co-teachers to work effectively as classroom partners, both need to understand their roles and responsibilities. Before meeting, each teacher should review the upcoming content, goals, and objectives and consider possible resources and other support services that some students may need. As ideas come to mind, it is helpful if partners individually write notes regarding potential practice activities, individual and group projects, evaluation procedures, student performance concerns, and accommodations (Walther-Thomas, 1998). For example, Margaret and Catherine are seventh-grade language arts co-teachers. Figure 9.5 on page 204 shows the pre-meeting form each partner uses before they meet. This example illustrates Catherine's notes for their next planning session. Effective preparation at this stage demands that both teachers have easy access to all classroom textbooks and supplementary resources. It is also helpful for specialist partners to see copies of past lesson plans, student worksheets, and other handouts to help them develop an accurate sense of their partners' expectations and to consider in which areas some students will need additional support.

Create Planning Meeting Routines

Establishing standard routines leads to efficient planning patterns that can facilitate teamwork (Walther-Thomas, 1997a; Walther-Thomas et al., 1996). For example,

FIGURE 9.5   Individual Co-Planning Preparation Guide.

Catherine's Weekly Co-Planning Preparation Guide

Class: 7th grade Language Arts   **Week of:**   12/15

Period: 3rd

Content to Be Covered

Chapter 6 language arts text: "Using Descriptive Language in Writing"

- Common writing motifs
- Use of descriptive language
- Use of dialogue in writing
- Story writing
- Imagination Express Software

Learning Goals/Objectives (Class goals)

1. Read and analyze fairy tales
2. Discuss motifs and describe language
3. Write a fairy tale in class with a group using story writing software (Hyper Studio or Imagination Express)
4. Develop a fairy tale individually for presentation; use story writing software

Resources/Additional Needs

- Fairy tale videotapes?
- *Rabbit Ears Radio* audiotapes from National Public Radio?
- Imagination Express and Hyper Studio software
- Ask library volunteer for easier versions of fairy tales for Paul, Marisa, Holzer, Felipe (3rd–4th grade reading levels)

Questions/Accommodations Needed

Remember to work on Jack's daily goals next week! He seemed to have a difficult time staying focused this week.

Ask Margaret about *The Princess Bride.* Has she seen it? Would it fit in with this chapter?

Work with Margaret to prioritize and modify learning goals for Paul, Jack, Holzer, Felipe, and Marisa.

Should be okay with basic class goals if easier stories are provided for low readers and writing software is provided.

---

starting the session with a brief review of the past week's activities may help set the stage for the coming week's plans. It also provides time for partners to celebrate classroom successes and acknowledge individual and team accomplishments. Finally, such a review helps co-teachers to address instructional problems that may exist.

During planning sessions effective co-teachers pose and revisit questions related to content, practice, student learning needs, and evaluation. They revisit major concepts, practice activities, and other concerns based on their previous experience. Over time they can refine existing units, create new ones, and modify lessons and activities within units. Following the discussion of the next week's "big picture" issues, specific needs of individual students can be discussed, as well as any learning strategies that may be appropriate. As teams progress, most feel more comfortable relying on their growing knowledge of their students' needs, abilities, and interests. Daily interaction with students and with each other also facilitates planning. They anticipate potential problems, identify topics of student interest, and customize learning experiences to meet individual and group needs more effectively.

It is important for teams to sort problems that arise during planning meetings. Instruction-specific issues (e.g., grading criteria for an upcoming assignment, poor scores on a recent quiz) should be addressed immediately. Other group and student-specific problems (e.g., a parent's telephone call regarding an upcoming IEP meeting, recent drug problems in the school) may need to be set aside and addressed at a later time. It is tempting to use co-planning time to discuss "hot" topics that may arise; however, this time must be held exclusively for instructional planning.

Once the learning objectives and content have been reviewed, most of the remaining time should be spent (1) planning content delivery (e.g., interactive teaching, station teaching, parallel teaching, alternative teaching); (2) designating corresponding practice activities (e.g., peer tutoring, cooperative learning groups, individual projects); and (3) determining appropriate monitoring and evaluation procedures (e.g., oral discussions, quizzes, worksheets, group presentations).

Develop Written Plans

Although it is difficult for new co-planners to finalize all of the details about the coming week's instruction during a 1-hour planning meeting, good co-planners develop a master plan and a daily instructional schedule. Critical roles and responsibilities should be determined before the conclusion of their meeting. All assigned preparation, teaching, supervision, and evaluation responsibilities should be written down and both partners should receive copies. This step is crucial to ensure that both partners are clear about their tasks for the coming week. Without written plans, important responsibilities can be easily confused or forgotten. If this happens repeatedly, it undermines team effectiveness and diminishes confidence in each partner's commitment to common goals.

Develop Predictable Daily Lesson Formats

Planning is facilitated when partners create a predictable but flexible format for sequencing many daily classroom activities, classroom management responsibilities, and teaching tasks. Lively, logical, and well-organized daily schedules allow all participants to feel more prepared and focused. In addition, a predictable format helps reduce the time needed for planning in advance. It becomes easier for partners to divide their ongoing preparation responsibilities, classroom "house-keeping" roles, and co-teaching assignments. This process facilitates ongoing rotation of daily classroom responsibilities such as greeting students at the door, collecting homework assignments, recording attendance, correcting homework, presenting "warm-up" (learning review) activities, and presenting new content. Rotating these jobs helps new collaborators establish parity and trust with one another and create a better sense of shared credibility with the students (Figure 9.6).

Over time Catherine and Margaret have developed a format they use as they develop daily lesson plans. It is based on a weekly routine that delineates various roles and responsibilities. For example, on Mondays, Wednesdays, and Fridays, Catherine plans and presents a warm-up activity at the beginning of class that is based on the previous day's lesson. On those days, Margaret takes responsibility for the 5-minute wrap-up session at the end of class designed to review the key concept(s), provide lesson closure, and prepare students for tomorrow's class. On Tuesdays and Thursdays, they reverse these roles. Figure 9.7 illustrates one of their daily plans.

FIGURE 9.6   **Rotating Classroom Roles and Responsibilities for Catherine and Margaret.**

Today Before Class

Catherine...
Checks today's homework assignment
Prepares a warm-up activity

While Margaret...
Greets students at the door
Sets up a learning station activity

During Class

Catherine...
Reviews last night's homework
Role plays teacher role
Monitors peer editing activity at station 2

While Margaret...
Discusses yesterday's lesson and key
   vocabulary words with two students
   who were absent
Role plays student role
Teaches 15-minute lessons on writing process at station 3

After Class

Catherine...
Grades homework on Tuesday &
   Thursday nights this week
Plans tomorrow's warm-up activity

While Margaret...
Grades homework on Monday &
   Wednesday nights this week
Keeps track of three student behavior
   contracts

FIGURE 9.7 Daily Co-Teaching Lesson Plan to Introduce a 2-Week Creative Writing Unit on Fairy Tales.

Date: 12/15	Teacher 1: Margaret (M)	Teacher 2: Catherine (C)	Time Required: 50 minutes	Accommodations
Preparation	Go to library and get multiple copies (6–8) of fairy tales	1. Pick up videotape for Tuesday (*Princess Bride*) 2. Make worksheet copies		Get some lower level versions of fairy tales for Paul, Marisa, Felipe, and Holzer
M—Greet at door C—Collect homework Warm-up	1. Quick unit overview—Both (5 minutes) 2. Write kids' ideas on the board 3. Think of favorite fairy tale. Why favorite? Discuss		10–15 minutes	Remind Jack about his daily goal—reduced talkouts
Content presentation	1. Both read *Little Red Riding Hood* to class; each take parts (e.g., narrator, Wolf, Little Red Riding Hood) 2. Discuss motifs kids recognize 3. Fill in missing motifs (e.g., clever hero, villain, 3 trials, happy ending)		10–15 minutes	
Practice activities M—Introduce C—Assign kids to activities pairs	1. Students read *Little Mermaid* or *Hansel and Gretel*, complete worksheet, and discuss answers with another pair. 2. Both monitor and assist 3. Get Betty S. (Sue's grandma) to help with monitoring. She's visiting class on Monday		10–15 minutes	Separate Paul and Marisa Pair Jack with Felipe, and Barbara with Holzer
Wrap-up	Check homework assign-ment	Assign homework—similar worksheet (*Billy Goat's Gruff*)	5 minutes	
Progress monitoring	Both—monitor worksheet completion participation C—keep track of Jack's talkouts (5 or less)			

Note: This example is presented in a typed format to facilitate its readability. In classroom use co-planners would plan at a computer workstation using a planning template or use handwritten plans.

Chapter Summary

Effective co-teaching provides direct and daily in-class support for students and ongoing opportunities for professional growth. Successful co-teaching partnerships are based on professional competency and trust, shared beliefs and commitment, and ongoing collaboration. Effective co-teachers plan and present appropriate instruction, offer guided practice to cultivate skill mastery, and monitor student performance. During student-focused efforts, many partners also report sharing their own knowledge and skills and growing professionally from information their partners provide.

Ongoing planning and participation in all aspects of classroom life are critical to the lasting effectiveness of these relationships. Inequities on either side can undermine co-teaching relationships (Karge, McClure, & Patton, 1995; Pugach & Wesson, 1995; Walther-Thomas, 1997b); problems between partners emerge quickly if the situation is not well structured. On one hand, if specialists are not involved in daily preparation, group teaching, grading, and student evaluation, classroom teachers may feel overburdened by their personal responsibilities to meet diverse student needs with little support. Resentment develops when limited classroom support and assistance exists. On the other hand, if specialists are not accepted and valued as equal partners in the classroom, they often feel frustrated and underutilized.

As noted earlier, co-teaching is not an exact science. Under the best of circumstances, unexpected events require changes in plans and routines. Consequently, although effective partners must be as well prepared as possible and fulfill their commitments to each other, partners must also stay open-minded and flexible. Given time, patience, commitment, and adequate resources, effective co-teaching partnerships provide appropriate learning environments for diverse learners and reflect the contributions of both professionals.

CHAPTER ACTIVITIES

1. Examine the characteristics of effective co-teachers and consider your own professional and personal strengths and weaknesses. Discuss your observations with a partner. Generate a list of ideas that you could use to increase your skills to become an effective co-teacher.

2. Work with a small group of classmates and make a list of typical roles and responsibilities of co-teachers. Individually prioritize the importance of the items your group identifies. Share your opinions with each other and discuss why competent and committed professionals might choose different priorities.

3. Design a 45-minute class presentation on co-teaching with a partner. Think about how you could demonstrate the four variations of co-teaching presented in this chapter during your presentation. Discuss your presentation ideas with others in a small-group setting. Provide an outline that illustrates each of your roles and responsibilities.

10 Individualizing Educational Programs

LEARNING OBJECTIVES

1. Describe the collaborative planning process to individualize students' educational programs in inclusive settings.
2. Explain the legal assurances for individualized education programs (IEPs) as outlined in the Individuals with Disabilities Education Act (IDEA).
3. Identify strategies for increasing active participation of families as team members in planning individualized student programs.

Six-year-old Quong is currently in a full-day kindergarten class at Townville Primary School. He had participated in an inclusive preschool program for 2 years after his family moved into the community. Quong responds well to his peers and enjoys being part of a group. Other children and adults describe him as friendly and likeable—a boy with "lots of personality." Quong has cerebral palsy with significant cognitive, language, and motor disabilities. He feeds himself and uses the bathroom but requires assistance with these self-help tasks. His speech is severely delayed and is often difficult for peers and teachers to understand.

* * *

Chet is a 10th grader at James Monroe High School. He has been receiving special education services since the third grade when he was identified as having a learning disability. Chet's teachers have consistently described him as bright, outgoing, and popular. This year, Chet started as tight end on the varsity football team and is determined to maintain his eligibility. Academically, he is interested in science and math and has maintained a "B" average in both courses. Chet hopes to be an engineer like his father and his uncle; he is highly motivated to go to the state university they attended. Chet's disabilities in reading and written expression have been most detrimental to his performance in English, foreign languages, and social studies classes. Although his decoding skills have improved, he reads slowly and has weak comprehension skills. Composition is especially difficult for Chet. When required to write papers or complete essay tests, he frequently gets failing grades. Overall, Chet has poor organization and study skills, which have been a major focus of his IEPs since middle school.

* * *

Lark is a seventh grader at Lewis Middle School. A year ago, she was identified with an emotional disorder and began to receive special education support. She is well known for her outlandish outfits and makeup, as well as her tattoos and body piercing. Three times this semester she has been sent home because her "skimpy and provocative" outfits violated school dress codes. Lark lives with her grandmother, who is unable to enforce curfews and other rules. She has told Lark's teachers that she fears Lark will get pregnant or into other serious trouble. Although Lark has average ability and is capable of getting good grades, she is failing most of her courses because she doesn't turn in her assignments. When teachers try to work with her, Lark is often disrespectful and rude. She also has difficulty getting along with peers. When things don't go her way, Lark strikes out with abusive language and, on occasion, with physical blows.

Students like Quong, Chet, and Lark receive appropriate special education support within general education classrooms. Meeting their unique needs requires a thorough understanding of their interests and skills, capabilities, and difficulties. It also requires that educators examine the general education curriculum and classroom environment and make necessary accommodations to enable students with disabilities and those at risk to succeed. This chapter describes the process of individualizing student programs as a particular application of reflective practice. It also addresses legal requirements for the development of individualized education programs (IEPs) for students who are eligible for special education services and strategies to enhance the IEP process to produce more meaningful and useful documents for educators, students, and family members. Although IEPs are required only for students with identified disabilities, the overall process for individualizing students' educational programs is applicable for all students with special needs in inclusive schools.

Individualizing Programs through Reflective Practice

Chapter 4 introduced reflective practice as a process for systematic planning and problem solving. The basic sequence of planning, acting, describing, and evaluating is the essence of effective teaching and professional practice. Reflective professionals continually frame and reframe the complex problems that they encounter, test out various solutions, and modify their next interventions as a result (Schön, 1983, 1987). As emphasized in Chapter 4, the value of reflective practice is enhanced when educators engage in dialogue with their peers; that is, when they plan and problem solve in collaboration with others.

Over the last three decades, experts have offered many different models for individualizing educational programs for students with special needs. In the 1960s and 1970s, some of the leading models were described as *systematic* (McCormack, 1976; Snell, 1978); *directive* (Haring & Schiefelbusch, 1976; Stephens, 1977); *programmed* (Tawney et al., 1979), *clinical* (Lerner, 1976; Smith, 1974); and *prescriptive* (Charles, 1976; Mercer, 1979; Moran, 1975; Peter, 1965). What all of these early models had in common was a focus on individual students. A thorough assessment of the learner served as the basis for the selection of instructional objectives, strategies, teaching methods, and materials. Continuous measurement of student performance was an integral part of each model, providing the primary means of evaluating program effectiveness (Laycock, 1982). Contemporary models have built on these earlier versions and emphasize planning for success in general education classes and other natural environments. Models such as MAPS (Forest & Pearpoint, 1992), VISTA (Giangreco, 1996a), and COACH (Giangreco, Cloninger, & Iverson, 1997) may be particularly helpful guides for team planning. Orelove and Malatchi (1996) found that effective program planning models share four common features:

1. *Individualized planning is emphasized.* Although some planning models rely more heavily than others on the value of standardized test scores and categorical labels, most inclusive planning models place greater emphasis on the hopes and dreams held by students and others significant in their lives (e.g., family members, teachers, transition specialists). The group's concerns provide the foundation for the goals and learning objectives written into students' individualized education programs.

2. *The IEP is the primary program planning document.* In many schools, IEPs are viewed negatively as bureaucratic nuisances rather than essential planning tools. In schools committed to inclusive education, IEPs become highly valued working documents. Inclusive IEPs reflect clear evidence of collaboration, creativity, and teamwork by all participants in the process. As a result, the goals and objectives that emerge from the IEP writing process are ones that are meaningful for the student and the planning team. They serve as the basis for most significant classroom learning experiences.

3. *Effective teaching techniques are used to achieve important student learning outcomes.* Students' learning needs are viewed holistically, and meaningful academic, social, and functional goals are established. Inclusive classrooms use methods such as cooperative learning, peer tutoring, cognitive strategies, and positive behavior support that are effective and encourage participation by all students.

4. *Individualized classroom supports and resources are established to ensure classroom success for students and adults.* Effective inclusive program planning does not stop with the establishment of appropriate goals and objectives. Time and attention are also devoted to implementation to ensure that students and teachers receive the support they need to achieve in inclusive classrooms. Monitoring plans are developed to measure the effectiveness of these efforts.

Although each model incorporates its own steps and planning tools, all are essentially variations or elaborations of reflective practice, that is, planning, implementing, describing, and evaluating. Recognition that reflective practice remains the essential and versatile framework helps to demystify the challenge of inclusion. Unfortunately, there is no "bag of tricks," just a recursive cycle of planning and problem solving to determine what is effective for individual students with disabilities or other special needs.

When the reflective cycle focuses intentionally on individual students, the planning step becomes especially critical. Planning for the purpose of individualizing educational programs is essentially a four-faceted task; it requires (1) assessment of student needs; (2) formulation of long- and short-term goals for students; (3) analysis of aspects of the general education program that meet and fail to meet the identified student needs, and (4) design of individualized programs that incorporate as much of the general education program as possible with appropriate accommodations and related services to enable students to attain defined goals.

Fortunately, teachers in inclusive schools do not have to plan and problem-solve on their own. As student needs become more complex, teachers collaborate with others to provide additional support. Working with assistance teams or consultants, for example, teachers can intervene in the classroom without referring some low-performing students for special education services. Similarly, in co-taught classes, many students at risk receive the support they need and may never require more intensive special education or related services. When teachers or families suspect that students have disabilities that interfere significantly with their ability to succeed in general education, they can initiate a formal referral to determine eligibility for special education services.

Legal Assurances of the Special Education Process

Assistance teaming and consultation are described in Chapters 7 and 8 as collaborative structures that allow teachers to meet the needs of students who demonstrate learning or behavioral problems. Although these prereferral processes are not always used prior to a full student evaluation, they help teachers document the need for more extensive interventions such as special education or related services. Prereferral is a best-practice approach that helps to guard against referral for unnecessary evaluations and subsequent misidentification of student disabilities (Turnbull, Turnbull, Shank, & Leal, 1995). This section outlines those procedural safeguards set forth legally to facilitate assessment and eligibility determination.

On June 4, 1997, the Individuals with Disabilities Education Act (IDEA, 1977) Amendments were signed into law. This reauthorization was viewed by many as an opportunity to review, strengthen, and improve IDEA to better educate children and youth with disabilities and enable them to achieve a quality education by ensuring greater access to the general education curriculum and reforms Council for Exceptional Children ([CEC], 1998). The 1997 Amendments sought to expand and promote opportunities for family members, special education, general education, related services and early intervention providers, and community-based agencies to work in new partnerships at both the state and local levels. An additional goal of the Amendments was to shift the focus of IDEA from paperwork and compliance to improving education outcomes for students with disabilities. IEPs are the primary vehicle for achieving this intent (Hallahan & Kauffman, 1997).

The Child Study Process

After a referral has been made by an educator, family member, or other person, a screening or child study committee meets to discuss available information and decide if an evaluation is warranted. Central to IDEA is the requirement for a non-discriminatory, multifaceted, multidisciplinary, and professionally sound evaluation. Specifically, the law requires that an initial comprehensive individual evaluation be conducted before the provision of special education or related services. Figure 10.1 cites the regulations pertaining to student evaluations.

The requirement that assessment tools and strategies provide information that directly assists the team in individualized planning for the student supports the increased use of alternative assessments (e.g., curriculum-based measures, portfolios) in addition to traditional standardized measures. This broadens the assessment process beyond basic eligibility determination to include information about how to teach students in the ways in which they are most capable of learning.

Eligibility determination is to be made by a team of qualified professionals and the student's parents or guardians. Basically, the team must answer two questions: first, does the student have a disability and, second, are special education or related services required to meet the student's specific educational needs. Copies of the evaluation reports and documentation of the student's eligibility determination are to be given to the family (IDEA, 1997, section 614). Following eligibility determination, an IEP must be developed prior to initiation of special education services.

The Individualized Education Program

In the context of federal special education law, the term *individualized education program (IEP)* means a written statement for each student with a disability that is

FIGURE 10.1   **IDEA Requirements for Evaluation.**

In conducting student evaluations for special education, the school district must: (1) use a variety of assessment tools and strategies to gather relevant functional and developmental information, including information from parents and family members; (2) not use any single procedure as the sole criterion for determining eligibility or for determining an appropriate educational program for the student; and (3) use technically sound instruments that may assess the relative contribution of cognitive and behavioral factors, in addition to physical or developmental factors.

In addition, the law requires a school district to ensure that: (1) tests and other evaluation materials used to assess a student are selected and administered so as not to be racially or culturally discriminatory, and are administered in the student's native language or other mode of communication, unless it is clearly not feasible to do so; (2) any standardized tests given to the child have been validated for the specific purpose for which they are used and are administered by trained and knowledgeable personnel in accordance with the instructions provided by the producers of such tests; (3) the student is assessed in all areas of suspected disability; and (4) assessment tools and strategies provide relevant information that directly assists persons in determining the educational needs of the student.

---

developed, reviewed, and revised, as required by IDEA (1997). As a core component of IDEA, the IEP is the major vehicle for assuring the provision of a free, appropriate public education (FAPE) for each student eligible for special education services. It is important to note that the IEP is both a process and a document. The IEP process involves all the previously described individualized planning steps performed by a multidisciplinary team that includes family members and general educators to assess the student, determine eligibility, and design an appropriate educational program. The IEP document is the concrete confirmation of the decisions reached by the team about the student's service needs and program.

Perspectives on the IEP document and process vary throughout the country. For many, it represents collaboration at all levels—families with schools, teachers with administrators, and teachers with specialists. The IEP is also envisioned as a problem-solving model that includes a reasonable degree of flexibility in addressing individual student needs (National Association of State Directors of Special Education [NASDSE], 1996). A review of the literature on IEPs yields both strengths and limitations (McDonnell, McLaughlin, & Morison, 1997; Smith, 1990; Smith & Slattery, 1993; Tanzman, 1997). However, the potential benefits of the IEP process and document are seen as far more significant than the limitations, which typically represent flaws in practice rather than in the IEP concept itself. Noteworthy is the growing trend in many educational reform efforts toward the use of individual learning plans for all students.

Components of the IEP.   Although IEPs vary greatly in format and detail from one school district to another, each must include the following information:

1. Documentation of the student's current levels of educational performance including how the student's disability affects involvement and performance in the general curriculum.
2. Statement of measurable annual goals including benchmarks or short-term objectives related to involvement and progress in the general curriculum and each of the student's other needs resulting from his or her disability.
3. Statement of special education and related services, supplementary aids and services, and program modifications or support for school personnel necessary for the student to advance appropriately toward annual goals, to be involved and progress in the general education curriculum, to participate in extracurricular and nonacademic activities, and to be educated and participate with other students with disabilities and nondisabled students in the general education classroom.
4. Explanation of the extent to which the student will not participate in general education.
5. Statement of individual modifications in the administration of state and districtwide student achievement tests, or if the IEP team determines the student will not participate, a statement of why that assessment is not appropriate and explanation of how the student will be assessed.
6. Projected date for beginning of services and modifications and anticipated frequency, location, and duration of those services and modifications.
7. Statement of how the student's progress toward annual goals will be measured, and how the parents will be kept informed of progress toward both annual goals and the extent to which that progress is sufficient to meet annual goals, on a regular basis (at least as often as parents of typical students).

In addition, a statement of transition service needs under the applicable components of the student's IEP is required beginning at age 14 and is updated annually. Beginning at age 16 (or younger if determined appropriate by the IEP team), the IEP must also include a statement of needed transition services including interagency responsibilities. Beginning at least 1 year before the student reaches the age of majority under state law, the IEP must indicate that a student has been informed of his or her rights under IDEA that will transfer from the parents or guardians to the student on reaching the age of majority.

Think About It...

If IDEA mandates the components of IEPs, should it also require that a standard IEP form be used by all schools? Why or why not?

A Process for Planning Individualized Programs

As noted, the IDEA Amendments of 1997 mandate important changes in both the focus and development of IEPs. One significant change is heightened emphasis on students' participation in the general education curriculum. This new focus necessitates more active dialogue among special educators, general educators, and families to develop IEPs that are truly tailored to the immediate and long-term needs of individual students (CEC, 1998; Yell & Shriner, 1997).

New IEP provisions require a paradigm shift among many school personnel. In the past, it was not uncommon for special educators to "draft" IEPs before meetings were convened to make efficient use of team members' time. Unfortunately, this practice precluded genuine collaboration in developing IEPs. Family members, community representatives, and even school personnel may have been reluctant to propose alternatives if a complete "draft" was presented at the meeting. To comply with the spirit of the new legislation, IEP meetings are now likely to require more time, as participants assume more active roles and teams deliberate individual student priorities. Chapter 6 includes some creative suggestions for making time in the schedules of school personnel to participate in IEP and other collaborative meetings. This new approach to IEP development represents a major change in most schools and will involve all of the challenges of organizational change described in Chapter 3. Many participants will need professional development and support to increase their communication and problem-solving skills.

Facilitating Family Participation

Facilitating meaningful participation of families on IEP teams is of special concern. Educators must ensure that families, including the students themselves, understand both their rights and their roles in the IEP process. Limited research on family participation reveals that, although some parents reported positive experiences, many others have not participated at all or found themselves in adversarial relationships with schools when they did not agree with the staff recommendations (National Council on Disability [NCD], 1995). A number of specific barriers to family participation have been identified: low meeting attendance, time constraints, educational jargon used by school professionals, undervaluing of family input, and a lack of information about the IEP process (McDonnell et al., 1997).

Professionals in K-12 schools can learn from their colleagues in early childhood special education who have designed more family-centered practices for planning and developing the individualized family service plans (IFSPs) required for serving preschool children with disabilities (Bailey, 1987; Dunst, Trivette, Starnes, Hamby, & Gordon, 1993; McGonigel, Kaufmann, & Johnson, 1991). In essence, family-centered approaches recognize the centrality of the family in the lives of individuals, focus on strengths and capabilities, and are guided by fully informed choices made by the family (Beach Center on Families and Disability, 1997).

> ## Think About It...
>
> Consider Bailey's points for family-centered services in light of your own beliefs and values. To what extent do you agree or disagree with specific recommendations?

To make services more family centered and to involve families as equal partners, Bailey (1991) offers educators the following suggestions:

1. Recognize that team meetings belong to both families and professionals. Like all other team members, families should be made aware of why a meeting is being held, who will be there, and what to expect.
2. Invite families to speak first in team meetings to share their perspectives and suggestions before staff give theirs.
3. Explain any medical, educational, or technical terms in everyday language every time they are used until all team members are familiar with the terms.
4. Be honest and open with families when team members disagree with one another or are uncertain about information.
5. Speak of families and students in the same manner whether or not they are present. In other words, if professional staff members are unwilling to address an issue with the family, they should not discuss it with other team members.

Many families are better prepared for full participation at team meetings when professionals provide help in identifying their concerns, priorities, and resources. Professionals begin gathering this information as soon as they meet families. The initial contact of family members may be with a classroom teacher, special educator, school social worker, or other team member. The contact person should be the school representative who seems most likely to establish rapport and trust with students' families. Use of open-ended questions and other interviewing techniques elicits more information. Questions such as, "How does Martin participate in family activities? What does he typically do after school?" may stimulate productive discussion of student interests, strengths, and needs. Written forms and checklists have also been developed to assist families in clarifying their thoughts prior to participating in IEP meetings. It is important that families have choices in the ways they share information with other team members. Language, culture, and literacy skills are critical considerations when professionals offer options for family input (Child Development Resources, 1995; Dennis & Giancreco, 1996; Harry, 1992). Whenever written instruments are used, professionals need to explain why the information is important, how exactly it will be used, and that sharing information about needs and concerns is voluntary (Dunst, et al., 1988). Professional honesty, openness, and inclusive attitudes help build trusting and supportive relationships with families.

FIGURE 10.2   **Strategies for Increasing Family Participation in IEP Team Meetings.**

- Schedule meetings before and after school or in the evenings to accommodate families.
- Provide sufficient advance notice for families to rearrange work and child care schedules.
- Arrange for a cab or bus ride through the school district or a local community action agency, if transportation is needed.
- Convene meetings in public libraries, community centers, churches, restaurants, or other sites that may be more convenient and less intimidating to families.
- Equip a van as an "IEP Mobile" to take professional team members to neighborhoods or other sites more convenient to families.
- Provide child care as needed; enlist the help of student service clubs, community volunteers, college student interns, and others.
- Invite members of extended families to participate as appropriate.
- Encourage families to invite trusted community leaders, ministers, coaches, and others if they are uncomfortable attending meetings alone.
- Loan families videotapes in advance to provide an overview of the IEP meeting.
- Create a family resource center or lounge with materials of interest to families as a waiting room before meetings get underway.
- Meet in settings in which all team members can sit comfortably around a table; avoid conference rooms that may be too formal or intimidating to families.
- Use name tags or name plates at meetings so families are not disadvantaged by not knowing the names and titles of all participants.

Many times family participation is curtailed by the logistics of scheduling team meetings. If meetings are only held during the school day, for example, some parents will be unable to attend because of job responsibilities. Other families require assistance with transportation or child care in order to participate. Schools that truly value family involvement find creative ways to overcome logistical barriers. Figure 10.2 presents strategies that some schools have used successfully to increase family participation at IEP meetings and other conferences.

An Individualized Education Program Planning Process in Inclusive Schools

Family members are not the only ones who benefit from guided preparation for IEP meetings as inclusive programs are planned. Professionals also need a process for organizing their input prior to the actual meetings. In particular, general educators who may be less experienced with IEP meetings can benefit from a guided preparation process. Traditionally, school psychologists, special educators, and others have relied primarily on their formal assessment reports. Although these reports should still be shared with families, the information needs to be translated into language that is more useful for IEP planning purposes. Many inclusive IEP planning teams ask members to do some "homework" before attending the planning meeting to make the most of their time together.

Figure 10.3 presents an IEP premeeting planning guide that can be used by all participants—students, family members, and professionals—to prepare for IEP meetings. Considering important planning questions before the actual meeting helps all parties involved to organize their thoughts, identify their primary planning concerns, and generally feel more confident about their participation in the discussion (Van Rusen, Bos, Schumaker, & Deshler, 1994). Some parents or guardians may choose to work with their children to complete one form as a family; other students and family members may choose to complete their forms individually. Some students may prefer to complete their planning forms at school with assistance as needed from one or more members of the team. Student participa-

FIGURE 10.3   IEP Premeeting Planning Guide.

Date: _____

Student name: _____   Date of birth: _____

Teacher: _____   Grade: _____   School: _____

Person completing form: _____   Relation to student: _____

1. What I know about _____.

   What are his/her interests and skills?

   How does he/she learn best?

   What are the areas of concern?

   Where is help needed?

2. My hopes and dreams for _____.

   What would you like to see happen this year?

   What would you like to see happen in 5 years?

3. What it will take to achieve these hopes and dreams?

   What does _____ need to learn and be able to do? (student goals)

   What kinds of strategies and supports are we (school, family) going to implement to help?

4. How will we measure progress?

   What will we see him/her doing?

   How will we keep track?

tion in IEP planning should be strongly encouraged, while respecting student and family preferences as well as other factors, such as the student's age, disability, cognitive skill levels, and possible adult concerns (Kochhar & West, 1996; Turnbull et al., 1995). Participation in IEP planning, starting at an early age, provides opportunities for students to learn and practice appropriate self-advocacy skills. Student involvement also helps ensure a higher level of student commitment to the goals that are developed (Lovitt, Cushing, & Stump, 1994; Peters, 1990; Van Rusen & Bos, 1994; Van Rusen et al., 1994). Similarly, teachers and specialists can complete their premeeting planning guides either individually or collaboratively. For example, a classroom teacher who serves on the IEP committee may elicit input from other teachers on the grade-level team who work with the same student.

When family members and professionals complete the same premeeting planning guide, a sense of parity is established early in the process. All participants come to the meeting prepared to offer their ideas on four basic topics: what they know about the student; their hopes and dreams for the student; what the student, family, school, and others can do to accomplish those hopes and dreams; and ways that they will know whether they are succeeding. The four basic questions shown in Figure 10.3 frame an agenda for IEP meetings as well as encourage all team members to participate fully in discussion of the student's present levels of performance, goals and objectives, and team intervention strategies. During the IEP meeting, the team leader's role is to facilitate discussion of each of these topics, ensuring that all team members have opportunities to contribute. It is also helpful for the team leader to note areas of agreement and instances in which team members hold different opinions. A recorder summarizes key points on a chart, so that all participants can follow the planning process. These notes become part of the permanent record of the IEP planning meeting, and team members conclude the meeting by signing-off on the team planning form. After the meeting, one team member, often the special educator, is delegated responsibility for converting the information into formal statements of present performance, measurable goals and objectives, and other required sections of the student's IEP. To maintain parity and active involvement, the roles of leader, recorder, and IEP transcriber should be rotated among professionals as appropriate. Recorders and transcribers may find it helpful to use word processors, specialized IEP software, or other computer applications in the preparation of the IEP document (Male, 1997).

The IEP team for Lark, the middle school student introduced in the opening vignette, included Lark, her grandmother, the lead teacher from her seventh-grade team, the special education teacher for students with behavior disorders, the school psychologist, and the assistant principal. Each member had completed the IEP premeeting planning guide in advance as the basis for their meeting agenda. All of the team members, including Lark and her grandmother, shared their "visions" for her future. They discussed her strengths and learning needs. School members took time to praise Lark's social and emotional growth during the past year. They also commended her grandmother for her efforts to work closely with the school members of the team.

Their collective contributions were captured on the team IEP planning form shown in Figure 10.4. Section I summarizes her present levels of performance (i.e., what is known about Lark). Participants have characterized Lark's interests and skills, learning style, and areas of concern and need. Section II, achievement of hopes and dreams, constitutes the heart of the intervention plan: specific goals and objectives, suggested resources and strategies, and success indicators. The most important decisions, those that are central to the IEP process, were made at this planning meeting.

Working together for consensus, the planning team defined five major goals to help Lark be successful in school this year and prepare her for the future. As potential goals were identified, the team leader deliberately asked Lark about each one. Did she think the goal was appropriate? Would she support it? What would it take for her to achieve the goal? Several of the goals address academic and social skills of particular concern to Lark and her grandmother. This learning plan also reflects the insights of the school professionals on her team who clearly understand the short- and long-term performance expectations for high school graduation. For example, they know that Lark must pass the district's eighth-grade math competency test with a score of 80% or better to enroll in a credit-bearing math class as a high school freshman.

To make the best use of group time, the special education teacher agreed to take the lead in transferring the content from this planning form to the actual IEP form used by the school district. The specific section of the IEP listing goals for Lark is shown in Figure 10.5 on page 224. Lark's team decided to meet again the following week to review and sign the IEP document.

Several key points should be kept in mind as teams plan IEPs. First, educators on the planning team must remember that IEPs define the curricular priorities for individual students with disabilities. The general education or core curriculum should serve as the appropriate initial frame of reference for planning IEPs because it maintains students' graduation and diploma options and enables them to participate as fully as possible in general education offerings (Laycock & Korinek, 1989). IDEA specifies that only when participation in the general curriculum with supplementary support and services can be demonstrated as not benefiting the student should an alternative curriculum be considered. For most students, therefore, the core curriculum constitutes their basic educational program. As students' support needs increase, the curriculum is adapted or individualized to serve them more appropriately. The curriculum for some students may focus more on the key concepts and skills considered the essential outcomes in a subject area. For the few students with significant support needs, their IEP goals are individualized to maximize their appropriate participation in current and future environments. For students with high ability, the curriculum should be adapted through enrichment to focus on more advanced concepts and skills.

FIGURE 10.4   IEP Team Planning Form.

Student Name: __Lark Myles__   Date: __November 10, 1997__   Grade: __7th__

Team Members: __Carol Myles (guardian), David Webster (special educator), Bonnie Castle (general educa-tor), Faye Gunnell (social worker), Deb Hawkins (Assistant Principal)__

What We Know: Present Performance Levels

Interests and Skills	Learning Style	Concerns and Needs
• Artistic; likes drama, reading, gothic; loves movies • Average ability, good thinking skills • Gets passing grades when she does the work • Very verbal • More mature than peers in some areas • Motivated by peer attention • Good attendance • Interested in her grandmother • Interested in her appearance	• Visual, creative, experiential learning • Has to see relevance • Responds to challenging experiences but requires support/monitoring • Works well with carefully selected peer • Good with details • Up and down days • Enthusiastic about things that interest her	• Frequently does not follow directions • Uses inappropriate language • Disrespectful to teachers • Doesn't hand in work; thus does not pass classes • Failing in math • Violates dress code • Concerns regarding sex • Difficulty getting along with peers

What We Need to Do: Achieving Hopes and Dreams

Hopes and Dreams	Student Goals	Instructional Activities and Support	Success Indicators
• For the year: stay in school and be success-ful • Complete and turn in work • Make friends; learn to work with others • Get along better with teachers and parents • Feel better about herself • Take responsibility for sexual behavior • Use appropriate language • High school diploma • Plans after graduation • Part-time job experi-ence • Develop outside school interest	Improvement in: • Social skills • Interactions with other (teachers, peers, grandmother) • "School-appropriate" appearance and language • Basic 7th grade math skills • "Good student" behaviors (e.g., fol-lowing directions, completing and turning in work)	• Weekly talks with trusted/knowledge-able adult • Reading materials • Journaling • Small-group discussion • Drama club teacher • Volunteering • Job training • Math tutor • Tues./Thurs. home-work group • Placement in co-taught math class • Computer-assisted math practice • Home–school contract • Check daily planner • Study skills through language arts class	• More positive class-room interactions • Lark's comments, par-ticipation in groups, grandmother's report • Teacher reports • Journal entries • More responsible sex-ual behavior (discuss this with guidance?) • Scores on homework, quizzes, computer practice, tests • Tutor reports • Decreased office referrals • Classwork in mini-class • Daily performance in content classes • 80% or better on behavioral contract reports and work completion scores • School activities participation

Note: Team members complete this form during their meeting. This document is handwritten. It is presented here in a typed format to make it easier to read.

FIGURE 10.5   Lark's IEP Goals.

Goal 1   Lark will master the basic 7th grade math skills as described in the district curriculum.

Goal 2   Lark will follow school and team rules.

Goal 3   Lark will improve interactions with peers and adults in school and in her home.

Goal 4   Lark will develop effective organizational and study skills.

Goal 5   Lark will complete daily assignments in her classes.

Those who are highly gifted pursue individualized goals that extend beyond the core curriculum. Figure 10.6 illustrates the range of curricular considerations for program planning in inclusive schools. The dotted lines on the figure indicate that options are not completely discrete and that student needs may vary across subject areas and time.

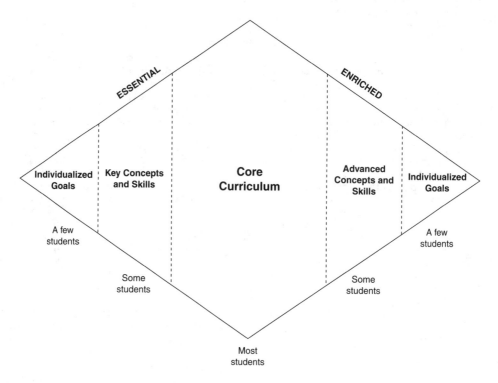

FIGURE 10.6   Instructional Planning Considerations in the Classroom.

Note: Although the underlying principle in inclusive classrooms is a belief that all students can learn, not all students need to learn everything. Some parts of the curriculum are more essential to individual students than others.

Educators must also keep in mind that IEPs should be written in "user-friendly" language for all team members, including the students themselves. Concern for writing technically correct goals and objectives should never overshadow the importance of clear statements that accurately communicate the team's IEP priorities for the individual student. IEP goals and objectives must also be stated in measurable terms. Figure 10.7 provides some alternative examples of evaluative procedures, schedules, and criteria that may help teams formulate more complete and useful goals and objectives. This matrix may assist teams in selecting specific evaluation approaches that are appropriate for the target skills or behaviors,

FIGURE 10.7   Examples of Evaluation Criteria, Procedures, and Schedules. This table is useful to create short-term objectives or benchmarks for IEP goals.

Procedures	Schedules	Criteria
Teacher-made tests	Daily	With ___ % accuracy
Behavior checklist	___ times per day	8 out of 10 trials
Duration recording	Weekly per class	For at least ___ minutes
Teacher observations with anecdotal records	___ times weekly	Every class period
Student self-evaluation	___ times each month	Within ___ minutes
Timed worksheets	Every ___ weeks	At a rate of ___ times per minute
Probe sheets	Each marking period	With < ___ errors
Assignment completion	During ___ classes	Legibly and within the lines
Teacher–student conferences	For a unit	Correctly for ___ consecutive days
Weekly work/behavior contracts	Before/after class	Without teacher prompts
Chapter/unit tests	By the end of the week	___ % improvement over baseline
Portfolio/journal entries	When asked to do so	___ times per interval or period

Sample Objectives:

Juan will compute fractions using mixed numbers with 80 percent accuracy on teacher-made weekly quizzes.

Regina will remain on task at least 30 of 45 minutes during class as measured by time-sampling observation two times a week.

Kimberly will complete all classwork assignments for 10 consecutive days as measured by records in teacher's grade books.

adequate as meaningful measures of performance, and feasible for implementation in classroom or other settings. The samples provided at the bottom of Figure 10.7 illustrate several different ways of stating complete behavioral objectives. Figure 10.8 provides further examples by listing specific behavioral objectives for two of Lark's IEP goals.

To ensure appropriate classroom support for students with IEPs and for their classroom teachers, planning teams should determine the daily, weekly, and monthly support and related services that will be needed. Services such as co-teaching, weekly consultation, daily paraeducator involvement, assistive technology, and other equipment should be specified on the IEP document. Any strategies, modifications, and accommodations that will be needed, including accommodations in mandated testing, should also be identified. Similarly, important medical, health, or emergency information that teachers, paraeducators, students, and others need to be aware of should be included. If the desired level of student participation is

FIGURE 10.8   Examples of Lark's IEP Goals and Objectives.

Goal 2: Lark will follow school and team rules.

Objectives	Criteria	Evaluation Procedures
Lark will wear appropriate clothing to school	0 occurrences per week of being sent home for dress code violations	Teacher observation using school dress code requirements
Lark will use appropriate language on the bus and at school	0 occurrences per week of inappropriate language	Number of referrals to office or disciplinary actions for inappropriate language
Lark will talk respectfully to teachers and other school personnel	0 referrals for inappropriate language per week	Number of referrals to office or disciplinary actions for inappropriate language

Goal 4: Lark will develop effective organizational and study skills.

Objectives	Criteria	Evaluation Procedures
Lark will record all class assignments in a daily planner	90%	Daily checks by teacher and grandmother
Lark will complete and submit assignments	4 of 5 days (80%) with 80% accuracy	Daily records in teacher grade books
Lark will attend and participate in the student homework support group	6 of 8 times/month (75%)	Student self-evaluation and peer evaluations of participation

limited in some areas or if ongoing classroom modifications will be needed, these details should be noted.

Supplementary Implementation Tools for Individualized Education Programs

Planning teams often supplement the formal IEP document with additional attachments. Some teams find it helpful to design more detailed support plans on large pieces of poster board or on a chalkboard. These plans should specify the IEP goals, daily instructional periods in which goals can be addressed, and support services that are needed to facilitate student success. An example of an instructional support matrix developed for Lark is presented in Figure 10.9 on page 228. The matrix outlines team recommendations to meet Lark's defined IEP goals across the entire school day. It specifies what Lark will do (e.g., use a calculator for modified tests) and what school and family members will do (e.g., check homework record weekly) to support her in each of her classes. Some strategies, such as a daily homework record and daily self-monitoring chart, are applicable across all subject areas. Others, such as the interventions for math, are specific to one class. Developing an IEP instructional support plan and the document itself ensure that there is a comprehensive and cohesive process for addressing IEP goals throughout the school day and that all team members, including the student, know what they are to do and why.

Given time limits, some teams may "draft" support service plans with the understanding that final versions will be developed after the meeting by one or more team members. Like the IEP, all participating team members should receive a copy of this document. This document allows teachers, paraeducators, substitute teachers, specialists, and others to identify "at a glance" student goals and objectives that may need additional attention or alternative instructional opportunities (Giangreco, 1996b). It takes extra time for planning teams to develop appropriate support plans after IEP goals are established. Admittedly, in some challenging cases, it may require additional team meetings for this essential activity. The importance of appropriate classroom support in inclusive programs for students with disabilities cannot be minimized (Kochhar & West, 1996). Determining the types of support that will be needed and the amount of support that schools will provide helps build trust, confidence in the process, and a shared commitment to achieve targeted goals. Knowing that support will be provided on an ongoing basis is reassuring to classroom teachers, families, and students. In addition, early attention to the support details facilitates ongoing instructional planning and promotes collaboration.

Think About It...

Using Figure 10.9, suggest additional strategies for addressing Lark's goals across the curriculum.

FIGURE 10.9 **IEP Instructional Support.** *Note:* Daily instructional periods serve as the reference point for planning classroom activities and support programs. This figure provides an example of Lark's instructional support plan in target subject areas as identified by the planning team.

DAILY INSTRUCTIONAL PERIODS

	Language Arts/Drama	Math	Social Studies	Science	PE/Health
Goal 1—Lark will master basic 7th-grade math skills as described in the district curriculum.		• Use calculator for modified tests • Math tutor—M&W • Computer practice at home			
Goal 2—Lark will follow school and team rules.		• Daily self-monitoring chart • Weekly conference with special education teacher • Weekly teacher reports			
Goal 3—Lark will improve interactions with peers and adults at school and in her home.	• Weekly participation in Friday social skills group during language arts • Weekly after-school drama club participation				• Weekly conference with physical education (PE) teacher during class time
Goal 4—Lark will develop effective organizational and study skills.	• Check homework record weekly		• Strategies instruction • Daily homework record		
Goal 5—Lark will complete daily assignments in her classes.			• Daily homework record • Weekly progress report		

Advantages of a Collaborative Process for Individualized Education Programs

This process for IEP development offers several advantages over more traditional approaches. It reflects the spirit of IDEA as well as specific requirements of the law. By engaging team members who are the key stakeholders more actively in program planning, the process facilitates creative discussion, brainstorming, and problem solving. Preplanning and team planning guides ensure that multiple perspectives are captured in IEP development. In particular, school personnel have opportunities to gain better understanding of family goals, expectations, and resources. The focus on student performance in general education classrooms promotes full participation by classroom teachers and produces clearer indicators of success. The recommended structure for collaborative IEP development encourages integration of data from multiple formal and informal sources for a more complete and accurate student profile. Explicit attention to student skills and interests provides team members with more information to build on student strengths. The more thorough understanding of student performance proves especially helpful when functional assessments and behavioral support plans are necessary to meet student needs. Overall, coordinated and cohesive IEP planning contributes to greater transfer and generalization of student skills across settings, because teachers, specialists, and family members have collaborated on the essential elements of the plan. Finally, active involvement by family members and professionals in IEP decision making increases the likelihood that all will be truly committed to the implementation and support of the program the team has developed, thus enhancing the chances of success for the student.

Chapter Summary

Planning appropriate, innovative, and most importantly, educationally relevant programs for students with disabilities in inclusive settings requires many seasoned program planners to think about the process in new ways. Many special educators, as well as their general education colleagues, must take a broader view of learning as they develop appropriate goals and objectives; this is especially true in planning programs for students with significant support needs. To achieve this, educators must be truly committed to the belief that all students can learn. Although this statement sounds painfully obvious at this point in the text, it is important to remember that for too long, many students' IEPs have been written as if they had little or nothing to gain from education (Orelove & Malatchi, 1996). To make inclusion meaningful for all students and manageable for all school professionals, the IEP planning process must change. It must reflect greater collaboration with families and communities, stronger transdisciplinary efforts, and more creativity than has been shown during the past 20 years of mandated IEPs. The process for individualizing education programs described in this chapter represents both a change and challenge for school professionals and families.

CHAPTER ACTIVITIES

1. Interview a classroom teacher, special educator, or other professional who has served on IEP teams. In their experience, how collaborative were the team meetings? What factors influenced the degree of collaboration? Share the process and planning guides from this chapter. To what extent might these enhance the IEP process in this person's school?

3. In what ways does the IEP process recommended by the authors differ from current practices? What obstacles might be encountered in attempting to implement the approach recommended in this chapter? Suggest specific ways that those obstacles might be overcome.

11 Teaching Academics in Inclusive Classrooms

LEARNING OBJECTIVES

1. Identify considerations in planning appropriate units and lessons for heterogeneous classes.
2. Describe effective practices for key phases of instruction for heterogeneous groups.
3. Explain a systematic process for analyzing and selecting accommodations for students with special academic learning needs.
4. Describe applications of promising accommodations for students with special academic learning needs.

Chanay Wells, a special educator, and Gloria Van Acker, a sixth-grade science teacher were planning a unit on natural resources that they would be co-teaching for the next 2 weeks. The unit focused on management of renewable and nonrenewable resources and the cost-benefit tradeoffs in conservation policies. The sixth-grade science objectives for the district emphasize data analysis, experimentation, and methods for testing the validity of predictions and conclusions. Although many students were ready to launch into scientific investigations related to natural resources, others were just learning to identify some resources around them.

Prior to their meeting, Chanay and Gloria had reviewed the textbook chapters and teacher's manual on natural resources and made notes about possible community sites, speakers, materials, activities, and projects that might be included in the unit. Although Chanay had been co-teaching science with Gloria for several months, she relied on Gloria to coordinate their units with districtwide learning objectives in science and identify the "big ideas" and content to be taught in their science lessons. Gloria depended on Chanay to help her plan for and meet the needs of the special education students included in their class of 26 students. Chanay also took the lead in developing learning and social skills strategies for a number of other at-risk students in the class.

The students in the class identified for special education included three students with learning disabilities, one with emotional disorders, and another with physical disabilities. Several other students showed difficulties in their study skills and social interactions. Standardized test scores for the group ranged from the bottom quartile for some to the top quartile for others. In addition, 4 students in the class participated in the gifted program at their school. These students used class time for special projects through curriculum compacting in some of their regular subjects. Planning effective lessons and units of instruction for this group was always a challenge.

The previous chapters addressed identification of instructional targets for students with special needs (i.e., the curriculum or *what* the students should learn). This chapter focuses on instruction (i.e., *how* the curriculum is delivered effectively) in inclusive classrooms. It is important to identify teaching techniques that maximize learning for a wide variety of students in inclusive classrooms and to tailor adaptations to meet specific learning needs. Considerations for classroom adjustments to facilitate student success are presented here within the context of differentiated curriculum and effective instruction with examples designed to meet a variety of student needs. As King-Sears (1997) noted, "The best academic practices for inclusion are instructional techniques that promote achievement, independence, and interdependence of individual students—with and without disabilities—within settings that include students who have a range of learning needs as a learning community" (p. 18). Many of these practices are reviewed in this chapter.

Numerous instructional practices are presented to stimulate readers' thinking and action and to remind educators of potential applications of techniques with which they may already be familiar. Professionals new to the field or to some of the practices that are discussed may need more extensive illustrations of specific adaptations and techniques than can be provided in this chapter. Readers are strongly encouraged to consult the references that have been provided to obtain more information regarding instructional implementation.

Context for Accommodations: Differentiated Curriculum and Effective Instruction

Traditionally, special education has focused on assessment, planning, and instruction for individual students with identified disabilities. Inclusive education and the mandates embodied in the latest amendments to the Individuals with Disabilities Education Act (IDEA, 1997) require educators to develop better collaborative relationships with others. Increasingly, research from general and special education is converging as classrooms become increasingly diverse and the needs of students become more complex (King-Sears, 1997; Simmons & Kameenui, 1996). As educators and specialists engage in reflective planning and practice, the needs of individual students must remain a focal point within the context of the general education curriculum and effective instruction. Accommodations are best considered within this same context. Appropriate curriculum and effective instruction benefit all learners and reduce the number of unique adaptations required by students with special academic learning needs, particularly those with mild to moderate disabilities.

Differentiated Curriculum

Tomlinson (1995) described a *differentiated classroom* as one in which "the teacher plans and carries out varied approaches to content (what students learn), process (how they learn), and product (how they demonstrate learning) in anticipation of and response to student differences in readiness, interest, and learning needs" (p. 11). Differentiation may take place with various aspects of curriculum and instruction including the type of knowledge emphasized (basic to transformational), the representational level of materials or ideas (concrete to abstract), pacing of instruction (slow to quick), task level (simple to complex), structure of the lesson or activity (more to less), and student independence required for completion and mastery (less to greater). Use of flexible groupings, different assignments and projects, learning or interest centers, varied texts and resource materials, multiple media, and technology can all facilitate the differentiation process. For example, at various times in the school day or class period, some students may engage in self-directed practice activities (e.g., journal writing, silent or partner reading, self-correcting exercises, basic skills practice, computer-assisted instruction) while others engage in peer- or teacher-facilitated learning (Tomlinson, 1995). The greater the range of learner differences, the greater the differentiation of content, process, and products needed to address those differences.

Even without the inclusion of students with identified disabilities, the vast majority of classrooms have students with a wide range of learning abilities, styles, and needs. Successful teachers recognize and respond to these differences by being student-centered; proactive in planning and instruction; and open to a variety of instructional strategies, arrangements, and supports. They also recognize the value of collaborating with families, specialists, and administrators to complement their expertise and bring additional perspectives, talents, and resources to their students.

Effective Instruction

Successful educators implement instructional practices that are supported by research and effective with a wide range of students. Some of these practices include using curriculum-based assessment; activating prior knowledge and making connections to new learning; clarifying objectives, expectations, and presentations; providing opportunities for active learning; and using specific positive and corrective feedback (Brophy & Good, 1986; Cohen, 1993; Englert, Tarrant, & Mariage, 1992; Rosenshine & Stevens, 1986). These techniques are employed during key phases of an instructional cycle comprised of (1) planning, (2) establishing a learning set, (3) presenting new material, (4) conducting guided and independent practice, and (5) evaluating student progress (Hudson, Lignugaris-Kraft, & Miller, 1993). The more effectively that educators differentiate instruction, the greater the likelihood that students will acquire critical concepts and skills across a variety of learning needs and preferences. Indeed, Wang, Haertel, and Walberg (1993) found that achievement correlates more powerfully with instruction than with other variables including demographics, policies, and organizational differences.

Several models have been proposed to determine appropriate accommodations in curriculum and instruction for students with learning and behavioral differences to help them benefit from educational programs (e.g., Cohen, 1993; Friend & Bursuck, 1996; Lewis & Doorlag, 1995; Warger & Pugach, 1996). Common to these models is the process of analyzing curricular content and demands; identifying strengths and needs of students in relation to these demands; brainstorming and selecting environmental, curricular, and instructional accommodations; implementing appropriate accommodations; and evaluating student progress. For students with special needs, this process is enhanced through professional collaboration that draws on the unique expertise of general educators and specialists, often assisted by paraeducators, working with the students and their families. Typically, general educators are well versed in the standard curriculum and subject matter expectations for students; specialists have been prepared to identify individual strengths, weaknesses, and learning preferences as well as alternative instructional strategies to address individual differences. Working as a collaborative team through assistance teaming, consultation, or co-teaching, professionals can determine the best matches between curriculum/instruction and accommodations for students with special needs. This is a dynamic process, as the demands of the curriculum and the skills of students change over time and vary across subject areas and tasks.

Considerations for Students with Significant Support Needs

Students with significant support needs in one or more areas comprise a very small percentage of students in special education (U.S. Department of Education [USDOE], 1998). Relevant tasks for these students that cut across subject areas include attending to teacher and task, following directions, managing materials, requesting help, expressing needs, responding to questions and comments, interacting with peers and adults, decision making, problem solving, and functional academics (Downing, 1996). Many general education students require explicit instruction and practice on these same skills. Students with significant support needs typically require more specialized adaptations such as the use of manipulatives, more functional assignments, and alternate communication systems. Even these more extensive adjustments can benefit other students in general education classrooms.

Allowing partial participation in classroom lessons and activities, incorporating community-based education and functional academics, and integrating therapies into class routines so that they support successful completion of classroom activities are ways to increase the level of participation and independence for students with significant support needs and their typical peers (Cohen, 1993). For example, Symbreel counts coins while her peers complete a worksheet on math calculations (partial participation), Harris works on recognizing survival vocabulary during spelling (functional academics), and Cindy's occupational therapist comes to her home living class to help her work on grasping skills in the context of a lesson on meal preparation (integrated therapy).

For educators new to inclusive education, selecting appropriate practice activities for students with significant support needs can be challenging. This process becomes easier as planners become more experienced. Despite lower levels of functioning by these students, care must be taken to provide age-appropriate materials and to ensure attention to functional or life skills. Lowell, York, Doyle, and Kronberg (1995) suggest a continuum of possibilities in selecting appropriate activities and assignments for students with more significant support needs. Some possible options include:

1. Using the same task and materials as are used with typical peers.
2. Using the same task but an easier step (for example, Quong, a student with severe motor problems, may point to pictures that begin with the letter *p* to meet his communication objectives, while the other kindergarten students cut and paste the *p* pictures onto a worksheet).
3. Using the same task with different materials (for example, Kevin, a nonreader, "reads" the story by following along with an audiotape while classmates read from the text).
4. Using a different task related to the theme of the lesson (for example, Liana, a student with oral language disabilities, brings a holiday decoration used in her family and tells the class about her family's German traditions while other students may write about winter holidays celebrated in different cultures).
5. Using a different objective and a different task from the rest of the class (for example, Jose who needs to improve self-help skills, works with the occupational therapist on toileting and dressing tasks in a private bathroom while the other students engage in writing workshop activities).

Collaboration among specialists, classroom teachers, family members, paraeducators, and others involved with students with significant support needs is essential to planning programs, selecting accommodations, and implementing services that address critical competencies.

Due to space limitations, the suggestions in this chapter focus primarily on students with less extensive support needs, who constitute the vast majority of students served in general education classes. Readers are encouraged to review some of the many helpful resources available for more in-depth information on program development and implementation for students with significant support

> ### Think About It...
>
> How do you address "fairness" issues with typical students in inclusive classes when they question adjustments made for students with disabilities?

needs (e.g., Block, 1994; Downing, 1996; Giangreco, Cloniger, & Iverson, 1997; Orelove & Sobsey, 1996; Rainforth & York-Barr, 1997; Snell & Janney, 1999).

Instructional Strategies and Accommodations

The following sections summarize recommended effective practices and describe possible accommodations that can be implemented at various phases of the instructional cycle. Figure 11.1 serves as an advance organizer or blueprint for this chapter by noting key techniques and potential accommodations used during the various instructional phases. Terms and techniques are described, but detailed descriptions of how to implement the instructional strategies and accommodations are limited. Readers are again encouraged to consult the references provided for more specific information on techniques of interest.

Planning Instruction

In the planning phase of instruction, educators select content to be covered in the unit or lessons as well as specify learning objectives, pretest students with some form of curriculum-based assessment, select presentation and practice activities, determine needed resources, group students, assign professional and paraeducator roles, structure the environment (e.g., space, seating, routines, rules, rewards, transitions), and allocate instructional time. Curriculum planning and instruction should focus on the *big ideas* or concepts and principles that facilitate the most efficient acquisition of knowledge in a domain (Carnine, 1994), rather than presentation and memorization of isolated facts. Big ideas represent themes that are fundamental to the domains and serve as *anchors* to which details or smaller ideas can be connected and understood in context. Examples of big ideas in various subject areas are presented in Figure 11.2 on page 238.

Today curricular content and skills in subject areas are often dictated by standards or benchmarks for learning set by state or local systems. Individual profiles of students' strengths, interests, preferred learning modalities, and difficulty areas help educators make decisions about expectations and appropriate lesson accommodations. Individually teachers can make many accommodations but, as noted in Chapter 4, consultation or co-teaching may be necessary when demands increase because of the complexity of the subject matter, learner needs, required resources, and the like.

FIGURE 11.1 Phases of Instruction and Examples of Potential Accommodations.

PHASES OF EFFECTIVE INSTRUCTION

POTENTIAL ACCOMMODATIONS	Planning	Learning Set	Presentation	Guided and Independent Practice	Evaluation
	• Select content • Specify objectives • Assess based on the curriculum • Select materials/resources • Group students • Design activities	• Check homework • Review prior learning • State objectives/expectations • Activate background knowledge	• Ensure attention • Provide rationale • Present in small steps at brisk pace • Model desired responses • Use examples and nonexamples • Check for understanding	• Provide numerous opportunities to respond/practice • Ask frequent questions • Correct mistakes • Reinforce correct responses • Lead initial work on assignments • Monitor students • Develop meaningful assignments • Reteach as necessary	• Monitor progress regularly • Provide for review/maintenance • Assess performance • Make decisions based on performance data
KWL		✓	✓		
Graphic organizers	✓	✓	✓	✓	✓
Study guides	✓	✓	✓	✓	✓
Notetaking			✓	✓	
Cognitive strategies	✓	✓	✓	✓	✓
Mediated scaffolding			✓	✓	✓
Peer-mediated practice			✓	✓	✓
Modified assignments				✓	✓
Authentic assessment	✓	✓		✓	✓

FIGURE 11.2   Examples of "Big Ideas" or Fundamental Themes in Content Areas.

History
Four factors relevant to group success in a war are capability, resources, quality of
leadership, and motivation (Carnine, Miller, Bean, & Zigmond, 1994).

Geography
All places on the earth have distinctive physical and human characteristics that give
them meaning and character and distinguish them from other places and regions
(Souza & Downs, 1994).

Language Arts
Story grammar (description of typical story elements such as theme, setting, characters,
goal or problem, attempts at resolution, resolution, and reactions) provides an
effective summary and indication of comprehension of most stories used for
classroom reading instruction (Carnine, Silbert, & Kameenui, 1990).

Math
Mathematics involves problem solving, communicating mathematical ideas,
mathematical reasoning, and connecting mathematics to real-life applications
(Commission on Standards for School Mathematics, 1989).

Science
Primary processes for science include observing, classifying, measuring, using spatial
relationships, communicating, predicting, and inferring (Mastropieri & Scruggs,
1994).

Several potential accommodations to be considered during lesson planning
are shown in Figure 11.3. In reviewing the list, readers will note that many suggestions may enhance learning success for *all* students but may not be absolutely
essential to their learning. However, for students with disabilities or those at risk
for failure, appropriate accommodations are critical for their success. For these
students accommodations make the vital difference between meaningful, productive participation in the inclusive classroom and academic or social failure.

Establishing a Learning Set: Getting Students Ready to Learn

Prior to beginning instruction on new concepts or skills, a number of effective
practices have been recommended (Brophy & Good, 1986; Cohen, 1993; Englert et
al., 1992; Rosenshine & Stevens, 1986). Prepresentation practices include checking
homework to hold students accountable for previous learning and to determine
understanding before moving on in the lesson, briskly reviewing previous learning, stating the objective of the lesson, and communicating expectations for performance. Educators try to spark student interest in the topic and create a mindset
or context for new learning.

FIGURE 11.3   **Potential Accommodations to Be Considered during Lesson Planning.**

- Develop instructional posters, bulletin boards, notebooks, and centers.
- Develop and/or adapt presentation and practice materials by changing the size, format, font, number of problems, and/or complexity of problems.
- Design flexible student grouping arrangements to facilitate individual, small-group, and large-group instruction and support.
- Provide concept, lesson, and unit organizers (e.g., unit study guides, weekly lecture outlines, graphic organizers).
- Use instructional resources such as films, guest speakers, labs, field trips, computer software, and audiotaped texts and materials on related topics.
- Use more examples, modeling, or a simpler explanation; facilitate accelerated students' completion of in-depth projects on the same topic.
- Cover less material in smaller steps and ensure mastery of essential prerequisite skills before moving on to the next concept or skill.
- Teach problem-based learning through teacher role plays, models, class demonstrations, simulation activities, or experiments.
- Teach students to use adaptive and assistive technology and software for composition, outlining, graphics, databases, presentation, and information searching; teach keyboarding skills.
- Teach cognitive strategies (e.g., mnemonics, comprehension, self-monitoring, paraphrasing, test taking) and study skills (e.g., highlighter use, note cards, notebook organization, time management).

Carnine (1994) pointed out the importance of *primed background knowledge* at the introductory phase of instruction. "Priming" background knowledge involves reminding students of previous experiences and learning relevant to the new concepts or skills to be presented. Guided discussion at this stage allows teachers to assess the depth and accuracy of students' knowledge and prerequisite skills related to the topic or skill. For example, a lesson on mammals may begin with a discussion of what students know about animals familiar to them in relation to critical characteristics of mammals. A lesson on probability could begin by having students predict the chances of drawing a white marble from a box of black and white marbles, given the numbers of each color contained in the mixture.

Simple techniques to capture students' attention, a prerequisite to their learning, and to enhance student interest in a lesson include providing novelty or props. For example, an interesting artifact such as an actual preserved brain may increase student interest in a lesson on the nervous system. Other attention-getters relate lesson concepts or examples to students' backgrounds and interests in phenomena such as sports, television characters, hobbies, social events, or food. Eliciting associations by asking students to recall experiences or perceptions related to the topic may also be effective. For example, one teacher asked students to recall their greatest vacation prior to "traveling" to a new region of study in geography. Educators must clarify connections between attention-getters and the topic being introduced to avoid students' remembering only the novel item or experience and missing the point being made.

Other techniques that can be used to get students ready to learn, spark student interest, and introduce new topics or skills include: (1) Know—Want to learn—Learned (KWL), (2) graphic organizers, (3) anticipation guides, and (4) study guides described in the following sections.

Know—Want to Learn—Learned (KWL).   KWL (Ogle, 1986) is a technique that helps students to identify what they already *know* about a topic, what they *want to learn* or questions they have about the topic, and what they *learned* as instruction and study on the topic progresses. Educators can record know (K) and want to learn (W) responses for the class in various formats (e.g., flipchart with columns for each heading, overhead transparency). In addition to priming background knowledge and enhancing motivation, KWL allows educators to discern the class range of experience with the subject of study, identify class "experts," and provide students an opportunity to raise questions and share interests. Periodically throughout the lesson, teachers and students can revisit the KWL to identify the questions that have been answered and new questions that have arisen, and to document knowledge and skills that have been learned in the course of the lessons. Using different-colored markers to record new learning highlights student progress throughout the unit.

Graphic Organizers.   Graphic organizers are "visual formats that help students organize their understanding of information being presented or read and the relationships between various parts of the information" (Friend & Bursuck, 1996, p. 486). Graphic organizers provide a visual means of helping students to generate, record, and organize their thoughts; make connections; and focus their learning and study (Archer & Gleason, 1990; Hyerle, 1996). They are also useful organizers for writing projects.

In constructing graphic organizers, Archer and Gleason (1990) recommend that educators determine the most critical content to be covered and organize these concepts, ideas, events, facts, or details as simply as possible in a diagram that best matches the structure of the important content. Students may be given partially completed diagrams on which to take notes as the teacher presents the information in class. This involves the class in constructing the visual aid, and provides a multisensory learning experience. Blank or partially completed visual tools may also be used for small group or individual practice and assessment activities. By varying the degree of structure provided to learners (e.g., complexity, amount of information included on the visual), graphic organizers can be used easily and effectively to differentiate instruction.

Examples of several types of graphic organizers are shown in Figure 11.4. These organizers include the following visual formats.

1. *Semantic maps or webs.* A semantic map or web depicts major categories and subcategories, or main ideas and details related to a topic or concept. For example,

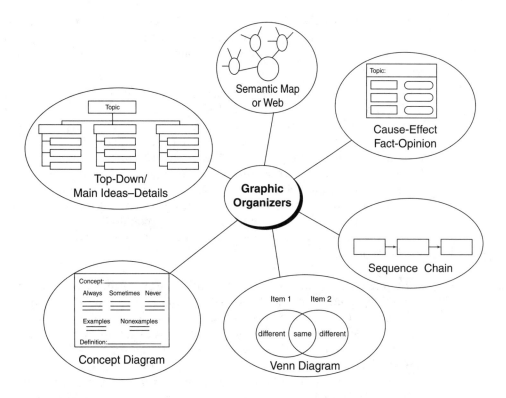

FIGURE 11.4   Samples of Graphic Organizers.

whales might be the major concept in the center circle with smaller circles radiating out from the center devoted to associated categories such as types of whales, what they eat, and where they live.

2. *Main idea—details or top-down tables.* These visuals show main ideas or topics, supporting details or subtopics, and related examples. For example, the U.S. Government may be the main topic with the three branches of government and their respective functions as subtopics and examples.

3. *Cause-effect or fact-opinion tables.* These tables demonstrate connections or contrasts, such as sources of pollution and environmental effects or facts versus opinions about people with disabilities.

4. *Sequence chains.* In a sequence chain, ordered steps of a process or procedure are displayed, such as the steps in oil refinement, paper production, a bill becoming a law, algorithms for solving mathematical problems, or chronological events in history.

5. *Venn diagrams.* These diagrams show similarities and differences between two concepts, such as mammals and reptiles, two characters in a play, physical features of two countries, or comparisons and contrasts between democracies and dictatorships.

6. *Concept diagrams.* Concept diagrams portray critical characteristics or attributes, definitions, examples and nonexamples of particular concepts (Bulgren, Schumaker, & Deshler, 1988). For example, polygons are plane figures with more than two angles and sides. "Always present" characteristics might include more than two sides, more than two angles, area, line segments joined at ends to form angles; "never present" attributes would be curves, open figures, rays; and "sometimes present" features may be varying numbers of sides. The examples might include triangles, hexagons, pentagons; nonexamples could be circles, rays, lines, and squiggles. After multiple models, students can be expected to discriminate and generate original examples and nonexamples of concepts using the critical attributes to justify their answers.

Anticipation Guides.   Anticipation guides are interesting lists of true-false, agree-disagree, truth-myth, or fact-fiction statements about a topic designed to generate interest and discussion among students prior to beginning formal instruction (Vacca & Vacca, 1986). For example, statements such as "Cookies are healthier breakfast food than cereal" or "Carrots are poison for most people with diabetes" may stimulate discussion, prompt independent reading and research to find or support answers, and increase student interest in a unit on nutrition. "Shakespeare and soap opera writers have a lot in common," and "The bigger the container, the cheaper (per unit) the product contained therein" are examples that can peak interest in literature and math lessons, respectively. Initial responses to these statements may be recorded, tallied, and revisited after reading, research, or instruction on the topic.

Study Guides.   Study guides are outlines or questions used to highlight important information to be learned (Lovitt & Horton, 1987) and are helpful to students at the beginning as well as throughout various phases of lessons. Study guides require educators to identify essential vocabulary, concepts, facts, and skills to be covered in a lesson or unit and then develop questions or items that prompt students to focus on these key elements. Item types may include short answer, cloze, matching, or a mixture of question types. Depending on the needs of the students, basic study guides can be adapted easily with wider margins to allow note taking next to related questions, page numbers to direct students to the location of answers in the text, or word banks from which to select answers. Students with significant learning difficulties may be required to answer fewer items on the study guide (e.g., circled or starred item numbers, the first three problems in each section, all even-numbered items) than students who perform at higher levels. In addition to serving as an overview of lesson essentials, study guides can also be used for note taking; independent, partner, or small group study; informal assessment and evaluation; and review.

> **Think About It…**
>
> Which of the suggested techniques for establishing a learning set (i.e., Know–Want to learn–Learned, graphic organizers, anticipation guides, study guides) would be most helpful to you as a learner in preparing for a new topic? Why?

Presenting New Material

New concepts and skills are explained and demonstrated during the presentation phase of lessons. Students with disabilities and others who are less successful typically need more structured, systematic presentations because they tend to make fewer connections to previous learning and experiences on their own. Recommended practices for instructional presentations include maintaining learner attention, providing a rationale or purpose for the new learning, presenting new material in small steps and at a brisk pace, using concrete and varied examples, and modeling desired responses (Brophy & Good, 1986; Cohen, 1993; Englert et al., 1992; Rosenshine & Stevens, 1986). Carnine (1994) stressed the need for *strategic integration* in presenting concepts and skills. Strategic integration refers to educators' clarifying critical connections between what students already know and understand and the new concepts or skills being taught to promote higher level learning. The objective of strategic integration is to link essential big ideas across lessons within a curriculum and to emphasize meaningful relationships (Simmons & Kameenui, 1996). For example, when covering various types of governments in social studies, educators could point out the connections between the characteristics of familiar governments recalled by the students in an initial discussion used to prime background knowledge and the critical attributes of new types of government under study.

Sharing the rationale or purpose for learning new ideas or skills enhances lesson relevance and motivation for learning (Deshler, Ellis, & Lenz, 1996). When students can see how they will benefit from the knowledge or skills being taught, they are more likely to put forth the effort required to learn. Rationales should be student-focused and meaningful, especially with students for whom grades are less of an incentive for achievement. Rationales also force educators to consider priorities and connections among concepts and skills.

Techniques to Engage Students during Teacher Presentations.   Opportunities for frequent, correct responses to multilevel questions about what is being learned or opportunities to use the information or skills to perform a variety of tasks strongly correlates with improved academic achievement (Cohen, 1993; Englert et al., 1992; Rosenshine & Stevens, 1986; Harper, Maheady, & Mallette, 1994). Techniques that may be used to engage students and ensure that *all* students, not just the most vocal volunteers, are given opportunities to respond include (1) choral responding, (2) think-pair-share, (3) note-taking techniques, and (4) the PAUSE strategy.

Choral Responding.   Choral responding involves students responding in unison to prompts or questions posed by the teacher following an agreed-on signal for responding (Heward, Courson, & Narayan, 1990). This technique is especially useful for responses to convergent questions or recall of factual information (e.g., math facts, sight vocabulary, steps for a strategy or procedure, spelling words, reiteration of key terms or phrases during instruction). With choral responding, less vocal students have numerous opportunities to hear classmates respond with correct answers which serve as additional models or prompts for their own answers.

Think-Pair-Share/Square.   Think-pair-share/square (Kagan, 1990; Lyman & Foyle, 1990), also known as *sharing pairs* (Harmin, 1994), gives all participants a brief chance to respond, become actively involved, share opinions, exchange ideas, check understandings, and work with a peer. This technique involves the educator posing a question, problem, or issue; giving students time to formulate individual responses and discuss their responses with a partner; then having students share ideas or answers with the entire class (think-pair-share) or another pair of students (think-pair-square). For example, Mr. Larkin asks his 10th-grade economics students to generate examples illustrating the law of supply and demand in their own town. After allowing individual think time, he instructs them to discuss their examples with a peer and then calls on various students during large-group sharing and continued discussion of the topic.

Note Taking.   A number of techniques have been proposed to facilitate accurate note taking and processing of information by students during the presentation phase of lessons. Rooney (1990) suggested that students record notes on main ideas and details of a lecture or reading material using only the left half of the page. Students use abbreviations for commonly used terms and insert question marks where they miss points in the lecture or where they are uncertain about the accuracy of their notes. Students write questions about the information recorded in their notes on the right side of the page and use these questions to facilitate comprehension and study of the material.

Other forms of note taking involve students writing in two or three columns across the entire page to record main ideas and details, as shown in Figure 11.5. For students who have great difficulty simultaneously listening, understanding, synthesizing, and writing critical information during lectures, accommodations in the form of modeled notes written on the board or overhead transparency, partially completed notes (students fill in key words), audiotaped notes, note-taking buddies, or copies of teacher notes may be logical initial accommodations to ensure accurately recorded information for study. If note taking is taught systematically over time, more independent note taking can be expected of many students.

FIGURE 11.5 Formats for Note Taking.

Topic: Structure of U.S. Government

Single-column Note-taking example

Main Idea and Details	*Questions*

1. Branches of government
   Legislative—make laws
   Executive—enforces laws
   Judicial—interprets laws
	1. What are the names and
	   functions of the three
	   branches of government?

Two-column Note-taking example

Main Idea	*Details*
3 branches of government	Legislative Executive Judicial

Three-column Note-taking examples

Main Idea	*Details*	*Questions*
3 branches of government	Legislative Executive Judicial	Name 3 branches of government.

Main Idea	*Details*	*Examples*
3 branches of government	Legislative Executive Judicial	Congress (House and Senate) President and Cabinet Courts

PAUSE Strategy. The PAUSE strategy (Bauwens & Hourcade, 1995) is a complementary strategy that can be used during lecture breaks to enhance active processing and retention of information. The steps of the PAUSE strategy include

> *P*—Partners gather.
> *A*—Ask yourself (the main idea or the most important points).
> *U*—Use your brains, notes, text, etc. to find the answer.
> *S*—See if you are both on track.
> *E*—Eagerly ask the teacher if unsure.

PAUSE steps cue students to partner with a peer to process the main ideas that were presented; check their notes for completeness and accuracy; and use each other, their notes, and the text as resources for information. Student responses to PAUSE exercises also help the educator to assess whether students understood the main points of the presentation or if additional explanation is needed.

Numerous instructional strategies and accommodations exist to enhance the effectiveness of lesson presentations and keep students engaged while learning new concepts, skills, and relationships. Educators are reminded, however, that effective instruction goes beyond isolated teacher, specialist, or paraeducator

Think About It...

If you were delivering a presentation on active student involvement in the classroom, how would you actively engage *your* audience in your presentation? Which techniques described in the presentation phase seem most appropriate for adults? For older students? For young children?

behaviors or techniques to the overall quality of instruction and the nature of adult-student interactions that affect achievement (Englert et al., 1992).

Providing Student Practice on Concepts and Skills

Guided or initial practice refers to the portion of the lesson in which educators carefully facilitate student practice of concepts and skills presented in the lesson. As the name implies, independent practice follows guided practice and involves students practicing individually to reach mastery and fluency (i.e., correct, confident, and rapid rates of responding). Between teacher-guided and independent practice, peer-mediated practice activities can be structured to reinforce learning. A number of techniques designed to maximize the benefits of guided, peer-mediated, and independent student practice are described in the following sections.

Guided Practice.   Educators enhance the results of guided practice by asking frequent questions, correcting mistakes, repeating instructional steps as needed, and leading initial work on assigned problems or examples (Brophy & Good, 1986; Cohen, 1993; Englert et al., 1992; Rosenshine & Stevens, 1986). The goal of this phase of the lesson is to provide frequent opportunities to respond, maximize participation by all students, provide feedback, and facilitate supervised student applications of the information and skills being studied before assigning independent practice.

Effective feedback to students during guided practice should be specific and tailored to student responses; that is, the educator should identify exactly what was correct or incorrect in the answers and prompt correct student responses before moving on to the next question or item. For example, if students provide firm, correct responses, teachers should quickly acknowledge these responses and keep up the pace of instruction. Student responses that are hesitant or show a lack of understanding should receive more elaborate teacher feedback to explain or prompt the correct answer. When explicit feedback is used, students require significantly fewer trials to reach mastery than when more general feedback is provided (Deshler, 1998). Researchers (e.g., Brophy & Good, 1986; Cohen, 1993; Rosenshine & Stevens, 1986) recommend that students reach at least 80 to 90% accuracy in guided practice before moving to independent practice.

Reteaching, additional practice, or both may be provided to individuals or small groups of students whose in-class responses indicate a need for more intensive instruction on basic skills and concepts. This additional help may be provided by the teacher while other students are engaged in independent practice, by co-teachers or paraeducators, or by volunteers under the supervision of the educator. If large numbers of students seem hesitant or confused in their responding, more teacher modeling and guided practice for the entire group is needed before advancing to peer-mediated or independent practice.

The principle of *a turn on every turn* is helpful during the guided practice portion of the lesson to ensure that *all* students respond or problem-solve in some way even though only one student may be designated to provide the answer to a specific question or prompt (Korinek, 1996). Also known as checking for understanding, this type of active involvement is especially important for students with limited language, those who are reluctant to speak in front of their peers, or those who need additional practice to build confidence in their responses. Voting techniques (Harmin, 1994) offer one way to provide a turn on every turn by having students raise "Yes" or "No" cards to respond to teacher questions. Students might note their agreement or disagreement with a classmate's answer using a "thumbs up" or "thumbs down" signal. Degree of understanding could be designated by students raising one, two, or three fingers to signal "don't know," "not sure," and "quite sure" answers to questions or problems. Educators may also require students to work problems, compose sentences, or generate examples at their desks (alone or with a partner) while a designated student answers at the board or on an overhead transparency.

Mediated scaffolding is the temporary assistance and support provided by teachers, peers, or materials to ensure student success in a task (Carnine, 1994) and is highly relevant to the guided practice stage of lessons. When students are learning new concepts or skills, educators can provide more supports or "scaffolds" by carefully structuring the types of cues, tasks, content, and materials used at different points in the students' learning. As learners demonstrate increasing proficiency, supports are faded or progressively withdrawn to promote independence and mastery. Students with special needs and others performing at a lower level may require more scaffolds and slower removal of these assistive devices in order to be successful. One illustration of scaffolding is use of a series of examples that range from simple to more complex to explain and practice a new skill. For instance, in teaching calculation of area, the area of rectangles or squares would be practiced before progressing to areas of more complex shapes. Another type of scaffolding involves designing task requirements that progress from recognition to production, such as requiring students to discriminate among examples of particular types of plant species given only a few choices before expecting them to generate original examples of various species and justify their answers. Prompts are gradually removed as students master the content or skills.

Scaffolds are determined by assessing learner ability, goals for instruction, and task complexity (Simmons & Kameenui, 1996). In heterogeneous classrooms, the need for mediated scaffolding or provision of instructional supports varies

FIGURE 11.6   **Potential Accommodations for Student Practice.**

- Clarify directions. Provide oral and written directions; use simpler language; highlight, underline, or color-code key information. Present directions one or two steps at a time or provide completed examples for reference.
- Design flexible student groups to facilitate individual and small-group practice through peer tutoring or cooperative learning.
- Provide additional guided practice with active student responding before moving on to independent practice.
- Prepare paraeducators, community volunteers, older students, and university interns to serve as tutors and/or practice supervisors.
- Establish small-group learning centers and workstations.
- Develop or adapt self-correcting worksheets, software, or games.
- Change requirements for success (e.g., fewer problems or questions, more time to complete assignments, completion of one part of assignment at a time).
- Allow alternative responses to demonstrate understanding (e.g., drawing, diagramming, oral recording or reporting, dictated answers).
- Enhance positive consequences for task completion through incentives, self-recording, charting, or rewarding successive approximations.

greatly across learning objectives and tasks. Educators who prepare scaffolds to meet a range of learning needs have fewer specialized accommodations to make for students with more significant special education needs. Examples of potential scaffolds and accommodations for practice activities are presented in Figure 11.6.

Peer-Mediated Practice.   Peer-mediated practice can serve as a bridge between guided and independent practice. A variety of peer-mediated structures for student practice exist to facilitate active involvement, increased opportunities to respond, and additional skill applications (Jenkins & Jenkins, 1985; King-Sears, 1997; Utley, Mortweet, & Greenwood, 1997). Peer-mediated learning has tremendous potential as an efficient and cost-effective way to improve performance of students with special needs. Some frequently used formats for peer practice include (1) partner learning, (2) peer tutoring, and (3) cooperative learning.

Partner Learning.   As the name implies, partner learning activities entail student peers working together in dyads to practice skills under study. Examples of partner learning include peer modeling and paired reading. *Peer modeling* refers to one student demonstrating appropriate behaviors for another student to imitate (Utley et al., 1997). Behaviors may involve completing various academic tasks, following classroom or school routines, or engaging in social interactions. For example, Annie shows her classmate, Matt, who has moderate mental retardation, how to use materials safely and how to record observations during science labs. Educators must prepare peer models to fulfill their roles and monitor the learning pairs to ensure that the less skilled partner is benefiting from the peer modeling (Utley et al., 1997).

Paired reading is an instructional device to keep more students simultaneously engaged in active practice in reading or content areas. Students are paired and sit facing each other to take turns orally reading text passages. They help each other decode difficult vocabulary, discuss content, and answer comprehension questions about the material. After reaching consensus on questions, students may be required to write responses independently. If the written responses pose significant challenges for some students, they may use alternate forms of response.

Peer Tutoring. Typically, peer tutoring is a more structured and ongoing form of peer-mediated practice. Peer tutoring offers an alternative for providing one-to-one academic and social skills instruction, enhancing individualization, and correcting and providing feedback to students. Studies have documented the benefits of peer tutoring with students from diverse ethnic, economic, language, age, achievement, and social groups in a variety of subject areas (Greenwood & Delquadri, 1995; Jenkins & Jenkins, 1985; King-Sears, 1997; Utley et al., 1997). Peer tutoring for students with identified disabilities may be done by same-age peers or older students. Students with special needs should not be placed constantly in the role of tutee. Through the use of answer keys, flash cards with answers on the back, and strengths these students possess, they too can be effective tutors for peers or for younger students.

Careful structuring of peer tutoring arrangements helps to maximize the benefits of this technique for both tutors and tutees (Fuchs & Fuchs, 1998; Greenwood & Delquadri, 1995; Jenkins & Jenkins, 1985; King-Sears, 1997; Utley et al., 1997). Experts recommend that lessons for peer tutoring be highly prescriptive, closely matched to classroom instruction, with little ambiguity about the learning task to be accomplished. The best results accrue when tutoring sessions are regularly scheduled (daily or several times weekly) for a moderate amount of time, and when tutees are required to master specific skills before progressing to new skills. In some cases, reward systems increase student incentives to engage in peer-mediated practice activities. Preparing tutors for their roles is also critical to the success of peer tutoring. Tutors should be taught to give clear directions, encourage without providing too much assistance, confirm accurate responses and correct errors, and manage required materials and recording. Peer tutoring pairs should be regularly monitored and provided with specific feedback regarding their efforts. Care should be taken not to overuse highly capable students as peer tutors.

A unique application of peer tutoring developed in general education classrooms to improve achievement of low-performing students and to include all students in subject matter instruction is *ClassWide Peer Tutoring* (CWPT) (Delquadri, Greenwood, Stretton, & Hall, 1983; Greenwood, Terry, Delquadri, Elliott, & Arreaga-Mayer, 1995). After the teacher reviews and introduces new material to be learned, each student in the class is paired with a partner and each pair is assigned to one of two competing teams. Students take turns being the tutor and tutee during the tutoring session (an example of reciprocal tutoring), while the teacher supervises student interactions. Lists, answer keys, or flashcards with questions, terms, or problems on one side and answers, definitions, or examples on the other side may be used to structure student practice and ensure correct responding. Bonus points may be awarded to tutors for engaging in correct teaching behaviors and to tutees for practicing the skill appropriately. Tutees earn points by giving correct answers to tutor questions and by correcting their errors when they make mistakes. Points earned during tutoring sessions are added to points earned on weekly individual quizzes or tests covering the information or skills being practiced to comprise the total team score. Public posting of team scores and social rewards for the winning team provide additional incentives for practice and performance (Greenwood & Delquadri, 1995).

Cooperative Learning.   Cooperative learning is a third option for peer-mediated practice. Cooperative learning puts concepts into context for students through group discussion and projects with peers (Johnson, Johnson, & Holubec, 1994; Goor & Schwenn, 1993). Like other forms of peer-mediated learning, when effectively implemented, cooperative learning promotes improved academic achievement and classroom climate, interactions among diverse students, acceptance of differences, and social skills development (Harper et al., 1994; Johnson et al., 1994). A number of specific variations of cooperative learning structures exist [e.g., Learning Together (Johnson et al., 1994); Student Team Learning (Slavin, 1984); Jigsaw (Kagan, 1992); Group Investigation (Sharan & Sharan, 1990)]. These variations differ in the amount of structure provided for students, the nature of the cooperative activities undertaken, and the relative emphasis on academic and social development. Generally, more structured cooperative activities are recommended for less experienced learners. Cooperative learning requires carefully planned and monitored learning experiences to ensure that task expectations are clear, roles are understood and implemented, everyone contributes equitably to accomplishing the task, and individual as well as group learning occurs. As with other forms of peer-mediated learning, students should be prepared for cooperative learning activities by articulating and practicing behaviors required for effective teamwork, such as sharing, listening, turn-taking, encouraging, and giving feedback.

In designing cooperative learning arrangements, educators must recognize that students with disabilities tend to be more teacher-focused and less likely to attend to key information. Without careful planning, they may have difficulty participating productively in group work, resulting in higher ability students bearing the burden for accomplishing group tasks. Providing role cards for each team member designating his or her task, such as timer, recorder, reporter, team leader, or materials manager and associated responsibilities; requiring students to share materials; and signing-off on completed tasks to indicate agreement and understanding helps to equalize participation and promote interdependence among group members. Posting group work rules and task directions, using prearranged signals (e.g., raised hand, caution sign) to control noise and to gain student attention, and providing clear criteria for task completion assist effective group functioning. Allowing processing time and providing evaluation sheets to prompt cooperative teams to self-evaluate their group behaviors also ensure that all students participate effectively and benefit from cooperative learning. Individual accountability (i.e., individual assessments of content or skill mastery) as well as group performance must be considered in evaluating the effectiveness of cooperative learning activities.

Independent Practice.   During independent practice students work alone to practice and demonstrate understanding, while educators and paraeducators circulate among students to ensure understanding and provide corrective feedback if necessary. In addition to being specific about what is correct and how to fix errors, feedback should encourage self-evaluation among students by pointing out the relationship between effort and performance, improvement over past performance, and the specific nature of the improvement. Answer keys, self-correcting materials, and peer checkers increase immediacy of feedback and student responsibility. For example, during independent practice in a fourth-grade math class, students are completing worksheets on basic calculations. Some students are working on pages of simple addition or subtraction problems while others are completing mixed-operation worksheets with regrouping. Some students are using manipulatives or multiplication grids to check their answers; others are taking turns at the computer to complete a drill and practice exercise. Two students have been assigned official "checker" roles to correct other students' worksheets when completed and mark problems that need to be redone. Advanced students check their completed work using the teacher's edition of a higher grade level text. Independent practice and feedback allows teachers to spend more time explaining and reteaching students who require additional instruction and allows students more timely feedback on their work. Figure 11.7 presents suggestions for enhancing the effectiveness of homework, an extension of independent practice.

FIGURE 11.7   Recommended Homework Practices.

- Establish clear routines for assigning, collecting, and checking homework.
- Begin homework assignments in class to ensure correct practice.
- Assign homework that students can complete independently. Use assignment notebooks to record assignments.
- Adjust assignments by reducing the length or number of problems, allowing alternate response formats, assigning related tasks, or permitting use of aids such as recordings, word processors, and calculators.
- Use groups during class time to support homework completion and check student work.

Think About It...

What are the advantages and disadvantages for students of individual practice versus practicing with peers? What are the advantages and disadvantages for teachers?

Cognitive Strategies

Students with disabilities and others at risk for school failure have few cognitive strategies or approaches for "learning how to learn" to meet academic and social demands at school. Strategies that successful learners use to acquire, organize, and express knowledge and skills and to solve problems should be made explicit to students with disabilities to help them learn efficiently and effectively. Carnine (1994) refers to these as *conspicuous strategies.* Examples include strategies for acquiring knowledge from texts (e.g., word identification, paraphrasing, interpreting graphics, and self-questioning); strategies for storing or remembering information, such as mnemonics or note taking; and strategies for expressing learning or demonstrating knowledge (e.g., sentence and paragraph writing, error monitoring, test taking) (Deshler, Ellis, & Lenz, 1996). Commonly used stages for acquiring and generalizing strategies are presented in Figure 11.8. As readers will note, these stages align closely with the phases and techniques for effective instruction described earlier.

Cognitive strategy instruction would be a critical part of the educational program for Chet Thompson, the 17-year-old student with a learning disability

---

FIGURE 11.8   Stages for Teaching Cognitive Strategies and Skills.

1. Pretest students on the strategy or skill to assess strengths and needs. Have students set goals for learning the strategy.
2. Describe the strategy to the student including the purpose for the strategy and instances in which it might be used.
3. Model use of the strategy.
4. Have students verbally rehearse strategy steps. Discuss the purpose for and processes involved in each step.
5. Practice the strategy steps using easy or familiar material with feedback.
6. Practice using more difficult or grade-level material with feedback.
7. Ensure mastery of the strategy and help students set goals for generalizing use of the strategy to other subjects and settings.
8. Work with others to help generalize the strategy to other subjects and settings. Check strategy use regularly to provide feedback and encouragement.

Source: Adapted from Deshler, D. D., Ellis, E. S., & Lenz, B. K. (1996). *Teaching adolescents with learning disabilities: Strategies and methods* (2nd ed.). Denver: Love.

described earlier in Chapter 10. His slow reading ability, weak comprehension, writing difficulties, and poor organizational and study skills require continued focus for improvement, while building on his strengths in math, science, athletics, and interpersonal skills. Instruction may include comprehension and writing strategies in the context of his English classes, required multiple drafts and peer reviews of his research papers, use of taped books to supplement his text reading on some assignments, and organizational strategies for recording and completing assignments on time.

Monitoring and Evaluating Student Performance and Progress

Limitations of traditional, standardized assessments for classroom-based instructional decision making are well known (Blankenship, 1985; Deno & Fuchs, 1987) and the call for more meaningful, authentic, or "real-world" assessment is a frequent topic in the professional literature. For students with disabilities, the results of traditional assessments frequently are more reflective of their disabilities than what they know. In inclusive classrooms, great variance in prior knowledge, attention spans, learning rates and preferences, abilities, and talents necessitates multiple assessment approaches. Various ways to measure student performance over time and suggestions for adapting evaluation measures for students with learning difficulties are listed in Figure 11.9 on page 254.

Research on teacher effectiveness and successful learning supports regular and repeated teacher monitoring of student progress on a daily, weekly, and monthly basis (Brophy & Good, 1986; Englert et al., 1992; Fuchs, Fuchs, & Hamlett, 1989; Rosenshine & Stevens, 1986). Whether at the state, local, or classroom level, appropriate assessment must be clearly linked to instructional objectives derived from the curriculum to produce the data needed to make sound decisions about how to improve student learning. Some alternatives for structuring assessments and monitoring student performance and progress include (1) curriculum-based assessment, (2) portfolio assessment, and (3) alternate grading systems, which are described in the following sections.

Curriculum-Based Assessment.   Curriculum-based assessment (CBA) can be thought of as precise, task-analyzed, teacher-made tests or commercially produced tests that are closely aligned with the content being taught. The CBA process involves direct and frequent measurement of student performance on objectives derived from the curriculum (Blankenship, 1985; Deno, 1985; Fuchs & Deno, 1991; Shinn & Hubbard, 1996; Taylor, 1993). In CBA, educators identify skill sequences for specific units, specify behavioral objectives for students, and focus on them in classroom instruction. Objectives may vary for students with disabilities based on team-developed individualized education program (IEP) goals and objectives. Once objectives have been delineated, the conditions for task performance (i.e., materials, directions, and methods for completing tasks) and criteria for mastery

FIGURE 11.9   Suggestions for Monitoring and Evaluating Student Progress.

Preparation for Assessment
- Establish written criteria for homework, projects, papers, and presentations.
- Provide study guides to highlight essential content for study.
- Develop alternative assessment tools such as projects, portfolios, presentations, and criteria for evaluation.
- Design a classroom management plan with involvement from students.
- Keep a daily journal to remember major classroom performance events.
- Teach self-monitoring through personal journals, daily rating sheets, or written critiques.
- Teach peer review techniques as appropriate.
- Teach test-taking strategies and conduct practice tests.

Evaluation Strategies
- Provide alternative assignments (e.g., skits, models, daily journals, videos, book reports, group reports, oral presentations); encourage students to create their own assignments.
- Maintain student-selected work portfolios throughout the year.
- Create individual student contracts as needed.
- Adapt weekly quizzes, unit tests, and assignments as needed by altering font size, length, number of problems or questions to answer, time allowed, or distractors provided for multiple-choice items. Simplify language in the directions and items. Use aids such as calculators, spellers, text, or notes to accommodate differences.
- Read questions to any student who requests this support.
- Conduct regularly scheduled progress meetings with individual students.
- Teach students to monitor and critique their own work according to class-developed criteria. Use peer editing and feedback as appropriate.
- Write narrative report cards and progress reports; include self-evaluations of progress by the students and send progress notes home regularly.

or *rubrics* for grading completed tasks are specified. Stimulus materials and scoring sheets are prepared, and the test administration and scoring procedures are determined. In addition to paper-and-pencil tests, students may be asked to perform tasks or solve problems using manipulatives or task materials, provide oral responses, submit work samples, or be observed using a checklist of behaviors during the course of the school day. The response mode should match the task being assessed in the most realistic way possible. For example, multiple choice items may be more appropriate to test knowledge of concepts, definitions, or relationships but role plays or observations using a checklist of steps may be more appropriate for assessing vocational, social, or self-help skills. A written report may be a more valid way to evaluate students' use of multiple sources of information and synthesis skills than matching items on a paper-and-pencil quiz.

After a curriculum-based test is administered, the results are analyzed with reference to the established criteria. Types of errors made by individual students, as well as error patterns demonstrated by the class, are noted. Instructional targets and strategies are identified based on student performance on the CBA. Parallel CBAs or subsections of parallel CBAs are administered throughout instructional units to monitor skill acquisition (performance) and progress through the curriculum over time. Few phenomena are as discouraging and frustrating to both students and teachers as reaching the end of an instructional unit only to realize that students missed the critical points or mastered few new skills. CBA allows educators to reteach in a more timely manner or accelerate instruction if warranted.

Male (1997), Greenwood and Rieth (1996), and Fuchs (1992) among others advocate the use of technology to assist assessment. Technology-based assessment is the "use of electronic systems and software to assess and evaluate the progress of individual children in educational settings" (Greenwood & Rieth, 1996, p. 279). This involves the use of computers and other electronic media such as video cameras for conducting assessment tasks including administering tests, scoring forms, providing simulation activities for problem solving, and completing student response analysis with suggestions for instruction. Programs are available for computer labs that track progress of individual students through basic skills acquisition as the students complete the software exercises and quizzes on the material.

Portfolio Assessment. Portfolio assessment involves selection and analysis of a varied collection of student work samples in one or more areas chosen to document student learning or progress over an extended period of time (e.g., unit, grading period, semester, school year). Portfolio contents may include logs, written work samples, audiotapes, videotapes, checklists, illustrations, projects, interviews, or other original products (Wesson & King, 1996; Swicegood, 1994). Electronic portfolios allow students to store their work on audiotapes, videotapes, computer disks, or some combination thereof. Work samples frequently integrate word processing, databases, and various media to allow students to share their ideas with pictures, tables, and video and audio clips (Male, 1997; Greenwood & Rieth, 1996).

Portfolios allow students to assume more ownership for learning and to show what they *can* do related to the topics and skills being addressed. Students can demonstrate their learning and performance on authentic tasks that have relevance beyond the classroom. Selection of portfolio items is typically a task shared by students and educators responsible for providing the basic parameters for item selection and evaluation. Students are asked to reflect on their portfolio selections and progress and to share these reflections in some form (e.g., interview, journal notes, audiotape) with the teacher. Portfolio entries provide insights into student interests, learning styles and strategies, strengths, and needs, thus providing opportunities for direct connections between assessment and instruction (Swicegood, 1994; Wesson & King, 1996; Wolf, 1991). Portfolios also provide a valuable tool for communicating with family members, other professionals involved with students, and with the students themselves.

Alternate Grading. A number of alternatives to traditional letter grades are used to represent more accurately students' with disabilities performance and progress in the general education or adapted curriculum. Friend and Bursuck (1996) reported that some commonly used options are pass/fail and credit/no credit to indicate whether minimum understanding and skills have been mastered, and competency lists to document achievement of specific concepts or skills. Polloway and colleagues (1994) described grading adaptations that included (1) grades based on amount of improvement, (2) separate grades for effort and achievement, (3) adjusted grading (e.g., more weight for effort and projects than for tests), and (4) grades based on student ability (e.g., grading on IEP objectives, requirements of academic or behavioral contracts, limited class content, modified grading scales for letter grades, effort). Written comments on progress have the potential to provide more detailed information to students, families, and others if competencies are clearly specified and monitored on a regular basis.

In inclusive classrooms it is essential that grading for students with disabilities be a shared process among teachers and specialists involved with the student's educational program. Basic philosophies about the meaning of grades, assignments and tasks that will be graded and how much each contributes to the total grade, how responsibility for grading will be shared, and how grades will be communicated are some of the basic issues that must be addressed.

Chapter Summary

Appropriate accommodations make the critical difference for students with disabilities between academic success and failure, and between meaningful inclusion in general education classes and meaningless placements in physical proximity to their peers. Collaboration among teachers, specialists, families, students, and others is essential for determining appropriate accommodations that promote both success and independence for students with special needs. Appropriate adjustments in curriculum and instruction allow students with disabilities to benefit from general education programs and ensure that they are able to demonstrate what they have learned rather than be restricted by the limitations of their disabilities. Accommodations are best considered within the context of differentiated curriculum and effective instruction for *all* students. Effective teaching practices at all phases of the instructional cycle help reduce the number of specialized accommodations needed for students with disabilities. Adjustments tailored to specific students may also facilitate learning for other members of the class.

CHAPTER ACTIVITIES

1. Many successful educators believe that "Good teaching is good teaching is good teaching" whether for general education or special education students. Do you agree? Are there significant differences in the way that students who are identified for special education learn or in how they must be taught to enable them to develop

concepts and skills? If so, what are those differences? Discuss your responses with your peers.

2. Identify at least three accommodations that might be appropriate for the following students:

   a. Beth is a 7th grader with limited reading skills.
   b. Tuwanda is a 3rd grader with low academic skills and poor attending behaviors.
   c. Scott is a 9th grader who has average abilities but is very disorganized.

3. Describe at least six ways to evaluate student progress.

12 Fostering Positive Student Behavior in Inclusive Classes

LEARNING OBJECTIVES

1. Describe the rationale for developing prosocial behaviors as an explicit part of the curriculum in inclusive programs.
2. Outline the process for integrating social and academic skill development into ongoing academic instruction.
3. Discuss special considerations for developing social skills among younger students, students with more significant support needs, and older students.

Mrs. Lanney walked her daughter to her prekindergarten class on a typical Thursday morning. When they arrived in the classroom, the teacher, Mrs. Samuels, was explaining to Dennis, one of her students, why he should not have hit his classmate, Jessie. Mrs. Lanney remembered that Dennis had come up as a subject of discussion during a recent family–school meeting when a parent complained that her child was afraid of Dennis's "mean" behavior. Some family members suggested that he didn't belong in this class; perhaps there were other schools that could better handle "kids like that." Several parents mentioned that Mrs. Samuels was vigilant to correct Dennis's behavior before he really hurt someone. One parent noted that, on a recent field trip, classmates seemed to tease Dennis and provoke his inappropriate behavior.

Mrs. Samuels was just about to deal with Jessie when Denisha ran up, grabbed the teacher's arm, and sobbed, "Albert won't let me play in housekeeping. He keeps making Batman capes out of the dress-up clothes! Make him stop!" Meanwhile, two other preschoolers thought that Albert's Batman impressions looked like fun, so they started chasing away the other children who had been playing "restaurant" before the housekeeping area was turned into Gotham City. One of the students chased from housekeeping screamed, "You always mess up our games. I hate you!" Another whined, "We never get to do what we want to do. You're so mean." Two other students who had been playing a game quietly stopped and ran toward the teacher who was now trying to referee the commotion. After several minutes, she calmed everyone by having them sit on the "quiet line" formed where the carpet met the linoleum in the classroom. The classroom assistant sighed, "It's going to be another one of those days."

* * *

Shanna Willis, a first-year high school special education teacher, was assigned to a combination resource/self-contained class of 10 students with mild to moderate disabilities. At the beginning of the year she was told that her enrollment numbers would increase as more students demonstrated learning and behavioral problems in their classes during the year. Although several more students were assigned to Shanna's class for short periods of time, only two of her students remained in school at the end of the school year. The other students had been suspended, expelled, incarcerated, or simply stopped coming to school. She was informed by veteran staff that this was typical for "those kids."

How do educators promote social success, build responsible behavior, and provide support in inclusive classes? How do professionals avoid situations like those depicted in the vignettes and foster a sense of school and classroom community? The classrooms described show signs of being places where some students feel frustrated and alienated. Clearly, the students would benefit from learning more effective interaction skills and reducing classroom confrontations and plays for teacher attention.

Successful inclusion requires meaningful social involvement as well as academic integration of students with disabilities into general education classrooms. Adult collaboration alone cannot accomplish successful integration. Student-to-student collaboration and support from genuine friends, peer advocates, cooperative learning partners, tutors, and others are critical for successful inclusion (Stainback & Stainback, 1994). Adult orchestration, facilitation, and modeling are needed to foster supportive relationships among students. Often the students who are most in need of support are the least skilled in developing and maintaining social relationships. Students for whom making friends and interacting with adults comes easily may have little awareness or experience supporting others in these endeavors. The vast majority of typical students as well as students with disabilities need adult guidance in developing skills associated with citizenship and social responsibility, such as assisting others, problem solving, decision making, and other skills characteristic of caring classrooms and communities.

This chapter builds on the concept of student support networks described in Chapter 4 and the strategies for building classroom communities proposed in

Chapter 6. It presents the context, rationale, and techniques for increasing pro-social student behaviors—the positive verbal and nonverbal behaviors that promote successful interactions with adults and peers. Strategies for integrating social skills development into the general education curriculum and for developing prosocial skills of all students in inclusive environments are shared. Special considerations for younger students, students with more significant support needs, and older students are also addressed. The emphasis here is on building positive behavior and preventing inappropriate behavior by providing the emotional, instructional, and environmental support all students need to be successful. Proactive and preventive strategies can lead to greater academic and social success for all students as more cohesive and supportive classrooms emerge.

The focus on student support and on building appropriate behavior is highly consistent with the Individuals with Disabilities Education Act (IDEA) Amendments (1997) requirements for school teams to conduct functional behavioral assessments and to provide positive behavioral intervention plans for students with disabilities who demonstrate challenging behaviors. Functional behavioral assessment assumes that students behave for purposeful reasons and in ways that get their needs met. Functional assessment is the process of analyzing the purpose or function of a student's problem behavior (e.g., control, attention, avoidance, affiliation) and environmental factors associated with it in order to meet that student's needs in more acceptable ways and to design interventions that teach and support appropriate behavior (Durand, 1993; Horner, O'Neill, & Flannery, 1993; Knoster, 1998; Quinn, Gable, Rutherford, Nelson, & Howell, 1998). This process represents a distinct departure from viewing challenging behavior from primarily a punishment perspective.

Functional assessment and positive behavioral support consider problem behavior as an indication that environmental or programmatic adjustments are required to help meet student needs more appropriately. Adjustments may include changing the level of the material, task demands, or response modes to allow more student success; providing varied activities of interest to the student; addressing medical issues; or providing more opportunities for attention and recognition within the school day. Intervention plans focus on teaching and supporting positive replacement behaviors (e.g., social skills, learning strategies, communication skills) rather than merely decreasing negative behaviors through some form of punishment. Long-term outcomes of more positive and supportive methods for changing behavior that offer convincing evidence of the efficacy of this approach are discussed later in this chapter.

Rationale for Social Learning as an Integral Part of the Curriculum

Most educators agree that development of responsible behavior, citizenship, and the ability to get along with others are worthwhile aims of schooling. National education goals established by the Goals 2000: Educate America Act (National

Education Goals Panel, 1995) included preparation for citizenship, rights and responsibilities, and provision of disciplined school environments conducive to learning. Many teachers, however, are concerned with where, when, and how to address social goals in an already crowded curriculum and a climate of increasing accountability for academic outcomes. Some professionals argue that social learning is the responsibility of families and not a topic for direct instruction in general education classrooms. An examination of the research and literature on social and emotional learning (including social skills development) provides rich insights into the value of and means for addressing social behavior as part of the school curriculum for all students.

Research Supporting Social Skills Development

Systematic attention to positive social behaviors and student support structures is vital to establishing a sense of classroom community—a sense that everyone belongs, is valued, has something to contribute, and has rights but also responsibilities for the welfare of others in the class and school. This sense of community benefits not only students with disabilities or those at risk for school failure but all students. Walberg and Greenberg (1997) reported on several research studies showing that classroom social environment had a significant effect on student attitudes, interest, productivity, engagement, and academic achievement. Johnson and Johnson (1995) found that effective student problem solving and conflict resolution also made classrooms more productive academically. Increased achievement and attachment to school and family and decreased aggression, suspensions, drug use, and delinquency were outcomes of the Raising Healthy Children project focused on social skills development (Hawkins et al., 1992). Goleman (1995) summarized research showing that social and emotional intelligence is highly predictive of postschool success. Numerous anecdotes from teachers involved in social and emotional learning programs—even those who had originally felt that they were too busy or their curricula were too crowded to include social skills instruction—revealed that time spent on building positive student behaviors saved time and energy in the long run by preventing problems and sharing the support role normally relegated to the teacher (e.g., Charney, 1991; Chuoke & Eyman, 1997; Dowd, 1997; Walberg & Greenberg, 1997; York, Doyle, & Kronberg, 1992). In contrast, there is "growing evidence that, in schools where community has not been established, there are increased problems with underachievement, student dropouts, drug abuse,...exclusion of students with disabilities from the mainstream, and gang activity" (Stainback & Stainback, 1994, p. xxiv).

For students with disabilities, social competence has been shown to be a major correlate of success both in school and in life (Bryan, 1991; Korinek & Polloway, 1993; Sugai & Lewis, 1996). Yet deficits in social skills are characteristic of students with emotional and behavioral problems (Elksnin & Elksnin, 1995; Kauffman, 1993; Odom, McConnell, & McEvoy, 1992; Sugai and Lewis, 1996), and students with learning disabilities (Lerner, 1997; Mercer, 1997; Vaughn, Zaragoza, Hogan, &

Walker, 1993). Similar deficits are found among students with other disabilities and those at risk for school failure (Downing, 1996; Friend & Bursuck, 1996; Sabornie & deBettencourt, 1997). Poor social skills often contribute to negative attitudes and lack of acceptance by teachers and other students in general education (Kemple, 1991; Montague, Bergeron, & Lago-Delello, 1997; Wentzel, 1993). Lack of understanding and inadequate preparation to deal with social and behavioral differences also contribute to teacher and peer reluctance to interact with students with disabilities.

Social skills taught in pull-out settings frequently fail to generalize to other situations (Forness & Kavale, 1996; Gresham, 1990; Rutherford, 1997). Students do not automatically transfer the interactional skills they learn in controlled settings to other environments that call for these skills. Many students have difficulty discriminating when to use the skills in natural interactions, or they may be unmotivated to do so (Forness & Kavale, 1996; Gresham, 1990). Social skills learned in isolation may not be systematically practiced or reinforced in other settings.

In short, many students in today's classrooms are not demonstrating the social competence necessary to develop and maintain friendships with peers or to interact appropriately with the adults in their environment. Peers are receiving little guidance in becoming more supportive and responsible for their classmates. Often the skills that are necessary for survival in nonschool environments are not well received or conducive to success in school. Without adult attention to increasing students' repertoires of prosocial skills and facilitating peer acceptance, many students fail to develop support networks or demonstrate socially responsible behaviors needed to be successful in school and life (Friend & Bursuck, 1996). Inclusive schools and classrooms afford numerous opportunities to practice social skills and develop social competence in natural environments (Forness & Kavale, 1996; Warger & Rutherford, 1993).

Context for Social Development

Typically discussions about social development and responsible behaviors focus on students. However, attempting to improve student behavior without considering the classroom and schoolwide structures that encourage, support, and reinforce positive behavior limits the success of even well-designed, student-specific programs. It is insufficient to address problems displayed by individual students without examining conditions in the classroom and school that are not student-centered and "student friendly" (Comer, as cited in O'Neil, 1997). If students feel disconnected, disenfranchised, unwelcome, or unsafe in school, they will have great difficulty changing their behaviors or benefiting from instruction.

Schools and classes in which the most academic and social progress is being achieved are places where the adults assume responsibility for modeling and facilitating community among themselves and among their students. Community building also requires direct instruction in prosocial behavior, guided and continued practice and feedback, and meaningful student involvement in decision making

(Berreth & Berman, 1997; Chuoke & Eyman, 1997; Meyer & Northup, 1997; Thousand, Villa, & Nevin, 1994; York et al., 1992). Efforts must be ongoing and sustained; single events and piecemeal programs seldom impact student engagement and responsibility in lasting ways (Berreth & Berman, 1997; Charney, 1991; Holden, 1997; Weissberg, Shriver, Bose, & DeFalco, 1997).

Comprehensive planning, clear communication, and coordinated efforts that involve faculty, families, and students in identifying valued outcomes and working to achieve them over time stand the best chance of success (Comer as cited in O'Neil, 1997; Elias, Bruene-Butler, Blum, & Schuyler, 1997). Some districts have a social development coordinator or planning committee to examine overlaps and distinctions among programs, facilitate selection of target behaviors, sequence development of core skills across grade levels, promote the development of instructional strategies, and create support structures across schools in the district (Elias et al., 1997). Other schools designate transition specialists, guidance counselors, school psychologists, or teachers to fulfill these roles.

Schoolwide intervention assistance teams, advisory committees, or grade-level teams may be other alternatives for addressing prosocial program issues and initiatives in districts with limited resources. Elias and colleagues (1997) recommended starting with pilot projects that address significant social concerns but that also have a high likelihood of succeeding (i.e., do not begin with the most serious and complex problem in the school but address areas that are manageable and will make a difference). They further suggest that persons charged with implementation observe in other schools with effective social development programs, work with others to tailor programs to local needs, and meet regularly to share successes and make program adjustments.

Social Skills Curriculum and Instruction

Although there is not a universally accepted definition of social skills, most authors describe verbal and nonverbal behaviors (e.g., words, tone of voice, facial expression, actions, body posture) used in interactions with peers and adults that result in positive social outcomes (Elliott & Gresham, 1991; Sugai & Lewis, 1996). Examples of specific skills addressed in a number of published social skills curricula include

- Peer/friendship skills (e.g., listening, asking and answering questions, initiating and maintaining interactions).
- Coping skills (e.g., following directions, getting help, responding to peer pressure, expressing anger, stress management).
- Problem-solving/decision-making skills (e.g., problem identification, goal setting, generating and selecting alternatives, negotiating).

Some of these skills are as specific as using "please" and "thank you" or giving eye contact; other skills such as negotiation, conversation, and problem solving are more complex.

Social competence involves social skills used effectively (as judged by others) in situational contexts (Foster & Ritchey, 1979; Gresham, 1986; Sugai & Lewis, 1996). Not only do students need to demonstrate specific verbal and nonverbal behaviors that comprise the social skills but also demonstrate appropriate use of those skills in varied social situations. This requires judgments about when, where, and how to apply specific social skills to achieve positive interactions with peers and adults. Again, professionals are reminded of the mediating effects of culture on choice and perceptions of social behaviors and should involve family members, as well as students themselves, in discussions of what constitutes socially competent behavior.

Numerous social skills curricula are available to help educators develop prosocial behaviors. (See Alberg, Petry, & Eller, 1994; Elksnin & Elksnin, 1995; and Quinn, Mathur, & Rutherford, 1995 for descriptions of published social skills programs.) Most of these programs provide for direct instruction and practice of social skills as separate instructional activities (Elliott & Gresham, 1991; Goldstein, Sprafkin, Gershaw, & Klein, 1980; Korinek & Polloway, 1993; McGinnis, Goldstein, Sprafkin, & Gershaw, 1984; Rutherford, Quinn, & Mathur, 1996; Sugai & Lewis, 1996; Walker, Todis, Holmes, & Horton, 1988). Social skills lessons typically involve (1) defining the skill and its substeps, (2) identifying situations in which the skill is used; (3) developing with students the rationale for using the skill, (4) modeling the skill using examples and nonexamples, (5) guiding student practice of the skill with feedback, and (6) promoting generalization of the skill to new situations. An example of a social skills lesson is presented in Figure 12.1. Students demonstrating significant social skills deficits who have not been exposed to systematic teaching and reinforcement of basic social skills are likely to require direct instruction and concentrated practice in social skills in order to demonstrate these skills in interactions with peers and adults. Classroom teachers are strongly encouraged to collaborate with specialists who have expertise in social skills development as they plan to meet the needs of students with social skill difficulties. Direct instruction in social skills typically takes place in smaller groups using Alternative Teaching or Parallel Instruction variations of co-teaching as described in Chapter 9. It is essential to prompt, practice, and reinforce these skills regularly in general education settings.

The Process for Integrating Academic and Social Skills Instruction

Although direct instruction for social skills is a necessary and viable option in many cases, educators are often reluctant to focus lessons exclusively on social skills in the face of societal and political demands for greater excellence as measured by academic achievement. The challenge of generalizing social skills taught in isolation is also well documented. One solution to help teachers address both academic and social learning in an efficient and effective manner is the following process for integrating academic and social skills instruction. Depending on one's primary orientation (academic or social skill emphasis), the point of entry into the

FIGURE 12.1   Illustrative Lesson Plan for Teaching Social Skills.

Skill: Resisting peer pressure (politely refusing to do something suggested by a peer). Instructor introduces the skill by defining "resisting peer pressure" and reviewing the steps of this skill.

Steps: 1. *Say something positive* to the peer.
2. *Say no* to what the peer is trying to get you to do.
3. *Tell why* you said no.
4. *Suggest something else* to do.
5. If the peer asks again, *say no again and leave.* (Don't argue.)

Conditions to Use the Skill—General Conditions: Instructor elicits general characteristics of situations requiring use of the skill, for example, peers ask students to do things they feel are wrong, against the rules or the law, might hurt someone, or get the student in trouble.

Conditions to Use the Skill—Specific Examples: Instructor asks for specific examples of situations in which the skill could be used. Examples include peers asking students to cut class, drink, cheat on tests or assignments, shoplift, use parent's car without permission. Students should generate and discuss realistic examples.

Rationale: Instructor elicits possible reasons for using the skill, such as avoiding trouble or hurting someone, building trust and keeping privileges, and keeping friends because the refusal was done in a positive way. Students should provide their own rationales before moving to the next step.

Model of the Skill: Two adults or an adult and a student role-play an interaction between two students in which one resists a peer's asking him or her to cut class to go to the convenience store. All steps of the skill are included in the role play and discussed after the demonstration. Additional role plays should be modeled by instructors and students and discussed before moving to student practice.

Student Practice with Feedback: Students develop their own role plays or are given situations to role-play. Students practice in dyads or small groups, checking off the steps of the skill as they are demonstrated in role plays. Feedback on steps performed effectively and those needing more practice is given by peers in the group and by instructors. All steps should be demonstrated effectively for mastery.

Generalization: Students keep a social skills log, recording each time they resist peer pressure, what they said and did, and results of the interaction. Situations are "debriefed" in class discussion after 1 week, 2 weeks, and periodically thereafter to note successes, difficulties with the skill, and potential adjustments.

process may differ, but the lesson plan that results from the thoughtful integration of the two skill areas can be basically the same. The steps of this integration process are presented in Figure 12.2 on page 266 and further explanation is provided in the following sections. Some of the content in this section is adapted from an article in *Preventing School Failure* (Korinek & Popp, 1997).

FIGURE 12.2   **Process for Integrating Academic and Social Skills in Inclusive Settings.**

1. Target an academic or social skill.

2. Pair social and academic skills.

3. Weave social skills into general curriculum and classroom routines.
   - Determine instructional arrangements and materials.
   - Plan and deliver lessons.
   - Evaluate academic and social skill attainment.
   - Provide reinforcement and generalization opportunities.

As is true for direct instruction of social skills, the most efficient and effective way to plan and implement this integrated social–academic skills process is through collaboration between general education teachers with expertise in the academic curriculum and specialists with experience teaching social skills. Ideally, integrated lessons would be co-planned and co-taught (Warger & Rutherford, 1993). Consultation from specialists could also provide support for successful programming by general education teachers if co-teaching could not be arranged.

Step 1: Target an Academic or Social Skill.   The general educator or specialist, or both select the primary skill to be taught. Typically, grade-level competencies established in school systems or subject matter skill hierarchies guide the selection of academic skills. Common academic skills that spiral throughout the various grade levels include listening and speaking skills such as paraphrasing, summarizing, and debating; literary skills dealing with characters, plot, inferences, relationships, and predictions; writing skills related to various types of sentences and kinds of composition; science skills dealing with experimentation and change; and social studies skills related to citizenship, responsibility, conflict resolution, and leadership. These academic skills readily lend themselves to meaningful connections with social skills, thus setting the stage for more integrated development in both areas.

In turn, if the major focus for instruction is social skills development, logical targets for instruction may include skills that enhance students' ability to work together to complete tasks, skills that have been identified as common student needs based on classroom disciplinary incidents, or skills targeted in one or more students' individualized education programs (IEPs). Many of the specific social skills mentioned previously in this chapter may be useful choices, depending on the needs and prerequisite skills of students in a particular classroom. Student characteristics and readiness, potential student benefits from the skill, the setting and subject demands, and the likelihood that the skill will be naturally reinforced across environments should be considered in selecting social skills (Elksnin & Elksnin, 1995; Elliott & Gresham, 1991; Rutherford et al., 1996). Social validity or the social importance of the skills to the student across multiple school and community settings and the acceptability to students, teachers, and families of the way in which the skills are taught and learned are additional concerns in targeting skills (Rutherford et al., 1996; York et al., 1992). As noted previously, family members should be consulted in determining social skills to be addressed to ensure that target behaviors are consistent with cultural, community, and family values and norms.

Step 2: Pair the Social and Academic Skills

Integration Beginning with an Academic Focus.   Although an academic or social skill may be targeted as primary, complementary skills from the secondary area (social skills or academics, respectively) should also be targeted early in the planning process to capitalize on opportunities for integration. If the academic objective has been selected as primary, educators need to consider how the academic skill can be taught in a way that incorporates writing, discussion, or practice of one or more of the social skills that have been identified as important. This process also lends authenticity to the lesson, since it provides opportunities to relate student learning to relevant aspects of their lives. Practice activities that require the use of cooperative learning, peer tutoring, or other types of interaction among students may be additional ways to match social with academic objectives.

A common academic objective found in English and the social sciences at the upper elementary through secondary levels is writing a persuasive argument. The persuasive argument can be used as practice for negotiating with others on issues of importance to students such as curfew times, homework policies, allowance, or school privileges. Since negotiating requires some ability to predict objections, role playing of debate scenarios may be incorporated into the plan. Best choice debates (Harmin, 1994) wherein opposing sides seek to understand and accurately summarize each other's arguments, then determine how they might work together in spite of their opposing views is another alternative for integration. The persuasive argument can also be used to target other skills such as the ability to disagree agreeably and to handle pressure from peers. Prompts for different students may be tailored to specific social skill needs or a current classroom crisis needing resolution. While focusing on persuasive arguments, teachers could also incorporate the social skill of positive self-talk in a written format. For example, students may be asked to record their arguments for persuading themselves to do their best work or exercise restraint in their comments to authority figures.

Another academic skill that often spirals through the curriculum from early elementary through secondary grades is understanding and applying the scientific method or experimental design. Although the number of steps and sophistication of the analyses vary, common elements include asking questions, observing, collecting data, identifying patterns, generating questions, making predictions, and conducting experiments. Students could use a similar procedure to observe social interactions, predict responses, and choose effective actions for given social situations.

Literature also offers a wealth of possibilities for integrating academic and social skill objectives. For example, the second-grade story, *Howdy* (Weir, 1989) could be used to incorporate work on greeting skills. This story depicts a young boy, Luke, whose pleasant greeting of "Howdy" changes the behaviors of those he meets in his daily activities. Extensions of this lesson could incorporate experimental design by having students identify social patterns in the story. A prediction may be that people respond to the mood or countenance of others. Students could conduct a simple experiment by greeting others in school with a smile and "hello," and observing their reactions. These reactions could be compared with reactions received when there is no greeting or when the greeter frowns.

Integration Beginning with a Social Skill.   A social skill that has been targeted schoolwide, classwide, or one that is needed by a student or group of students may provide the primary focus for a lesson. Skill selection may be based on informal observation or the collection of baseline data. Families and students should also have a clear voice in designating skills that will be most useful and valued in their culture and communities. Another important source for targeting specific social skills is the IEPs of class members.

If educators start with the social skill as the primary objective, they then "pair" skills by taking instruction beyond the singular focus of social skill development to integrate a secondary focus on academic skills. For example, if students are learning greeting and conversation skills, they could also read Dr. Seuss stories that repeat the pattern of characters meeting one another; write or dictate a script for an interaction between two characters (which could be acted out and requires language, writing, and reading skills); keep data on the number of greetings they initiate with others in a designated period of time and the types of reactions they receive; graph these data; or rephrase greetings or sentences from a conversation in a way that clarifies meaning or elicits a more positive reaction.

Decision-making skills (e.g., problem identification; goal setting; generating, selecting, and evaluating a solution) are critical social skills that can be practiced through the general academic curriculum. Crises presented in literature, conflicts prominent in historical events, ethical issues in science, and current events lend themselves to having students practice the decision-making process. An outline or graphic organizer of the decision-making steps (i.e., problem, goal, first alternative with advantages and disadvantages, second alternative with advantages and disadvantages, third alternative with advantages and disadvantages, selected solution, and rationale) may be helpful to guide students through the problem-solving process, while giving them additional practice in writing and organizational skills. Many additional examples of social and academic skill integration are described in the literature. Some of these are summarized in Figure 12.3.

Planning, practicing, and observing social skills within the general education curriculum promotes accountability. For example, initiating interactions with others may be targeted on the IEP. The next step for integration would be to determine where in the required academic curriculum this skill could be practiced. Initiating skills may align with citizenship objectives, basic group skills, or oral language skills of initiating and carrying on a conversation. Depending on the level of direct social skills instruction needed and the number of students being targeted, integrated lessons may involve the whole class or be a part of differenti-

FIGURE 12.3   **Examples of Social and Academic Skill Integration.**

1. Interviews with senior citizens were conducted by seventh graders as part of a 6-week interdisciplinary unit on twentieth-century American history. Students collaborated to develop interview guides, debriefed after interviews, edited and produced the adults' biographies to meet competencies in language arts, history, and other social studies (Smith, 1997).

2. Strategies used by real diplomats to diffuse international conflicts were studied and analyzed for school-classroom use by students as part of a history unit (Berreth & Berman, 1997).

3. Questions regarding literature examples and media were posed to fourth graders as part of the *Raising Healthy Children Project* to help them reflect on friendship skills (e.g., Which character in the novel or story would you like for a best friend? What social skills does he or she have that you admire? How many put-downs and put-ups did you observe in this dialogue or a 30-minute television show?) (Cummings & Haggerty, 1997).

4. Urban middle school students were asked to "write for their lives" in an interdisciplinary project in which they constructed their life stories, developed questions about their experiences, and then conducted research to try to find answers to questions that touched them personally (e.g., "Why do kids join gangs or take drugs?" "Why do parents get divorced?"). Students held class meetings, developed life graphs, constructed "identity boxes," reviewed each others' work, and reflected on their lives and what they learned (Appelsies & Fairbanks, 1997).

5. At an elementary school, students were taught noncompetitive games and, in "Play Fair Squads" of five or six students, presented to other classes, coached other students, and monitored the playground to promote peaceful recreational activities for their peers (Chuoke & Eyman, 1997).

ated lessons for the targeted students. In either case the lesson is contextualized by the general education curriculum or theme being studied in class.

Step 3: Weave Social Skills into the General Curriculum and Classroom Routines.   Steps 1 and 2 of the process address the integration of social and academic objectives for specific lessons. Integration must become an integral part of ongoing planning and implementation of the general curriculum; the social skills must become institutionalized as a component of general classroom routines. If this does not happen, opportunities for emphasizing, reinforcing, and increasing social skills development in a proactive way will be lost, and more time will likely be spent reacting to negative classroom behaviors.

The "howdy" greeting lessons described in previous steps can be used to illustrate weaving social skills into the general curriculum. Greetings could be adopted as daily classroom practice. To reinforce the importance of appropriate greetings, students may agree to exchange pleasant "hellos" when entering class.

Official greeters could be appointed each day to help students learn each other's names and make everyone feel welcome.

As students become more proficient in moving through the steps, the scientific method could be applied to real-life problem solving in the classroom. Students can be empowered to settle disagreements systematically. Bus, hallway, classroom, or playground conflicts can become opportunities to describe observations, note reactions to stimuli and any patterns that emerge, predict future responses, and select "an experiment" (i.e., an alternative response to the conflict) to employ next time. Peer mediation for conflicts can be approached within this model as students support each other through the problem-solving process. Teachers may further integrate the scientific method and awareness of social interactions by sharing their observations of classroom behaviors and subsequent management decisions with students.

Peer tutoring and cooperative learning groups described in Chapter 11 provide excellent vehicles for integrating academic and social skills development in classroom operating procedures. Social skills such as following directions, active listening, turn-taking, sharing, criticizing ideas and not people, providing feedback, and reaching consensus are critical skills that must be performed within peer tutoring and cooperative group arrangements while students practice and complete academic assignments. Deliberately targeting social skills needed for peer work early in the school year leads to more effective and efficient groups as students work and learn together throughout the year.

Providing appropriate peer models within groups and classes is also critical. One of the surest ways to invite challenging behaviors and frustrating situations for both students and teachers is to "load" classes with students with identified needs, those at risk for failure, and those performing at the lowest levels. This inappropriate arrangement severely limits student access to appropriate models and invites problems because students tend to contribute to one another's negative rather than positive behaviors. Educators can also capitalize on natural class leaders to help shape other students' behaviors. Student leaders are not always those who already demonstrate exemplary behavior. Sometimes "bullies" or students who have a tendency toward noncompliance can be involved in a positive manner through peer mediation, problem-solving groups, student representation to faculty, or other positions of responsibility after some preparation to acquire necessary skills. These students may have even more influence on peers than "model" students because peers may more readily identify with them than with students who never seem to have any difficulties in school.

Virtually every academic skill can be taught and practiced in a way that incorporates some dimension of social skills development. Materials, examples, student groupings, practice activities, or assignments used in lessons offer a wide array of options for integrated instruction. Targeting and teaching the most essential academic and social skills make instruction and learning more focused, relevant, and strategic, thus more likely to produce the intended social and academic outcomes.

In selecting strategies to build responsible student behaviors and increase peer support and acceptance of diverse students in the classroom, Harper, Maheady, and Mallette (1994) note that the most acceptable interventions are those that benefit heterogeneous groups of students, not just a select group; are feasible to implement within a classroom; and are "socially acceptable to…classroom teachers, students, and peers" (p. 230). The social-academic skill integration process provides a vehicle for addressing both areas to ensure that these criteria are met.

Special Considerations in Developing Prosocial Skills with Various Groups

The guidelines for teaching social skills and integrating social skills development into the general curriculum offered in this chapter are widely applicable across ages, grade levels, and diverse students. Some special considerations, however, are helpful to keep in mind when working with young children, students with more significant support needs, and older students.

Considerations for Developing Prosocial Skills with Young Children

Preschoolers with disabilities frequently demonstrate delays in social development, and these delays are often related to development in other domains such as cognition, language, and motor skills (Elksnin & Elksnin, 1995; Odom et al., 1992). Consequently, interventions to promote social development must take into account children's skills and limitations in these other areas. Inclusive classrooms afford ongoing opportunities to foster prosocial development among typical students and their peers with disabilities or other risk factors. Typically, play situations are the context for preschoolers' social interactions and the avenue for assessing and developing skills across domains.

A variety of peer-mediated and adult-mediated approaches exist to increase the quantity and quality of children's social interactions. Peer-mediated interventions generally involve teaching socially competent peers to initiate interactions with target students, prompting and reinforcing these students for engaging in prosocial behaviors, and structuring activities that promote identified students' interactions with peers. One peer-mediated intervention is the *Stay, Play, and Talk* strategy (English, Goldstein, Kaczmarek, & Shafer, 1996) in which selected peers are paired with children with disabilities. For example, Norma, a typical peer is taught to participate in her "buddy" Karl's activity or invite Karl to engage in another activity. Norma and Karl talk about their actions during play, the toys they are using, and respond to each other's communicative attempts.

Adult-mediated approaches involve coaching students through social interactions with peers and teaching social skills (e.g., sharing, helping, inviting) in the context of classroom routines, such as cooperative games, art time, or snack time. Modeling, role playing, prompting, and encouraging prosocial behaviors in natural interactions are emphasized in social skills instruction. The *Win/Win Approach* to settling disputes that arise during class activities (Smith, 1995) exemplifies an adult-mediated intervention for teaching young children to solve classroom problems. First, educators help students define the dispute in terms of a shared problem by all involved (e.g., for Dennis and Jessie in the opening vignette, "There is only one toy and you both want it."). Second, students generate several potential solutions to the problem, with prompting if necessary (e.g., share, take turns, find another toy to play with, find another activity). Finally, the students involved select a solution that pleases both sides (e.g., play with another toy). The entire class can be involved in generating mutual problem statements and possible solutions to provide modeling and practice in problem solving. Teacher assistance with the process is gradually faded and students are encouraged to resolve disputes on their own.

Research has shown that both peer-mediated and adult-mediated approaches have been successful in increasing prosocial behaviors in young children (Elksnin & Elksnin, 1995; Hundert, 1995; Odom et al., 1992). Hundert (1995) cautioned, however, that adult-mediated interventions may not be consistently feasible given other teacher responsibilities, children may become dependent on adult intervention, and the teacher's presence may sometimes interfere with natural student–student interactions. Gradual withdrawal of educator assistance and external reinforcement as typical students become more supportive and as identified students become more socially competent helps to avoid potentially negative effects of adult mediation.

Use of puppets; familiar television or story characters; dramatizations with figures they can see and hear; and stories, songs, and other participation activities enhance the relevance and appeal of social skills lessons given young children's concrete thinking, short attention span, and need for movement. Wittmer and Honig (1994) also suggested that early childhood educators specifically label prosocial and antisocial behaviors using terms such as "helpful," "sharing," "hurtful," rather than the general terms "good" or "naughty." They further recommend attributing positive social behaviors to each child in the class, encouraging prosocial behaviors but limiting external reinforcement, developing understanding and expression of feelings, and emphasizing the consequences of behavior (e.g., "He feels hurt," "No one can play with a broken toy," "You helped him clean up so now we can all go to lunch"). Educators should respond to and provide alternatives for aggressive behavior by modeling, redirecting (telling students what to do rather than what not to do), and coaching (prompting students to engage in particular behaviors).

A number of social skills programs that incorporate many of these suggestions and various peer- and adult-mediated strategies have been developed to promote the integration of young students with disabilities and improve social skills among preschoolers (Elksnin & Elksnin, 1995). Some of these programs include *Transdisciplinary Play-Based Intervention* (Linder, 1993), *Play Time/Social Time* (Odom & McConnell, 1993), *Using the Supported Play Model* (Sheridan, Foley, & Radlinkski, 1995), *Skillstreaming in Early Childhood* (McGinnis & Goldstein, 1990), and *Taking Part: Introducing Social Skills to Young Children* (Cartledge & Kleefeld,

1991). Working together, teachers and specialists can tailor programs to the specific needs of students and staff in a particular setting.

Considerations for Students with More Significant Support Needs

Many of the suggestions for working with younger students also apply to students with more significant support needs, because they often exhibit developmental delays across domains. In addition, their physical conditions may complicate social interactions by limiting their comprehension of verbal and nonverbal messages from others, restricting their movement or activities, making their communications difficult to understand, and attracting negative attention from peers through their appearance or behaviors. Students with significant support needs are extremely diverse but generally do better when they are actively involved and given tactile cues, pictures, or objects; models in addition to verbal input; and extra time and opportunities for repetition in their learning.

Despite the fact that students needing extensive support may be functioning at younger developmental levels than many of their peers, it is imperative that educators strive to use age-appropriate materials and instruction (e.g., referring to sports figures or rock stars rather than Sesame Street or other preschool characters in lessons; using materials with pictures of same-age peers). Further, professionals must constantly be focused on transitional goals related to daily living, use of community resources, and career education to prepare students for life beyond school and provide more normalized educational experiences. These considerations are formalized in the individualized transition planning and implementation process for students with identified disabilities described in Chapter 10. Occupational therapists, physical therapists, transition specialists, community agency representatives, and other resource personnel can assist in making classroom curricula relevant to students' immediate needs as well as longer-term goals.

Downing (1996) stressed the need to teach typical peers how to communicate with students with significant support needs included in their classes (e.g., using computer-assisted or picture board communication systems, sign language, object or touch cues—whatever the students are using to interact). Classmates need to learn what they can do to assist effectively but also what is expected of the students. They should avoid helping too much, that is, doing something for the student with disabilities that he or she can and should do independently. Another necessity may be to explain to peers the reasons for stereotypical and aggressive behaviors that students with significant support needs may exhibit. Explaining that a student may be trying to calm or stimulate himself or herself through these behaviors or may be aggressive out of frustration and discussing how it feels to be frightened, upset, or frustrated, helps to lessen fears and promote acceptance. Classmates might even be involved in brainstorming better ways to meet the student's needs, include him or her more fully in class activities or extracurricular offerings, or make lesson adaptations from a peer perspective.

Specific tools that have been developed to garner support for students with more significant support needs include *Circle of Friends* (Forest & Lusthaus, 1989; Perske, 1989), *Making Action Plans* (MAPs) (Forest & Lusthaus, 1989, 1990; Forest & Snow, 1987), and *Planning Alternative Tomorrows with Hope* (PATH) (Pearpoint, O'Brien, & Forest, 1993). These approaches are described briefly in the following paragraphs, but professionals are urged to consult the original sources for rich examples, support materials, and strategies for implementing these techniques with students. As with other methods to enhance the quality of school and classroom communities and to build prosocial behaviors, these techniques require time, commitment, and attention over the course of students' educational careers to maximize their benefits.

Circle of Friends (Forest & Lusthaus, 1989; Perske, 1989).   Circle of Friends is a technique whereby typical students individually complete a diagram of four concentric circles to help them articulate their own groups of friends and the support offered by each group. The innermost circle represents people closest to each student (e.g., family, intimate friends). The second circle includes those considered "best friends," that is, people students like, but not as much as those in circle one. Individuals with whom students like to do things, but who are not as close comprise the third circle (e.g., church or club members, teammates, neighbors, volunteers). The outermost circle consists of "paid friends" (e.g., doctors, dentists, teachers, tutors) with whom students interact because of the services they provide. Peers then consider the circles of students with disabilities, new students in their class, or students who do not have a rich network of support enjoyed by most others. Frequently their circles include family members and paid professionals as friends but these students have few names in the "best friends" or "social acquaintances" categories (circles two and three). Students discuss how this might feel and how they would react if this represented their social network. They then generate ideas about how their peers with limited friends could garner more support and how they, as classmates, might be more actively supportive (Falvey, Forest, Pearpoint, & Rosenberg, 1994).

MAPs (Forest & Lusthaus, 1989, 1990; Forest & Snow, 1987).   MAPs is another process that can be used to help students with significant support needs assess their lives and plan for their futures in inclusive communities. The MAPs process facilitates the collection of information about a student that is focused on his or her strengths and positive attributes (Falvey et al., 1994). The student and family volunteer for the process and invite others who are involved with the student (e.g., relatives, friends, classmates, teachers) to participate in helping them think about the student's future. Siblings can also play a vital role in the MAPs process given their knowledge of their brother's or sister's likes and dislikes. A facilitator who knows the process but generally does not know the people invited to the meeting guides the student and other participants through answering a series of questions. Questions are related to the process itself; the student's history or story; his or her dreams—life goals or what the student really wants to become in the future; nightmares—what he or she is afraid of in the future (e.g., loneliness, poverty, institutionalization); student descriptors; strengths and talents; and needs. Finally, to avoid the nightmares and realize the dreams, the group develops an action plan, which is the aim of the entire process. Frequently part of the action plan involves identifying ways for the student to increase the circle of friends, participate in self-advocacy and other groups, and build on strengths to promote participation in "dream-related" activities. The session is recorded in pictures and on audiotape or videotape as a public record, a reminder of the discussion, and a framework for planning.

PATH (Pearpoint et al., 1993).   PATH is similar to the MAPs process and can also be used to develop services and supports for students with significant support needs. Participants develop short- and long-range action plans specifying who will do what, where, and when to implement these plans (Falvey et al., 1994).

Family involvement is essential in using these or other approaches to implement relevant inclusive programs for students with significant support needs. Searcy (1996) further recommended that professionals work with families to develop friendship goals and plans for their children, identify ways to encourage positive social skills, find playmates to invite to their homes, observe children work and play with peers in school, learn games or activities that foster positive play and friendships, host student study groups at their homes, and take advantage of other opportunities for their child to interact with children outside of school.

Considerations for Adolescents and Young Adults

Sabornie and deBettencourt (1997) summarized physical, cognitive, and behavioral attributes of adolescence as falling between the worlds of childhood and adulthood, sharing characteristics of both. Although adolescents may think like adults in some ways, they lack autonomy. They may not be ready to assume the responsibilities of adulthood, yet they see themselves as being light years away from childhood demands. It often feels to them as if society, family, and school are pulling them in different directions. Peer relationships, issues of identity and control, and dealing with the demands of home, school, and life are paramount at this stage of development.

As noted in Chapter 10, the individualized transition planning process is mandated for adolescents with disabilities and the transition IEP provides the framework for educators in designing and delivering educational experiences for these students. Appropriate programs may include career/vocational opportunities or community-based instruction in addition to more traditional academic coursework, depending on needs, the nature of the disability, and the strengths and interests of the students.

Although academic instruction at the secondary level is primarily content-focused, the suggestions for integrating social skills into academic instruction presented earlier in this chapter are highly relevant to this level. Co-teaching with a special educator, guidance counselor, school psychologist, or other specialist versed in social skills development affords important support for the integration process as well as for more concentrated work with students who are demonstrating significant social skills difficulties when compared with their peers. For more severe behavioral issues such as chronic truancy, physical aggression, and depression, educators are urged to access colleagues or specialists who have expertise in functional assessment, behavior intervention planning, and dealing with challenging behaviors through assistance teams, consultation relationships, or interdisciplinary or interagency teams as described in Chapter 4 and other chapters. These collaborative structures provide much-needed support for individuals faced with serious behavioral problems. In general, the more complex and long-standing the problem, the greater the expertise and involvement of others across settings are needed to change the situation for the better.

Whether or not secondary-level educators are involved in specific collaborative arrangements with colleagues, they can implement classroom strategies that promote positive student behaviors. Some of these strategies are described in Figure 12.4.

The importance of providing appropriate adult and peer models for adolescents cannot be overemphasized. Educators should consistently model respectful, considerate behavior in their interactions with students. Those who treat students with dignity and are genuinely concerned about helping students develop more effective prosocial behaviors for their own benefit elicit more respectful, prosocial behavior from students in return. Educators can also call attention to actions of celebrities, figures related to course topics, or persons held in esteem by adolescents who did the "right thing."

Chapter Summary

Developing prosocial behaviors of students as part of the curriculum in inclusive classrooms yields rich dividends in terms of building classroom community, student motivation, and learning—both academic and social. This chapter has presented rationales and strategies for building positive student behaviors and integrating social skills development into academic instruction and class routines. Special considerations for working with young children, students with more significant support needs, and adolescents and young adults were also offered. The dividends of developing prosocial student behavior come with adult commitment to providing needed supports, careful planning, and consistent implementation over time. Contrary to being a waste of time or robbing time from the academic curriculum, social skills development is fundamental to learning and to life. As Charney (1991) wrote:

> I have grown to appreciate the task of helping children learn to take better care of themselves, each other and their classrooms. It's not a waste. It's probably the most enduring thing that I teach. In a world filled with global violence, threats of

FIGURE 12.4   **Strategies to Promote Prosocial Behavior in Secondary Classes.**

1. Clearly articulate expected behaviors (e.g., arrival times, task completion, cooperation with peers) and ensure consistency with follow-up and accountability.

2. Provide time for groups to discuss specific behaviors that contributed to effective class or group functioning.

3. Connect positive classroom behaviors to success in life outside of school. Relate behaviors to social relationships with peers, family, coworkers, and community members (e.g., dating, negotiating home privileges, job interviewing).

4. Have students set specific individual and group goals for social and academic learning. Designate time for weekly goal monitoring and celebrating attainment.

5. Provide specific opportunities to practice prosocial skills (e.g., during pair work, group work, discussions, debates, role plays).

6. Remind students of expected behaviors at the beginning of lessons or activities (e.g., "Now would be a good time to compare notes").

7. Encourage and reinforce demonstrations of positive behaviors by individuals and by groups. For example, comment when students have participated actively, cooperated well in groups, or individuals have displayed improved behavior. Frequently, older students prefer to have individual encouragement offered privately rather than in front of their peers.

8. Have students monitor and record their own behaviors individually or in group work using checklists, tally sheets, or other counting systems.

9. Draw attention to the social aspects of subject matter (e.g., problem solving in science or social studies, effective or ineffective behaviors of leaders or groups, consumer significance of math concepts).

10. Offer choices such as student selection of research topics, formats for demonstrating learning, and negotiated dates for projects or assignments.

nuclear and environmental devastation, where drugs and guns are available on nearly every street corner, learning to be more decent and to build caring communities is hardly a waste of time. Safe and effective communities in the classroom are rarely by-products. They are built through our commitment and conscious design; they grow from our best energies, time and attention. (p. 10)

CHAPTER ACTIVITIES

1. Design a social skills lesson to teach a specific social skill to a student or group of students. Implement the lesson, if possible, noting what went well and any needed adjustments to your lesson.

2. Select a content area text and identify the skills targeted in a chapter. Identify complementary social skills that could be paired with these academic skills. Work with

a partner to brainstorm ways to integrate the social and academic skills into your instruction and classroom routines following the integration process presented in this chapter.

3. Use the circle of friends procedure with a group or classroom of students. Have students construct a list of specific suggestions to help individuals with more significant support needs develop richer circles of friends and a list of actions that typical peers could take to be more supportive of these students.

13 Collaboration for Inclusive Education

Realizing the Promise

1. Discuss multiple perspectives on the essential features for inclusive education.
2. Summarize the current controversy surrounding inclusive education.
3. Describe a "vision" for students with disabilities in the future.

Listening to Voices about the Future of Special Education

*"It is my vision that one day 'all students' will truly mean **all** students."*

* * *

"I see a future for education where 'different' is no longer synonymous with 'deficit,' a future where diversity is celebrated."

* * *

"I am concerned that we not continue to ask more and more of educators without providing them with the support and resources necessary for student success."

As the voices above reflect, this is a period of both optimism and concern for the future of education for students with disabilities and others with special learning needs. As a new millennium arrives, professionals in every field are taking inventory of past performance and accomplishments, reviewing periods of challenge, and projecting future needs and possible courses of action. In contemplating the future of inclusive education for all students, it is helpful to consider present challenges and future possibilities. Chapter 1 provided a review of evolving practice to respond more effectively to the needs of students with disabilities, students at risk, and their families. It offered a glimpse of the tradition of care and concern for students with special needs that has been a cornerstone of public education. Such a perspective also revealed the ongoing struggle for inclusion, equal access, and educational opportunities for individuals with disabilities and other learning differences. There have been numerous celebrations as well as setbacks along the way.

Widespread educational reform efforts signal a period of change, now more than ever before, as issues of appropriate programming for all students have become the education agendas at federal, state, and local levels. In many arenas, as decisions are made and plans formulated, there appears to be an increased sense that "we are all in this together." This book has described the essential features required to ensure the quality of collaborative endeavors on behalf of all students. This final chapter revisits these key features and provides opportunities to reflect on varying perspectives and common themes that emerge from conversations about the future of special education with professionals and family members around the country. It also provides a framework for considering both organizational and personal "visions" for unified, collaborative approaches to serving all students together in the future.

Essential Features and a Focus on the Future: Voices from the Field

It may be useful to review briefly the seven essential features of inclusive education programs that were introduced in Chapter 2. These features, drawn primarily from research on effective and lasting organizational change, provide collaborators with the structure and support needed to modify existing practices, create more inclusive approaches, and sustain them over time. These concepts have served as the guiding principles for this text. Realistically, few school districts have all seven elements fully in place when new initiatives are launched. It is important, however, for stakeholders to understand their importance. Simply put, without attention to these features it will be difficult, if not impossible, to build a lasting base of support for professional collaboration and inclusive education.

This section summarizes these essential features and incorporates divergent perspectives on their importance to the future of inclusive service delivery. These key perspectives are provided by various individuals whose experiences and education have shaped their respective hopes and visions. Figure 13.1 introduces the professionals and family members who participated in a "virtual" dialogue about their visions for the future of collaboration and inclusive education. Questions about these topics were posed to each participant; however, space does not permit reporting their entire responses. Such ongoing dialogue facilitates understanding between individuals with different personal and professional backgrounds who share a common interest in improving education for all students.

Collaborative Culture

Collaborative cultures are working environments in which teamwork, cooperation, and trust are valued and encouraged. In inclusive schools, all participants are

FIGURE 13.1   Dialogue Participants.

Mimi Bryant, high school English teacher, in Jacksonville, Florida.

Sue Land, special education instructional specialist, in Williamsburg-James City County (Virginia) Public Schools.

Lee Martin, director of special education, in Ypsilanti (Michigan) Public Schools.

Paula Miller, parent of a high school student who receives services from programs for students with learning disabilities and emotional disabilities in Tampa, Florida.

Jane Quenneville, occupational therapist/assistive technology specialist, in Virginia Beach(Virginia) Public Schools.

Steve Staples, superintendent of York County (Virginia) Public Schools

Ann Turnbull, special education professor and researcher at the University of Kansas at Lawrence, co-director of the Beach Center on Families and Disability, parent of a young adult with disabilities.

members of their schools' team—administrators, teachers, specialists, students, and families—working together to make their educational programs stronger. Collaborative cultures are environments in which resources are shared, personal and team efforts are recognized and valued, and all team members—students and adults—have opportunities for growth and leadership. Collaborative cultures facilitate innovative thinking and risk taking. Schools that lack a collaborative culture are often competitive and stressful workplaces because there is limited trust among participants. Without a collaborative culture for support, highly skilled and competent participants may be reluctant to offer new suggestions or try alternative practices for fear of failure.

On collaborative culture

There needs to be more consistency between elementary, middle, and high school levels. I feel that teachers need to take more ownership in educating all children. —Jane Quenneville, occupational therapist

I see a future where teams of professionals will work with groups of students to direct their learning, provide assistance and tutoring for areas of difficulty, make needed accommodations for specific learning needs, and teach self-help skills that permit students to become independent learners, regardless of the labeling affixed to students. —Steve Staples, superintendent

The outspoken acceptance of ownership for all students is critical. —Lee Martin, director of special education

Parents need to be involved as much as possible. —Paula Miller, parent

Shared Leadership

Shared leadership is the process of involving stakeholders in meaningful decision making. All stakeholder groups have representation in planning, implementing, and evaluating inclusive programs. Comprehensive planning teams address potential concerns in a proactive manner. For example, planning teams help ensure the appropriateness of student placements. They make well-reasoned decisions about co-teaching assignments and design professional schedules to facilitate meaningful classroom support and involvement. In general, shared leadership promotes greater trust, commitment, collaboration, and more creative problem solving. Without shared leadership, potential stakeholders may feel "left out" of the process. As a result of limited involvement and communication, many potential program supporters may feel little investment in changes and become passive or active resisters.

On Shared Leadership

In the future I see more excellent schools than we have now and the distinguishing characteristic of these schools is empowered leaders and collaborative planning/support among students, families, educators, and community members. We need to learn more about how to transform energy into synergy by the whole becoming greater than the sum of the parts. —Ann Turnbull, special education professor and parent

More consensus building is needed to get all individuals involved to agree on certain issues. Not just teachers—administrators, too. We need more role-release training of others to be competent in areas supportive of academic success for all children. —Jane Quenneville, occupational therapist

Coherent Vision

A coherent vision is a clear, well-defined, and shared view of what "should be." This is the "big picture" of what the school will look like when more inclusive practices are used consistently to support students and their teachers. A coherent vision of the school's future that is shared by administrators, teachers, specialists, students, and families enables teams to make more informed decisions, and it facilitates better collaboration. A well-articulated vision induces commitment among stakeholders and enhances efforts in goal setting, planning, and project management. It helps team members to understand how their individual and collective efforts fit together and reinforces their belief in the value of these efforts. Without a coherent vision of the future, a significant change effort can create feelings of confusion as familiar practices are replaced by new ones.

On Coherent Vision

For all students to be educated together successfully we need to work on a plan that everyone believes in and can support. The plan for these students is also a plan for

society. Schools cannot fix all the problems of society but they can start by preparing all children to learn together. —Mimi Bryant, high school teacher

Inclusion must remain a viable part of the vision for schools and this vision must be articulated repeatedly to reinforce the commitment. —Steve Staples, superintendent

I envision schools providing more inclusive services for all students. Students with identified needs will be served in their "home" schools, and there will be less transporting to special programs or special schools. Because of these changes there will be an even stronger emphasis on collaboration among general educators, special educators, parents, and other service providers. We'll see more creative approaches to providing services to children. —Sue Land, special education instructional specialist

Comprehensive Planning

Comprehensive planning and shared leadership go hand in hand. Comprehensive planning ensures that inclusive education is considered from every angle as decisions are made. This facilitates effective use of resources, and ongoing information sharing. By weaving inclusive education goals and collaborative working opportunities into the existing organizational fabric in a meaningful way, lasting stakeholder involvement is established. A carefully developed planning process helps stakeholders understand how new ideas can enrich established and valued goals and practices. Synergy is created as meaningful links between programs are made. Without ongoing comprehensive planning, daily implementation and evaluation problems are likely to continue over time without satisfactory resolution. Consequently, implementation progress is often very limited and even enthusiastic implementers may feel like they are on a treadmill, going nowhere fast.

Our dialogue participants agree on the importance of comprehensive planning and its relationship to the other essential features. When asked to identify what might be considered the greatest obstacle to inclusive practice, Steve Staples, a superintendent recognized for his leadership in inclusive education, responded, "Failing to plan adequately." He added, "It is not enough to simply believe in the concept. Doing the 'right thing' in the wrong way is no better than ignoring the right thing all together. Schools considering an inclusive approach must be prepared in practice as well as philosophy before taking giant steps forward. A poorly implemented attempt will simply confirm naysayers' attitudes and keep the issue off the table for another 20 years."

Adequate Resources

Adequate resources are the essential tools that inclusive education advocates need to do the job successfully. These tools span a broad resource spectrum. Tangible resources may include special materials, assistive technology, and paraeducator assistance. Many competent professionals may need opportunities to learn new skills in order to work with a more diverse student population. In addition, most educators have had little preparation for working in classrooms with other adults on a daily basis. Some may need advanced instruction on co-teaching, collaborative consultation, and team problem solving. Planning time is another essential resource that specialists and teachers need to consult and co-teach effectively with their partners. Unwavering administrative support is perhaps the most valuable resource. This ensures that classroom collaborators and school wide planning teams get the other resources they need. Administrative support also provides the essential "go ahead" signals that enable individuals and teams to create and implement more inclusive practices. Without adequate resources, even the most committed inclusive education advocates become frustrated and discouraged by the hurdles they face. Daily frustrations because of inadequate resources can lead to questions about leaders' true commitment to inclusive education and their own abilities to change practices that exclude students with disabilities from general education opportunities.

On Adequate Resources

Teacher training programs and professional development activities must prepare all personnel to educate students with disabilities in the general education classroom. —Lee Martin, special education director

You also need administrative support for planning, staffing, and continual reevaluation. —Mimi Bryant, high school educator

The teachers are our greatest assets. They need support to meet the many needs of our children. —Paula Miller, parent

I think creative options need to be explored that provide opportunities for all students but that also provide intensity of instruction and services in a cost-efficient way. —Ann Turnbull, professor and parent

Because of my frame of reference with assistive technology I see it being used in the classroom to enable children with disabilities to access the general education curriculum. —Jane Quenneville, occupational therapist

Professional staff will need intensive re-training to 'undo' our former emphasis on sorting and selecting students by program or other labels. Specifically, this training must (1) prepare teachers and other professionals to work effectively in a collaborative setting instead of the current one-adult to 25-students arrangement, and (2) emphasize individualized student learning approaches instead of large-group or whole-class activities. —Steve Staples, superintendent

Parent and student preparation would also be necessary. —Sue Land, special education instructional specialist

Sustained Implementation

Sustained implementation is the ability of program supporters to stay focused and committed over time while recruiting others to their ranks. For inclusive education to succeed in schools, it must remain a priority at the school and district levels. This maintenance of focus allows time to correct initial implementation problems that are inevitable and to demonstrate results that can help build a broader base of support. Time and sustained effort allow good ideas to become accepted practice. Historically, many schools have had difficulty maintaining long-term commitment to new ideas and initiatives. This could be attributed, in part, to a lack of understanding of the time required for effective change. Last year's "innovation" is often replaced by a competing initiative the following year. Many seasoned educators can easily identify a number of innovative ideas that were implemented briefly and then lost the attention and support of key individuals.

On Sustained Implementation

The "islands of excellence" throughout the country are some of the greatest assets to ensure sustained implementation of inclusive practice. The success stories need to be collected and shared as broadly as possible. —Ann Turnbull, professor and parent

To avoid such a scattering of successful projects and perpetuate larger systemic changes, I propose the creation of an educational roundtable to address long-standing barriers to educational change. This group must be comprised of legislators, industry executives, community leaders, higher education personnel, educators (preK–12), policymakers, families, and students. —Lee Martin, director of special education

I see greater acceptance of differences among populations and students. Our communities must have a heightened awareness to become more inclusive. That spirit can have a carryover effect into our schools and classrooms. —Steve Staples, superintendent

Continuous Evaluation and Improvement

Ongoing quantitative and qualitative evaluation provides implementers with the information they need to make well-reasoned, data-based decisions. Ideally, these data provide supportive evidence that shows new initiatives are working well. More likely, they show aspects of innovations that are proceeding as well as planned and indicate other areas in which additional changes are needed. Ongoing evaluation allows stakeholders to assess progress accurately and answer typical questions posed by many inclusive education supporters and critics. For example, how does inclusive education affect the academic performance of students with disabilities? How does it affect typical students? Do classroom communities change as a result of this new approach? What will make the process work more effectively?

Data can help reduce the natural resistance of many experienced educators when new and unproven initiatives are introduced. This information can also help sustain the commitment and motivation of program supporters during difficult periods. Without data it is difficult to gauge accurately the true efficacy of ongoing efforts and it is impossible to make appropriate program improvement decisions.

On Continuous Evaluation and Improvement

The one area that has to be consistently evaluated is that of academic integrity. It is wrong to have children sit in classrooms and not receive the education they need to function in society. —Mimi Bryant, high school educator

Remember, you are establishing an evaluation of an inclusive approach that will last a long time. —Steve Staples, superintendent

Evaluation efforts should consider the impact of inclusive practice on peer relationships and quality of life for students with disabilities and for typical students. —Ann Turnbull, professor and parent

In essence, these seven essential features represent sound and effective educational practice—regardless of the innovation. They are the building blocks of effective schools. Thoughtful consideration and implementation of these features will facilitate development of effective and lasting inclusive education programs.

Continuing Controversy: Inclusive Practice

Meaningful involvement in all important dimensions of life is what policy makers, educators, and families want for students. All students need educational opportunities that will enable them to gain the knowledge and skills they need to live life to the fullest. This is true for all students—those with and without disabilities or other special needs (Hallahan & Kauffman, 1997; Lipsky & Gartner, 1997a; McDonnell, McLaughlin, et al., 1997). Advocates hope that when students leave school they are as well prepared as possible for the academic, social, and vocational opportunities and challenges they will face as adults. Even the most outspoken critics of inclusive education believe in the value and importance of meaningful involvement in the "mainstream" of life for all students. This being the case, opposing inclusion seems to make as much sense as opposing healthy babies or computer technology. So, why do many committed professionals and family members still resist inclusive education programs for students with disabilities?

Most critics readily admit that they are not opposed to the concept of inclusion as much as they are opposed to versions so poorly implemented in many sites. Most anti-inclusion arguments stem from implementation issues rather than the conceptual framework. Many school districts jumped on the inclusion "bandwagon" without carefully considering what these changes would mean for students, families, and professionals. Many of the "horror stories" about "bad" inclusion are real in schools that have failed to address the seven essential features of effective programs adequately. Inclusion, as it is intended to work, will fail if it is not properly supported—like any other innovation poorly implemented. For program planners, questions related to inclusive education cannot be distilled to simply "Is inclusion good or bad?" There are many complex questions that need to be addressed as decision makers consider the issues, the resources, and their commitment to improve educational opportunities for all learners.

Inclusion, as a conceptual model, is gaining respect in public schools. Inclusive practice is steeped in shared values and beliefs, legal mandates, and educational common sense. Critics and advocates alike would agree that instilling a sense of belonging and acceptance, being valued by others, and achieving success in "real-life" contexts are important and appropriate goals for all students. Collaboration provides an opportunity for continued dialogue on the most appropriate means to achieving these goals.

Emerging Themes

In some ways designing and developing inclusive and effective schools is much like the creative work of a jazz ensemble. Each score of music is unique and represents an exciting problem-solving challenge for jazz musicians. Although variations exist among instruments, musicians understand the process that must be followed to produce an appealing rendition. There is often a band leader, but the leadership is shared as respective instruments are tapped for solo performances at a time agreed on by the group.

Together, the group reviews the musical score to develop a better understanding of their ideal vision for an outstanding performance and clarify their contributions. As they do, respective band members offer improvisations or variations on the musical theme based on past experiences and understanding of the talents, skills, and areas of difficulty for others in the band. Following this, they begin to plan performances together. They rehearse various arrangements as they plan. Individually and as a group they consider how the melodies might best fit together to create rich variations on each musical theme. Although they do their best to anticipate troublesome sections prior to performances, they also problem-solve and support one another as they play. Sometimes the most powerful performances come from this interplay between different musicians willing to assume both prominent and background roles as needed. This is a continuous process that improves over time. The longer the ensemble plays together, the better it gets. Members develop trust and appreciation for one another's skills and talents as they communicate through their instruments, verbally and nonverbally. An almost intuitive sense of the right thing to do for the good of the group is developed.

This metaphor holds true for schools that make the commitment to orchestrate inclusive programs that are in harmony with all students' needs. Although most districts share many common features, each one is unique, with a rhythm of its own, in terms of relative strengths and weaknesses. Some school systems have more assets than others. For example, some may begin with strong central office leadership, more committed parent advocates, or previous successes related to collaborative projects. Undoubtedly, some schools face many complex social concerns, community resistance, and other competing priorities. Ultimately, with commitment and perseverance, all schools can become more collaborative.

Recommendations for the Future

Problem solving to create inclusive schools is a process that is basically the same for all schools, no matter what their history. This book has provided fundamental strategies to help teams realize the promise of collaboration for inclusive education. The basic set of recommended practices is the same for all schools, regardless of their starting points.

• *Promote inclusive education to make schools stronger for all students.* Inclusive education provides a vision and focus for collaboration among schools, families, and communities. Effective programs for students with special needs strengthen learning environments for all students.

• *Help all participants comprehend the complex nature of change in educational organizations.* Appropriately implemented, inclusive practice represents a radical change in meeting the educational needs of students with disabilities. Understanding the change process enables the quality of collaborative interactions to improve as teams move from sharing a vision to planning to implementation to evaluation activities.

• *Develop implementation strategies based on commitment and teamwork at federal, state, district, school, and classroom levels.* Federal and state educational leaders can provide the vision, policies, and resources to guide local efforts. District and school teams should make inclusion a long-term priority by providing lasting support. Classroom teams must design, implement, and monitor programs that provide student support and meet the unique needs of learners.

• *Recognize that effective, efficient communication is crucial to collaboration.* The success of collaborative interactions rests on the continuously improving communication skills of all participants. Overcoming identified barriers to communication enhances the planning and problem-solving process for collaborators. Diversity should be viewed as a strength as teams work together to plan creatively to better serve all their students. It takes time and skill to integrate multiple perspectives.

• *Deepen and extend individual reflective practice through collaborative interactions.* The basic processes for reflective planning and problem solving are the same whether they are applied by individuals, dyads, or small groups. A collaborative or team approach heightens the power of reflective practice because others contribute unique perspectives and expertise.

- *Ensure that educators have access to a full array of options for collaborative support.* Although each school differs in terms of the particular structures and resources available, a collaborative network enables professionals to develop the types of support best suited to meet student needs, the curriculum and setting, their personal skills and preferences, and the configuration of students in specific classes.

- *Actively involve students, families, classroom teachers, and other key members of the service delivery team in the development of individualized education plans.* Meaningful participation by all members of the team produces more complete student assessment profiles, more cohesive and appropriate educational programs, and increased commitment for success.

- *Conceptualize special education as a continuum of student support services—not simply a range of placement options.* Planning teams must consider the specific conditions conducive to student success, the nature and extent of support needs, and ways to mobilize the necessary resources to provide appropriate support for students in inclusive environments.

- *Provide both indirect and direct collaborative support for inclusive program planning and problem solving.* Structures such as assistance teaming, consultation, and co-teaching facilitate both student and professional success. In addition, student supports, such as peer tutoring, help ensure greater levels of peer support and social skills development.

- *Base academic programs for students with disabilities on appropriately differentiated curriculum and effective instructional techniques for all students.* All students benefit from more intensive academic programs. If educators begin with differentiated curriculum and effective instruction, they can more easily ensure that students with disabilities have the accommodations and modifications necessary for success.

- *Approach social skills like academic skills—with the same commitment to teaching directly, focusing on positive behavior, and stressing prevention through meeting student needs.* Educators should ensure that students have access to a full array of options for student-centered collaborative support and social skills development in an inclusive learning community.

- *Make data-based decisions regarding the efficacy and improvement of programs and services.* Ultimately, decisions about individual students need to be based on continuous monitoring of performance and progress. Similarly, ongoing program improvement should be based on information from multiple sources incorporated into a comprehensive evaluation plan.

Chapter Summary

It is evident that there are numerous influences or forces that may impact the future reality of educational services for students with disabilities. Achieving inclusive education for *all* students will require careful, reflective consideration of the essential features and recommended practices by committed and skilled collaborators. In addition, effective programs require continuous review of the impact of values and beliefs, legal mandates, and school reform initiatives on evolving practice. These factors will all have significant implications for the future of inclusive education. Sustained commitment to the promise of inclusive education through collaboration can be encouraged by remembering the late jazz great, Duke Ellington, who attributed his success to two rules—Rule 1: Don't quit. Rule 2: Remember rule 1!

CHAPTER ACTIVITIES

1. When you think about special education 10 years from now, what do you envision? What factors or experiences have helped to shape your vision?

2. How might a person's role affect his or her perspective in the development of an inclusive education program?

3. What are the three to five most important concepts you have learned from reading this text? Explain your rationale for each.

BIBLIOGRAPHY

Adams, L., & Cessna, K. (1991). Designing systems to facilitate collaboration: Collective wisdom from Colorado. *Preventing School Failure, 35*(4), 37–42.

Aiello, B. (1976). Especially for special educators: A sense of our own history. *Exceptional Children, 42,* 244–252.

Aksamit, D. L., & Rankin, J. L. (1993). Problem-solving teams as a prereferral process. *Special Services in the Schools, 7*(1), 1–22.

Alberg, J., Petry, C., & Eller, A. (1994). *A resource guide for social skills instruction.* Longmont, CO: Sopris West.

Algozzine, B., & Ysseldyke, J. (1995). *Strategies and tactics for effective instruction.* Longmont, CO: Sopris West.

Algozzine, B., Ysseldyke, J. E., & Campbell, P. (1994). Strategies and tactics for effective instruction. *Teaching Exceptional Children, 26*(3), 34–35.

Allen, M., Hale, L., Mongeau, P., Berkowitz-Stafford, S., Stafford, S., Shanahan, W., Agee, P., Dillon, K., Dickson, R., & Ray, C. (1990). Testing a model of messagesidedness: Three replications. *Communication Monographs, 57,* 275–291.

Anderson, M. G. (1992). The use of selected theater rehearsal technique activities with African American adolescents labeled "behavior disordered." *Exceptional Children, 59*(2), 132–140.

Anderson, M. G., & Webb-Johnson, G. (1995). Cultural contexts, the seriously emotionally disturbed classification, and African American learners. In B. A. Ford, F. E. Obiakor, & J. M. Patton (Eds.), *Effective education of African American exceptional learners* (pp. 151–187). Austin, TX: Pro-Ed.

Appelsies, A., & Fairbanks, C. (1997). Write for your life. *Educational Leadership, 54*(8), 70–72.

Archer, A., & Gleason, M. (1990). Direct instruction in content area reading. In D. Carnine, J. Silbert, & E. Kameenui (Eds.), *Direct instruction reading* (2nd ed., pp. 339–393). Columbus, OH: Merrill.

Artiles, A. J., & Trent, S. C. (1994). Overrepresentation of minority students in special education: A continuing debate. *The Journal of Special Education, 27*(4), 410–437.

Ashton, P. T., & Webb, R. B. (1986). *Making a difference: Teachers' sense of efficacy and student achievement.* New York: Longman.

Association for Supervision and Curriculum Development. (1992). *Resolutions 1992.* Alexandria, VA: Author.

Ayers, E. J. B. (1991). An alternative approach to staff development. *Journal of Visual Impairment and Blindness, 85*(7), 302–305.

Babcock, N. L., & Pryzwansky, W. B. (1983). Models of consultation: Preferences of education professionals at five stages of services. *Journal of School Psychology, 21,* 356–359.

Bagin, D., Gallagher, D., & Kindred, L. (1997). *The school and community relations* (5th ed.). Boston: Allyn and Bacon.

Bailey, D. B. (1987). Collaborative goal-setting with families: Resolving differences in values and priorities for services. *Topics in Early Childhood Special Education, 7*(2), 59–71.

Baker, E. T., Wang, M. C., & Walberg, H. J. (1994/95, December/January). The effects of inclusion on learning. *Educational Leadership,* 33–34.

Barker, L. (1990). *Listening behavior.* Dillon, CO: Spectra.

Baron, K. S., & Chalfant, J. C. (1987). *Specific learning disabilities: Guidelines for identification and assessment.* Charleston, WV: West Virginia Department of Education.

Barth, R. S. (1990). *Improving schools from within: Teachers, parents, and principals can make a difference.* San Francisco: Jossey-Bass.

Bauwens, J., & Hourcade, J. J. (1995). *Cooperative teaching: Rebuilding the schoolhouse for all students.* Austin, TX: Pro-Ed.

Bauwens, J., Hourcade, J. J., & Friend, M. (1989). Cooperative teaching: A model for general and special education integration. *Remedial and Special Education, 10*(2), 17–22.

Bauwens, J., & Korinek, L. (1993). IEPs for cooperative teaching: Developing legal and useful documents. *Intervention in School and Clinic, 28*(5), 303–306.

Bay, M., Bryan, T., & O'Connor, R. (1994). Teachers assisting teachers: A prereferral model for urban educators. *Teacher Education and Special Education, 17,* 10–21.

Beach Center on Families and Disability. (1997, Summer). Family-centered service delivery. *Families and Disability Newsletter, 8*(2), 1–2.

Beck, R. & Gabriel, S. (1989). *Project RIDE: Responding to individual differences in education* (4th ed.). Great Falls, MT: Great Falls Public Schools.

Bender, W. N. (1992). *Learning disabilities: Characteristics, identification, and teaching strategies.* Boston: Allyn and Bacon.

Benes, K. M., Gutkin, T. B., & Kramer, J. J. (1991). Micro-analysis of consultation and consultee verbal and nonverbal behaviors. *Journal of Educational and Psychological Consultation, 2*(2), 133–149.

Beninghof, A. M. (1996, summer). Using a spectrum of staff development activities to support inclusion. *Journal of Staff Development, 17*(3), 12–15.

Bergan, J. R. (1995). Evolution of a problem-solving model of consultation. *Journal of Educational and Psychological Consultation, 6*(2), 111–123.

Bergan, J. R., & Tombari, M. L. (1975). The analysis of verbal interactions occurring during consultation. *Journal of School Psychology, 13,* 209–226.

Berreth, D., & Berman, S. (1997). The moral dimensions of schools. *Educational Leadership, 54*(8), 24–27.

Billingsley, B. S., & Cross, L. H. (1992). Predictors of commitment, job satisfaction, and intent to stay in teaching: A comparison of general and special educators. *The Journal of Special Education, 25,* 453–471.

Billingsley, B. S., Farley, M., & Rude, H. A. (1993). A conceptual framework for program leadership in the education of students with disabilities. In B. S. Billingsley (Ed.) *Program leadership for serving students with disabilities* (pp. 1–20). Blacksburg, VA: Virginia Tech.

Bishop, K. K., Woll, J., & Arango, P. (1993). *Family-professional collaboration for children with special health needs and their families.* Burlington, VT: University of Vermont.

Blankenship, C. (1985). Using curriculum-based assessment data to make instructional decisions. *Exceptional Children, 52*(3), 233–238.

Bliss, J., Firestone, W., & Richards, C. (Eds.). (1991). *Rethinking of effective schools: Research and practice.* Englewood Cliffs, NJ: Prentice-Hall.

Block, M. E. (1994). *A teacher's guide to including students with disabilities in regular physical education.* Baltimore: Brookes.

Boudah, D. J. (1994). *The development and evaluation of a model of collaborative instruction for teachers in inclusive classrooms.* Unpublished doctoral dissertation. Lawrence, KS: University of Kansas.

Bracey, G. W. (1996). The sixth Bracey report on the condition of public education. *Phi Delta Kappan, 78*(2), 127–138.

Brammer, L. M. (1993). *The helping relationship: Process and skills* (5th ed.). Boston: Allyn and Bacon.

Briggs, A. (1994). Achieving educational change through technical assistance. *Journal of Visual Impairment and Blindness, 88*(4), 310–316.

Brinckerhoff, R. F. (1989). Resource centers serve the needs of school science teachers. *School Science and Mathematics, 89*(1), 12–18.

Brophy, J., & Good, T. (1986). Teacher behavior and student achievement. In M. C. Wittrock (Ed.), *Handbook of research on teaching* (3rd ed., pp. 328–375). New York: Macmillan.

Brown, L., Ford, A., Nisbet, J., Sweet, M., Donellan, A., & Gruenewald, L. (1983). Opportunities available when severely handicapped students attend chronological age appropriate regular schools. *Journal for the Association of Persons with Severe Handicaps, 8,* 16–24.

Brown, L., Long, E., Udvari-Solner, A., Davis, L., VanDeventer, P., Ahlgren, C., Johnson, F., Grenewald, L., & Jorgenson, J. (1989). The home school. *Journal of the Association for Persons with Severe Handicaps, 14,* 1–7.

Bryan, T. (1991). Social problems and learning disabilities. In B. Wong (Ed.), *Learning about learning disabilities* (pp. 190–231). San Diego: Academic Press.

Buckley, J. M. D. (1994). New perspectives on training and technical assistance: Moving from assumptions to a focus on quality. *Journal of the Association for Persons with Severe Handicaps, 19*(3), 223–32.

Bulgren, J. A., Schumaker, J. B., & Deshler, D. D. (1988). Effectiveness of a concept teaching routine in enhancing the performance of LD students in secondary-level mainstream classes. *Learning Disability Quarterly, 11,* 3–17.

Bunch, G. (1997). From here to there: The passage of inclusion education. In G. Bunch, & A. Valeo (Eds.), *Inclusion: Recent research.* Toronto, Ontario, Canada: Inclusion Press.

Bunch, G., Lupart, J., & Brown, M. (1997). *Resistance and acceptance: Educator attitudes to inclusion of students with disabilities.* Toronto, Ontario, Canada: York University, Faculty of Education.

Bunch, G., & Valeo, A. (1997). *Inclusion: Recent research.* Toronto, Ontario, Canada: Inclusion Press.

Burrello, L., Burrello, J., & Winninger, J. (1993). *Facing inclusion together through collaboration and co-teaching.* Bloomington, IN: Council for Administrators of Special Education.

Byrd, H. B. (1995). Curricular and pedagogical procedures for African American learners with academic and cognitive disabilities. In B. A. Ford, F. E. Obiakor, & J. M. Patton (Eds.), *Effective education of African American exceptional learners* (pp. 123–150). Austin, TX: Pro-Ed.

Callahan, R., Fleenor, C., & Knudson, H. (1986). *Understanding organizational behavior: A managerial viewpoint.* Columbus, OH: Merrill.

Caplan, G. (1970). *The theory and practice of mental health consultation.* New York: Basic.

Caplan, G., Caplan, R. B., & Erchul, W. P. (1995). A contemporary view of mental health consultation: Comments on "Types of Mental Health Consultation." *Journal of Educational Psychological Consultation, 6*(1), 23–30.

Carlberg, C., & Kavale, K. (1980). The efficacy of special versus regular class placement for exceptional children: A meta-analysis. *Journal of Special Education, 14,* 459–462.

Carlson, E. (1997). *In-school and post-school outcomes of students declassified from special education.* Unpublished doctoral dissertation. College of William & Mary: Williamsburg, VA.

Carlson, R., & Awkerman, G. (Eds.). (1991). *Educational planning: Concepts, strategies and practices.* New York: Longman.

Carnine, D. (1995). Shifting the focus of state education legislation from innovative schools to high-performing schools. *Education Week, 15,* 40–43.

Carnine, D. (1994). Introduction to the mini-series: Educational tools for diverse learners. *School Psychology Review, 23,* 341–350.

Carnine, D., Miller, S., Bean, R., & Zigmond, N. (1994). Social studies: Educational tools for diverse learners. *School Psychology Review, 23,* 428–441.

Carnine, D., Silbert, J., & Kameenui, E. (Eds.) (1990). *Direct instruction reading* (2nd ed.). Columbus, OH: Merrill.

Cartledge, G., & Kleefeld, J. (1989). Teaching social communication skills to elementary school students with handicaps. *Teaching Exceptional Children, 22*(1), 14–17.

Casey, C. M., & Dozier, P. W. (1994, October). Cutting costs in special education. *The American School Board Journal,* 27–30.

Cawelti, G. (1994). *High school restructuring: A national study.* Arlington, VA: Educational Research Service.

Center for the Future of Children. (1997, Summer/Fall). Children and poverty. (Executive Summary) *Future of Children, 7*(2), 1–7.

Chalfant, J. C., & Pysh, M. V. (1989). Teacher assistance teams: Five descriptive studies on 96 teams. *Remedial and Special Education, 10*(6), 49–58.

Chalfant, J. C., Pysh, M. V., & Moultrie, R. (1979). Teacher assistance teams: A model for within building problem solving. *Learning Disability Quarterly, 2,* 85–96.

Charles, C. M. (1976). *Individualizing instruction.* St. Louis: Mosby.

Charney, R. S. (1991). *Teaching children to care: Management in the responsive classroom.* Greenfield, MA: Northeast Foundation for Children.

Child Development Resources. (1995). *Project Trans-Team.* Norge, VA: Author.

Children's Defense Fund. (1998). *The state of America's children yearbook 1998.* Washington, DC: Author.

Choate, J. S. (1997). *Successful inclusive teaching: Proven ways to detect and correct special needs.* Boston: Allyn & Bacon.

Chuoke, M., & Eyman, B. (1997). Play fair—And not just at recess. *Educational Leadership, 54*(8), 53–55.

Clift, R. T., Houston, W. R., & Pugach, M. C. (Eds.). (1990). *Encouraging reflective practice in education.* New York: Teachers College Press.

Clift, R. T., Veal, M. L., Holland, P., Johnson, M., & McCarthy, J. (1995). *Collaborative leadership and shared decision making: Teachers, principals, and university professors.* New York: Teachers College Press.

Cohen, E. G. (1973). Open-space schools: The opportunity to become ambitious. *Sociology of Education, 46,* 143–161.

Cohen, P. (Ed.). (1990). *Intentions in communications.* Cambridge, MA: MIT Press.

Cohen, S. B. (1993). Effective instruction: Principles and strategies for programs. In B. Billingsley (Ed.), *Program leadership in special education manual* (pp. 169–203). Richmond, VA: Department of Education.

Cole, D. A., & Meyer, L. (1991). Social integration and severe disabilities: A longitudinal analysis of child outcomes. *Journal of Special Education, 25*(3), 340–351.

Collicott, J. (1991). Implementing multi-level instruction: Strategies for classroom teachers. In G. Porter & D. Richler (Eds.), *Changing Canadian schools: Perspectives on disability and inclusion* (pp. 191–218). Ottawa, Ontario, Canada: Allan Roeher Institute.

Commission on Standards for School Mathematics of the National Council of Teachers of Mathematics (1989). *Curriculum and evaluation standards for school mathematics.* Reston, VA: National Council of Teachers of Mathematics.

Conoley, J. C., & Conoley, C. W. (1992). *School consultation: Practice and training,* (2nd ed.). Boston: Allyn & Bacon.

Cook, L., & Friend, M. (1995). Co-teaching: Guidelines for creating effective practices. *Focus on Exceptional Children, 28*(3), 1–16.

Coombs, C. (1987, April). The structure of conflict. *American Psychologist, 42,* 355–363.

Coontz, S. (1995). The American family and the nostalgia trap. *Phi Delta Kappan, 76*(7), k1–k20.

Corrigan, D., & Bishop, K. K. (1997). Creating family-centered integrated service systems and interprofessional educational programs to implement them. *Social Work in Education, 19*(3), 149–163.

Council for Exceptional Children. (1994a). *CEC Policies for delivery of services to exceptional children.* Reston, VA: Author.

Council for Exceptional Children. (1994b). *Creating schools for all our students: What 12 schools have to say.* Reston, VA: Author.

Council for Exceptional Children. (1996). Crises in the classroom. *CEC Today, 3*(6), 1.

Council for Exceptional Children. (1998). *IDEA 1997: Let's make it work.* Reston, VA: Author.

Council of Administrators of Special Education. (1993). *CASE future agenda for special education: Creating a unified education system.* Albuquerque, NM: Author.

Cox, P. L. (1983, November). Complementary roles in successful change. *Educational Leadership,* 10–13.

Cramer, S. F. (1998). *Collaboration: A success strategy for special educators.* Boston: Allyn and Bacon.

Creasey, M. S., & Walther-Thomas, C. S. (1996). Using planning teams to implement inclusive education effectively. *Preventing School Failure, 41,* 39–43.

Crowther, S. (1998). Secrets of staff development support. *Educational Leadership, 55*(5), 75–76.

Cuban, L. (1990). Reforming again, again, and again. *Educational Researcher, 19*(1), 3–13.

Cummings, C., & Haggerty, K. P. (1997). Raising healthy children. *Educational Leadership, 54*(8), 28–30.

Darling-Hammond, L. (1997). *Doing what matters most: Investing in quality teaching.* New York: The National Commission on Teaching and America's Future.

Deal, T. & Peterson, K. (1998). *Shaping school culture: The school leader's role.* San Francisco: Jossey-Bass.

De Bevoise, W. (1986). Collaboration: Some principles of bridgework. *Educational Leadership, 43*(5), 9–12.

DeFleur, M., Kearney, P., & Plax, T. (1993). *Mastering communication in contemporary America.* Mountainview, CA: Mayfield.

Delquadri, J., Greenwood, C. R., Stretton, K., & Hall, R. V. (1983). The peer tutoring game: A classroom procedure for increasing opportunity to respond and spelling performance. *Education and Treatment of Children, 6,* 225–239.

Dennis, R. E., & Giangreco, M. F. (1996). Creating conversation: Reflections on cultural sensitivity in family interviewing. *Exceptional Children, 63*(1), 103–116.

Deno, E. (1973). *Instructional alternatives for exceptional children.* Reston, VA: Council for Exceptional Children.

Deno, S. L., & Fuchs, L. S. (1987). Developing curriculum-based measurements systems for data-based special education problem solving. *Focus on Exceptional Children, 19*(8), 1–16.

Deshler, D. D. (1998). Grounding intervention for students with learning disabilities in "powerful ideas." *Learning Disabilities Research and Practice, 13*(1), 29–34.

Deshler, D. D., Ellis, E. S., & Lenz, B. K. (1996). *Teaching adolescents with learning disabilities: Strategies and methods* (2nd ed.). Denver: Love.

Dettmer, P. A., Dyck, N. J., & Thurston, L. P. (1996). *Consultation, collaboration, and teamwork for students with special needs* (2nd ed.). Needham Heights, MA: Simon & Schuster.

DeVito, J. A. (1994). *The interpersonal communication book* (7th ed.). New York: HarperCollins.

Dickinson, T. S., & Erb, T. O. (Eds.). (1996). *We gain more than we give: Teaming in middle schools.* Columbus, OH: National Middle School Association.

DiGeronimo, J. M. (1993). A buddy system for rookie teachers. *Phi Delta Kappan, 75*(4), 348.

Dollase, R. H. (1992). *Voices of beginning teachers: Visions and realities.* New York: Teachers College.

Dowd, J. (1997). Refusing to play the blame game. *Educational Leadership, 54*(8), 67–69.

Downing, J. E. (1996). *Including students with severe and multiple disabilities in typical classrooms: Practical strategies for teachers.* Baltimore: Brookes.

Drucker, P. (1985). *Innovation and entrepreneurship: Practice and principles.* New York: Harper and Row.

Dryfoos, J. (1994). *Full service schools: A revolution in health and social services for children, youth, and families.* San Francisco: Jossey-Bass.

Dryfoos, J. (1998). *A look at community schools in 1998.* New York: National Center for Schools and Communities, Fordham University.

Dunn, L. M. (1968). Special education for the mildly retarded—Is much of it justifiable? *Exceptional Children, 53,* 5–22.

Dunst, C. J., Trivette, C. M., & Deal, A. (1988). *Enabling and empowering families.* Cambridge, MA: Brookline Books.

Dunst, C. J., Trivette, C. M., Starnes, A. L., Hamby, D. W., & Gordon, N. J. (1993). *Building and evaluating family support initiatives: A national study of programs for persons with developmental disabilities.* Baltimore: Brookes.

Durand, V. M. (1993). Functional assessment and functional analysis. In M. D. Smith (Ed.), *Behavior modification for exceptional children and youth.* Boston: Andover Medical Publishers.

Edgar, E. (1988). Employment as an outcome for mildly handicapped students: Current status and future directions. *Focus on Exceptional Children, 21*(1), 1–8.

Edgar, E., Levine, P., & Maddox, M. (1986). *Statewide follow-up studies of secondary special education students in transition.* Working paper of the networking and evaluation team. Seattle: University of Washington.

Edgar, E., & Polloway, E. A. (1994). Education for adolescents with disabilities: Curriculum and placement issues. *The Journal of Special Education, 27,* 438–452.

Ehly, S. W., & Macmann, G. M. (1994). Reinventing consultation. *Journal of Educational and Psychological Consultation, 5*(2), 169–172.

Eisner, E. (1991). What really counts in schools. *Educational Leadership, 48*(5), 10–17.

Eitington, J. (1989). *The winning trainer.* Houston, TX: Gulf.

Elam, S., Rose, L., & Gallup, A. (1996, September). The 28th annual Phi Delta Kappa/Gallup poll. *Phi Delta Kappan, 78*(1), 41–59.

Elias, M. J., Bruene-Butler, L., Blum, L., & Schuyler, T. (1997). How to launch a social and emotional learning program. *Educational Leadership, 54*(8), 15–19.

Elksnin, L. K., & Elksnin, N. (1995). *Assessment and instruction of social skills* (2nd ed.). San Diego: Singular Publishing Group.

Elliott, D., & McKenney, M. (1998). Four inclusion models that work. *Teaching Exceptional Children, 30*(4), 54–59

Elliott, S. N., & Gresham, F. M. (1991). *Social skills intervention guide: Practical strategies for social skills training.* Circle Pines, MN: American Guidance Service.

Ellis, E. S. (1997). Watering up the curriculum for adolescents with learning disabilities: Goals for the knowledge dimension. *Remedial and Special Education, 18*(6), 326–346.

Ellis, E. S. (1998). Watering up the curriculum for adolescents with learning disabilities: Goals for the affective dimension. *Remedial and Special Education, 19*(2), 91–105.

Elmore, R. (1992). The role of local school districts in instructional improvement. Paper presented at the annual meeting of the American Educational Research Association, San Francisco.

Engeström, Y. (1994). Teachers as collaborative thinkers: Activity-theoretical study of innovative teacher team. In I. Carlgren, G. Handal, & S. Vaage, (Eds.), *Teachers' minds and actions: Research on teachers' thinking and practice* (pp. 43–61). London: Falmer Press.

Englert, C. S., Tarrant, K. L., & Mariage, T. V. (1992). Defining and redefining instructional practice in special education: Perspectives on good teaching. *Teacher Education and Special Education, 15*(2), 62–86.

English, K., Goldstein, H., Kaczmarek, L., & Shafer, K. (1996). "Buddy skills" for preschoolers. *Teaching Exceptional Children, 28*(3), 62–66.

Enos, R. (1990). *Oral and written communication: Historical approaches.* Newbury Park, CA: Sage.

Epstein, J. (1995). School/family/community partnerships: Caring for the children we share. *Phi Delta Kappan, 76*(9), 701–712.

Evans, S. B. (1991). A realistic look at the research base for collaboration in special education. *Preventing School Failure, 35*(4), 10–13.

Falvey, M. A. (1995). *Inclusive and heterogeneous schooling: Assessment, curriculum and instruction.* Baltimore: Brookes.

Falvey, M. A., Forest, M., Pearpoint, J., & Rosenberg, R. L. (1994). Building connections. In J. S. Thousand, R. A. Villa, & A. I. Nevin (Eds.), *Creativity and collaborative learning: A practical guide to empowering students and teachers* (pp. 347–368). Baltimore: Brookes.

Feichtner, S. (1993). VERS: Improving local programs across the nation. *Journal for Vocational Special Needs Education, 15*(2), 20–25.

Felner, R., Jackson, A., Kasak, D. T., Mulhall, P., Brand, S., & Flowers, N. (1997). The impact of school reform for the middle years: A longitudinal study of a network engaged in Turning Points-based comprehensive school transformation. *Phi Delta Kappan, 78*(7), 528–532.

Ferguson, M. (1982). *The aquarian conspiracy.* London: Granada.

Fine, M. J. (1985). A systems-ecological perspective on home-school intervention. *Professional Psychology: Research & Practice, 16,* 262–270.

Firestone, W. A., Rossman, G. B., & Wilson, B. L. (1983). *Only a phone call away: Local educator's views of regional educational service agencies.* Philadelphia: Research for Better Schools.

Fishbaugh, M. S. E. (1997). *Models of collaboration.* Boston: Allyn and Bacon.

Forest, M., & Lusthaus, E. (1989). Promoting educational equality for all students: Circles and MAPs. In S. Stainback, W. Stainback, & M. Forest (Eds.), *Educating all students in the mainstream of regular education* (pp. 43–58). Baltimore: Brookes.

Forest, M., & Lusthaus, E. (1990). Everyone belongs with the MAPs action planning system. *Teaching Exceptional Children, 22*(2), 32–35.

Forest, M., & Pearpoint, J. (1992). MAPS: Action planning. In J. Pearpoint, M. Forest, & J. Snow, *The inclusion papers: Strategies to make inclusion work* (pp. 52–56). Toronto, Ontario, Canada: Inclusion Press.

Forest, M., & Snow, J. (1987). *More educational integration.* Downsview, Ontario, Canada: Allan Roeher Institute.

Forness, S. R., & Kavale, K. A. (1996). Treating social skill deficits in children with learning disabilities: A meta-analysis of the research. *Learning Disability Quarterly, 19,* 2–13.

Foster, S. L., & Ritchey, W. L. (1979). Issues in the assessment of social competence in children. *Journal of Applied Behavior Analysis, 12,* 625–638.

Fraser, B. J., Anderson, G. J., & Walberg, H. J. (1991). *Assessment of learning environments: Manual for Learning Environment Inventory (LEI) and My Class Inventory (MCI).* Perth, Western Australia: Curtin University of Technology, Science and Mathematics Education Center.

French, N. K. (1996). *Teacher as executive: Preparing special educators to supervise paraeducators.* Paper presented at the 18th International Conference on Learning Disabilities, Nashville, TN.

French, N. K., & Gerlach, K. (1998, February). *What does it mean to be a professional educator? Role differentiation for paraprofessionals and professionals.* Paper presented at the annual meeting of the American Association of Colleges for Teacher Education, New Orleans, LA.

Freshour, F. (1989). Listening power: Key to effective leadership. *Illinois School Research and Development, 26,* 17–23.

Friend, M. (1984). Consulting skills for resource teachers. *Learning Disability Quarterly, 7,* 246–250.

Friend, M., & Bursuck, W. (1996). *Including students with special needs: A practical guide for classroom teachers.* Boston: Allyn and Bacon.

Friend, M., & Cook, L. (1996). *Interactions: Collaboration skills for school professionals* (2nd ed.). New York: Longman.

Friend, M., Reisling, M., & Cook, L. (1993). Co-teaching: An overview of the past, a glimpse at the present and considerations for the future. *Preventing School Failure, 37*(4), 6–10.

Fuchs, D., & Fuchs, L. S. (1989). Exploring effective and efficient prereferral interventions: A component analysis of behavioral consultation. *School Psychology Review, 18*(2), 260–283.

Fuchs, D., & Fuchs, L. S. (1995). Inclusive schools movement. In J. M. Kauffman & D. P. Hallahan (Eds.), *The illusion of full inclusion: A comprehensive critique of a current special education bandwagon* (pp. 213–243). Austin, TX: Pro-Ed.

Fuchs, D., Fuchs, L. S., Dulan, J., & Roberts, H. (1992). Where is the research on consultation effectiveness? *Journal of Educational and Psychological Consultation, 3*(2), 151–174.

Fuchs, D., Fuchs, L. S., & Fernstrom, P. (1993). A conservative approach to special education reform: Mainstreaming through transenvironmental programming and curriculum-based measurement. *American Educational Research Journal, 30,* 149–177.

Fuchs, L., & Fuchs, D. (1998). General educators' instructional adaptation for students with learning disabilities. *Learning Disability Quarterly, 21,* 23–33.

Fuchs, L. S. (1992). Classwide decisionmaking with computerized curriculum-based measurement. *Preventing School Failure, 36*(2), 30–33.

Fuchs, L. S., & Deno, S. L. (1991). Paradigmatic distinctions between instructionally relevant measurement models. *Exceptional Children, 57,* 488–500.

Fullan, M. (1993). *Change forces: Probing the depths of educational reform.* Bristol, PA: The Falmer Press.

Fullan, M. (1996, February). Turning systemic thinking on its head. *Phi Delta Kappan, 77*(6), 420–423.

Fullan, M., & Hargreaves, A. (1992). *Teacher development and educational change.* London: Falmer Press.

Fullan, M., & Hargreaves, A. (1996). *What's worth fighting for in your school?* New York: Teachers College Press.

Fullan, M., & Stiegelbauer, S. (1991). *The new meaning of educational change* (2nd ed.). New York: Teachers College Press.

Gable, R., Arllen, N., & Cook, L. (1993). But let's not overlook the ethics of collaboration. *Preventing school failure, 37*(4), 32–36.

Gable, R. A., Friend, M., Laycock, V. K., & Hendrickson, J. M. (1990). Interview skills for problem identification in school consultation. *Preventing School Failure, 35*(1), 5–10.

Gable, R. A., Korinek, L., & McLaughlin, V. I. (1997). Collaboration on the schools: Ensuring success. In J. S. Choate (Ed), *Successful inclusive teaching: Proven ways to detect and correct special needs* (2nd ed., pp. 450–471). Boston: Allyn and Bacon.

Gallagher, J. J. (1995). The pull of societal forces on special education. In J. M. Kauffman, & D. P. Hallahan (Eds.). *The illusion of full inclusion: A comprehensive critique of a current special education bandwagon* (pp. 91–103). Austin, TX: Pro-Ed.

Ganser, T. (1996). What do mentors say about mentoring? *Journal of Staff Development, 17*(3), 36–39.

Ganser, T., Freiberg, M., & Zbikowski, J. (1994). The perceptions of school principals about a mentoring program for newly hired urban school teachers. *The Teacher Educator, 30*(2), 13–23.

Garcia, S. B., & Malkin, D. H. (1993). Toward defining programs and services for culturally diverse and linguistically diverse learners in special education. *Teaching Exceptional Children, 26*(1), 52–58.

Garmston, R. J. (1998, Summer). Graceful conflict. *Journal of Staff Development, 19*(3), 56–58.

Garratt, B. (1987). *The learning organization.* London: Fontana/Collins.

Gartner, A., & Lipsky, D. K. (1987). Beyond special education: Toward a quality system for all students. *Harvard Educational Review, 57,* 367–395.

Garvar, A., & Papanla, A. (1982). Team teaching: It works for the student. *Academic Therapy, 18*(2), 191–196.

George, M. & George, N. (1993). Planning vision and descriptions. In B. Billingsley (Ed.), *Program leadership for serving students with disabilities* (pp. 21–54). Richmond, VA: Virginia Department of Education.

Gersten, R. (1998). Recent advances in instructional research for students with learning disabilities: An overview. *Learning Disabilities Research and Practice, 13*(3), 162–170.

Giangreco, M. F. (1996a). *Vermont Interdependent Services Team Approach: A guide to coordinating education support services.* Baltimore: Brookes.

Giangreco, M. F. (1996b). What do I do now? A teacher's guide to including students with disabilities. *Educational Leadership, 53*(5), 56–59.

Giangreco, M. F., Cloninger, C. J., Dennis, R. E., & Edelman, S. W. (1994). Problem-solving methods to facilitate inclusive education. In J. S. Thousand, R. E. Villa, & A. I. Nevin (Eds.), *Creativity and collaborative learning: A practical guide to empowering students and teachers* (pp. 321–346). Baltimore: Brookes.

Giangreco, M. F., Cloninger, C. J., & Iverson, V. S. (1997). *Choosing options and accommodations for children (COACH): A guide to planning inclusive education* (2nd ed.). Baltimore: Brookes.

Giangreco, M. F., Dennis, R. E., Cloninger, C. J., Edelman, S. W., & Schattman, R. (1993). "I've counted Jon": Transformational experiences of teachers educating students with disabilities. *Exceptional Children, 59*(4), 359–372.

Giangreco, M. F., & Putnam, J. W. (1991). Supporting the education of students with severe disabilities in regular education environments. In L. H. Meyer, C. A. Peck, & L. Brown (Eds.), *Critical issues in the lives of people with severe disabilities* (pp. 245–270). Baltimore: Brookes.

Girard, K., & Koch, S. (1996). *Conflict resolution in the schools: A manual for educators.* San Francisco: Jossey-Bass.

Goldstein, A. P., Sprafkin, R. P., Gershaw, N. J., & Klein, P. (1980). *Skillstreaming the adolescent: A structured learning approach to teaching prosocial skills.* Champaign, IL: Research Press.

Goleman, D. (1995). *Emotional intelligence.* New York: Bantam Books.

Goodwin, T., & Wurzburg, G. (1988). *Regular lives.* Washington, DC: WETA-TV, Department of Educational Activities.

Goor, M. (1995). *Leadership for special education administration: A case-based approach.* Fort Worth, TX: Harcourt Brace.

Goor, M. B., Schwenn, J. O., & Boyer, L. (1997). Preparing principals for leadership in special education. *Intervention in School and Clinic, 32,* 133–141.

Goor, M. B., & Schwenn, J. O. (1993). Accommodating diversity and disability with co-operative learning. *Intervention in School and Clinic, 29*(1), 6–16.

Graden, J. L., Casey, A., & Bonstrom, O. (1985). Implementing a prereferral intervention system. Part II: The data. *Exceptional Children, 51,* 487–496.

Green, J. W. (1982). *Cultural awareness in the human services.* Englewood Cliffs, NJ: Prentice-Hall.

Greenwood, C. R., Carta, J. J., Hart, B., Kamps, D., Terry, B., Arreaga-Mayer, C., Atwater, J., Walker, D., Risley, T., & Delquadri, J. (1992). Out of the laboratory and into the community: 26 years of applied behavioral analysis at the Juniper Gardens Children's Project. *American Psychologist, 47,* 1464–1474.

Greenwood, C. R., & Delquadri, J. (1995). Classwide peer tutoring and the prevention of school failure. *Preventing School Failure, 39*(4), 21–25.

Greenwood, C. R., & Rieth, H. J. (1996). Current dimensions of technology-based assessment in special education. In E. L. Meyen, G. A. Vergason, & R. J. Whelan (Eds.), *Strategies for teaching exceptional children in inclusive settings* (pp. 279–291). Denver, CO: Love.

Greenwood, C. R., Terry, B., Delquadri, J., Elliott, M., & Arreaga-Mayer, C. (1995). *ClassWide Peer Tutoring (CWPT): Effective teaching and research review.* Kansas City, KS: Juniper Gardens Children's Project.

Gresham, F. M. (1986). Conceptual and definitional issues in the assessment of children's social skills: Implications for classification and training. *Journal of Clinical Child Psychology, 15*(1), 3–15.

Gresham, F. M. (1990). Best practices in social skills training. In A. Thomas and J. Grimes (Eds.), *Best practices in school psychology—II* (pp. 695–709). Washington, DC: The National Association of School Psychologists.

Gutkin, T. B. (1996). Core elements of consultation service delivery for special service personnel. *Remedial and Special Education, 17*(6), 333–340.

Haley, P. H., VanDerwerker, W., & Power-deFur, L. A. (1997). Supporting inclusive education through interagency collaboration. In L. A. Power-deFur & F. P. Orelove (Eds.), *Inclusive education: Practical implementation of the least restrictive environment* (pp. 117–130). Gaithersburg, MD: Aspen.

Halford, J. M. (1998). Easing the way for new teachers. *Educational Leadership, 55*(5), 33–36.

Hallahan, D., & Kauffman, J. (1997). *Exceptional children: Introduction to special education* (7th ed.). Boston: Allyn and Bacon.

Hallahan, D. P. (1998). Sound bytes from special education reform rhetoric. *Remedial and Special Education, 19*(2), 67–69.

Halverson, A. T., & Sailor, W. (1990). Integration of students with severe and profound disabilities: A review of the research. In R. Gaylord-Ross (Ed.), *Issues and research in special education* (pp. 124–148). New York: Teachers College Press.

Hanson, M. J. (1992). Ethnic, cultural, and language diversity in intervention settings. In E. W. Lynch and M. J. Hanson (Eds.), *Developing cross-cultural competence: A guide for working with young children and their families* (pp. 3–18). Baltimore: Brookes.

Hanson, M. J., & Carta, J. J. (1995). Addressing the challenges of families with multiple risks. *Exceptional Children, 62*(3), 201–212.

Hargreaves, A. (1994). Changing teachers, changing times: Teacher's work and culture in the post modern age. New York: Teachers College Press.

Haring, N. G., & Schiefelbusch, R. L. (1976). *Teaching special children.* New York: McGraw-Hill.

Haring, T. G. (1991). Social relationships. In L. H. Meyer, C. A. Peck, & L. Brown (Eds.), *Critical issues in the lives of people with severe disabilities* (pp. 195–217). Baltimore: Brookes.

Harmin, M. (1994). *Inspiring active learning.* Alexandria, VA: Association for Supervision and Curriculum Development.

Harper, G. F., Maheady, L., & Mallette, B. (1994). The power of peer-mediated instruction: Why and how does it promote success for all students? In J. S. Thousand, R. A. Villa, & A. I. Nevin (Eds.), *Creativity and collaborative learning: A practical guide to empowering students* (pp. 229–241). Baltimore: Brookes.

Harry, B. (1992). Restructuring the participation of African-American parents in special education. *Exceptional Children, 59*(2), 123–131.

Haslam, M. B. (1992). *Assisting educators to improve education: A review of the research.* (Report Contract No. LC 89089001). Washington, DC: U.S. Department of Education.

Hatton, N., & Smith, D. (1995). *Reflection in teacher education: Towards definitions and implementation* [On-line]. Available: http://alex.edfac.usyd.edu.au/resources/hattonart.

Hawkins, J. D., Catalano, R. F., Morrison, D. M., O'Donnell, J, Abbott, R. D., & Day, L. E. (1992). The Seattle Social Development Project. In J. McCord & R. Tremblay (Eds.), *The prevention of antisocial behavior in children* (pp. 139–161). New York: Guilford Publications.

Hayek, R. A. (1987). The teacher assistance team: A prereferral support system. *Focus on Exceptional Children, 20*(1), 1–7.

Henderson, A. T., & Berla, N. (Eds.). (1994). *A new generation of evidence: The family is critical to student achievement.* Washington, DC: National Committee for Citizens in Education.

Herman, J. J., & Herman. J. L. (1994). *Making change happen: Practical planning for school leaders.* Thousand Oaks, CA: Corwin Press.

Hernandez, D. J. (1994). Children's changing access to resources: A historical perspective. *Society for Research in Child Development Social Policy Report, 8*(1), 1–23.

Hersey, P., Blanchard, K., & Johnson, D. (1996). *Management of organizational behavior* (7th ed.). Upper Saddle River: Prentice-Hall.

Heumann, J., & Hehir, T. (November 23, 1994). *Memorandum to the Chief State School Officers with questions and answers on the least restrictive environment requirements of the Individuals with Disabilities Education Act (IDEA) in relationship to inclusion.* Washington, DC: US Office of Education, Office of Special Education and Rehabilitative Services.

Heward, W. L., Courson, F. H., & Narayan, J. S. (1990). Using choral responding to increase active student responding. *Teaching Exceptional Children, 21*(3), 72–75.

Hill, E. B. (1996). *Comprehensive services for students with serious emotional disturbance: An analysis of state legislation and policy.* Unpublished doctoral dissertation, The College of William and Mary, Virginia.

Hodgkinson, H. (1993). American education: The good, the bad, and the task. *Phi Delta Kappan, 74*(8), 619–623.

Hogan, K. (1996). *The psychology of persuasion: How to persuade others to your way of thinking*. Gretna, LA: Pelican.

Holden, G. (1997). Changing the way kids settle conflicts. *Educational Leadership, 54*(8), 74–76.

Honig, B. (1994). How can Horace best be helped? *Phi Delta Kappan, 75*(10), 790–796.

Hord, S. H., & Hall, G. E. (1987). Three images: What principals do in curriculum implementation. *Curriculum Inquiry, 17*, 55–89.

Hord, S., Rutherford, W., Huling-Austin, L., & Hall, G. (1987). *Taking charge of change*. Arlington, VA: Association for Supervision and Curriculum Development.

Horner, R. H., O'Neill, R. E., & Flannery, K. B. (1993). Effective behavior support plans. In M. Snell (Ed.), *Instruction of students with severe disabilities*. New York: MacMillan.

Howe, K., & Miramontes, O. (1992). *The ethics of special education*. New York: Teachers College Press.

Hoyle, J., English, F., & Steffy, B. (1990). *Skills for successful school leaders* (2nd ed.). Arlington, VA: American Association of School Administrators.

Hudson, P., Lignugaris-Kraft, B., & Miller, T. (1993). Using content enhancements to improve the performance of adolescents with learning disabilities in content classes. *Learning Disabilities Research and Practice, 8*(2), 106–126.

Hundert, J. (1995). *Enhancing social competence in young students: School-based approaches*. Austin, TX: Pro-Ed.

Hyerle, D. (1996). *Visual tools for constructing knowledge*. Alexandria, VA: Association for Supervision and Curriculum Development.

Hynes, M. G. (1995, Fall). Children with disabilities in detention: Legal strategies to secure release. *District of Columbia Law Review*, pp. 1–11.

Hyun, J. K., & Fowler, S. A. (1995). Respect, cultural sensitivity, and communication: Promoting participation by Asian families in the individualized family service plan. *Teaching Exceptional Children, 28*(1), 25–28.

Idol, L. (1990). The scientific art of classroom consultation. *Journal of Educational and Psychological Consultation, 1*(1), 3–22.

Idol, L., Paolucci-Whitcomb, P., & Nevin, A., (1986). *Collaborative consultation*. Austin, TX: Pro-Ed.

Idol, L., & West, J. F. (1987). Consultation in special education: Training and practice (Part II). *Journal of Learning Disabilities, 20*(8), 474–497.

Idol, L., & West, J. F. (1991). Educational collaboration: A catalyst for effective schooling. *Intervention in School and Clinic, 27*(2), 70–78, 125.

Idol-Maestas, L., & Ritter, S. (1985). A follow-up study of resource/consulting teachers: Factors that facilitate and inhibit teacher consultation. *Exceptional Children, 48*, 121–131.

Individuals with Disabilities Education Act [IDEA] Amendments of 1997, P.L. 105-17, 20 U.S.C. 1401 *et. seq.*

Janas, M. (1998). Shhhhh, the dragon is asleep and its name is resistance. *Journal of Staff Development, 19*(3), 13–16.

Janney, R., Korinek, L., McLaughlin, V. K., & Walther-Thomas, C. S. (1994). *Report of focus group research on HJR 102: Integrating students with disabilities into general classes*. Richmond, VA: Virginia Department of Education.

Janney, R., & Meyer, L. H. (1990). A consultation model to support integrated educational services for students with severe disabilities and challenging behaviors. *Journal of the Association for Persons with Severe Handicaps, 15*(3), 186–199.

Jenkins, J. R., & Jenkins, L. M. (1985). Peer tutoring in elementary and secondary programs. *Focus on Exceptional Children, 17(6),* 1–12.

Jenson, W. R., Rhode, G., & Reavis, H. K. (1995). *The tough kid tool box.* Longmont, CO: Sopris West.

Jerald, C. D., & Curran, B. K. (1998). By the numbers: The urban picture. *Education Week, 17*(17), 56–69.

Johnson, D. W., & Johnson, R. T. (1995). *Reducing school violence through conflict resolution.* Alexandria, VA: Association for Supervision and Curriculum Development.

Johnson, D. W., Johnson, R. T., & Holubec, E. J. (1994). *The new circles of learning: Cooperation in the classroom and school.* Alexandria, VA: Association for Supervision and Curriculum Development.

Johnson, L. J., & Pugach, M. C. (1991). Peer collaboration: Accommodating the needs of students with mild learning and behavior problems. *Exceptional Children, 57*(5), 454–461.

Johnson, R. (1986). *Reaching out: Interpersonal effectiveness and self-actualization.* Englewood Cliffs: Prentice-Hall.

Johnson, R. (1993). *Negotiation basics.* Newbury Park, CA: Sage.

Jordan, L., Reyes-Blanes, M. E., Peel, B. B., Peel, H. A., & Lane, H. B. (1998). Developing teacher-parent partnerships across cultures: Effective parent conferences. *Intervention in School and Clinic, 33*(3), 141–147.

Joyce, B., & Showers, B. (1983). *Power in staff development through research on training.* Alexandria, VA: Association for Supervision and Curriculum Development.

Joyce, B. & Showers, B. (1995). *Student achievement through staff development: Fundamentals of school renewal* (2nd ed.). White Plains, NY: Longmont.

Joyce, B., Wolf, J., & Calhoun, E. (1993). *The self-renewing school.* Alexandria, VA: Association for Supervision and Curriculum Development.

Kagan, S. (1990). The structural approach to cooperative learning. *Educational Leadership, 46*(4), 12–15.

Kagan, S. (1992). *Cooperative learning.* San Juan Capistrano, CA: Resources for Teachers.

Karasoff, P. (1998). Collaborative partnerships: A review of the literature. In J. K. Jones (Ed.), *Profiles in collaboration: A comprehensive report of the professional development partnership projects* (pp. 7–22). Washington, DC: Technical Assistance Center for Professional Development Partnerships, Academy for Educational Development.

Karge, B. D., McClure, M., & Patton, P. L. (1995). The success of the collaboration resource programs for students with disabilities in grade 6 through 8. *Remedial and Special Education, 16*(2), 79–89.

Karp, N. (1993). Collaborating with families. In B. S. Billingsley (Ed.), *Program leadership for serving students with disabilities* (pp. 67–90). Richmond, VA: Virginia Department of Education.

Kauffman, J. M. (1989). The regular education initiative as Reagan-Bush education policy: A trickle-down theory of education of the hard to teach. *Journal of Special Education, 23,* 256–278.

Kauffman, J. M. (1993). *Characteristics of emotional and behavioral disorders of children and youth* (5th ed.). New York: Merrill.

Kauffman, J. M. (1994). Places of change: Special education's power and identity in an era of educational reform. *Journal of Learning Disabilities, 27*(10), 610–618.

Kauffman, J. M., & Hallahan, D. P. (1981). *Handbook of special education.* Englewood Cliffs, NJ: Prentice-Hall.

Kauffman, J. M., & Hallahan, D. P. (Eds.). (1995). *The illusion of full inclusion: A comprehensive critique of a current special education bandwagon.* Austin, TX: Pro-Ed.

Kaufman, R., & Herman, J. (1991). *Strategic planning in education: Rethinking, restructuring, and revitalizing.* Lancaster, PA: Technomic.

Kayser, T. (1994). *Building team power: How to unleash the collaborative genius of work teams.* Burr Ridge, IL: Irwin.

Keilitz, I., & Dunivant, N. (1986). The relationship between learning disability and juvenile delinquency: Current state of knowledge. *Remedial and Special Education, 7*(3), 18–26.

Kemple, K. M. (1991). Preschool children's peer acceptance and social interaction. *Young Children, 46*(5), 47–54.

Kerr, M. M., & Nelson, C. M. (1998). *Strategies for managing behavior problems in the classroom.* Columbus, OH: Merrill.

King-Sears, M. E. (1997). Best academic practices for inclusive classrooms. *Focus on Exceptional Children, 29*(7), 1–22.

Klinger, J. K., Vaughn, S., Hughes, M. T., Schumm, J. S., & Elbaum, B. (1998). Outcomes for students with and without learning disabilities in inclusive classrooms. *Learning Disabilities Research and Practice, 13*(3), 153–161.

Kmetz, J., & Willower, D. (1982). Elementary school principals' work behavior. *Education Administration Quarterly, 18,* 62–78.

Knoster, T. (1998). Questions and answers…Behavioral issues under IDEA '97. *The Positive Behavior Support Newsletter, 2*(1), 4.

Knudson, D. & Wood, F. (1998, Summer). Support from above. *Journal of Staff Development, 19*(3), 27–32.

Kochhar, C. A., & West, L. L. (1996). *Handbook for successful inclusion.* Gaithersburg, MD: Aspen.

Korinek, L. (1991). Self-management for the mentally retarded. In R. Gable (Ed.), *Advances in mental retardation and developmental disabilities* (Vol. 4, pp. 143–177). London: Jessica Kingsley Publishers.

Korinek, L. (1996, October). *Large group management strategies for inclusive classes.* Paper presented at the International Council for Learning Disabilities Conference, Nashville, TN.

Korinek, L., & McLaughlin, V. K. (1996). Preservice preparation for interdisciplinary collaboration: The intervention assistance teaming project. *Contemporary Education, 68*(1), 41–44.

Korinek, L., McLaughlin, V. L., & Gable, R. A. (1994). A planning guide for collaborative service delivery. *Preventing School Failure, 38*(4), 37–40.

Korinek, L., McLaughlin, V. L., & Walther-Thomas, C. S. (1995). Least restrictive environment and collaboration: A bridge over troubled water. *Preventing School Failure, 39*(3), 6–12.

Korinek, L., & Popp, P. A. (1997). Collaborative mainstream integration of social skills with academic instruction. *Preventing School Failure, 41,* 148–152.

Kovaleski, J. F., Tucker, J. A., & Stevens, L. J. (1996). Bridging special and regular education: The Pennsylvania initiative. *Educational Leadership, 53,* 44–46.

Kratochwill, T. R., Elliot, S. N., & Busse, R. J. (1995). Behavior Consultation: A five-year evaluation of consultant and client outcomes. *School Psychology Quarterly, 10,* 87–117.

Kraus, W. (1984). *Collaboration in organizations: Alternatives to hierarchy.* New York: Human Sciences Press.

Krug, S. E. (1992). Instructional leadership: A constructivist perspective. *Educational Administrative Quarterly, 28*(3), 430–433.

Kruger, L. J., Struzziero, J., Watts, R., & Vacca, D. (1995). The relationship between organizational support and satisfaction with teacher assistance teams. *Remedial and Special Education, 16,* 203–211.

Kuhn, T. (1970). *The structure of scientific revolutions.* Chicago: University of Chicago Press.

Kunc, N. (1992). The need to belong: Rediscovering Maslow's hierarchy of needs. In R. A. Villa, J. S. Thousand, W. Stainback, & S. Stainback (Eds.), *Restructuring for caring and effective education: An administrative guide for creating heterogeneous schools* (pp. 25–39). Baltimore: Brookes.

Langone, J. (1998). Managing inclusive instructional settings: Technology, cooperative planning, and team-based organization. *Focus on Exceptional Children, 30*(8), 1–15.

Larson, C. E., & LaFasto, F. M. J. (1989). *Teamwork: What must go right-What can go wrong.* Newbury Park, CA: Sage.

Laycock, V. K. (1982). Basic educational practices. In J. G. Greer, R. M. Anderson, & S. J. Odle, (Eds.), *Strategies for helping severely and multiply handicapped citizens* (pp. 43–76). Baltimore: University Park Press.

Laycock, V. K., Gable, R. A., & Korinek, L. A. (1991). Alternative structures for collaboration in the delivery of special services. *Preventing School Failure, 35*(4), 15–18.

Laycock, V. K., & Korinek, L. A. (1989). Toward least restrictive curriculum for behaviorally disordered adolescents. In S. L. Braaten, R. B. Rutherford, Jr., T. F. Reilly, & S. A. DiGamgi (Eds.), *Programming for adolescents with behavioral disorders* (Vol. 4, pp. 11–25). Reston, VA: The Council for Children with Behavior Disorders.

Lee, V., Bryk, A., & Smith, J. (1993). The organization of effective secondary schools. In L. Darling-Hammond (Ed.). *Review of research in education 1993* (pp. 171–267). Washington, DC: American Educational Research Association.

Lerner, J. (1997). *Learning disabilities: Theories, diagnosis, and teaching strategies* (7th ed.). New York: Houghton Mifflin.

Lerner, J. L. (1976). *Children with learning disabilities* (2nd ed.). Boston: Houghton Mifflin.

Levin, E. K., Zigmond, N., & Birch, J. (1985). A follow-up study of 52 learning disabled adolescents. *Journal of Learning Disabilities, 18,* 2–7.

Levin, H. M. (1997). Doing what comes naturally. In D. K. Lipsky, & A. Gartner, (Eds.), *Inclusion and school reform: Transforming America's classrooms.* Baltimore: Brookes.

Lewis, R. B., & Doorlag, D. H. (1995). *Teaching special students in the mainstream* (4th ed.). New York: Merrill.

Lilly, M. S. (1971). A training based model for special education. *Exceptional Children, 37,* 745–749.

Lilly, S. (1970). Special education: A tempest in a teapot. *Exceptional Children, 32,* 43–49.

Lipsky, D. K., & Gartner, A. (Eds.) (1997a). *Beyond separate education: Quality education for all.* (2nd ed.). Baltimore: Brookes.

Lipsky, D. K., & Gartner, A. (1997b). *Inclusion and school reform: Transforming America's classrooms.* Baltimore: Brookes.

Little, J. W., & McLaughlin, M. W. (Eds.). (1993). *Teachers' work: Individuals, colleagues, and contexts.* New York: Teachers College Press.

Littlejohn, S. (1991). *Theories of human communication.* Belmont, CA: Wadsworth.

Lloyd, J. W., Repp, A. C., & Singh, N. N. (Eds.). (1991). *The regular education initiative: Alternative perspectives on concepts, issues, and models.* Sycamore, IL: Sycamore.

Lovitt, T. C., Cushing, S. S., & Stump, C. S. (1994). High school students rate their IEPs: Low opinions and lack of ownership. *Intervention in School and Clinic, 30*(1), 34–37.

Lovitt, T. C., & Horton, S. V. (1987). How to develop study guides. *Journal of Reading, Writing and Learning Disabilities, 3,* 333–343.

Lowell, J., York, J., Doyle, M. E., & Kronberg, R. (1995). *Module 3. Curriculum as everything students learn in school: Individualizing learning opportunities.* Baltimore: Brookes.

Lyman, F., & Foyle, H. C. (1990). *Cooperative grouping for interactive learning: Students, teachers, and administrators.* Washington, DC: National Educational Association.

Lynch, E. W., & Hanson, M. J. (1992). *Developing cross-cultural competence: A guide for working with young children and their families* (3rd ed.). Baltimore: Brookes.

Lynch, E. W., & Stein, R. (1987). Parent participation by ethnicity: A comparison of Hispanic, Black and Anglo families. *Exceptional Children, 54,* 105–111.

Lyon, G. R., & Moats, L. C. (1993). An examination of research in learning disabilities: Past practices and future directions. In G. R. Lyon, D. B. Gray, J. F. Kavanagh, & N. A. Krasnegor (Eds.), *Better understanding learning disabilities: New views from research and their implications for education and public policies.* Baltimore: Brookes.

MacMillan, D. L. & Hendricks, I. G. (1993). Evolution and legacies. In J. L. Goodlad & T. C. Lovitt (Eds.), *Integrating general and special education* (pp. 23–48). New York: MacMillan.

Madden, N. A., & Slavin, R. E. (1983). Mainstreaming students with mild handicaps: Academic and social outcomes. *Review of Educational Research, 53*(4), 519–569.

Maeroff, G. (1993). *Team building for school change: Equipping teachers for new roles.* New York: Teachers College Press.

Male, M. (1997). *Technology for inclusion: Meeting the special needs of all students* (3rd ed.). Boston: Allyn and Bacon.

Malmgren, K., Edgar, E., & Neel, R. S. (1998). Postschool status of youths with behavioral disorders. *Behavioral Disorders, 23*(4), 257–263.

Mannino, F. V., & Shore, M. F. (1975). The effects of consultation: A review of the literature. *American Journal of Community Psychology, 3,* 1–21.

Martin, J., & Willower, D. (1981). The managerial behavior of high school principals. *Education Administration Quarterly, 17,* 69–90.

Mastropieri, M. A., & Scruggs, T. E. (1994). Text versus hands-on science curriculum: Implications for students with disabilities. *Remedial and Special Education, 15,* 72–85.

Maurer, R. (1991). *Managing conflict: Tactics for school administrators.* Boston: Allyn and Bacon.

McCormack, J. E. et al. (1976). *Systematic instruction for the severely handicapped: Teaching sequences.* Medford, MA: Massachusetts Center for Program Development and Evaluation.

McDonnell, J., Thorson, N., McQuivey, C., & Kiefer-O'Donnell (1997). Academic engaged time of students with low-incidence disabilities in general education classes. *Mental Retardation, 35*(1), 18–26.

McDonnell, L. M., McLaughlin, M. J., & Morison, P. (Eds.). (1997). *Educating one and all: Students with disabilities and standards-based reform.* Washington, DC: National Academy Press.

McGinnis, E., & Goldstein, A. (1990). *Skillstreaming in early childhood.* Champaign, IL: Research Press.

McGonigel, M., Kaufman, R., & Johnson, B. (Eds.). (1991). *Guidelines and recommended practices for the individualized family service plan* (2nd ed.). Bethesda, MD: Association for the Care of Children's Health.

McLaughlin, J. A. (1997, November). *A framework for strategic planning.* Paper presented at the annual meeting of the American Evaluation Association, San Diego, CA.

McLaughlin, J. A., & McLaughlin, V. L. (1993). *Program evaluation.* In B. S. Billingsley (Ed.), *Program leadership for serving students with disabilities* (pp. 343–370). Blacksburg, VA: Virginia Tech.

McLaughlin, M., & Warren, S. (1993). Do inclusionary practices cost more? Impressions of special education at eleven sites. Unpublished manuscript, University of Maryland.

McLaughlin, V. (1998). Listening: A self-check. Unpublished class material, The College of William and Mary, Williamsburg, VA.

McMurry, C. (Ed.) (1904). *The relation of theory to practice in the education of teachers: Third yearbook of the National Society for the Scientific Study of Education.* Chicago: University of Chicago Press.

Medway, F. J. (1979). How effective is school consultation? A review of recent research. *Journal of School Psychology, 17,* 275–282.

Melaville, A., & Blank, M. (1991). *What it takes: Structuring interagency partnerships to connect children and families with comprehensive services.* Washington, DC: Education and Human Services Consortium.

Mercer, C. D. (1979). *Children and adolescents with learning disabilities.* Columbus, OH: Charles E. Merrill.

Mercer, C. D. (1997). *Students with learning disabilities* (5th ed.). Columbus, OH: Merrill.

MetLife. (1998). *The Metropolitan Survey of the American Teacher 1998: Building family-school partnerships, views of teachers and students.* New York: Louis Harris and Associates.

Meyer, A. L., & Northup, W. B. (1997). What is violence prevention, anyway? *Educational Leadership, 54*(8), 31–33.

Miles, M. B. (1995). Mapping basic beliefs about learner centered schools. *Theory Into Practice, 34*(4), 279–287.

Montague, M., Bergeron, J., & Lago-Delello, E. (1997). Using prevention strategies for general education. *Focus on Exceptional Children, 29*(8), 1–12.

Moran, M. R. (1975). Nine steps to the diagnostic prescriptive process in the classroom. *Focus on the Exceptional Children, 6*(9), 1–14.

Morse, W. C. (1971). The crisis or helping teacher. In N. L. Long, W. C. Morse, & R. G. Newman (Eds.), *Conflict in the classroom: The education of children with problems,* (2nd ed., pp. 294–301). Belmont, CA: Wadsworth.

Murnigham, J. (1981, February). Group decision-making: What strategies should you use? *Management Review, 12,* 59–62.

Murphy, C. (1997). Finding time for faculties to study together. *Journal of Staff Development, 18*(3), 29–32.

Murphy, J. (Ed.). (1990). *The educational reform movement of the 1980s.* Berkeley, CA: McCutchan.

Murphy, J. (1993). Restructuring: In search of a movement. In J. Murphy and P. Hallinger (Eds.), *Restructuring schooling: Learning from ongoing efforts.* Newbury Park, CA: Corwin Press.

National Association of State Boards of Education. (1992, October). *Winners all: A call for inclusive schools.* Alexandria, VA: Author.

National Association of State Directors of Special Education, Inc. (NASDSE). (1996). *Enhancing individual student accountability through the IEP.* Alexandria, VA: Author.

National Center for Children in Poverty. (1996–97, Winter). One in four: America's youngest poor. *News and Issues, 6*(2), 1–2.

National Center for Family-Centered Care. (1990). *What is family-centered care?* Washington, DC: Association for the Care of Children's Health.

National Center on Educational Restructuring & Inclusion, (1995). *National study on inclusive education.* New York: City University of New York.

National Commission on Excellence in Education. (1983). *A nation at risk: The imperative for educational reform.* Washington, DC: Author.

National Commission on Teaching and America's Future (NCTAF). (1996). *What matters most: Teaching for America's future.* New York: Author.

National Council on Disability (NCD). (1995). *Improving the implementation of the Individuals with Disabilities Education Act: Making schools work for all of America's children.* Washington, DC: Author.

National Education Association (1992). *Status of the American public school teacher: 1990–91.* Washington, DC: National Education Association.

National Education Goals Panel. (1995). *Goals 2000: Educate America Act.* Washington, DC: U.S. Government Printing Office.

National Governors' Association. (1986). *A time for results.* Washington, DC: Author.

National PTA. (1998). *National standards for parent-family involvement programs.* Chicago: Author.

National Research Council, (1997). *Educating one and all: Students with disabilities and standards-based reform.* Washington, DC: National Academy Press.

Nelson, C. M., Rutherford, R. B., & Wolford, B. I. (Eds.) (1987). *Special education in the criminal justice system.* Columbus, OH: Merrill.

Nelson, F. H., & O'Brien, T. (1993). *How U.S. teachers measure up internationally: A comparative study of teacher pay, training, and conditions of service.* Washington, DC: American Federation of Teachers.

Newmann, F. (1991). What is a restructured school? A framework to clarify means and ends. *Issues in Restructuring Schools: Issue Report #1,* p. 3–13, 16. Madison, WI: Center on Organization and Restructuring of Schools.

Nias, J., Southworth, G., & Yeomans, R. (1989). *Staff relations in the primary school.* London: Cassells.

Oakes, J., & Quartz, K. H. (Eds.) (1994). *Creating new educational communities, schools, and classrooms where all children can be smart.* Chicago: University of Chicago Press.

Odom, S. L., & McConnell, S. R. (1993). *Play time/social time: Organizing your classroom to build interactional skills.* Tucson, AZ: Communication Skill Builders.

Odom, S. L., McConnell, S. R., & McEvoy, M. A. (1992). Peer-related social competence and its significance for young children with disabilities. In S. L. Odom, S. R. McConnell, & M. A. McEvoy (Eds.), *Social competence of young children with disabilities: Issues and strategies for intervention* (pp. 3–36). Baltimore: Brookes.

O'Hair, M. J., & Odell, S. J., (Eds.). 1995. *Educating teachers for leadership and change: Teacher education yearbook III.* Thousand Oaks, CA: Corwin.

O'Neil, J. (1997). Building schools as communities: A conversation with James Comer. *Educational Leadership, 54*(8), 6–10.

Orelove, F. P., & Malatchi, A. (1996). Curriculum and instruction. In F. P. Orelove & D. Sobsey (Eds.). *Educating children with multiple disabilities* (3rd ed.). pp. 377–411. Baltimore: Brookes.

Orelove, F. P., & Sobsey, D. (1996). *Educating children with multiple disabilities: A transdisciplinary approach* (3rd ed.). Baltimore: Brookes.

Ostroff, C. (1992). The relationship between satisfaction, attitudes, and performance: An organizational level analysis. *Journal of Applied Psychology, 77,* 963–974.

Ozer, M. N. (1980). *Solving learning and behavior problems of children: A planning system integrating assessment and treatment.* San Francisco: Jossey-Bass.

Paolucci-Whitcomb, P., & Nevin, A. (1985). Preparing consulting teachers through a collaborative approach between university faculty and field-based consulting teachers. *Teacher Education and Special Education, 8*(3), 132–143.

Patterson, J. (1993). *Leadership for tomorrow's schools.* Alexandria, VA: Association for Supervision and Curriculum Development.

Patton, J. (1998, November). *Attitudes, beliefs, and teacher efficacy do matter.* Presentation at the Council for Exceptional Children-Division of Diverse Exceptional Learners' Symposium on Culturally and Linguistically Diverse Exceptional Learners. Washington, DC.

Pearpoint, J., O'Brien, J., & Forest, M. (1993). *PATH: A workbook for planning positive possible futures.* Toronto: Inclusion Press.

Pelco, L. E., & Ries, R. R. (in press). Teachers' attitudes and behaviors towards family-school partnerships: What school psychologists need to know. *International Journal of School Psychology.*

Pellicer, L. O., & Anderson, L. W. (1995). *A handbook for teacher leaders.* Thousand Oaks, CA: Corwin.

Perloff, R. (1993). *The dynamics of persuasion.* Hillsdale, NJ: Lawrence Erlbaum Associates.

Perske, R. (1989). *Circles of friends.* Nashville: Abingdon Press.

Peter, J. L. (1965). *Prescriptive Teaching.* New York: McGraw-Hill.

Peters, M. T. (1990). Someone's missing: The student as an overlooked participant in the IEP process. *Preventing School Failure, 34*(4), 32–36.

Pfeiffer, S. I. (1980). The school-based interprofessional team: Recurring problems and some possible solutions. *Journal of School Psychology, 18*(4), 388–394.

Phillips, V., & McCullough, L. (1992). *Student/staff support teams: Administrative handbook.* Longmont, CO: Sopris West.

Pickett, A. L. (1996). *A state of the art report on paraeducators in education and related services.* New York: Center for Advanced Study in Education, City University of New York.

Pickett, A. L., & Gerlach, K. (1997). *Supervising paraeducators in school settings.* Reston, VA: Council for Exceptional Children.

Pitner, J., & Ogawa, R. (1981). Organizational leadership: The case of the superintendent. *Education Administration Quarterly, 17,* 45–65.

Polloway, E. A., Epstein, M. H., Bursuck, W. D., Roderique, T. W., McConeky, J. L., & Jayanthi, M. (1994). Classroom grading: A national survey of policies. *Remedial and Special Education, 15*(3), 162–170.

Pounder, D. G. (1998). Teacher teams: Redesigning teachers' work for collaboration. In D. G. Pounder (Ed.), *Restructuring schools for collaboration* (pp. 65–88). Albany, NY: State University of New York Press.

Prouty, R. & Prillaman, D. (1970). Diagnostic teaching: A modest proposal. *Elementary School Journal, 70,* 265–270.

Pryzwansky, W. B., & Noblit, G. W. (1990). Understanding and improving consultation practice: The qualitative case study approach. *Journal of Educational and Psychological Consultation, 1*(4), 293–307.

Pugach, M. C., & Johnson, L. J. (1988). Rethinking the relationship between consultative and collaborative problem-solving. *Focus on Exceptional Children, 21*(4), 1–8.

Pugach, M. C., & Johnson, L. J. (1990). Fostering the continued democratization of consultation through action research. *Teacher Education and Special Education, 13*(3–4), 240–245.

Pugach, M. C., & Johnson, L. J. (1995a). Unlocking expertise among classroom teachers through structured dialogue: Extending research on peer collaboration. *Exceptional Children, 62*(2), 101–110.

Pugach, M. C., & Johnson, L. J. (1995b). *Collaborative practitioners: Collaborative schools.* Denver: Love.

Pugach, M. C., & Wesson, C. (1995). Teachers' and students' views of team teaching of general education and learning-disabled students in two fifth-grade classes. *Elementary School Journal, 95*(3), 279–295.

Quinn, M. M., Gable, R. A., Rutherford, R. B., Nelson, C. M., & Howell, K. W. (1998). *Addressing student problem behavior: An IEP team's introduction to functional behavioral assessment and behavior intervention plans.* Washington, DC: Center for Effective Collaboration and Practice.

Quinn, M. M., Mathur, S. R., & Rutherford, R. B. (1995). *Social skills and social competence of children and youth: A comprehensive bibliography of articles, chapters, books, and programs.* Paper presented at the Behavioral Disorders Conference, Scottsdale, AZ.

Rainforth, B., & York, J. (1997). *Collaborative teams for students with severe disabilities: Integrating therapy and educational services* (2nd ed.). Baltimore: Brookes.

Rasmussen, K. (1998, January). Making parent involvement meaningful. *Education Update, 40*(1), 1, 6, 7.

Rea, P. J. (1997). *Performance of students with learning disabilities in inclusive classrooms and in pull-out programs.* Unpublished doctoral dissertation, College of William and Mary, Williamsburg, VA.

Reardon, K. (1991). *Persuasion in practice.* Newbury Park, CA: Sage.

Renyi, J. (1996). *Teachers take charge of their learning: Transforming professional development for student success.* Washington, DC: National Foundation for the Improvement of Education.

Repetto, J. B., & Correa, V. I. (1996). Expanding views on transition. *Exceptional Children, 62*(6), 551–563.

Reynolds, M. C. (1962). Framework for considering some issues in special education. *Exceptional Children, 28,* 367–370.

Reynolds, M. C., & Birch, J. W. (1977). *Teaching exceptional children in all of America's schools: The first course for teachers and principals.* Reston, VA: Council for Exceptional Children.

Reynolds, M. C., Wang, M. C., & Walberg, H. J. (1987). The necessary restructuring of special and regular education. *Exceptional Children, 53,* 391–398.

Richardson, J. (1997, October/November). Consensus: Tap into a powerful decision-making tool. *Tools for schools.* Oxford, OH: National Staff Development Council.

Richardson, V. (1990). The evolution of reflective teaching and teacher education. In R. T. Clift, W. R. Houston, & M. C. Pugach (Eds.), *Encouraging reflective practice in education* (pp. 3–19). New York: Teachers College Press.

Robbins, P. (1991). *How to plan and implement a peer coaching program.* Alexandria, VA: Association for Supervision and Curriculum Development.

Rooney, K. (1990). *Independent strategies for efficient study* (2nd ed.). Richmond, VA: J. R. Associates.

Rosenfield, S. (1992). Developing school-based consultation teams: A design for organizational change. *School Psychology Quarterly, 7,* 27–46.

Rosenkoetter, S. E., Hains, A. H., & Fowler, S. A. (1994). *Bridging early services for children with special needs and their families: A practical guide for transition planning.* Baltimore: Brookes.

Rosenshine, B., & Stevens, R. (1986). Teaching functions. In M. C. Wittrock (Ed.), *Handbook of research on teaching* (3rd ed., pp. 376–391). New York: Macmillan.

Ross, R. (1994). *Understanding persuasion.* Englewood Cliffs, NJ: Prentice-Hall.

Rutherford, R. B. (1997). Why doesn't social skills training work? *CEC Today, 4*(1), 14.

Rutherford, R. B., Quinn, M. M., & Mathur, S. R. (1996). *Effective strategies for teaching appropriate behaviors to children with emotional/behavioral disorders.* Reston, VA: Council for Children with Behavioral Disorders Mini-Library, Council for Exceptional Children.

Sabornie, E. J., & deBettencourt, L. U. (1997). *Teaching students with mild disabilities at the secondary level.* Columbus, OH: Merrill.

Safran, S. P. (1991). The communication process and school-based consultation: What does the research say? *Journal of Educational and Psychological Consultation, 2*(4), 343–370.

Safran, S. P., & Safran, J. S. (1996). Intervention assistance programs and prereferral teams. *Remedial and Special Education, 17*(6), 363–369.

Sage, D., & Burrello, L. (1994). *Leadership in educational reform: An administrator's guide to changes in special education.* Baltimore: Brookes.

Salend, S. J. (1994). Strategies for assessing attitudes toward individuals with disabilities. *School Counselor, 41*(5), 338–342.

Salend, S. J. (1995). Modifying tests for diverse learners. *Intervention, 31*(2), 84–90.

Sapon-Shevin, M. (1992). Celebrating diversity, creating community: Curriculum that honors and builds on differences. In S. Stainback & W. Stainback (Eds.), *Curriculum considerations in inclusive classrooms: Facilitating learning for all students.* Baltimore: Brookes.

Sapon-Shevin, M., Dobbelaere, A., Corrigan, C., Goodman, K., & Mastin, M. (1998). Everyone here can play. *Educational Leadership, 56*(1), 42–45.

Sarason, S. (1993). *The case for change: Rethinking the preparation of educators.* San Francisco: Jossey-Bass.

Schaffner, C. & Buswell, B. (1996). Ten critical elements of creating inclusive and effective school communities. In Stainback, S., & Stainback, W. (Eds.), *Inclusion: A guide for educators.* Baltimore: Brookes.

Schein, E. H. (1969). *Process consultation: Its role in organizational development.* Reading, MA: Addison-Wesley.

Schmuck, R. A. (1995). Process consultation and organization development. *Journal of Educational and Psychological Consultation, 6*(3), 199–205.

Schön, D. (1983). *The reflective practitioner: How professionals think in action.* New York: Basic Books.

Schön, D. (1987). *Educating the reflective practitioner.* San Francisco: Jossey-Bass.

Searcy, S. (1996). Friendship interventions for the integration of children and youth with learning and behavior problems. *Preventing School Failure, 40,* 131–134.

Senge, P. (1990). *The fifth discipline: The art and practice of the learning organization.* New York: Doubleday.

Senge, P., Kleiner, A., Roberts, C., Ross, R., & Smith, B. (1994). *The fifth discipline fieldbook: Strategies and tools for building a learning organization.* New York: Doubleday.

Sharan, Y., & Sharan, S. (1990). Group investigation expands cooperative learning. *Educational Leadership, 46*(4), 17–21.

Sharpe, N. M., York, L. J., & Knight, J. (1994). Effects of inclusion on the academic performance of classmates without disabilities. *Remedial and Special Education, 15*(5), 281–287.

Shartrand, A. M., Weiss, H. B., Kreider, H. M., & Lopez, M. E. (1997). *New skills for new schools: Preparing teachers in family involvement.* Cambridge, MA: Harvard Family Research Project.

Sheridan, M. K., Foley, G. M., & Radlinkski, S. H. (1995). *Using the supportive play model: Individualized intervention in early childhood practice.* New York: Teachers College Press.

Sheridan, S. M., Welch, M., & Orme, S. F. (1996). Is consultation effective? A review of outcome research. *Remedial and Special Education, 17*(6), 341–354.

Sherman, A. (1997). *Poverty matters: The cost of child poverty in America.* Washington, DC: Children's Defense Fund.

Shinn, M. R., & Hubbard, D. D. (1996). Curriculum-based measurement and problem-solving assessment: Basic procedures and outcomes. In E. L. Meyen, G. A. Vergason, & R. J. Whelan (Eds.), *Strategies for teaching exceptional children in inclusive settings* (pp. 243–278). Denver: Love.

Shinn, M., & Weitzman, B. C. (1996). Homeless families are different. In J. Baumohl (Ed.), *Homelessness in America.* Phoenix, AZ: Oryx.

Simmons, D. C., & Kameenui, E. J. (1996). A focus on curriculum design: When children fail. *Focus on Exceptional Children, 28*(7), 1–16.

Sindelar, P. T., Griffin, C. C., Smith, S. W., & Watanabe, A. K. (1992). Prereferral intervention: Encouraging notes on preliminary findings. *The Elementary School Journal, 92,* 245–259.

Skirtic, T. (1991). *Behind special education: A critical analysis of professional knowledge and school organization.* Denver: Love Publishing.

Skirtic, T. M., & Sailor, W. (1996). School-linked services integration: Crisis and opportunity in the transition to postmodern society. *Remedial and Special Education, 17*(5), 271–283.

Slavin, R. E. (1984). Team assisted individualization: Cooperative learning and individual instruction in the mainstream classroom. *Remedial and Special Education, 15*(6), 33–42.

Slavin, R. E., Karweit, N. L., & Madden, N. A. (1989). *Effective programs for students at risk.* Boston: Allyn and Bacon.

Smith, B. H. (1995). *Helping children cope with violence.* Presentation at the Child Development Research Early Intervention Institute, Williamsburg, VA.

Smith, D. B. (1997). Celebrating life's experiences. *Educational Leadership, 54*(8), 50–52.

Smith, R. M. (1974). *Clinical teaching: Methods of instruction for the retarded.* New York: McGraw-Hill.

Smith, S. W. (1990). Individualized education programs (IEPs) in special education: From intent to acquiescence. *Exceptional Children, 57,* 6–14.

Smith, S. W. & Slattery, W. (1993). Individualized education programs for students with disabilities: How do we move beyond compliance? In B. Billingsley (Ed.) *Program leadership for serving students with disabilities* (pp. 111–148). Richmond, VA: Virginia Department of Education.

Smolowe, J. (1993). Intermarried...with children. *Time, 142*(21) 64–65.

Snell, M., & Janney, R. (1999). *Teacher's guide to inclusive practices: Modifying schoolwork.* Baltimore: Brookes.

Snell, M. E. (Ed.). (1978). *Systematic instruction of the moderately and severely handicapped.* Columbus, OH: Merrill.

Snell, M. J., & Drake, G. P., Jr. (1994). Replacing cascades with supported education. *Journal of Special Education, 27,* 393–409.

Southern Regional Education Board (SREB). (1998). *SREB Educational Benchmarks 1998.* Atlanta: Author.

Souza, A. R., & Downs, R. M. (1994). *Geography for life: Executive summary, National Geography Standards 1994.* Washington, DC: National Council for Geographic Education.

Special Education Report. (1997). Study finds inclusion aides hampering class efforts. *Special Education Report, 23*(18).

Speck, M. (1996). The change process in a school learning community. *School Community Journal, 6*(1), 69–79.

Stainback, S., & Stainback, W. (1984). A rationale for the merger of special and regular education. *Exceptional Children, 51,* 102–111.

Stainback, S. & Stainback, W. (1996). *Inclusion: A guide for educators.* Baltimore: Brookes.

Stainback, W. & Stainback, S. (Eds.). (1990). *Support networks for inclusive schooling: Interdependent integrated education.* Baltimore: Brookes.

Stainback, W., & Stainback, S. (Eds.). (1996). *Controversial issues confronting special education: Divergent perspectives* (2nd ed.). Boston: Allyn and Bacon.

Stainback, W. C., & Stainback, S. B. (1994). Introduction. In J. S. Thousand, R. A. Villa, & A. I. Nevin (Eds.), *Creativity and collaborative learning: A practical guide to empowering students and teachers* (pp. xxi–xxvi). Baltimore: Brookes.

Stainton, T. (1994, August). *Tools for participatory citizenship: The necessity of inclusive education.* Paper presented at the Excellence and Equity in Education Conference, Toronto.

Stedman, P., & Stroot, S. A. (1998). Teachers helping teachers. *Educational Leadership, 55*(5), 37–39.

Steel, M. (1995, Spring). New colors. *Teaching Tolerance, 44–49.*

Stephens, T. M. (1977). *Teaching skills to children with learning and behavior disorders.* Columbus, OH: Merrill.

Stevens, R. J., & Slavin, R. E. (1995). The cooperative elementary school: Effects on students' achievement, attitudes, and social interactions. *American Educational Research Journal, 32*(2), 321–351.

Stigler, H. W., & Stevenson, J. W. (1992). *The learning gap: Why our schools are failing and what we can learn from Japanese and Chinese Education.* New York: Summit Books.

Stokes, T. F., & Baer, D. M. (1977). An implicit technology of generalization. *Journal of Applied Behavior Analysis, 10,* 349–367.

Sugai, G., & Lewis, T. (1996). Preferred and promising practices for social skills instruction. *Focus on Exceptional Children, 29,* 1–16.

Sullivan, C. J., & Sugarman, J. M. (1996). State policies affecting school-linked integrated services. *Remedial and Special Education, 17*(5), 284–292.

Swap, S. M. (1991, April). *Can parent involvement lead to increased student achievement in urban schools?* Paper presented at the Annual Meeting of the American Educational Research Association, Chicago, IL.

Swicegood, P. (1994). Portfolio-based assessment practices. *Intervention in School and Clinic, 30*(1), 6–15.

Tal, Z., & Babad, E. (1990). The teacher's pet phenomenon: Rate of occurrence, correlates, and psychological costs. *Journal of Educational Psychology, 82,* 637–645.

Tanzman, G. I. (1997, November). *IEP's for the next millennium: Remembering the past, designing the future.* Paper presented at the annual meeting of the Teacher Education Division of the Council for Exceptional Children, Savannah, GA.

Tapasak, R. & Walther-Thomas, C. S. (in press). Evaluation of a first-year inclusion program: Student perceptions and classroom performance. *Remedial and Special Education.*

Tawney, J. W. (1979). *Programmed environments curriculum: A curriculum handbook for teaching basic skills to severely handicapped persons.* Columbus, OH: Merrill.

Taylor, R. L. (1993). *Assessment of exceptional students: Educational and psychological procedures* (3rd ed.). Boston: Allyn and Bacon.

Tewel, K. (1995). New schools for a new century. Delray Beach, FL: St. Lucie Press.

Thomas, C. C., Correa, V. I., & Morsink, C. V. (1995). *Interactive teaming: Consultation and collaboration in special programs* (2nd ed.). Englewood Cliffs, NJ: Prentice-Hall.

Thousand, J. S., Villa, R. E., & Nevin, A. I., (Eds.). (1994). *Creativity and collaborative learning: A practical guide to empowering students and teachers.* Baltimore: Brookes.

Tilton, L. (1996). *Inclusion: A fresh look.* Shorewood, MN: Covington Cove.

Tindall, E. (1996). *Principal's role in fostering teacher collaboration for students with special needs.* Unpublished doctoral dissertation. College of William and Mary, Williamsburg, VA.

Tomlinson, C. A. (1995). *How to differentiate instruction in mixed-ability classrooms.* Alexandria, VA: Association for Supervision and Curriculum Development.

Tripp, T. (1995). Action inquiry. PARnet PARchives document. Retrieved May 4, 1998 from the World Wide Web: http://www.PARnet.org/PARchive/docs/tripp_96.

Trump, J. L. (1966). Secondary education tomorrow: Four imperatives for improvement. *NASSP Bulletin, 50*(39), 87–95.

Turnbull, A. P., & Turnbull, H. R. (1997). *Families, professionals, and exceptionality: A special partnership.* Upper Saddle River, NJ: Prentice-Hall.

Turnbull, A. P., Turnbull, H. R., III, Shank, M., & Leal, D. (1995). *Exceptional lives: Special education in today's schools.* Englewood Cliffs, NJ: Merrill.

U.S. Department of Education. (1995, April). *School linked comprehensive services for children and families—What we know and what we need to know.* Washington, DC: Author.

U.S. Department of Education. (1996, August). *A back to school special report: The baby boom echo.* Washington, DC: Author.

U.S. Department of Education. (1998). To assure the free appropriate public education of all children with disabilities. *Twentieth Annual Report to Congress on the Implementation of the Individuals with Disabilities Education Act.* Washington, DC: U.S. Government Printing Office.

U.S. Office of Juvenile Justice & Delinquency Prevention (1994). *Juvenile correctional education: A time for change.* Washington, DC: U.S. Department of Justice.

Ury, W. (1991). *Getting past no: Negotiating with difficult people.* New York: Bantam.

Utley, C. A., Mortweet, S. L., & Greenwood, C. R. (1997). Peer-mediated instruction and interventions. *Focus on Exceptional Children, 29*(5), 1–23.

Vacca, R. T., & Vacca, J. L. (1986). *Content area reading* (2nd ed.). Boston: Little Brown.

Van Dyke, R., Stallings, M. A., & Colley, K. (1995, February). How to build an inclusive school community. *Phi Delta Kappan,* 475–479.

Van Dyke, R. E., Pitonyak, C. R. & Gilley, C. T. (1997). Planning, implementing, and evaluating inclusive education within the school. In L. A. Power-deFur & F. P. Orelove (Eds.), *Inclusive education: Practical implementation of the least restrictive environment* (pp. 27–41). Gaithersburg, MD: Aspen.

Van Rusen, A. K., & Bos, C. S. (1994). Facilitating student participation in individualizing education programs through motivation strategy instruction. *Exceptional Children, 60*(5), 466–475.

Van Rusen, A. K., Bos, C. S., Schumaker, J. B., & Deshler, D. D. (1994). *The self-advocacy strategy for education and transition planning.* Lawrence, KS: Edge Enterprises.

Vaughn, S. (1997, October). *General education classrooms and students with learning disabilities: Success, failures, and suggestions for changes with implications for inclusion.* Panel presentation at the annual meeting of the Council for Learning Disabilities, Arlington, VA.

Vaughn, S., & Schumm, J. (1995). Responsible inclusion for students with learning disabilities. *Journal of Learning Disabilities, 28*(5), 264–270, 290.

Vaughn, S., Schumm, J. S., Klingner, J., & Saumell, L. (1996). Teachers' views of instructional practices: Implications for inclusion. *Learning Disabilities Quarterly, 18*(3), 236–248.

Vaughn, S., Zaragoza, N., Hogan, Z., & Walker, J. (1993). A four-year longitudinal investigation of the social skills and behavior problems of students with learning disabilities. *Journal of Learning Disabilities, 26,* 404–412.

Villa, R. E., & Thousand, J. S. (1990). Administrative supports to promote inclusive schooling. In W. Stainback, & S. Stainback (Eds.), *Support networks for inclusive schooling: Interdependency integrated education* (pp. 201–218). Baltimore: Brookes.

Villa, R. E., & Thousand, J. S. (Eds.) (1995). *Creating an inclusive school.* Alexandria, VA: Association for Supervision and Curriculum Development.

Villa, R. A., Thousand, J. S., Nevin, A. I., & Malgeri, C. (1996). Instilling collaboration for inclusive schooling as a way of doing business in public schools. *Remedial and Special Education, 17,* 169–181.

Villa, R. A., Thousand, J. S., & Rosenberg, R. L. (1995). Creating heterogeneous schools: A systems change perspective. In M. A. Falvey (Ed.), *Inclusive and heterogeneous schooling.* Baltimore: Brookes.

Virginia Department of Education. (1993). *Accept learning together: Integrating students with disabilities.* Richmond, VA: Author.

Vissing, Y. M. (1996). *Out of sight, out of mind: Homeless children and families in small-town America.* Lexington, KY: University Press of Kentucky.

Vobejda, B. (1991). Asian, Hispanic numbers in U.S. soared in 1980's, Census reveals: Groups accelerate ethnic diversification in every region. *The Washington Post,* pp. D1–7.

Wagner, M., Blackorby, J., Cameto, R., Hebbeler, K., & Newman, L. (1993). *The transition experiences of young people with disabilities. A summary of findings from the national longitudinal transition study of special education students.* Menlo Park, CA: SRI International.

Wagner, M., Newman, L., D'Amico, R., Jay, E. D., Butler-Nalin, P., Marder, C., & Cox, R. (Eds.). (1991). *Youth with disabilities: How are they doing? The first comprehensive report from the national longitudinal transition study of special education students.* Menlo Park, CA: SRI International.

Wagner, M. M., & Blackorby, J. (1996). Transition from high school to work or college: How special education students fare. *Future of children, 6*(1), 103–120.

Walberg, H. J., & Greenberg, R. C. (1997). Using the learning environment inventory. *Educational Leadership, 54*(8), 45–47.

Walker, H. M., Todis, B., Holmes, D., & Horton, G. (1988). The Walker Social Skills Curriculum: The ACCESS Program. Austin, TX: Pro-Ed.

Walker, M., & Harris, G. (1995). *Negotiations: Six steps to success.* Upper Saddle River, NJ: Prentice-Hall.

Walling, D. R. (Ed.) (1994). *Teachers as leaders: Perspectives on the professional development of teachers.* Bloomington, IN: Phi Delta Kappa.

Walther-Thomas, C. S. (1997a). Co-teaching: Benefits and problems that teachers and principals report over time. *Journal for Learning Disabilities, 30*(4), 395–407.

Walther-Thomas, C. S. (1997b). Inclusion and teaming: Including all students in the mainstream. In T. S. Dickinson & T. O. Erb (Eds.), *We gain more than we give: Teaming in middle schools.* (pp. 487–522). Columbus, OH: National Middle School Association.

Walther-Thomas, C. S., Bryant, M., & Land, S. (1996). Planning for effective co-teaching: The key to successful inclusion. *Remedial and Special Education, 17,* 255–265.

Walther-Thomas, C., Korinek, L., McLaughlin, V. L., & Williams, B. T. (1996). Improving educational opportunities for students with disabilities who are homeless. *Journal of Children in Poverty, 2*(2), 57–75.

Walton, D. (1989). *Are you communicating? You can't manage without it.* New York: McGraw-Hill.

Wang, M. C., Haertel, G. D., & Walberg, H. J. (1993). Toward a knowledge base for school learning. *Review of Educational Research, 63,* 249–294.

Ward, S. B., Korinek, L., & McLaughlin, V. (1998). An investigation of intervention assistance teams at a preservice level. *School Psychology International, 19*(3), 279–286.

Warger, C. D., & Pugach, M. C. (1996). Curriculum considerations in an inclusive environment. *Focus on Exceptional Children, 28*(8), 1–12.

Warger, C. L., & Rutherford, R. B. Jr. (1993). Co-teaching to improve social skills. *Preventing School Failure, 37*, 21–27.

Waxman, L., & Hinderliter, S. (1996). *A status report on hunger and homelessness in America's cities: 1996.* Washington, DC: U.S. Conference of Mayors.

Weir, L. V. (1989). Howdy! In P. D. Pearson (Ed.), *Garden gates* (pp. 104–113). Needham, MA: Silver, Burdett, & Ginn.

Weissberg, R. P., Shriver, T. P., Bose, S., & DeFalco, K. (1997). Creating a districtwide social development project. *Educational Leadership, 54*(8), 37–39.

Welch, M., Sheridan, S. M., Fuhriman, A., Hart, A. W., Connell, M. L., & Stoddart, T. (1992). Preparing professionals for educational partnerships: An interdisciplinary approach. *Journal of Educational and School Consultation, 3*(1), 1–23.

Wentzel, K. (1993). Does being good make the grade: Social behavior and academic competence in middle school. *Journal of Educational Psychology, 85*, 357–364.

Wesson, C. L., & King, R. P. (1996). Portfolio assessment and special education students. In E. L. Meyen, G. A. Vergason, & R. J. Whelan (Eds.), *Strategies for teaching exceptional children in inclusive settings* (pp. 293–302). Denver: Love.

West, J., & Cannon, G. (1988). Essential collaborative consultation competencies for regular and special educators. *Journal of Learning Disabilities, 21*, 45–53.

West, J. F., & Idol, L. (1987). School consultation: An interdisciplinary perspective on theory, models, and research. *Journal of Learning Disabilities, 20*(7), 388–408.

West, J. F., & Idol, L. (1990). Collaborative consultation in the education of mildly handicapped and at-risk students. *Remedial and Special Education, 11*(1), 22–31.

Whitaker, P. (1993). *Managing change in schools.* Philadelphia: Open University Press.

Whitten, E., & Dieker, L. (1995, November). *What are the characteristics of effective assistance teams?* Paper presented at the annual meeting of the Teacher Education Division of the Council for Exceptional Children, Washington, DC.

Whitten, E., Bahr, M. W., Hodges, D., & Dieker, L. (1996, November). *What are the characteristics of effective intervention assistance teams?* Paper presented at the annual meeting of the Teacher Education Division of the Council for Exceptional Children Conference, Washington, DC.

Wiederholt, J. L., Hammill, D., & Brown, V. (1978). *The resource teacher: A guide to effective practices.* Boston: Allyn and Bacon.

Will, M. (1986). Educating children with learning problems: A shared responsibility. *Exceptional Children, 52*, 411–415.

Wittmer, D. S., & Honig, A. S. (1994). Encouraging positive social development in young children. *Young Children, 49*(5), 4–12.

Wolf, K. (1991). The school teacher's portfolio: Issues in design, implementation, and evaluation. *Phi Delta Kappan, 73*(2), 130–136

Wolfensberger, W. (1972). *The principle of normalization in human services.* Toronto, Ontario, Canada: National Institute on Mental Retardation.

Yell, M. L., & Shriner, J. G. (1997). The IDEA amendments of 1997: Implications for special and general education teachers, administrators, and teacher trainers. *Focus on Exceptional Children, 30*(1), 1–20.

Yinger, R. J. (1990). The conversation of practice. In R. T. Clift, W. R. Houston, & M. C. Pugach (Eds), *Encouraging reflective practice in education* (pp. 73–94). New York: Teachers College Press.

York, J., Doyle, M. B., & Kronberg, R. (1992). A curriculum development process for inclusive classrooms. *Focus on Exceptional Children, 25*(4), 1–16.

Zigmond N., & Baker, J. (1990). Mainstreaming experiences for learning disabled students: A preliminary report. *Exceptional Children, 57*(2), 176–185.

Zigmond, N., & Miller, S. E. (1991). Improving high school programs for students with learning disabilities: A matter of substance as well as form. In F. R. Rusch, L. DeStefano, J. Chadnsey-Rusch, L. A. Phelps, & E. Szymanski (Eds.), *Transition from school to adult life*. Champaign, IL: Sycamore.

Zorfass, J. (1994). The National Center to Improve Practice: Promoting the use of technology in special education. *Educational Media and Technology Yearbook, 20,* 126–131.

INDEX

Note: Page numbers in *italics* indicate illustrations.

in guided practice, 246
positive, 128–129
Filtering, communication and, 96
Finances *see* Resources
Fishbowl Technique, 103, 105
Fleenor, C., 97
Force, in conflict management, 108
Frame of reference, in communication, 95
Friend, M., 5, 168, 256
Friendship clubs, 87
Friendship interventions, 127–128
Friendships, 6–7
fostering of, 127–129 *See also* Social skills
development
Fuchs, L. S., 255
Fullan, M., 52, 54, 63, 93
Full-service schools, 85
Functional analysis, 165–166
Funding *see* Resources

Garratt, B., 57
Generalists, vs. specialists, 137–138
Giangreco, M. F., 133
Gifted students, IEP for, 224, *224*
Gilley, C. T., 29
Gleason, M., 240
Goals 2000: Educate America, 260–261
Goleman, D., 261
Government, collaboration with, *32*
Grade level teams, 79
Grading, alternate, *254*, 255–256
Graphic organizers, *237*, 240–242, *241*
Greenberg, R. C., 234, 261
Greenwood, C. R., 255
Guided practice, 246–248
Gutkin, T. B., 164

Haertel, G. D., 234
Hall, G., 54
Hanson, M. J., 78
Harper, G. F., 270
Harris, G., 112
Harry, B., 77
Hendricks, I. G., 20
Herman, J. J., 55
Herman, J. L., 55
Heterogeneous grouping, 9–10
Higher education personnel, collaboration
with, 32

High schools
balanced rosters in, 9, 124
collaborative planning in, 125
co-teaching in, 187, 189 *See also* Co-teaching
social skills development in, 275–276
Holistic learning opportunities, 9–10
Homework hotlines, 87
Homework practice, 251, *251*
Honig, A. S., 272
Hord, S., 54
Hourcade, J. J., 46, 155
Howdy, 267
Huling-Austin, L., 54
Hundert, J., 272

IDEA *see* Individuals with Disabilities Education Act (IDEA)
Idol, L., 165, 179
IEP *see* Individualized education programs (IEPs)
IEP team, 83, 229
family participation in, 217–219, *219*
Implementation
administrative leadership in, 117–119
balanced rosters and, 122–124
case study of, 115–117
collaboration in, 120–121 *See also*
Collaboration
planning for, 117, 118–120
professional development and, 121–122
recruitment for, 120–121
resources for, 121
school-leadership in, 117–119
steps in, 41–42
sustained support for, 40–42
Implementation dips, 40
Improvement, continuous, 42–46
Incarceration rates, for special education
students, 17
Inclusive education
adequate resources for, 38–39, 283–284
benefits of, 3–4, 20–23
for peers, 22–23
for professionals, 23
for students with disabilities, 22
coherent vision in, 282–283
collaboration in *see* Collaboration
collaborative culture in, 28–29, 63–64, 92,
280–281